ST.
ST.
W9-ANP-391
D
20686

EXPLORING THE CITY
Inquiries Toward an Urban Anthropology

EXPLORING the CITY

Inquiries Toward an Urban Anthropology

ULF HANNERZ

New York Columbia University Press *1980*

Library of Congress Cataloging in Publication Data
Hannerz, Ulf.
Exploring the city.

Bibliography: p. 343
Includes index.
1. Urban anthropology.   2. Cities and towns.
I. Title.
GN395.H36   307.7′6   79-29707
ISBN 0-231-03982-4

Columbia University Press
New York   Guildford, Surrey

Copyright © 1980 Columbia University Press
All rights reserved
Printed in the United States of America

Contents

———•·•———

Acknowledgments

The acknowledgments which begin a book, but are usually the last part of it to be written, are evidence of a part of a personal network, and of phases of a life career. They may document a passage through many milieux, a series of significant experiences, and a variety of dialogues, ongoing or discontinued.

Toward the end of the introductory chapter, I sketch some of the personal factors which have gone into making *Exploring the City* the kind of book it is, and I mention there three field experiences, in Washington, D.C., in Kafanchan, Nigeria, and in the Cayman Islands. It seems fitting to make note first of what I learned in these places about what is urban and what is not, and to thank friends, acquaintances, and informants there collectively for what they did to push my understanding along. Those who were most helpful I have in some cases been able to single out, or will in the future, in other publications. But some, due to the ethics of field work and publishing, will remain anonymous. It is very likely, of course, that many of them would find it difficult to see the links between the concrete things we were through together and some of the more abstract notions of the following pages. All the same, the connections are there.

Turning to academia, it is rather more often possible to discern the direct influence of particular network partners on what has gone into this book, although reference must in some cases inevitably be made to other collectivities. The most diverse and far-flung one of these consists of those colleagues and students who have responded to my views on urban anthropology in a number of seminars and conferences in the United States, Canada, England, and Scandinavia, and allowed me to share theirs. What made up more of a real group, although by now it may well be almost equally scattered, were the participants in an urban anthropology seminar in the Department of Anthropology, University of Pittsburgh, where I was a visiting member of the faculty in 1971–72. Although by then I had not yet given serious thought to writing a book on the subject, this seminar helped me begin arranging my ideas. Leonard Plotnicov and Keith Brown, with whom I gave the seminar, were equally interested in discussing what they saw as characteristic of urban life and urban anthropology, in or out of the seminar room, and did much to make that year memorable. I expect that they will recognize in this book a number of issues first brought up in our conversations in Pittsburgh—whether by one of them or by me, I must confess, I cannot always quite remember.

Another academic excursion came at a later stage in the development of this book. During the spring of 1976, I was a Simon Senior Research Fellow in the Department of Social Anthropology, University of Manchester. Since this gave me the rather rare opportunity to spend a longer period reading, thinking, and writing without major distractions and in a stimulating milieu, I am very grateful to my then colleagues in Manchester for taking me in. John Comaroff, Chris Fuller, and Keith Hart were especially helpful as conversation partners. Because the role of the Manchester department has been so prominent in the development of anthropological urban studies, however, the advantages of that period also varied from something as concrete as specialized library holdings to a rather less tangible but still real sense of a proper ambience for my concerns.

Yet it has naturally been in my home department, at the University of Stockholm, that I have had the greatest opportunity to try out various ideas over the years during which this book has been in (not always lineal) progress, and that the book has also taken shape in other ways. Seminars on Urban Anthropology, Personal Information in Social Relations, Career Analysis, and Cultural Analysis between 1970 and 1978 have been especially useful in this regard, and the participants in these constitute another rather tightly-knit group which I must thank collectively. Stefan Molund, Kristina Bohman, and Tomas Gerholm have also at one time or another been through various chapter drafts and have often helped me clarify my assumptions and straighten out my argument through their criticisms, also bringing illuminating ethnography and other references to my attention. A group of colleagues, present or former graduate students of the department, again including the three just named, also have my gratitude for having been among the best guides an urban anthropologist could have, when I have visited them in the field, in cities in three continents. And four conscientious assistants in the department, Kerstin Lagergren, Ulla Forsberg Fröman, Gunnel Nordström, and Lena Haddad, have given their careful attention to typing parts and versions of the manuscript in a way for which I am very thankful.

Apart from the Pittsburgh, Manchester, and Stockholm network clusters, a few other persons should be recognized for the interest which they have taken in this book. Through conversations or correspondence, I have been pleased to have the views of Gerald D. Berreman with regard to chapter 1, A. L. Epstein and J. Clyde Mitchell with regard to chapters 4 and 5, Jeremy Boissevain and Alvin W. Wolfe with regard to chapter 5, and Erving Goffman with regard to chapter 6. An anonymous reader who looked over the completed manuscript on behalf of Columbia University Press made several helpful suggestions, only some of which I have in the end been able to follow. And John D. Moore of Columbia University Press has been a most friendly editor, even as the completion of the manuscript was repeatedly delayed.

As it will now come before the reader, *Exploring the City* is a somewhat different book from that which I first expected to write, when I began the project of organizing my view of urban anthropology. This is partly because I realized, after a while, that the time would seem to move ever farther ahead of me, like a mirage, when I could expect to finish a volume of the very wide scope originally intended. And it would hardly fit between two covers anyway. Even as it is, *Exploring the City* is not a very small book. It may be that I will find other opportunities to deal with issues and materials that must now be left out. But another reason why the book has perhaps expanded a little here, contracted a little there, and struck out in some directions which I had not first thought of, has of course been the ongoing influence of friends and colleagues. It will not, I hope, be the end product of my dialogues with them, as I wish to have many of them in my network when I move on to other aspects of the anthropological study of cities.

Whatever merit this book may have, then, I think I should share with those who have helped and encouraged my undertaking. Unlike a handful of recent authors, however, I think it would be unfair of me to suggest that those who have offered such support should also be prepared to take a part of the blame for its various faults. The convention that this burden should be carried by the author alone is one which I accept. After all, if this were a book that my friends and colleagues would wholeheartedly want to be associated with, would they not have written it themselves?

In other ways as well, writing tends in the end to be a lonely undertaking. The solitude required I have found for the most part during periods away from the entanglements of urban life, in a secluded summer house with a garden full of weeds and aged fruit trees, with visiting cats and a resident hedgehog, in southern Sweden. This, perversely, is where this book on urban anthropology was begun, and this is where I now reach its completion. Even for a committed urbanite, it may finally be acknowledged, the country may have its uses.

Utvälinge, April 1980   ULF HANNERZ

EXPLORING THE CITY
Inquiries Toward an Urban Anthropology

CHAPTER ONE

The Education of
an Urban Anthropologist

Only a little more than a decade ago, there was hardly an urban anthropology. A concern with urbanism as a part of civilization, and an interest in defining its properties cross-culturally, had already taken a handful of scholars to Timbuktu and other faraway places. But as late as in the early 1960s one student of comparative urbanism could remark that anthropologists were "a notoriously agoraphobic lot, anti-urban by definition" (Benet 1963a:212). Only in that decade did the tendency of anthropologists to go to cities (or simply to remain in them) become really pronounced. There were several reasons for this. In the exotic societies to which anthropologists habitually gave most of their attention—and which they were now learning to describe as "the Third World"—people increasingly left the villages for new and mushrooming urban centers, and the students of their lives could hardly disregard the fact. In the United States, many anthropologists were more directly touched by developments at home. In the 1950s, the American self-image had been one of an affluent, homogenized mass society; intellectuals complained of an excess of mediocre conformism. In the 1960s, ethnicity and poverty were rediscovered, and more often than not they were defined as "urban problems." In Europe at the same time, international labor migration, and to a lesser extent an influx of refugees from political upheavals, were changing the character of many cities. There was a search for new understandings, and anthropologists felt they could play a part in it. They had specialized in "other cultures" but had looked for them far away. Now they found them across the tracks.[1]

From the presence of anthropologists in cities to the emergence of an urban anthropology, however, there was yet another step. The collective identification of the new academic specialty and the regular use of the label of urban anthropology have been even more a thing of the 1970s than of the decade preceding it. The first book bearing the title *Urban Anthropology* appeared in 1968. Since 1973, authors and editors have (somewhat unimaginatively) used it for another five volumes.[2] The journal *Urban Anthropology* began publication in 1972. Obviously, by now urban anthropologists are forming a community. They apply for their own specialist slots in anthropology departments, they meet in their own conferences, and they write in no small part for each other when they do not write textbooks to teach students about cities.

To these developments reactions have been rather mixed. Urban anthropology as it now stands can claim certain accomplishments. It also confronts several unresolved issues, and there is no general agreement about its prospects. One practitioner suggests that "urban anthropology can become the creative new core of modern comparative social anthropology" (Gutkind 1968:77); another considers the delimitation of such a field "a spurious and retrograde one in that it tends to make an excuse for maintaining a subject matter within a discipline which cannot and should not handle it" (Leeds 1972:4). To some, the theoretical and methodological resources of the anthropological tradition seem insufficient for urban research; for others, the problem is precisely that the new urbanologists are not paying sufficient heed to the ideas developed by anthropologists in other social contexts. Those with some awareness of what goes on in the sister discipline of sociology may have noticed that the bases for an urban specialty, theoretical or substantive, have been in some doubt there. Others may have made their way independently, and perhaps more slowly, toward similar uncertainty. What is a concern for relevance to some may be mere opportunism to others—an "undignified scramble to find substitute savages in slums" in the words of Robin Fox (1973:20).

It might thus seem that urban anthropology has no past, and reason to worry about its future. Yet this book is largely retrospective, an attempt to trace some of the steps to the present. What reasons could there be for such an undertaking?

For a large part, I submit, they can be found in the manner the anthropologists entered the city. It was not so much their own reflections over the nature and state of their discipline that led them there, but rather external events that insisted on attention. In a headlong rush into a field defined by racial strife, malfunctioning institutions, and the growth of shantytowns, they often took little time to ponder over what is urban in urban anthropology, and what is anthropological about it. There was only the simplest and least self-conscious transfer possible of basic anthropology into the new context. The specialties of anthropology which were taken for granted were a sensitivity to cultural diversity, the closeness to ongoing everyday life which comes with participant observation as a dominant research method, and a readiness to define problems broadly, "holistically," rather than narrowly. Such characteristics of method and perspective tended to bring the anthropologist, not least in the United States, to the ethnic enclave, the ghetto, which had cultural and organizational characteristics with which he could—in his own curious way—feel comfortable. But what was often most important in drawing him there, of course, is that this sort of community is also frequently faced with social problems. Particularly American urban anthropology has thus become, in Tylor's phrase, "a reformer's science." It has applied itself to questions of health and welfare, law and justice, schools and jobs, the physical environment and its changes.

This is certainly no cause for regret. The concern with good works will certainly remain a part of urban anthropology, which we are apt to feel can be quite useful in such areas. It would also be inexcusable for an anthropologist with roots in a much more homogeneous society to suggest that American urban anthropologists should stop paying attention to the ethnic quarters of their cities. Obviously ethnicity remains a live force in American society. What has thus resulted, however, is rather a commonsense anthropology, the quality of which tends to be measured more by its practical relevance and results than by its sheer intellectual worth. Although theoretical contributions may result from such work, they are likely to be unanticipated by-products.

It is another fact of the same realities of research that the field of urban anthropology has been quite widely defined. More often than not it is taken to include all the studies where the city is the locus rather than the focus. [3] Ethnicity and poverty, for example, may occur *in* the city, but they are not by definition phenomena typical of the city. The euphemistic use of "urban problems" in political rhetoric is no trustworthy guide here. Investigations of urban family life, or the activities of youth gangs, or occupational cultures, need not be much concerned with any intrinsically urban characteristics either. This generous inclusiveness of all sorts of interests, ideas, and findings, together with a relative unconcern for what might be their common denominator, also contribute to the picture of an urban anthropology which seems to lack a coherent, unifying structure of ideas.

In this book we will try to sort out some of the elements of such a structure. Probably inevitably, this also leads us to aim first of all for an urban anthropology more strictly conceived, where the focus is on urbanism itself—whatever this statement will turn out to mean. To a great extent we will disregard what appears to be merely the routine practice of anthropology within city limits. But this need not mean that we have to start again from scratch. We can get a better overview of the territory to be explored if we use the opportunities which come our way to observe it from the shoulders of giants—or sometimes even of little people like ourselves. In other words, we will try to pull together some components of a usable past for the urban anthropology we have in mind. Urban anthropology needs its own history of ideas, a collective consciousness of the growth of understandings concerning the essentials of the city and city life. Some of these understandings may already be of a venerable age. Others are the products of a very recent past, even merging with the present. They have made their appearance in varied contexts, and it may often be helpful (or at least intellectually pleasing) to view them first in these. Others, of course, have recurred in slightly different guises in many times and places. Much of the work of tracing their interconnections and combining them into a pattern remains to be done.

To describe what follows as a partial history of urban anthropological thought, however, would only be in some ways correct, and in other ways misleading. Above all it would imply too great an autonomy for the field. Much of what may be the usable past for the urban anthropology of today originated on the other side of academic boundaries, congenial as the ideas in question may now seem to an anthropological perspective. They must be appropriated for example from history, sociology, and geography. There is also the question of the relationship of the urban branch discipline to anthropology as a whole.

One can perhaps see urban anthropologists either as urbanologists with a particular set of tools, or as anthropologists studying a particular kind of social arrangement. The two ways of looking at their work are not totally unrelated but suggest different emphases. I believe much recent urban anthropology lends itself mostly to the former view; its question has been "What is the contribution of anthropology to urban studies?" The complementary question is, "What is the contribution of urban studies to anthropology?" Both questions deserve to be asked, time and time again to see if new answers may be developing. But if to the first question there have hitherto been mostly standard answers concerning the characteristics of anthropology, the latter may be more theoretically provocative and can perhaps ensure that the communication between general comparative anthropology and its branch in the city becomes more of a two-way flow.

In order to live up to its claim of being "the science of humanity," anthropology must be reconstructed to include an awareness of urban life. It cannot draw only on research in small, uncomplicated communities, mostly in non-western parts of the world. The special contribution of the urban part to the anthropological whole consists of understandings of a range of social and cultural phenomena less often or never found elsewhere, to be seen against the background of human variation in general.

From this point of view, it must be added, the flocking of urban anthropologists to the ethnic enclaves of our cities may seem to be an evasion. These may be as similar to the traditional anthropological research site as one can find in the city, "urban villages" in Gans's (1962a) terms. In the ideal case, a large proportion of the social relationships of the population is contained within the enclave. The urban villager's compatriots form a pool from which not only his neighbors but also his friends and kinsmen are drawn, and he interacts with them in these capacities mostly within the village territory. The smaller the population is, the more likely is it that it will form a dense web of relationships in which one can start out from one person, trace a few links and return on a circuitous path to the same person—and one can do this by a number of different paths. As Gans puts it, everyone might not know everyone else, but they know something about everyone else. Furthermore, there may be considerable continuity over time in these relationships, as villagers see one another day after day and do not frequently experience such changes in their lives as must disrupt their ties to one another. Children who grew up together may well be, as adults, one another's friends, neighbors, and perhaps affinal relatives.

All ethnic quarters are not like this. To contribute maximally to the ethnographic panorama which is one of the greatest resources of anthropology, however, anthropologists of the city perhaps ought to give much of their attention to the very opposite of the urban village. We tend to think of the city rather as a place where people do not know one another too well (at least not initially), where mutual acquaintances are discovered rather than assumed, and where quick passages may be made through the social structure. Against this it may be held that such phenomena are really no more typical of the city than is the urban village. This may be true in one way but is quite beside the point in another. There is a sense in which we are likely to agree that they are "more urban" than the urban village—they are more likely to be found in the city than elsewhere. If true to our anthropological heritage we are more concerned with form variations than with averages, it is in this sense they are important as manifestations of urbanism.

Throughout this book, our inquiries will thus be directed toward identifying particular insights that the study of city life can offer to anthropology. At the same time it must be understood that our very way of selecting and conceptualizing phenomena may in itself be a contribution of anthropology to urban studies. Urban anthropological thought is fundamentally anthropological thought. Both what may be original about it and what will be borrowed from other sources (and thereafter possibly transformed) are determined by the confrontation of the anthropological mind with urban realities. This may turn out to be a somewhat paradoxical experiment in the adaptability of anthropological analysis. After decades of work in constructing a conceptual apparatus for the understanding of distant traditional societies, constantly fearing the moral and intellectual captivity of ethnocentrism, we now face the test of the apparatus in our own cities. Its effects, I would hope, would include the development of ideas which could prove valuable in other arenas of anthropology as well, although the nature of urban life may show their usefulness in particularly dramatic ways.

I would expect the perspective sketched here to satisfy those anthropologists who are critical of the notion of an urban anthropology because they feel that its differentiation, with a label of its own, would mark its secession from the mother discipline. They are concerned that the establishment of a separate identity would lead to a rejection of anthropological method and theory as unsuitable to urban studies. This is obviously not my conception of urban anthropology. As a branch of anthropology, urban anthropology is no more separate than studies of, say, peasant or nomad societies. Nobody suggests that the anthropological study of peasants has divorced itself from anthropology proper; nobody denies that anthropology has benefited from the growth of peasant studies which not so long ago also constituted a new emerging interest. Yet at the same time it is recognized that the study of peasant societies involves a cluster of concepts and ideas for which it is practical to have a common designation. Neither more nor less is what I think should be claimed for urban anthropology. It is a recognizable specialization, but at the same time an integral part of anthropology.

On the other hand, a concern with the intellectual contribution of urban studies to anthropology could seem like mere academicism, a retreat from relevance. One may respond to this objection first of all that there is room for more than one urban anthropology. At least at this early stage, certainly, we should be prepared to let a thousand flowers grow, and hope that they will find ways of flourishing in the concrete environment. But furthermore, one may reply that the anthropologist whose field is in Boston or Berlin ought to have as much or as little of a license—whichever way one wants it—to cultivate his curiosity for its own sake as he who goes to live among the Bongo Bongo. To think otherwise would seem to smack of ethnocentrism, however well-intentioned. True, if Boston or Berlin happened to be part of one's own home society, one may be better able to play the active part of an anthropologist-advocate than one can do where one is "only visiting." Yet there seems to be little difference in principle between rejecting that role while staying home and avoiding it by going to Bongo Bongo.

Naturally we may also hope that a more critical attention to theory and conceptualization in the meeting grounds of anthropology and urbanism could lead to a more powerful, more exactly calibrated practical application of anthropology to urban affairs. And, in addition, we should not fall into the trap of seeing only narrowly academic work, and equally narrowly defined involvement in piecemeal social engineering, as the only alternatives facing anthropologists. The relevance of anthropology lies also in its potential, not always realized, of making people reflect on the variability of the human condition and on their own particular situation.

I might elaborate a little on this power of anthropology. In 1935, an English satirist, Charles Duff, published an *Anthropological Report on a London Suburb,* a parody of what an anthropologist of that time might have to say were he to turn his attention to his own society.[4] To follow Professor Vladimir Chernichewski, that fictive "eminent scientist" in whose name Duff wrote:

> the science of anthropology is not only concerned with the naked savage, but with the man or woman in plus fours or evening dress. To the true man of science it matters little whether he is dealing with suburb or jungle, modern

jazz dancing or savage sex orgy, forest magic or the anthropomorphic deism of a suburban green-grocer, the cures and charms of the Bantu medicine-man or the work of a Fellow of the Royal College of Physicians. The difference between ourselves and savages is often more apparent than real; plus fours may conceal a brute, and a coat of paint may cover a tender heart. (Duff 1935:12)

Up to a point the urban anthropologist of today may concur in the relativism of Professor Chernichewski. But Chernichewski uses his licence to make the suburbanite and the savage seem equally ludicrous, and draws ridicule himself by appearing unable to reach a close understanding of either. The tactic we may prefer is one where anthropology, because of the awareness it fosters of any life style as one of an almost infinite number of alternatives, can contribute to an exoticization of the familiar; its newly acquired strangeness may then make possible fresh and incisive thought. Not only should the grassroots perspective of anthropology toward the interrelationships of social life lend itself well to what C. Wright Mills (1961:5) called the sociological imagination, enabling its possessor "to understand the larger historical scene in terms of its meaning for the inner life and the external career of a variety of individuals." There is also a peculiarly anthropological imagination, entailing a sharpening of his understanding by implicit or explicit comparisons with life under other social and cultural arrangements. It rests on the possibility of understanding oneself by understanding others. This is also a contribution of anthropology to urban studies: urban anthropology as an instrument by which city dwellers can think in new ways about what goes on around them.

It may be useful if I elaborate a little further here on my understandings of the nature of anthropology, as they will continue to color what follows. Perhaps the most characteristic product of anthropological work is ethnography; predominantly qualitative, richly contextualized accounts of human thought and action. Slightly schematically, one may think of such ethnography on the one hand as something intimately connected with the way the anthropological field worker approaches reality, on the other hand as the source from which anthropological theory is extracted and refined, then used to guide the further production of ethnography. This complex of intellectual industry may not seem very efficient. Some observers could feel that too much of the ethnography becomes only dross. One would surely have to see this, however, against the background of the anthropologist's natural concern with discovery. Because it is his tradition to explore unknown social and cultural terrain he wants to maximize sensitivity to the unexpected—new facts, new connections between facts. It is easy to understand the emphasis on participant observation and "holism" as at least partly motivated by the exploratory character of the enterprise. That use of the anthropological imagination by which even familiar scenes can be made strange and thus available for new discoveries also fits in here.

But at this particular point we may concern ourselves less with anthropological field procedure and more with anthropological thought, with the conceptual structure which is also a part of the anthropological stance toward reality. The perspective I develop here is that of a *social* anthropologist, and it suggests to me one way of drawing the contrast between myself and a kind of archetypical sociologist. This is possibly useful since urban anthropologists seem often to develop a chronic anxiety about not being sufficiently different from urban sociologists—especially from early urban sociologists. Beals (1951:4), many years ago, quoted a sociologist to the effect that if anthropologists continued as they had begun in the study of modern culture, they would in time reinvent sociology, only at least fifty years behind the rest of the field. More recently, Shack (1972:6) has lamented that much urban anthropology seems to be only "the sociology of the 1940s revisited." Instead, he proposes, urban anthropology should draw on the anthropological tradition of comparative analysis of institutional behavior—as examples he suggests that the principle of complementary opposition or the analysis of developmental cycles in domestic groups may well be of value in urban studies.

I have no objections to these examples, and the extension of general anthropological concepts into the urban field is certainly well in line with my conception of urban anthropology as an integral part of a general comparative view of human society. But this must not degenerate into scholasticism, a neglect of the ways in which urban life has its own peculiar characteristics, the understanding of which can itself help to develop ideas for general anthropology. For such reasons, one may find even "comparative analysis of institutional behavior" too constraining a definition of anthropology, for one of the areas in which the anthropology of complex societies has made important contributions is indeed that of non-institutionalized behavior—entrepreneurship, network manipulation, and so forth.

What difference there is between urban anthropology and sociology, I believe, is better understood in another way. The distinction I have in mind is made most forcefully by Leach (1967) in his comments on a social survey in rural Ceylon. The premise of the sociologist with his statistical orientation, Leach suggests, is that the field of observation consists of "units of population," "individuals." The social anthropologist instead thinks of his data as made up of "systems of relationship." The anthropological image of society, that is, is more specifically one of episodes of interaction and of more durable interdependencies between people. Individuals, as social anthropologists deal with them, are engaged in contacts with others; they are entities constructed from the roles through which they participate in these varied situations. Sociologists more often try to cope with the paradox of abstracting people from the real diversity of their ongoing linkages, decontextualizing them, yet defining them in some way as social animals. This difference of tendency is what is fundamental. The greater ease with which numbers can be used in dealing with individual as compared to relational data is secondary, conspicuous as it may be as a symptom.

Our emphasis here is thus on a relational perspective—on social situations, on people's shares in these, and on the way a complex social life can be assembled from them. This is admittedly not quite sufficient in dividing urban anthropology strictly from all that passes for urban sociology, or indeed anthropology from sociology. Anthropologists at times find reason to count individuals, and one will find sociologists who think as much in relational terms as any anthropologist. In the urban field the latter is exemplified by classics as well as by a number of scholars with a sociological professional affiliation who have recently become the cool ethnographers of strip joints, after-hours clubs, and massage parlors.[5] Even so, we may discern that as they have evolved, anthropology and sociology have different centers of gravity, not only in choice of subject matter but also analytically. Anthropology as it moves into the city need not become utterly indistinguishable from sociology, and on a moment's reflection we may perhaps realize that the "urban sociology" which as anthropologists we find most congenial is really according to this criterion "urban anthropology." A little arrogantly, we may even sometimes feel that its analysis could have been taken further had this been realized. On the other hand, a rather vague definition of the boundary between sociology and anthropology need not be particularly disturbing. The territorial imperative ought not to be intellectually respectable, and the mutual visiting between anthropology and sociology has often been rewarding when it has occurred. To no small extent the fuzzy dividing line we have is an accident of history. In this book we will not be very respectful toward it.

Those who are not so emphatically *social* anthropologists may be surprised that I have chosen the relational point of view, rather than the concept of culture, as the distinguishing mark of anthropology. In American academia in particular, one often comes across the rather whimsical notion that "sociologists study society, while anthropologists study culture." One might think they could hardly study either without to some extent studying both. Yet certainly the idea contains some truth. There are some anthropologists who deal in cognitions without developing much of a conception of social structure, and sociologists sometimes pay very little attention to such things as ideas, knowledge, beliefs, or values in their depictions of society. In urban anthropology as well, I believe the idea of culture will be much more central than it has customarily been in urban sociology. My reason for giving first place to the relational conception of society may have some resemblance to Fortes' (1953:21) well-known statement that social structure can be seen as "the entire culture of a given people handled in a special frame of theory," but it has a more direct connection to our understanding of urbanism. The latter is considerably more likely to be defined in social than in cultural terms; we tend to generalize about urbanism first of all as a characteristic kind of system of social relationships, and only secondarily and derivatively as a set of ideas held by urbanites. Urban culture, consequently, may be most readily conceptualized when the description of social structure is already well under way.

It seems quite possible, at the same time, that urban studies could help give anthropologists a much more sophisticated conception of cultural processes and organization than they often have. Culture, it has been said, is a matter of traffic in meanings. The image is a felicitous one for our purposes, for it is immediately apparent that urban traffic patterns have some peculiarities, and that some vehicles may be better suited for them than others. The urban social system may foster certain kinds of ideas, or give rise to particular problems of organizing culture. There may be ideas about managing contacts with strangers, if there is an abundance of them in the environment. Or if, as is fairly likely in a complex social system, some individuals at least can be said to be involved in several cultures, the ways of handling this diversity may be a problem for analysis. We will touch on such questions, but hardly more, in this volume.

Such, then, is in the most general terms possible my conception of the anthropological view of society, the background of my treatment of assorted ways of describing and analyzing urban life in the chapters to come. I might have gone on here to state something similarly synoptically about what I assume to be the realities of urbanism, the other part of the equation in the encounter of the anthropologist with the city. But I will let these understandings unfold gradually in what follows. Instead I will add just a few notes of a more personal kind, which may throw light on the kind of book I have written.

Although I believe it would be useful for urban anthropologists to draw together more tightly for a while, working over some apparatus of concepts of varying scope to see how far these could be helpful in organizing the field intellectually, it may be obvious from what has been said that in my personal choice of such ordering ideas, I am not very loyal to any one anthropological tradition. I have said that I write as a *social* anthropologist; this may be understood as the chosen identity of someone favorably inclined toward the British strand in anthropological thinking. Indeed, I do find the latter's efforts toward a systematic, comprehensive analysis of social relations admirable. But many of its central ideas have a longer history, and over the years they have also spread to other corners of the world, where they have been reshaped. These earlier and later developments, it will probably be seen, have been of as great an interest to me as those of the established center.

Furthermore, the view of urban anthropology presented here is influenced by a couple of other predilections of my own. I want to give some fairly close attention to the shaping and handling of meaning in interactions, thus aiming for a cultural analysis which is flexible enough to match the so far more well-developed social analysis of complex structures. For this purpose I was drawn rather early toward symbolic interactionism, a tendency in American social thought, although mostly just outside its academic anthropology. While my interest in it has not been particularly systematic, it certainly plays a part in the pages which follow. By now, however, I see a rather strong affinity between it and the symbolic anthropology which has more recently become a major component of anthropology in the United States.

My interest in social history will only be in evidence in a more scattered fashion. I do believe, however, that urban anthropologists will do well to acquaint themselves more thoroughly with historical scholarship, especially as they start engaging in more systematic comparative studies of urbanism. I hope to have more to say on this in later work.

Possibly this personal synthesis, incompletely worked out as it may yet be, has something to do with my own academic experience. I have had the opportunity to do some participant observation among both American and British anthropologists, and since urban anthropology has developed with far greater breadth in the United States than elsewhere, I find myself conducting a sort of dialogue particularly with these developments. But I spend most of my time in an academic milieu without a settled national tradition of its own in the kind of anthropology with which I am concerned. It may be that this has left me with slightly greater freedom to pursue ideas in somewhat idiosyncratic directions, across boundaries of universes of thought which elsewhere might be more clearly demarcated.

But commitments and experiences other than those arising within the circle of professional peers may also have had their effects on what I take urban anthropology to be about. Although I propose that a certain knowledge of ideas about the city, of the works where these ideas have been prominent, and of the people behind these works, are all part of the education of an urban anthropologist, it must also draw considerably on the intertwining of urban themes with his own biography. Like a great many other anthropologists, I have spent virtually all my life in urban areas. (Perhaps we glimpse here a further reason why the discipline has turned increasingly to studies in cities—many of us do not know very much about the practicalities of farming, keeping domestic animals, and other aspects of living closer to nature, and are in this respect ill prepared for learning about rural ways of life.) I also like cities, using other habitats mostly briefly for contrast. Going off for a holiday, I am more likely to seek out distant streets than the mountains or the beach. I have been an ordinary inhabitant for fairly lengthy periods of Swedish, American, and English cities, and more briefly I have been able to do some anthropological sightseeing in urban communities in Africa, Asia, Australia, Oceania, Latin America, and the Caribbean, as well as elsewhere in Europe. This has provided opportunities for reflecting over what is different and what remains in some way the same between towns and cities in varied places. Furthermore, three experiences of anthropological field work have also influenced my thinking about urban life—one more indirectly, two very directly.

In the late 1960s, I spent two years in Washington, D.C., doing what I would now consider (in line with what has been said above) anthropology in the city, but for the greater part not urban anthropology in the strict sense. In other words, the focus of my interest was not on the specifically urban character of the life styles I became involved with, although I gradually became more aware of such a line of inquiry, and more concerned with it. This was a study centered on a black low-income neighborhood, conducted almost wholly through participant observation in order to make my researcher role minimally ambiguous in a rather tense atmosphere. The book which resulted (Hannerz 1969) dealt with the interplay of ethnic boundedness and limited economic opportunity in the shaping of a range of collective adaptations; a complex culture anchored both in the past and in the present. Among the specific themes were the dynamics of ghetto sex roles, shared knowledge which served as a source for a common identity among ghetto inhabitants, and the relationship between their thoughts and deeds and American mainstream culture. Less conspicuously, however, I was dealing also for instance with the uncertainties both I and they faced in handling street life. More than before, I realized that one could sometimes be forced to think of the unknown people in the urban setting as problems. I also became conscious of the difficulties of choosing and delimiting a unit for observation in urban study. My neighborhood could be seen as in certain ways like an urban village, but for some people it was not as equally significant an arena of their lives as it was for others. If certain individuals hardly ever moved far away from it, others mostly came home to sleep, and sometimes not even that all too regularly. There could be close ties of kinship and friendship with people in the rural South, and a general lack of personal acquaintances outside the black community. Since Washington had such a large black population, however, the ghetto as a whole sufficed for arrangements of social relationships which were neither compact nor static. As a further example of the way problems of urbanism mingled with those of poverty and ethnicity, I could note that I occasionally wondered about the differences between black ghetto life in Washington and other cities, like Newark or Detroit. To what extent did the nature of the entire community affect the ethnic community nested within it? If you have seen one ghetto, have you really seen them all?

My second field experience, in 1970 (and reported in Hannerz 1974a), was a rather brief study of local politics in the Cayman Islands in the Caribbean, and its relationship to urban anthropology is hardly obvious. I was indeed based in the capital—named George Town, like so many other places in what were once parts of the British Empire—but it was little more than the main village in a very small territory. Actually, the relevance of the experience to my understanding of urbanism is that it offered a considerable contrast. Caymanian society is the closest I have come as a practicing ethnographer to a small-scale social structure, and this was not least evident in its politics. The formal machinery of government was based on ideas imported from a mass society, with highly differentiated roles and impersonal procedures. The Caymanians' acquaintance with each other, on the other hand, was sometimes too close for comfort, and more or less their entire personalities tended to become involved in interactions. This was also the way they preferred to do their politicking, and so its clash with the niceties of government had some dramatic moments. For me it was food for thought about the part played by personal information in the variable constructions of social relationships.

My most recent field work has been in Nigeria, in the mid-1970s, and in this case the objectives of research have been urban anthropological in the strict sense. Having behind me a study of life in an enclave of a large city, I now wanted to experiment conceptually and methodologically with the study of an entire urban community. The field site chosen was Kafanchan, a town which has grown up at an important railroad junction during the past fifty years and which now exhibits great occupational and ethnic diversity.[6] The mosaic is a popular metaphor when we try to summarize the character of such a community, and it is certainly in some ways an appropriate one. But if some of the groups which constitute the community are relatively well-bounded, hard-edged in a mosaic-like fashion, others overlap or blend into one another. Furthermore, the history of Kafanchan has in some ways reflected the volatile past of Nigeria as a whole, and this is one of the reasons why the diachronic dimension of its social structure is of great importance. The mosaic turns into a kaleidoscope, where the multitude of parts again and again take on new configurations.

I have made a beginning in Kafanchan toward grasping the totality of the clusters of relationships ordered along ethnic, occupational, religious, recreational, and other lines. It is a goal the pursuit of which takes one into churches, law courts, market places, palm wine bars, tenement yards, and a variety of other settings. Ideally—and the study has certainly not yet reached there—one would want a picture of the urban social structure from top to bottom, from the most to the least inclusive sets of linkages, even if the latter can be no more than sampled. In the process, also, one gains an appreciation of the way these varied components of community life are ordered into physical co-existence in a restricted space. Undoubtedly this spatial and visual organization must impress itself on the minds of urban ethnographers in many settings. Kafanchan has also sharpened my awareness, however, of the fact that to understand an urban community as a whole, one must see it in its wider context. The town would not have come into existence if it were not for the construction of a Nigerian railroad system. Its site might still have been a piece of savanna land, partially used by subsistence cultivators in a nearby hamlet and occasionally traversed by cattle herders. Now that things turned out differently, Kafanchan has become the hub of a small region, served (or perhaps sometimes rather ruled or exploited) by the bureaucrats, traders, doctors, nurses, teachers, religious leaders, and artisans of the town. Peasants go there to sell their produce, but also sometimes for the pleasures of watching the urban scene. Leaving out all these connections between town and country, one would get a very odd picture of a place like Kafanchan.

These impressions from three fields, then, may adumbrate many of the questions raised in this book, as they have been a major part of my own course work in urban anthropology. In the pages to follow, however, Washington, George Town, and Kafanchan are not conspicuously present. The materials for an urban anthropology that I will emphasize are such as have received rather wide recognition for their importance in urban research, although putting them together in this way, and interpreting them as we do, may be unusual. The chapters do not all cut out similar slices of urban thought. First, in the next chapter, we concentrate on Chicago, and the remarkable pioneering work in urban ethnography carried out there particularly in the 1920s and 1930s. This is one instance where we disregard the boundary between sociology and anthropology, since what we are dealing with is "the Chicago School of sociology." But in the end, we find the contrasting styles of conceptualization which mark the boundary of some significance after all. From here, we move in chapter 3 to a more wide-ranging search for ideas of what urbanism may be about. This could be regarded as the central chapter of the book, and at the same time the one of most diverse contents. All kinds of cities appear in it, and several disciplines. In chapter 4, there is a more distinct focus resembling that on the Chicago School. We deal here again with a particular form of urbanism, that of the Central African mining towns, as studied during the late colonial era by the anthropologists of the Rhodes-Livingstone Institute (also identifiable as members of "the Manchester School of anthropology"). There is a close connection also between this group and the topic of chapter 5, network analysis, since it has played a prominent part in developing that mode of conceptualizing social relations. But we draw here on a more varied collection of contributors to network thinking, not all within academic anthropology. Network analysis, of course, is not confined to urban research, but it seems useful to deal with it here since it may be of particular utility in understanding aspects of life in the city. The lead part in chapter 6 is played by Erving Goffman, a brilliant and somewhat controversial thinker who is again positioned so as to straddle sociology and anthropology. With his work as a point of departure, we consider the problem of defining the person—both the construction and the presentation of self—under urban circumstances. This is also a return to where we started, as Goffman is a Chicagoan of a later generation. In the last chapter, we will try to pull together the threads hanging loose from its predecessors, delineating what we have made urban anthropology out to be.

A small army of guides will thus be enlisted to help us explore the city. There are yet others who could have taken us on additional tours, but I have also seen reasons to leave out some of the more obvious candidates. The *Yankee City* studies of Lloyd Warner and his associates surely constitute an important body of research with an acknowledged anthropological inspiration. Yet their impact has been greater in the field of social stratification than in that of urbanism, and it is perhaps no cause of great surprise that urban anthropologists today pay little attention to them. Besides, enough may already have been said—"there have been so many criticisms of Warner that it might well be time to call for a moratorium on them" (Bell and Newby 1971:110). A similar case can probably be made for excluding the Lynds on Middletown, and (closer to us in time) the "culture of poverty" debate, so central to what was understood as urban anthropology in the United States in the late 1960s. I was involved in it myself through my Washington study; it seems sufficiently exemplified by the volumes authored by Lewis (1966) and Valentine (1968) and edited by Leacock (1971). A complex of research which I would have been more tempted to deal with is that of Latin American urbanism, carried out not least by anthropologists from the United States and Britain. For one thing, it could have been a useful counterpart to what is said about African towns and cities in chapter 4. The earlier work, however, mostly on squatter settlements, seems less rich in analytical ideas about urbanism, while the theoretically important second wave with its concern for wider regional and international connections is so much a thing of the present that it would be difficult here to handle its continuing development. We are, to repeat, mostly concerned with retrieving a usable past.

So let us begin with Chicago, as it was in its adolescence.

CHAPTER TWO

Chicago Ethnographers

The growth of Chicago in the nineteenth and early twentieth centuries, from practically nothing to a great metropolis, was spectacular. From the eastern states and from much of Europe people flocked to get some share, large or small, of the wealth created by the meat-packing industry, the steel works, the wheat exchange, and industry and commerce of other varieties. Now and then a newcomer would be successful beyond imagination. Others found themselves in that hopeless poverty which was so often the reverse side of a rapidly industrializing society under laissez-faire conditions. Some of the recent arrivals succeeded only by turning to crime, but surely this was no certain road to a comfortable life for everyone who tried it. In the young working class, unions and political groups were organizing toward collective action; on May 1, 1886, what was probably the world's first May Day demonstration marched up Michigan Avenue in favor of the eight-hour work day. A few days later, a workers' protest meeting in Haymarket Square ended in chaos, as the police moved in to break it up and a bomb exploded, provoking indiscriminate shooting with the death of a number of policemen and protesters as a result. The "Haymarket Affair" for a long time remained a symbol of the threats of foreign ideologies such as anarchism and socialism to American society.

This volatile Chicago was also a point of entry to the West, so some newcomers moved on again. But toward the end of the nineteenth century this option was no longer as attractive as before. In conjunction with the Chicago World's Fair of 1893—an event of pride to those Chicagoans who saw their city as a success story—that meeting of historians was held where the young Frederick Jackson Turner noted the end of the frontier era, at the same time as he speculated on its significance for American culture. In the decades which followed, the further expansion of American society would be even more concentrated in its cities, with Chicago continuing to take a prominent place.

Like many other changing cities, Chicago has covered up much of the tracks of its earlier history. Hull House, the early settlement house out of which a small band of idealists led by Jane Addams operated, trying to ameliorate conditions in the surrounding slums, still stands, but now somewhat isolated as a small museum on the outskirts of a new academic complex. A few hundred yards away, Haymarket Square has been cut into two by a thruway system, and of a monument erected to commemorate the part of the policemen in "defending the city" on that disastrous May evening, only the base remains, hardly noticeable if one is not looking for it. Several versions of the statue which used to be on top have been blown up over the years, one of them by Weathermen in 1969.

But if the city no longer looks quite the same, Chicago's youth has been documented forcefully in many other ways. There were the novelists. Theodore Dreiser, in *Sister Carrie,* showed a city which seemed to make growth itself, and the corruption of young newcomers, its main business; Upton Sinclair traced the dismal career of the Lithuanian immigrant Jurgis Rudkus from slaughterhouse worker to jail inmate to steelworker to tramp to robber to political crook in *The Jungle.* There are Jane Addams' recollections of *Twenty Years at the Hull House.* There is the chapter devoted to Chicago politics in Lincoln Steffens' *The Shame of the Cities,* in which perhaps surprisingly he found that the city, in 1903 at least, was not really among the most corrupt.

Not least, however, one local institution which is still alive and well has played an important role in shaping our understanding not only of early twentieth-century Chicago but of urbanism in general. From World War I and on into the 1930s, sociologists at the University of Chicago turned out a series of studies based on investigations in their own city which have been generally recognized as the beginning of modern urban studies, and as the most important body of social research on any single city in the contemporary world. Although it has been reviewed before, we may remind ourselves of it once more in order to incorporate it explicitly into the heritage of urban anthropology.[1]

THE BEGINNINGS: THOMAS and PARK

Young institutions, unless they are too respectfully intent on imitating their venerable predecessors, stand a chance of doing some innovating. The University of Chicago opened its doors in 1892 and soon had the first sociology department in an American university. This was a period when recruits to the new discipline generally came in from other more established fields, and perhaps for such reasons American sociology at the time could be divided into two major tendencies: a speculative social philosophy, theorizing on a grand scale about the bases of human society and social progress, and a social survey movement, conceptually weak but intensely concerned with getting together the data about undesirable features of the growing industrial society. (A half century or so later the latter would have a parallel in the first wave of research in Third World cities; see Mitchell 1966b:39–40.) Both tendencies were concerned with improving the human condition, but between them there was a great gap. Because of what he did to close it, the most important appointment in the first twenty years of the department, at least as far as lasting intellectual influence is concerned, was probably that of William Isaac Thomas.

Thomas insisted on systematic empirical investigation and took part in gradually removing the study of social organization from the biologistic inclinations which had characterized it earlier. He emphasized the need to understand the participants' view, the "definition of the situation" as he termed it, and as a methodological counterpart to this theoretical innovation, he pioneered in the use of "personal documents"—diaries, letters, and autobiographies as well as accounts of life experience collected by psychiatrists, social workers, or social scientists. In an autobiographical statement of his own, Thomas has suggested that he first stumbled onto this method accidentally:

> I trace the origin of my interest in the document to a long letter picked up on a rainy day in the alley behind my house, a letter from a girl who was taking a training course in a hospital, to her father concerning family relationships and discords. It occurred to me at the time that one would learn a great deal if one had a great many letters of this kind. (Baker 1973:250)

He was able to demonstrate many of his ideas in his great study of European immigrant groups, which took him on wide-ranging travels in search of new materials. In the end it narrowed down to the Poles, in a collaboration with the young Polish social philosopher Florian Znaniecki, who thereby launched his own American career. The five volumes of *The Polish Peasant in Europe and America* were published between 1918 and 1920, a landmark in American sociology.

At about the same time, Thomas left the University of Chicago, under the threat of a personal scandal. (A detective found him in a hotel room with someone else's wife and was in little doubt about how to define the situation; Thomas defended himself against the charges, but in a rather provocative manner. The moral climate at the university was apparently much the same as when Thorstein Veblen left it under similar circumstances a decade or so earlier.) He left behind him a complex of important ideas, including, apart from those already mentioned—and a little ironically perhaps, under the circumstances—a concept of social disorganization, "the decrease of the influence of existing social rules of behavior upon individual members of the group," which emphasized social process rather than individual characteristics. This idea would have a central place in Chicago urban studies. Yet for all his own contributions, the most important part Thomas played in the growth of urban sociology probably consisted in bringing to the university Robert Ezra Park.

When he arrived to take up a post in Chicago, Park already had fifty years of varied life behind him. He had grown up in a Minnesota town, in a neighborhood where Scandinavian immigrants dominated, gone to the University of Michigan, and soon afterwards joined the *Minneapolis Journal*. His many years as a journalist did much to develop his point of view toward urban life, for as his city editor realized that he would stay longer on a story than anybody else, Park became an investigative reporter. It was a period when the popular press went in for reform, muckraking had begun, although not yet under that label. Park only wanted to carry on this work more systematically. He reported on opium dens and gambling houses, discussed the causes of alcoholism on the basis of case materials, and tracked down the source of a diphtheria epidemic by drawing a spot map of its spread. With a beginning in these experiences, he later wrote in an oft-quoted passage, he had probably "covered more ground, tramping about in cities in different parts of the world, than any other living man."

But in the long run the progress of journalism left Park dissatisfied, and he moved on to become a student of philosophy at Harvard. After a year there, he continued his academic work in Germany where he acquired a thorough knowledge of European intellectual currents, attended lectures of Georg Simmel and others, and took his doctorate at Heidelberg with a slim dissertation on collective behavior. This could seem to be a long way from the life of the journalist, but in a way it was all an outgrowth of his earlier experiences. Public opinion, he wrote in his dissertation, was too easily manipulated by catch words; "modern journalism, which is supposed to instruct and direct public opinion by reporting and discussing events, usually turns out to be simply a mechanism for controlling collective attention."

Returning to America, Park soon wanted out of the academic world again, and turned once more to reform. He became a press agent of the Congo Reform Association, an organization of Baptist missionaries who wanted to draw attention to King Leopold's misrule in the Congo, and he contributed articles to *Everybody's,* a leading muckraking publication. He was planning to go and study the situation on the spot when he was drawn instead to become involved with American race relations. Booker T. Washington, the most influential Negro leader at the time, invited Park to his institute at Tuskegee, and there he remained as Washington's assistant for many years. He got to know the South intimately, and he also accompanied Washington on a study tour of Europe to compare the situation of southern Negroes with that of European peasants and workers. At Tuskegee Washington and Park also held an international conference on the race problem, and it was at this conference, in 1911, that Thomas first encountered Park. A couple of years later he was able to bring him to the University of Chicago. To begin with, it was supposed to be a short-term appointment only; as it turned out, Park remained for twenty years.

A VISION of URBANISM

Throughout these Chicago years there was a steady flow of analytical comment on contemporary life from Park's pen. Given his experience of American race relations and the continuous impact of immigration on American society, it is not surprising that minority problems constituted one of his major substantive areas of concern; the other was urbanism, and the two were not always easily separated. He expressed himself mostly through articles and prefaces to the books of his students. In this way he kept adding continuously to a structure of ideas, but the outline of the structure was apparently quite clear in his mind by the time this period began. In the first and most famous of his urban papers, "The City: Suggestions for the Investigation of Human Behavior in the Urban Environment," published in 1915 not long after his arrival in Chicago, one could see a vision of urbanism which was at once the product of long experience and the statement of a research program for years to follow.

Park was capable of thinking about urbanism both on a grand scale and in minute detail. His familiarity with writers such as Simmel and Spengler told him that the city was a force in world history, capable of shaping and releasing human nature in new ways. At the same time he was the man who had spent a decade of his life on the newsbeat, observing what was going on in the streets and behind the façades. In his first paper on urban research both these sides of his interests were visible. On the one hand, he noted the varying characteristics of urban neighborhoods; how some were isolated little worlds to themselves, homes of immigrant populations with few ties to the surrounding society, while others were anonymous agglomerations of individuals on the move, and others again, such as the vice areas, were better characterized by how they were used then by who lived there. These different neighborhoods all needed to be described and understood. But at the same time the big change which urbanism brought was that of an increasing division of labor which served to break down or modify the older type of social organization based on such factors as kinship, caste, and ties of locality. The division of labor created a new kind of rational, specialized man—or rather many kinds, for each occupation could set its own stamp on people. The practical implication for research was that a variety of ways of making a living ought to be investigated:

> the shopgirl, the policeman, the peddler, the cabman, the nightwatchman, the clairvoyant, the vaudeville performer, the quack doctor, the bartender, the ward boss, the strikebreaker, the labor agitator, the school teacher, the reporter, the stockbroker, the pawnbroker; all of these are characteristic products of the conditions of city life; each, with its special experience, insight, and point of view determines for each vocational group and for the city as a whole its individuality. (Park 1952:24–25)

A number of institutions also deserved study. What happened in the city to the family, the church, the courts of justice? What new organizational forms arose under urbanism? There was, again, the newspaper and its part in molding public opinion. What kind of person was the newspaperman? A detective? A historian? A gossip? There was the stock market: what were the psychology and the sociology of its fluctuations? There was political organization: what was the nature of social relationships in machine politics and in reform politics? Partly, these were questions in the field of collective behavior, and so Park could return to some of his past academic preoccupations.

There was a constant concern with "the moral order." [2] In any society, Park felt, the individual is engaged in a struggle to preserve his self-respect and his point of view, but he can succeed in this only by earning the recognition of others. This is what turns the individual into a person. But in the city this moral order of relationships is fraught with special difficulties. Money rather than civility becomes the medium of exchange. People hardly know one another: "Under these circumstances the individual's status is determined to a considerable degree by conventional signs—by fashion and 'front'—and the art of life is largely reduced to skating on thin surfaces and a scrupulous study of style and manners" (Park 1952:47).

This idea of the superficiality of urban social relations would be a recurrent theme in Chicago urban studies. Yet Park was fully aware that close and stable ties also existed in the city, and that the urban conditions had an influence on the way in which these would sort themselves out. In the city there were enough people to sustain a variety of styles of life, and enough freedom for many groups not to have to be excessively bothered with the disapproval of others.

> . . . social contagion tends to stimulate in divergent types the common temperamental differences, and to suppress characters which unites them with the normal types about them. Association with others of their own ilk provides also not merely a stimulus, but a moral support for the traits they have in common which they would not find in a less select society. In the great city the poor, the vicious, and the delinquent, crushed together in an unhealthful and contagious intimacy, breed in and in, soul and body . . . We must then accept these "moral regions" and the more or less eccentric and exceptional people who inhabit them, in a sense, at least, as part of the natural, if not normal, life of a city. (Park 1952:50–51)

There is at least a part of theory of urban cultural process here, some of which we are perhaps willing to accept, and some of which we will most likely find unsatisfactory. The vocabulary is by now no longer ours, and we may feel ill at ease with it. The emphasis on the interactional basis of cultural growth, which one might see as the core of the statement, appears sound, and we will return to it. Park also carefully noted that it was a general analytical point, not one concerning only the criminal or abnormal. The city makes it possible for different people to keep different company; and a company of like characteristics can provide the moral underpinnings for behavior which others might frown upon. In the small community each one of these people might have been the only person of a kind, and the pressures of conformity would have hindered expressions of what would then be mere idiosyncracy. Park dealt less effectively, however, with just what it was that people brought to interact over. Here he tended to fall back on an individual psychology, treating personal inclinations to one kind of behavior or other as more or less given. Thus the city was seen more as a permissive than as an actively shaping influence—it tended to "spread out and lay bare to the public view all the human characters and traits which are ordinarily obscured and suppressed." By now we would probably want to push our inquiry rather further into the social-structural determinants of behavior in the city.

To describe the separate "moral regions" or "social worlds" became one of the major tasks of the Chicago sociologists. But the fact of the coexistence of these worlds in the city could also lead to further questions about the relationships between them. In a passage which could by itself seem enough to stimulate much research, Park gave a glimpse of one way in which they could interact:

> The processes of segregation establish moral distances which make the city a mosaic of little worlds which touch but do not interpenetrate. This makes it possible for individuals to pass quickly and easily from one moral milieu to another, and encourages the fascinating but dangerous experiment of living at the same time in several different contiguous, but otherwise widely separated, worlds. (Park 1952:47)

This facet of cultural organization in the city, however, was to a much greater extent left unattended by his followers in the years to come. One might perhaps see the writings on the "marginal man," launched in 1923 by Park himself, as taking up this thread, although many of them lost themselves in a quagmire of inadequate conceptualization. But here as elsewhere in their work on the moral order, Park and the other Chicagoans tended to leave behind them unfinished business rather than failure in developing an understanding of urban life.

As with PLANTS: The SPATIAL ORDER of the CITY

There was rather more systematic effort in illuminating what was seen as the other major dimension in urban life—indeed in all human life—that of the raw struggle for existence. Already in his first major paper on the city Park had noted the extremely varying characteristics of the neighborhoods; he could also witness that these characteristics did not remain stable over time. In the words of one of his students (Zorbaugh 1929:235), an observer of the Chicago scene in the early twentieth century could see how fashionable residential streets have become the heart of the rooming house district; rooming houses have become tenements, tenements have been reclaimed for studios and shops. Group has succeeded group, the world of fashion has become the world of furnished rooms, and into this world have come the slatternly residents of the slum. The Irish Kilgubbin has become the Swedish Smoky Hollow; the Swedish Smoky Hollow, a Little Sicily; and now Little Sicily becomes a Negro quarter.

Park reflected on these changing patterns in a series of papers in which he developed his "human ecology." This was an analytical perspective where the peculiarly human phenomena of consensus and communication were of negligible importance, and where the inspiration from social Darwinism was obvious. There was a stratum of human life in which people tended to behave like other living things, a "subsocial" or "biotic" stratum where competition was the basic form of coexistence. While such tendencies might or might not be checked by higher-order factors, such as moral constraints, they had a great impact in shaping the modern city. Park found the analogy with plant ecology particularly fitting and elaborated on the utility for urban studies of such concepts as dominance, symbiosis, and succession. Most important, however, was competition, and he saw it as a competition for space. Thus the strongest inhabitants of the urban environment would occupy the most advantageous locations, and others would adjust to their demands. Over time, the former might expand so that others would have to relocate. The principle of symbiosis, according to which different inhabitants could benefit mutually from coexistence in an environment, was a modifying factor in the general scheme.

Park's own writings on human ecology were mostly statements of general principles coupled with apt illustrations. It fell to younger associates of his, particularly Roderick McKenzie and Ernest Burgess, to elaborate on the concepts and show practical applications. The latter especially did so within the Chicago context. As human ecology was conceived as a sociology of space and since competition was the major force of regulation, it was understood that the various human activities would be distributed according to land values. From this Burgess derived his famous ideal-type diagram of the city as a series of concentric circles (figure 1). Inside the first circle was the central business district—in Chicago "the Loop"—with the highest land values. The second circle contained a "zone in transition," which was being invaded from the center by business and light industry. This made it unattractive to most inhabitants who therefore escaped to the residential areas of the more peripheral zones. But the zone in transition still contained artists' colonies, immigrant neighborhoods, and rooming-house areas. They would only move on as they could afford to reject their deteriorated environment or as the affluent center forced them further out by its growth. Economic processes thus created "natural areas," as the Chicago sociologists put it—neighborhoods which had not been consciously designed but just grew.

This view of the city has come in for much criticism, partly due to the tendency of Burgess and others to equivocate on the question whether their interpretations were supposed to hold true for Chicago only, or for any industrial city, or for any city of whatever kind.[3] In fact, it would have been prudent to make only more limited claims. The scheme appeared for example to presuppose a far-reaching division of labor with very differentiated land uses and a separation between residence and work; it ignored the fact that travel in the city would be much more inconvenient under some circumstances than others (depending not least on transport technology), so that suburban living could be a nuisance to people who still had some choice; it excluded consideration of the natural features of the urban site; and not least, the assumption need not always hold true that land was indeed on the market, and held no values of other kinds.

Of course, the model did apply quite well to Chicago, even if Burgess' circles had to extend into Lake Michigan on one side and north-south differences had to be played down. This was a new city where no sentiments attached to particular areas had become strong enough to upset economic processes, and it was a flat place. And whatever limitations the frame of thinking had, it was important in orienting the Chicago sociologists. In the case of the studies to which we will give particular attention below, it gave them an anchorage in particular territories, mostly within the zone in transition. But as we shall see, in these instances locating the phenomena in space was generally only the prolegomenon to ethnographic work where the ecological concepts as they stood were overtaken by cultural and other factors of human consciousness. In other studies, the spatial dimension remained more central, as they focused on the large scale study of the distributions of particular social phenomena in the city. We have seen that Park, as a journalist, had already experimented with spot maps of things he was investigating. At the University of Chicago the idea was taken up as a major research tool, and Burgess in particular devoted classes in "social pathology" regularly to such mapmaking. The outcome of the accumulating knowledge of this sort was a series of correlative studies using

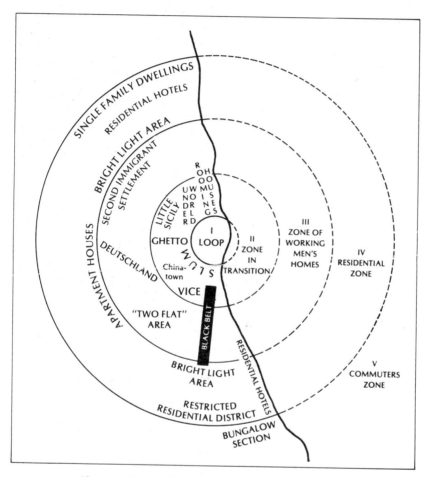

Figure 1. Burgess' Ideal-Type Diagram of the City

abstracted quantitative data—not, it was suggested in the preceding chapter, the manner of conceptualization and research which anthropologists usually favor. But in sociological urban ecology it became increasingly dominant, not changing fundamentally as later scholars tried to reconstruct the perspective so as to avoid some early Chicago errors. In concentrating on aggregate data and disregarding the inside view, it has thus taken another road than that which appeals most to anthropologists. Park, for his part, had his doubts about the wisdom of neglecting qualitative data, but also had a stake in making sociology scientific. And science, at the time, was big on measurement. So around 1930, at the University of Chicago and elsewhere, what was termed urban sociology began to grow away from ethnography.

The CHICAGO STUDIES as ANTHROPOLOGY

It seems justified to suggest, then, that two kinds of urban studies were created in Chicago; conceived in unity but drifting apart in terms of present-day markers of disciplinary inclinations. One became more narrowly sociological, and there is an unbroken line of descent from it to much present-day urban sociology. The other was more anthropological. It may be held that it can become part of the ancestry of urban anthropology only by adoption; in passing, we may note that the connection is a little stronger than this.

When the urban research program got under way, the divorce between sociology and anthropology had not yet taken place at the University of Chicago. Only in 1929 was a separate department of anthropology established. It is not so widely known that Leslie White was a product of this joint department, since his later evolutionary anthropology bore little obvious resemblance to the concerns of the Chicago urbanists. White has later commented that Park was the most stimulating teacher he had at Chicago, although he did not quite know what he learned from him (Matthews 1977:108). Robert Redfield, on the other hand, coming out of the department with his doctorate at about the same time, took Chicagoan concerns into the heartlands of anthropology, as we shall see in the next chapter; he was also Park's son-in-law.

What is equally important to note is that this was a time when sociologists still took more care to familiarize themselves with the current state of anthropology (and anthropologists with that of sociology) than they have tended to do more recently. The University of Chicago, moreover, had an intellectual atmosphere in which contacts between the various social sciences were unusually strong. It is against this background one should view the fact that Thomas, as early as 1909, had published the *Source Book for Social Origins,* an important compendium of ethnological facts, with a revised edition under the new title *Primitive Behavior* in 1937. And in a widely quoted remark in his 1915 article on urban studies, Park noted that anthropological method could be one source of inspiration for the urban research to come:

Anthropology, the science of man, has been mainly concerned up to the present with the study of primitive peoples. But civilized man is quite as interesting an object of investigation, and at the same time his life is more open to observation and study. Urban life and culture are more varied, subtle and complicated, but the fundamental motives are in both instances the same. The same patient methods of observation which anthropologists like Boas and Lowie have expended on the study of the life and manners of the North American Indian might be even more fruitfully employed in the investigation of the customs, beliefs, social practices, and general conceptions of life prevalent in Little Italy on the lower North Side in Chicago, or in recording the more sophisticated folkways of the inhabitants of Greenwich Village and the neighborhood of Washington Square, New York. (Park 1952:15)

Yet Park certainly also had other sources for an ethnographic approach to urban life—his journalistic experience was one of them, the literary naturalism of Zola, Dreiser, and Upton Sinclair was another—and what is important is not just intellectual genealogy. The point, rather, is that wherever the original influences came from, and wherever they went immediately afterwards, many of the studies turned out rather like the urban anthropology of today. This is not so much true as far as explicit theory is concerned, but more true when it comes to choice of methods and topics, and to the form of presentation. The methodological battery of these Chicagoans was similar to that of anthropologists in emphasizing observation of social phenomena in their natural setting but including also informal interviews, surveys, and the collection of personal documents such as life histories, in mixes which varied from one study to another. As the data gathered by these means were woven together, the results were well-rounded ethnographies with an emphasis on qualitative presentation. And as the following sketches of five of the best-known studies may show, the topics selected were institutions and ways of life of types which have tended to draw the interests of latter-day urban anthropologists as well.

HOBOES and HOBOHEMIA

The first in the series of well-known studies of Chicago's social worlds to be published was Nels Anderson's *The Hobo,* in 1923. The hobo as Anderson knew him was a migrant worker, mostly American born and bred, moving around the country according to no fixed plans. Construction work and farm work, forestry and fishing, and any number of temporary odd jobs, all found room for the hobo. But not so long after Anderson's study, it became obvious that this particular kind of modern nomad was a vanishing species. The hobo had been part of a second American frontier, moving westward two decades or so behind the first frontier, in the wake of the railroads. New towns and cities, new farms and industries, made possible and partly even demanded a mobile work force. As this frontier also closed, the openings for transient laborers became much fewer. And so the hobo moved into frontier history.

Much of the territory covered by hobo society, of course, lay farther west, but Chicago was still the hobo capital. To Chicago the men would travel between jobs. It was the terminus of important railroads, and hoboes were habitués of stolen rides on freight trains. They had themselves taken part in building the railroads, and in Chicago and elsewhere their squatter settlements, known as "jungles," were often located next to the tracks. But in Chicago the jungles were only a part of the hobo's world. Anderson's hobohemia was a part of the transitional zone, an area with cheap lodging houses which could compete with the uncomfortable squatter settlements, but also one where the hobo would mix with a variety of other people and institutions.

Nels Anderson was peculiarly well equipped to undertake a study of the hobo life. He had in fact himself dropped out of high school to become a young hobo, drifting around in the West for some time until a farm family in Utah who had given him work encouraged him to go back to school and then continue through college. He worked himself through school by doing occasional migrant labor, and was then advised by a teacher to do graduate work in sociology at Chicago. After he made use of his previous experience as materials for term papers there, funding was arranged so that he could continue his studies in this field. For Anderson as a sociologist, this was participant observation; for Anderson as a hobo, the study was a way of "getting by." And the research site was the same streets, alleys, and saloons where he had sold newspapers as a boy.

Anderson estimated that some 300,000–500,000 homeless men passed through Chicago each year, staying for just a few days or for longer periods, depending on a variety of factors such as the state of the job market and the time of year. During the winter many would remain in the city for longer periods. At any one time there would be between 30,000 and 75,000 of these men in Chicago. But the homeless men who thus assembled along the "main stems" of Chicago's transitional neighborhoods were not all hoboes. Five major types could be distinguished, according to Anderson, and the hobo was only one of them. The first was the seasonal

worker, who followed a more or less steady annual cycle, mostly of agricultural work, like today's American migrant farm laborers. In the terminology of nomadism, their migratory pattern could be seen as a kind of
transhumance. The second type was the hobo, also a migrant worker, but
not one to follow a predictable and recurrent itinerary. The third type was
a migrant, but not a worker; this was the tramp, who made his living
through begging and perhaps stealing. The fourth type was the home
guard, a worker but not a migrant. While the hobo would not usually take
jobs in Chicago, the home guard was a kind of localized urban counterpart
of his; he remained in the same community but drifted between ill-paid
and unskilled jobs, with his roots, if he had any, in hobohemia's street society. The fifth type was the bum, more down-and-out than any of the
others, not working and not migrating. Between these types there were, of
course, gradations, and men were constantly transferring from one category to another.

Exactly why homeless men became homeless men was not always easy to
find out, since every man's past was his own secret, although less personal
news about conditions on the road was willingly exchanged. But a variety
of reasons could be gleaned. Some simply went in search of new experiences. Others were pushed out of steady work by contractions in the job
market. Yet others left family crises behind them. Some suffered from
physical or mental disabilities. With the conditions of life and work encountered by the homeless man, more of them would later end up in this
last category. Alcoholism also took its toll, as did drug use on a smaller
scale.

The men had very few female counterparts.[4] Most were unmarried,
some had separated from their families. Homosexual practices occurred
with some frequency, perhaps especially in the work camps, as in other situations of sexual isolation. In Chicago there was a better chance of finding
feminine company, in the dance halls, among the girls of the burlesque
theatres, or among prostitutes. Some settled down with their partners and
left the world of homeless men, but for the majority there were only transient relationships. The relationships between men and women in hobohemia were only one of many examples of symbiosis between the homeless
and other groups and institutions. There were the fifty some employment
agencies which kept the hoboes shuttling between Chicago and the West.
There were the pawnbrokers, the restaurants where one could have an
uninspiring meal for ten cents, and the cheap hotels and flophouses where

one could stay. There were the barber colleges where trainees needed somebody to practice on, somebody who would not complain about the results as long as the price was right.

While in the city the hoboes had plenty of time on their hands, but little money, much of their time was spent walking up and down the streets, window-shopping for meals and jobs. They could go over to Washington Square, "Bughouse Square" on hobo maps, to listen to the soap-box orators holding forth on assorted subjects of science, politics, economics, and religion. They might stop and listen to the singing of choirs from the missions or the inspired salesmanship of street hawkers. If their economic situation was particularly bad they could themselves turn to peddling or begging. Although perhaps most of the homeless men were hostile to organized religion, some might submit to being "converted" in exchange for bed and board, but these would more often be bums or tramps than hoboes. The designation for them was "mission stiffs"; the homeless men had a well-developed vocabulary of social types which allowed them to communicate efficiently about adaptations and personalities in their world of flux. A "jungle buzzard" made his living by begging in the jungles and would wash pots and kettles for the other men in exchange for the privilege of eating what was left in them. A "jack roller" would rob fellow tramps while they were drunk or asleep; it was about a young man of this type that Clifford Shaw (1930), another Chicagoan, did a well-known life-history study. A "gun moll" was a dangerous female tramp. As Eskimos have an elaborate set of designations for different kinds of snow, the hoboes needed terms by which to think and talk about kinds of people. Although he did little more than note the existence of these terms, Anderson's attention to them could be seen as a first step in the direction of an ethnoscientific study of urban nomadism, taken further more recently by Spradley (1970, 1972), whose tramp studies showed that some of the same terms were still in use close to fifty years later.

The mobile way of life of the hobo obviously permitted no very tight social organization, and the men kept such outside agencies as missions and charities at arm's length. Yet a couple of organizations existed which were not only for the hobo but to some extent also of the hobo. Both had the political objective of improving the lot of the migrant working man, but their strategies differed. One of them was the reformist International Brotherhood Welfare Association, founded by James Eads How, heir to a family fortune, who hoped to erase poverty through education. To this end he supported "hobo colleges," lecture halls where the men could come to listen to lectures and discuss the issues of the day. The IBWA also ran hostels. Because of How's control over the funds, however, it could be only partly an organization of the homeless men themselves; partly it remained a charity, even if it was dedicated to the goal of "a classless society." Thus it differed significantly from the other organization with some major impact on hobo society—the Industrial Workers of the World, the "Wobblies." The IWW, of course, did not aim only at organizing hoboes, but among them it found its strongest support, and this contributed to making Chicago the capital of Wobblydom. Its organizers traveled widely throughout the West, however, selling the red membership cards, sometimes through ideological persuasion, at other times by the use of threat. Some of the hoboes, at least, could thus be considered a politically conscious part of a lumpenproletariat. They were the men who supported hobohemia's radical bookstores, read the *Hobo News* and the *Industrial Solidarity,* and according to an IWW recommended reading list of April 1922, could reflect on the meaning of Lewis Henry Morgan's *Ancient Society.* They would try to spread the message further by speaking in "Bughouse Square," and some of them would themselves try to write, although few, like Joe Hill with his songs, would gain any recognition even among other hoboes for their efforts.

Perhaps because Anderson with his background could make it an "inside job," *The Hobo* ranks among the best of the Chicago monographs in terms of ethnographic richness. If there was a streak of romanticism involved in his picture of the world of the homeless men, it might be partly due to a general tendency among the Chicago sociologists, and partly to some nostalgia of his own. But this nostalgia in its turn could perhaps be grounded in an awareness that at least for the hobo, this world could contain a reasonably viable way of life and a coherent world view. The hobo, Park wrote in *The City,* was "the bohemian in the ranks of common labor." But if some could feel that it was a way of life with some satisfactions, it was clearly not so to every hobo, and even less probably to the tramp and the bum. With the hobo gone and only these latter left, the Skid Row of American cities, successor to hobohemia as the quarter of homeless men, remains with little but the elements of human tragedy.

1,313 GANGS

Chicago in the 1920s had a multitude of organizations with such names as "Buckets of Blood," "the Dirty Sheiks and Wailing Shebas," and "the

Hawthorne Toughs." These, and other examples of boys and young men in groups (with female partners seldom included), were the subject of Frederic M. Thrasher's *The Gang,* first published in 1927, a pioneering inquiry into delinquency in urban life. Its subtitle described it as "a study of 1,313 gangs in Chicago," an enormous figure considering that more recent students of gangs have often been satisfied to cover one, and also a figure which might suggest that this would be a study revolving around the statistical manipulation of massive quantitative data. This is not the case, however, as Thrasher's data on the various gangs were not strictly comparable, and thus not generally amenable to such treatment. Some data came out of newspaper reports, others from personal observation, yet others from personal documents by members of gangs and by observers of the gang scene. (Thrasher apparently won the favor of many gang boys by showing his skills as a magician.) In fact, it does not seem clear exactly how Thrasher enumerated his gangs. Counting them and separating them as discrete entities would certainly entail some difficulties, as "the ganging process is a continuous flux and flow, and there is little permanence in most of the groups." Some of them had as little as three members; others included thousands. In the former case, of course, a "now you see it, now you don't" quality must have been inescapable.

While Thrasher could offer tables of numerical data for some characteristics of the gangs—but only for very variable proportions of the populations of 1,313—he thus used the breadth of his information mostly to indicate themes and variations. A latter day reader of *The Gang,* apart from becoming perhaps a little impatient with some of the psychological arguments, might find this presentation at times somewhat unfocused, or at worst contradictory. Trying to generalize about groups of quite different orientations and membership characteristics, such problems can be expected. Although most gang members were adolescents, for example, Thrasher had groups with members as little as six years old, and others with members up to fifty years old. Certainly it would have been a more manageable task to deal with some smaller number of groups, or groups of some more sharply delimited type. What Thrasher gave his readers instead was an overview of the entire ganging complex, irritatingly obscure in some ways but very illuminating in others. [5]

A major finding was that the formation of gangs had a territorial aspect. They arose in a gangland, and this largely coincided with the zone of transition in Burgess' ecological scheme.

Probably the most significant concept of the study is the term *interstitial*—that is, pertaining to spaces that intervene between one thing and another. In nature foreign matter tends to collect and cake in every crack, crevice, and cranny—interstices. There are also fissures and breaks in the structure of social organization. The gang may be regarded as an interstitial element in the framework of society, and gangland as an interstitial region in the layout of the city. (Thrasher 1963:20)

The point was important, for one thing, in that it suggested that gangs were part of the social characteristics of the area itself, rather than of any particular group of people who happened to find themselves there. Thrasher noted that a variety of immigrant groups had passed through the transitional zone as an area of first settlement, and that while they all tended to form gangs while they were there, their rates of gang formation generally declined drastically as they moved out of it. Gangs would thus have to be regarded as an integral part of the social disorganization which he found typical of the transitional zone.

Even so, he could not entirely ignore the ways in which ethnicity channeled gang life. Of the 880 gangs for which he had data on ethnic composition, about sixty percent were exclusively or dominantly of one ethnic group. Naturally, some ethnic groups would furnish more gangs than others, simply by being a greater proportion of the population. But there was also some variation relative to this proportion. Poles, Italians, Irish, and blacks had many gangs from this point of view. Germans, Jews, and Swedes had few. Partly, but not altogether, this would be a function of which ethnic groups had already begun to move out of the transitional zone, as Thrasher calculated with the population figures of Chicago as a whole. Furthermore, his figures do not tell us if any ethnic group gave rise to larger gangs than others, so that a small number of gangs could encompass a relatively large part of the population. Probably, however, there were also some real cultural and organizational differences between ethnic groups—Thrasher used the contrast between the Jews and the Irish as an example.

Yet ethnicity was not the only, perhaps not even the major basis of gang formation and gang conflict. There was antagonism between groups at different economic levels, and ethnic homogeneity may often have been a coincident of territoriality. Gangs were mostly recruited on a neighborhood basis, and since much of the transitional zone consisted of a variety of ethnic quarters, ethnic gangs were a natural consequence. If these quarters were threatened by the invasion of another ethnic group, ethnic solidarity in the gang might be heightened, as gang conflict became one expression of the struggle. Where mixed neighborhoods had achieved some stability, on the other hand, gangs were also mixed.

Thrasher found the origin of gangs in the small and informal play groups of children even below school age; this was one reason he felt it necessary to view everything from these groups to machine politics and organized crime as a single social field. Gradually, the groups would develop an internal structure and shared traditions. What finally turned a group into a gang, however, was the reaction of opposition and disapproval from its surroundings—the gang was a conflict group.

Certainly it was not constantly engaged in acute conflict. Thrasher noted that much of its activity simply involved roaming about and exploring the world, trying out new patterns of behavior and creating romantic fantasies to take their minds at least momentarily out of their restricted environment. Hikes, sports, burlesque theatres and movie thrillers played as much of a part in this as gang fights. In this Thrasher saw an endless quest for new experience, one of the "four wishes" which Thomas has formulated as the mainsprings of human motivation.[6] But he did not relate this quest very clearly to the structural position of gang boys. While more recent sociologists of delinquency, with their more socialized conception of man, have often seen gang behavior in terms of status insecurity and similar problems, for Thrasher it was a sign of independence. Gangland was a moral and cultural frontier, where human nature could be expressed in the raw, and the gang boy was a frontiersman.

Let us return, however, to the involvement with conflict. This did not take an identical, or equally acute, form in all gangs, and Thrasher outlined a typology to allow us some understanding of the variations. The "diffuse type" was only a rudimentary gang. Its members might live in the same neighborhood and thus interact with one another daily, and occasionally they would fight together. But loyalties or internal structure were not strongly developed. Out of this type, usually through more extended conflict, the "solidified type" could develop, "a well-integrated fighting machine, by means of which the gang presents a solid front against its foes." This was the most pure type of conflict group, one which valued conflict in itself, treasured its reputation for toughness and maintained a strict code of loyalty. Usually it was a teenage group. As its members grew older, and if they did not simply drop out of gang life, some alternative sequences of development could occur. The gang could turn into a secret society, developing rituals apparently mostly motivated by the thrills of mysticism. This would probably be a largely peaceful group, pursuing a pattern of group organization with some prestige in the wider society and continuing to provide sociability for its members. Another possibility was that it could become a "conventionalized type" of gang, discarding its most blatant conflict orientation and achieving legitimacy as a club with some socially acceptable purpose. The most common variant was the athletic club, whereby at least some members would establish contact with organized sports.

But often it would also be linked to politics, as a machine politician would give it his patronage in exchange for various kinds of support, such as bringing out the vote on election day. This was one of integrating the gang into the wider structure of the adult world. Another was to take on a more instrumental orientation to crime and link up more definitely to the underworld. Many gangs, of course, had been in the habit of occasional thieving, from a mixture of economic and expressive motives, and their neighborhoods were sometimes strongholds of organized crime which could play some part in their informal socialization. Some gangs had their own Fagins, Thrasher observed. And in the prohibition era, there was a wide scope for illicit activities.

When gangs became secret societies or athletic clubs, they would necessarily take on a more formal structure. In other types of gangs, internal relationships would more often be informally ordered, and such an order could exist intertwined with formal organization as well. In his attention not only to the leaders but also to the role of the "funny boy," the "sissies," the "show-offs," and "the goofy guys" in the instrumental and expressive division of labor in the gang, Thrasher became more specifically microsociological than most of the Chicago sociologists and showed a notable awareness of small-group dynamics. In this, as well as in noting the embeddedness of gangs in the structures of machine politics and organized crime, he adumbrated the achievements of William F. Whyte in *Street Corner Society* (1943). Whyte, of course, could be in some ways more systematic, as he dealt with only a single gang, and he decisively made the point that the slum has a social organization of its own, rather than merely disorganization. But Thrasher, while sticking to the vocabulary of his peers, was not so far removed from such an insight:

Gangs represent the spontaneous effort of boys to create a society for themselves where none adequate to their needs exists . . . The failure of the normally directing and controlling customs and institutions to function efficiently
in the boy's experience is indicated by disintegration of family life, inefficiency
of schools, formalism and externality of religion, corruption and indifference
in local politics, low wages and monotony in occupational activities, unemploy-
ment, and lack of opportunity for wholesome recreation. All these factors
enter into the picture of the moral and economic frontier, and, coupled with
deterioration in housing, sanitation, and other conditions of life in the slum,
give the impression of general disorganization and decay.

The gang functions with reference to these conditions in two ways: It offers
a substitute for what society fails to give, and it provides a relief from suppression and distasteful behavior. (Thrasher 1963:32–33)

In other words: the gang itself was organization rather than disorganization, an adaptation to an unresponsive environment. As an example of
how Chicago concepts sometimes betrayed Chicago observations, this one
should be obvious enough.

The JEWISH QUARTER in EUROPE and AMERICA

Louis Wirth's *The Ghetto* (1928) was, to a greater extent than the other
monographs dealing with particular Chicago neighborhoods, a work of
social history—not surprisingly, since the Jewish neighborhood made its
appearance in the United States with a ready-made and obvious past in the
Old World. Wirth thus spent almost the first half of his book discussing
the ghetto phenomenon in Europe, from the time of the diaspora to the
nineteenth century, characterized by emancipation in western Europe and
by increasing repression in the East. In their beginning, the ghettos were
voluntary concentrations of Jews in particular quarters; as time went on,
their segregation there became publicly regulated, at the same time as the
livelihood of the Jews became increasingly circumscribed to a limited
number of niches. On the one hand, the history of the ghetto in Europe is
thus that of the institutionalization of an ethnic boundary. The Jews were
useful at least to some parts of the surrounding society, and therefore
largely tolerated, but with continuous harassments and with outbreaks of
persecution which a member of the minority could hardly afford ever to
forget. On the other hand, the ghetto had considerable autonomy as far as
its internal affairs were concerned. The outside world tended to treat it as
a corporate community, responsible as a whole for the conduct of its members. Its taxes, for example, were exacted as a lump sum from the officials

of the synagogue. Within this community, religious, legal, educational, and welfare institutions grew, enmeshing the ghetto dwellers in a web of life which connected them to one another and separated them from outsiders. But it also had an informal, emotional dimension which was hardly less important for the man of the ghetto.

> While his contacts with the outside world were categoric and abstract, within his own community he was at home. Here he could relax from the etiquette and the formalism by which his conduct in the gentile world was regulated. The ghetto offered liberation. The world at large was cold and strange, his contact with it being confined to abstract and rational intercourse. But within the ghetto he felt free . . . Whenever he returned from a journey to a distant market, or from his daily work which had to be carried on largely in a gentile world, he came back to the family fold, there to be re-created and reaffirmed as a man and as a Jew. Even when he was far removed from his kin, he lived his real inner life in his dreams and hopes with them. With his own kind he could converse in that homely and familiar tongue which the rest of the world could not understand. He was bound by common troubles, by numerous ceremonies and sentiments to his small group that lives its own life oblivious of the world beyond the confines of the ghetto. Without the backing of his group, without the security that he enjoyed in his inner circle of friends and countrymen, life would have been intolerable.

In his discussion of the European ghetto Wirth used particularly the example of Frankfurt, the most famous of Jewish quarters in western Europe. But during the nineteenth century, western European Jews were drawn increasingly into the mainstream of life in their respective societies. Many were in the frontline of cosmopolitan intellectual enlightenment. In eastern Europe, the situation was quite different. Often isolated in the midst of a peasant society, Jews there continued to turn inward to their own community, their world view strongly tinged by mysticism. While the western ghettos began to dissolve, the eastern communities were still encapsulated in their minority status. This difference between East and West in Europe was a fact of major importance as the history of the American ghetto began.

What, then, was the Chicago ghetto like, as Wirth described it? To begin with, for a period of several decades of Jewish life in the city, there was really nothing that could well be called a ghetto. The small Jewish community, recruiting new members only through a slow trickle, was not exactly randomly scattered in space, but neither was it isolated. Its members were mostly fairly successfully engaged in commerce and had a wide range of contacts with other Chicagoans. Since most of them were of

German background they felt little inclination to raise barriers against the society around them, and they strove to shape the institutions which they built so as to fit into the general pattern of respectable life in urban America. In the latter part of the nineteenth century, however, the number of Jewish newcomers continued to grow, and now they were mostly Eastern Europeans—Poles, Russians, Romanians. This was the period when the growth of a ghetto really began on the West Side of Chicago, continuing until, with a population of more than a quarter million by the time of Wirth's study, the Jewish community of Chicago was the second-largest of any American city, although yet vastly outnumbered by that of New York. But of course, the entire number did not live in the ghetto. For one thing, the better-established Jews remained in those more satisfactory neighborhoods where they had by then rooted themselves. And those for whom the ghetto was the point of entry would gradually move on from there.

Where the Jewish Chicagoan chose to live is in fact the focus of Wirth's study, as, true to the ecological inclinations of his sociological fraternity, he observed that "where the Jew lives is as good an index as any other as to the kind of Jew he is." The West Side ghetto, indeed, became in some ways like the old ghettos of Europe. A wall, although now invisible, seemed still to encircle it and shield its community life from outside influences. Orthodox synagogues flourished, making up in numbers for their frequently modest size and appearance. The language was Yiddish, and social life, both formal and informal, revolved around the *Landsmannschaften* of people from the same town or region in the old country. Synagogues, mutual aid societies, burial societies, and religious schools were formed on this basis, and countrymen could reminisce together about the past and exchange thoughts about their new country. Yet institution-building also took place on a community-wide basis. There was a Yiddish press and a Yiddish theater. Zionism and socialism had wide support, as they had already had in eastern Europe.

But despite all the intensity of its internal life, the ghetto was a vulnerable community. From the very beginning, its inhabitants saw that there were Jews who preferred to live outside it, who had apparently rejected ghetto ideas of the Jewish identity. The German Jews, of course, were prominent among these. The Eastern Europeans of the ghetto now often saw them as apostates. At the same time, other ties drew the two groups together. The Eastern Europeans had arrived just about penniless, and life in the ghetto for these newcomers was characterized by stark poverty. Motivated undoubtedly in part by humanitarianism and ethnic solidarity, the German Jews undertook a variety of projects to aid the ghetto poor; partly, they were also driven by that desire for respectability which has so often been a strong motive among more advantageously situated members of American minorities, understanding that the reputation of ghetto Jews would also reflect on them. For many of the Eastern Europeans one of these already successful ethnic compatriots would also become the first employer. Yet if the two groups were thus in some ways linked, the hierarchical nature of the linkages could also add to discord.

As time went on, the German Jews would no longer stand alone as symbols of the problematic relationship between Jewishness and success, as understood in the ghetto. Men who graduated from a pushcart in the Maxwell Street market to a small store to a wholesale enterprise began to move away from customs which interfered with progress, and the next generation was even more likely to question the old values.

This dilemma of adaptation led to the differentiation of the ghetto community and also to its decline as a center of ethnic life. The inhabitants had a vocabulary for it. There were successful Jews who were *Menschen,* who had done well without sacrificing much of their Jewishness. But there were also the *Allrightnicks,* regarded as cultural opportunists whose economic mobility was accompanied by disrespect for traditional community standards. [7] Those who seemed to model their new behavior on that of the German Jews became known as *Deitchuks:* and as they moved away from the West Side ghetto, gradually taking over the Lawndale area from the Irish and the Germans, this new neighborhood, socially superior but with a much less distinct ethnic flavor, became known to the ghetto dwellers as *Deutschland.* More and more moved up and out of the ghetto, however, until those who had come to Lawndale to escape the ghetto found that it had followed them to the new location, even if it had lost some of its characteristics. And thus a new wave of dispersal began, to neighborhoods which would never have so strong an ethnic concentration.

The Ghetto shows the usual influences of Chicago ecological thought. We have seen that Wirth found residence a useful index of life style. Some particular cultural factors, like access to a market and relations to other ethnic groups, may have had some influence on the location of the ghetto; yet the laws of economic competition were supreme, and so basically the ghetto was the same sort of "natural area" as Little Sicily, the Black Belt,

or even a vice area. Each area had its own life, while between them contacts were superficial. Again Wirth brought out the image of symbiosis
among plants.

Even more than it is a work of Chicago ecology, however, *The Ghetto*
may be seen as an expression of the influence of Park's thought on race
relations.[8] The typical "race relations cycle" would lead from isolation
through competition, conflict, and accommodation to assimilation—the
ghetto represented accommodation, and the move out of it was the beginning of assimilation. This, however, was a difficult phase. The individual
involved in it would be, in the term coined by Park, a "marginal man." In
the preceding stage, Wirth suggested rather harshly, "the ghetto Jew is
provincial and has a dwarfed personality." As he enters the wider society,
"he stands on the map of two worlds, not at home in either."

Later writers, as we have noted, have made much use of the marginal
man concept; others have been sharply critical of it. This, however, is
tangential to our concerns here. What should perhaps instead be emphasized is that the state of flux which Wirth described as following the
departure from the ghetto would not necessarily end in assimilation. As
Amitai Etzioni (1959) has pointed out in a critique of *The Ghetto,* an ethnic community, albeit of a somewhat different kind, could stabilize again
without a territorial basis. For Wirth, an agnostic of German Jewish background, such a proposition might have been neither interesting nor desirable. But perhaps also his lack of concern with such an alternative is the
price he had to pay for his ecological frame of mind.

LOWER NORTH SIDE PANORAMA

In his introduction to Harvey W. Zorbaugh's *The Gold Coast and the
Slum* (1929), Robert Park drew a distinction between "descript" and "nondescript" communities. The former were places of unity and charm; the
latter lacked these qualities. The Lower North Side of Chicago, the subject of Zorbaugh's monograph, was clearly nondescript. It was more questionable whether it could really be termed a community, since the area
shared little more than a common designation. It was not really, as the title
of the volume might lead one to believe, a matter of only two communities
either. Zorbaugh in fact delineated six "natural areas" on the Lower North
Side—The Gold Coast, the rooming-house zone, Bohemia, the dilapidated
business and entertainment area centering on North Clark Street, the

slum, and Little Sicily. Again, of these, some were more communities than others. Anyway, the scope of this study was thus wider than those of most of its contemporaries. It also overlapped partly with these, so that it could draw to some extent, for example, on Thrasher on the gang, Anderson on the hobo, and Cressey on the taxi-dance hall.

More often than not, the Chicago urbanists reported on the poor, the foreign, or the more or less disreputable. Zorbaugh's chapter on the Gold Coast marked an exception. The Gold Coast, lining the shore of Lake Michigan, was the home of many well-to-do Chicagoans, but most notably of the Four Hundred, the self-conscious upper class of the city. The guide to who was who in this group, with their universities, clubs, and marriages listed, was that thin blue book, the *Social Register,* and Emily Post's *Blue Book of Etiquette* was the codification of its style of life.

Several members of this group wrote documents for Zorbaugh's study, representing "friendly insights and half amused self-analysis," and the chapter was constructed around these. This was a world of leisure. One had to attend first nights at the opera and the right balls and club meetings, and one had to fit the hairdresser, the manicure, the massage, and the French language class into one's weekly schedule. For a considerable part of the year, of course, one might not be in Chicago at all, but in Europe or at American resorts. Yet there were also responsibilities to society. One could participate in one or another of the uplift organizations active in poorer neighborhoods, and one had to give willingly to charities. This was in fact one of the ways by which a family of new wealth could enter the real elite: giving conspicuously to an established society woman's pet charity and thus eliciting an invitation to join her social circle, if only at its periphery to begin with. Another way would be to send one's children to the right schools, making connections through them. The Chicago social elite at this time was becoming less closed and caste-like, a cause for some regret among the Four Hundred. But the newcomers would at least have to assimilate themselves to the hierarchy of style. One could not arrive at the opera in a Yellow Cab, one ought not carry packages or an umbrella, and by the time the shopgirls moved up to a new clothing fashion, the socially ambitious Gold Coaster would have to abandon it.

Some of these shopgirls made their home—or what they might somewhat hesitatingly refer to as their home—not so far from the Gold Coast, in that "world of furnished rooms" which adjoined it on the west. This had once been an area of fashionable residences, but one by one they had been taken over by rooming houses, and thus it had become a natural area of a very different kind. If the Gold Coast had its cliques of quite intensive interaction and if its inhabitants kept a close check on personal reputations, the rooming-house area was one of severe social atomism and anonymity. At some points it merged with the slum, in its more northerly and respectable part, young unmarried men and women of a modest white-collar stratum made up much of the population, in an unsensational interlude between two family cycles. Naturally such a neighborhood would be marked by transiency, not only because it was part of a stage in a person's life. People would also move in and out of rooming houses, hoping that somehow the next would be less dreary a place. Even the landlords were rootless. Zorbaugh found that half of them had been no more than six months at their current address.

The rooming-house zone provided the sociologist with a platform for a dramatic formulation of what urban living may be like:

> The conditions of life in the world of furnished rooms are the direct antithesis of all we are accustomed to think of as normal in society. The exaggerated mobility and astonishing anonymity of this world have significant implications for the life of the community. Where people are constantly coming and going; where they live at best but a few months in a given place, where no one knows any one else in his own house, to say nothing of his own block (children are the real neighbors, and it is a childless world); where there are no groups of any sort—where all these things are true it is obvious that there can be no community tradition or common definition of situations, no public opinion, no informal social control. As a result, the rooming-house world is a world of political indifference, of laxity of conventional standards, of personal and social disorganization.
>
> The rooming-house world is in no sense a social world, a set of group relationships through which the person's wishes are realized. In this situation of mobility and anonymity, rather, social distances are set up, and the person is isolated. His social contacts are more or less completely cut off. His wishes are thwarted, he finds in the rooming-house neither security, response, nor recognition. His physical impulses are curbed. He is restless, and he is lonely. (Zorbaugh 1929:82)

Clearly there was some basis for an interpretation such as this. Documents provided Zorbaugh with illustrations of roomers whose past and present lives were unknown to their neighbors, and who left without a trace, or of people whose isolation may have led them onto paths they might not otherwise have taken. The suicide rate of the rooming-house area was high. Yet one may wonder whether in the case of such a footloose population a focus on its neighborhood would really lead to an understanding of its way of life—or more realistically perhaps, of its variety of life styles. For while some undoubtedly were lonely in the big city, others may simply have had their significant contacts outside the territory, and among the young men and women some most likely formed there those close relationships which ultimately led them away from the area of rented rooms.

The bohemian quarter of Chicago was also known as Towertown, after the old water tower which remained as a sole reminder of the early North Side from before the great fire of 1871. It had what such a quarter should have: studios, art shops, bookstores, and small restaurants. In gathering places like the Dill Pickle Club, its intellectuals would air radical views on sex and politics. Even if many of its inhabitants would also turn out to be only temporary residents, it was more of a community than the rooming-house area. It provided freedom not merely through anonymity but through assertion of principle. Unmarried couples who were living together could find a haven there, as could sexual minorities. Women found a freedom of initiative in its cultural life which they did not have elsewhere in American society.

Towertown had also had its share of successful artists and authors. But most of them had gone on to bigger and better bohemias elsewhere, in New York and overseas. To Zorbaugh this was one sign of decline, for he was not impressed with what was left behind—"egocentric poseurs, neurotics, rebels against the conventions of Main Street or the gossip of the foreign community, seekers of atmosphere, dabblers in the occult, dilettantes in the arts, or parties to drab lapses from a moral code which the city has not yet destroyed." Self-expression was the avowed goal, but to those with little talent this became a matter of playing roles and wearing masks. As on the Gold Coast, those who had a more authentic claim to the values of the community were being joined by newcomers whose hold on these values was more precarious. But again the latter as well were concerned with maintaining the symbolic boundaries toward the wider society by rejecting what it accepted.

Even in this state, however, Zorbaugh felt that bohemia could not maintain itself. Not only were land values rising, forcing people out of their cheap studio apartments before encroaching business buildings. More importantly, perhaps, the tolerance of bohemia would spread over the city with mobility and anonymity. There would no longer be a need for a Towertown.

Going from the Gold Coast through the rooming-house zone and bohemia to North Clark Street, one was clearly descending through the class system. This was a part of hobohemia as described by Anderson. It was also Main Street to much of the rooming-house zone and the slum, and "the Rialto of the half-world," in a turn of phrase popular among the Chicago sociologists. It was lined with dance halls, cabarets, restaurants, pool halls, pawn shops, and cheap lodging houses. The young singles of the rooming houses might seek their entertainment here, in the smaller dance halls. The larger halls had a mixed public of workingmen, shopgirls, gang members, prostitutes, and criminals. The sidewalks were the territory of panhandlers and hawkers.

The slum of which North Clark Street was in part a commercial extension was itself an area of great diversity. Only cheap rents had pulled people of many kinds together there. For many it would only be a stopover on the way to somewhere else. Others spent their entire lives there. Some of the inhabitants, single people or families, were economically, mentally, and physically down-and-out. Another category included the personnel of the underworld. A third category were simply working-class people of modest incomes, often of ethnic minorities. Zorbaugh found representatives of twenty-eight nationalities. There were the largest colony of Assyrians in the United States, a Greek settlement, a growing Black Belt, and groups of Germans and Swedes remaining after most of their compatriots had left the area. To Zorbaugh the slum was preeminently an area of social disorganization. Yet we may suspect that these varied categories of people on closer inspection would show more varied social patterns than such a label would allow, and that particularly the ethnic minorities could in some cases be described as rather closely knit groups.

The sixth and last area described by Zorbaugh was one of the ethnic colonies, part of the slum although large and distinct enough to be singled out for special treatment. This was Little Sicily, also known as "Little Hell." The area had turned Italian—and practically all Sicilian—soon after the turn of the century, and even more than before, when it had been the home of other immigrant groups, it had become a world of its own. Perhaps one should even say that it had turned into many smaller worlds, for the consciousness of kind of the Sicilian was intensely local. Like the Jews of the West Side ghetto with their *Landsmannschaften,* the Sicilians thus began by organizing their social life on the basis of origin in the same place in the old country.

This inward turn of the community had many implications. It could maintain a Mediterranean social code of intense family loyalties, strict control over women, and ideas of honor and shame. It allowed some members to set themselves up in business by catering to culturally-derived needs unfamiliar to the outside world, and others to establish themselves as brokers, trusted, for example, with finding work for the others in that world, or with using their collected voting power in machine politics. It made it possible for some to terrorize others through acts of violence, since no one would be an informer to the police. And this rule of silence would also protect those who were to climb the ladder of organized crime. But this to Zorbaugh was already a sign of change, for the delinquent gang was a response of the second generation to the increased contacts with American life. As with other immigrant groups, the younger generation would have to go through disorganization as it took its first steps into the wider social arena and left old norms behind.

The panoramic perspective of *The Gold Coast and the Slum* remains impressive. Noting that Zorbaugh had achieved one of the aspirations of Robert Park, David Matza (1969:48) has suggested that "it was as if an anthropologist let loose in Chicago had discovered urban America in its full diversity." Yet one may feel that if he gained in breadth of coverage compared to most of his colleagues, he lost something in depth. While his descriptions provide fascinating glimpses of the variety of lives on the lower North Side, they seem more like the ethnographic notes supplied to colonial archives by touring district officers (although perhaps more lively) than they conform to the Malinowskian ideals of professional anthropologists. As far as giving an inside view is concerned, Wirth's study of the ghetto and Anderson's of hobohemia are considerably superior to *The Gold Coast and the Slum*. Nor did Zorbaugh do much with the proximity of his six natural areas to one another, even though the last part of the book is devoted to a discussion of the problems faced by voluntary agencies and associations in trying to make one community of the Lower North Side. By and large, the reader is still likely to remember this as a study of a series of separate social worlds. This was most likely the intention, but perhaps a closer attention to what happened at social boundaries, and to the perspectives of these worlds toward each other, could have done something to tie the parts more closely into a single whole. More specifically, if the Gold Coast was not just a community at leisure but a social world in which power was exercised in ways which affected much of the city, Zorbaugh had little to say about it. This became only one more portrait of a style of life, to be set alongside other vignettes of a similar nature.

Despite such criticisms, drawing on almost another half-century of developments in the social sciences, however, *The Gold Coast and the Slum* deserves to be noted among the Chicago classics. For someone wanting a capsule introduction to the work of the early Chicago urbanists, this (or Short's anthology, *The Social Fabric of the Metropolis*) would be a good choice. It has their characteristic form of presentation, a good outline of their theoretical views, and ethnography which should still stimulate the thought of urban anthroplogists.

DANCING for a LIVING

"Feminine society is for sale, and at a neat price." Thus Paul G. Cressey described the essence of the new urban institution which was the topic of his *The Taxi-Dance Hall*. Published in 1932, it was one of the last of the well-known ethnographies associated with the early Chicago school of sociology. Field work for it had begun in 1925, however, and it was based on a thesis for which the Master's degree had been granted in 1929, so that the setting is really Chicago in the twenties rather than the thirties.

The taxi-dance hall was a somewhat disreputable kind of establishment which traced its origins both to dancing schools and to regular dance halls open to both sexes. Some managers of dancing schools found that certain male pupils were willing to pay for the opportunity to dance with their female instructors far beyond the stage where they really needed lessons; owners of dance halls on the other hand sometimes found themselves with large numbers of socially unattractive male patrons for whom there was no female company. The logical solution was to pay girls to dance with the customers. Ten cents a dance was the usual price. The men would buy tickets at the gate, and the girl chosen as partner for a dance would collect the ticket. She then got half the earnings from her tickets, while the other half went to the proprietor who paid for the hall, the orchestra, and other operating expenses. This system, naturally, ensured the most popular girls of the best earnings and put the girls on a competitive footing toward each other.

Something could be said about the ecology of the taxi-dance halls (which still tended to describe themselves as dancing academies, although few customers would be fooled by this claim to pedagogy). They would be located where rents were low, and in areas which were conveniently accessible for their patrons—now all male. In practice, this often meant a rooming-house area, not too far from the central business district. But ecology was not a topic to which Cressey devoted many pages. He was more concerned with the taxi-dance hall as "a distinct world, with its own way of acting, talking, and thinking. It has its own vocabulary, its own activities ·and interests, its own conception of what is significant in life, and—to a certain extent—its own schemes of life" (Cressey 1969:31).

This world had three major groups of inhabitants: the owners, the taxi-dance girls, and the patrons. In Chicago, almost all the pioneers in establishing taxi-dance halls were Greek-Americans. Cressey saw the explanation for this in their geographic mobility, whereby they could learn of a new business opportunity such as this in other cities where it had made an earlier appearance, and in their relatively low prestige which was likely to shut them out of the regular ballroom business but which would put them in close touch with the inhabitants of the rooming-house zone. He also noted that as the taxi-dance halls grew more economically successful, there was a tendency toward ethnic succession, as they became interesting as business propositions to members of ethnic groups with more powerful political connections—always an important factor in an enterprise operating on the edge of respectability and legality.

The second group, the taxi-dance girls, drew most of Cressey's attention. Many of them, he found, were "giddy young girls in the first flush of enthusiasm over the thrills, satisfactions, and money which this transient world of the dance hall provides"—Sister Carries some forty years after the original. Others were already more blasé, and less concerned about moral conventions. Their ages varied between fifteen and twenty-eight. In the taxi-dance hall, they went through a socialization process; the talk in the restroom during intermission was an important part of this. The effect was on the one hand to loosen the hold of conventional etiquette, on the other hand to regulate the relationships between the girls. The dominant stance toward the patrons was that they were "fish," persons to be exploited. It could happen, however, that a girl took a liking to a partner, and one way of expressing this was to give him free dances, that is, without collecting his ticket. But this practice had to be hidden from the management. The latter had its code of conduct for the girls, the girls had one of their own, and theirs was more effectively enforced on the floor.

Who were these girls? Often they were apparently already rather detached from the controlling influences of family and neighborhood before, by various routes, they entered the taxi-dance hall. Many had grown up in incomplete families, and considering their youth, the fact that about two-fifths of them had gone through a divorce might be surprising. In most cases, their parental families lived in or near Chicago, but there were also a fair number of immigrant girls. Cressey noted that there were hardly any Italian girls, or girls from the Jewish ghetto, but that there were some girls from the Jewish area of second settlement (Lawndale or similar areas) and a rather large proportion of girls of Polish background. A great many of the girls took new "professional" names for use in the hall. If Cressey's camouflaged list of such names is a true indication, this tended to involve a change from Slavic to French, Anglo-Saxon, and Celtic names. [9]

One of the most notable sets of findings of Cressey's study involved the social mobility of the taxi-dance girls. Unlike the typical occupational career, that of the taxi-dance girl went downward rather than upward. Certainly, it could become stabilized at some point; but there was, Cressey felt, a pattern of decline. The first step involved a move from a dissatisfactory situation in conventional society into the world of the taxi-dance hall, where the newcomer might well enjoy popularity and prestige. If, as time passed on, she could no longer maintain her status, however, she might seek to reestablish it in new circles—at a less competitive dance hall, for example, or by accepting the attentions of patrons of lower status, such as the Orientals who made up a considerable part of the taxi-dance hall population. She could only maintain her popularity with the latter, however, as long as they did not regard her as "common." The next downward step might be to the cabarets of Chicago's Black Belt, and the final move might be to prostitution in a black neighborhood. The pattern thus involved a move from low personal esteem in a sphere of higher prestige to high esteem in a sphere of lower prestige. This could be seen as a short upward move; but once inside the new sphere, the girl was liable to suffer continuous decline.

About the patrons Cressey was less able to offer systematic information, partly because the men flowing through this institution made up a rather varied group. There were hoboes and workers, businessmen from out of town, and once-only slummers from higher social strata; Filipinos, Slavs, Greeks, Chinese, Mexicans, black sheep from upper-class families (but no real blacks); the dwarfed, the maimed, the pock-marked. Obviously varied kinds of needs were met by the taxi-dance hall. It was a convenient way of enjoying feminine company for transients who had no time to make acquaintances through conventional channels. It was a way of spending a night on the town for young men of ethnic groups which kept their own young female members under strict family surveillance. It provided relief for middle-aged single men for whom well-meaning acquaintances would tend to suggest much duller female company. But clearly, the taxi-dance hall also found many of its patrons in stigmatized groups who were not competitive. Among these were the Orientals; and the Filipinos made up the larger number of these, at least one-fifth of the entire patron population according to Cressey's estimate. The Filipinos suffered racial discrimination and thus had great difficulties finding company of the other sex, and of the Filipinos arriving in the United States during the 1920s only about one in fifteen was a woman. The fact that taxi-dance halls also existed in the Philippines could have been an additional reason for the readiness of men from there to seek them out in American cities.

For the categories of men who could not easily establish contacts with women through other channels, it was natural that they would sometimes want to take their relationships to the taxi-dance girls beyond dancing. The management of the dance halls would normally discourage such contacts, but they occurred anyway. Occasionally they led to marriage, but more often the relationships thus formed would be more or less mutually exploitative. Among those which involved sexual affairs Cressey delineated three types: those where a girl became for a period the mistress of one man; those where a kind of short-term polyandry was established, with several men contributing to the support of one girl, while aware of one another's existence or even friendly with one another; and overnight dates. Such relationships could obviously mark a step on the downward career to prostitution. But this was not always the consequence, nor did all taxi-dance girls engage in them.

Cressey gave some emphasis to his understanding of the taxi-dance hall as a self-contained world, "a moral milieu rather completely removed from the other more conventional forms of city life." Indeed, a girl could become almost fully enveloped by the institution, living with other taxi-dance girls, making a living from the hall, and meeting her boy friends on its floor. Yet it seems reasonable to hesitate before this claim of moral isolation, in view of evidence elsewhere in the text. The girls came from other kinds of life, and after a rather short period they would again move on to something else.

Many of them maintained some sort of contact with their families, and Cressey even described them as leading "double lives," shielding their families from knowledge about their occupation. Although he formulated a typical career pattern as a downward movement, he also noted that the anonymity of urban society made it possible for both taxi-dance girls and prostitutes to move back and forth between these livelihoods and positions in conventional society. The patrons of the taxi-dance hall, of course, were drawn from many circles, and the proprietor's network might include politicians and law enforcement officers. It could all be a matter, naturally, of what is meant by the "isolation" of a social world. But considering this variety of outside links, we could as well consider *The Taxi-Dance Hall* a pioneering study of one of these nodal institutions where many urban worlds meet.

The CHICAGO SCHOOL in RETROSPECT

In his introduction to a new edition of Shaw's *The Jack-Roller,* Howard Becker (1966) has commented on the way in which the Chicago studies form a mosaic—again this metaphor—each one of them a piece contributing to the whole and serving as background reading for the others. When one comes to the part of that life history where Stanley, the jack-roller, engages in stealing with other boys, one may recall Thrasher's discussion of gangs and theft, and when for a time the scene of his life is West Madison Street, one can turn to Anderson for a more detailed description of this hobo "main stem." This is cooperative ethnography; if the mosaic does not form a picture of Chicago as a whole, then at least we get a broader picture of the urban environment of any particular group or institution than we can normally find in any single study. The achievement is worth noting because it has scarcely been paralleled elsewhere.

In large part, however, it is up to the reader to ferret out for himself the facts on which to base this wider-scope understanding. The authors themselves tended rather to exaggerate the isolation of the social world they studied—as David Matza (1969:70–71) has put it in his important critique of the Chicagoans in *Becoming Deviant,* "there was a certain blindness to overlap and connection," to the fact that, for example, deviant groups "existed in the context of conventional America, drew sustenance from that milieu, dispensed services to it, recruited persons from it, and frequently delivered repentant deviators back to it."

If one considers each study by itself, it actually turns out that the Chicago School had more or less the pioneers in virtually all the kinds of topical anthropologies in the city which we are used to by now: studies of ethnic enclaves, gang studies, studies of deviant occupations, studies of behavior in public places or of public entertainment, studies of mixed neighborhoods. But they share with many of the urban ethnographies of a later generation that "certain blindness." The shortcoming may seem surprising, in view of Park's interest in the passage of persons between different moral milieux.

Possibly the Chicagoans were sometimes closer to a breakthrough in this area than later scholars have often been. One way in which this is true is their awareness of the time dimension. Relationships between different segments of urban society may frequently be understood as relationships emerging over time, and as Short (1971:xliv) has noted, "the Chicago School, more than any other, developed a sensitivity to process." Park's race relations cycle, Thrasher's tracing of the gang from play group to politics or organized crime, or Cressey's interpretation of the stages of the taxi dancer's career are examples of this. If the Chicagoans had given greater recognition to the relative open-endedness of these developmental sequences, the variable passages of groups and individuals through the urban social structure could have been better illuminated.

The fact that they got no further, under circumstances which would seem to have been propitious, is perhaps best understood against the background of a general weakness in the group in the analysis of social organization, where developments lagged behind those in ecology, and also in social psychology. The interplay between ethnography and conceptual growth never really worked very well. The ethnographic contributions of the Chicago School have sometimes been described, with an explicit or implicit reference to Park's past, as "mere journalism." Such a judgment at least underestimates Park's own learning—as we have seen, his academic experience was far from parochial, and he had a profound sociological imagination. While many of his ideas remain of considerable interest, however, it is true that not all were really taken any further by his followers. They neglected some of them; others they cited faithfully, or even strained in order to incorporate as much as possible, but there was little theoretical cumulativity. One could have wished, moreover, that Park had transmitted more effectively his inspirations from the emergent classics of European sociology to all, rather than some, of his students and colleagues. In several of the ethnographies, there is little sign of direct influence from them. Nels Anderson, in the new preface to a reissue of *The Hobo,* has noted that the most important piece of advice he had from Park was indeed to "write down only what you see, hear, and know, like a newspaper reporter," and that at the stage of writing his famous book his empirical knowledge outweighed his theoretical sophistication by far. Park, while sharing some of the nostalgia of a great many social theorists for the small community, also had a sharp sense of the unique possibilities of urban life. This appreciation again seemed often to be lacking among others in his group, who could appear, to one more recent critic (Feuer 1973:86), "like a bevy of small-town YMCA secretaries" with their strait-laced moral vocabulary which later generations might not have thought would be a contribution to sociology from the Roaring Twenties.

Rather too much, for one thing, became "disorganization." There is surely a need for some such concept in the study of social relationships, and present-day anthropologists may at times take their cultural relativism too far in order to avoid it. But the Chicagoans made the opposite mistake. Thomas' definition emphasized the decreasing influence of norms—but which norms? Although, as Park had shown, urban social structure could allow groups to go separate ways and assert their own norms, there was a strong tendency in this group of scholars to regard everything but conformity with the standards of conventional society as a matter of disorganization. And so, in Matza's (1969:48) phrasing, they conceived disorganization when they described diversity. As a partial exception, they could readily admit that the standards of immigrant groups were really different, and norms in their own right; but in line with the assimilationist beliefs of Park and others, they felt this was a passing phenomenon. When the second generation in immigrant groups showed another kind of behavior without seeming to be quite conventional Americans, their way of life was already more likely to be termed disorganized. The generous use of this label could obviously conceal systematic variation in the form of social relationships.

Behind this kind of vocabulary, and behind the relatively limited interest in theoretical development, one may sense the fact that the interests behind the studies were often rather more of a practical nature. Despite the rather provocative contempt which Park, in the Chicago phase of his meandering career, used to express on the subject of "do-gooders"—reputedly resulting from his disillusionment over the missionaries he had worked with on the Congo affair—sociology at Chicago was still deeply involved in reform. And if ecology seemed on its way to hardnosed science, ethnography was more often aligned with the tenderhearted wing and its tradition of fact-finding surveys. This also implied an involvement with outside agencies, with Burgess frequently in the role of liaison man. For the hobo study, Anderson had the sponsorship of the Chicago Council of Social Agencies and the Juvenile Protective Association, the latter also supported Cressey in his research on the taxi-dance hall, Zorbaugh's study related to the work of community organizations such as the Lower North Side Community Council, and Thrasher listed no less than twenty-six agencies which cooperated with his study of the gang. Under such circumstances, these students found themselves writing not only for their professional peers but to a high degree for people with an immediate practical interest in their findings. Certainly, if "there is nothing as practical as a good theory," this need not have constrained the development of theoretical ideas in their studies. But ideas with less obvious relevance to social reform might have been in little demand, and could even have been counterproductive if their inclusion in publications would have made these less intellectually accessible to lay readers.

As far as ecology was concerned, where the theoretical push did occur, we have seen that it was of mixed value to the work in urban ethnography. It offered to the latter what one might consider a largely useful sense of place. The Chicago studies are quite clearly set in a particular territory, not in a vacuum as certain more purely organizational analyses seem to be. At the same time, it created problems of its own. Now and then the Chicagoans themselves made this sense of place ambiguous by implying that the Chicago spatial order was the spatial order of any city. The analogy with plant ecology also had limits which are very obvious but which the Chicago School did not really take very fully into account. People, unlike plants, move around. Not all their relationships are based on enduring territorial sharing or on competition for land. And urbanites especially, as we shall have opportunity to point out again, typically do not draw their sustenance directly out of the earth, but to a great extent from their dealings with one another. A narrow concern with spatial relations and the sorts of facts relating most closely to them would thus probably lead to an impoverished view of urban life, even if clearly the city must be recognized as in part a spatial phenomenon.

From the very beginning, of course, Park had noted that ties of locality were likely to be of decreasing importance within the city. In an area like Zorbaugh's "world of furnished rooms" this is conspicuous enough. The alternative suggestions Park had made for occupational studies in his first research program did inspire some work, notably that of Everett Hughes, who with Redfield inherited Park's wide-ranging interests and essayist style. Hughes's interactionist perspective and concern with field observation provide a strong link between the early Chicago School and such later ethnographer-sociologists as Erving Goffman, Howard Becker, and Anselm Strauss. Yet work like his did not become an integral part of urban research but rather a separate occupational sociology.

Park's 1915 paper marked the beginning of the first period of Chicago ethnography; a little more than two decades later, another paper by Louis Wirth in a way summarized much of what it had been about. As we shall see next, there were obvious similarities between the two. This could be taken as another sign that in the area of social organization at least, there had been some theoretical stagnation, even if both papers have been of great importance. But we should not be too harsh. Half a century after it came out, the work of the Chicago ethnographers is still well worth reading. Some of the criticisms which may be aimed at it are equally to the point, we have suggested, in the case of a great many recent studies. And if we want to move ahead toward a more systematic anthropology of city life, it offers just as many useful pieces as these.

As far as Chicago itself is concerned, of course, ethnography has come back. One can think of some of the latter studies, furthermore, as more or less close counterparts of studies in the first period. Zorbaugh's multifaceted neighborhood has its 1960s parallel in Suttles' *The Social Order of a Slum* (1968), not quite so mixed and considerably more intensively analyzed. The *Jack-Roller* is matched by *Hustler!* (1965), the life history of Henry Williamson, black criminal, as edited by Lincoln Keiser. Gang studies range from Keiser's of one large organization, *The Vice Lords* (1969), to Short's and Strodtbeck's (1965) of a great many, which may thus more resemble Thrasher's with his 1,313. If transvestite actors (Newton 1972) and urban blues singers (Keil 1966) are in some ways very different from taxi-dance girls, they are still the centers of social worlds where entertainment is business. But participant observers are also turning up in new places—as a worker in a steel mill, like Kornblum (1974), or as a precinct captain in the dominant political machine, like Rakove (1975). Obviously Chicago continues to attract as a laboratory for social research, as Park once envisaged it.

CHAPTER THREE

The Search for the City

Louis Wirth published his "Urbanism as a Way of Life" in 1938, one of the most widely-known papers in the social sciences. At about the same time, another Chicagoan, Robert Redfield, was at work formulating his idea of the anti-city, the folk society. In this chapter we will take our point of departure in Wirth's city, as illuminated by the contrast with Redfield's folk, in trying to come to grips with the idea of urbanism. To identify its boundaries, to define it in a way which is valid for all times and in all places, for small town and megalopolis, has turned out to be far from easy. It is "one of the most protean of terms," in the words of one recent authoritative commentator (Wheatley 1972:601). But a bird's-eye view of some of the shapes it has taken on, in the eyes of different interpreters, should at least allow us to find out something about what urban anthropologists could do with it. Thus we will go on to note the relationships between urbanism and particular cultural traditions; the impact of different economies and technologies on the form of city life; the perspectives toward comparative urban history held by Marx, Weber, and others; and ideas of urban systems developed by geographers. And then, in the last third or so of this chapter, we will begin to draw together the elements of an analytical framework of our own.

While Redfield was personally and intellectually linked to the Chicago sociologists, his interest ranged more widely over the world, focusing initially on its small traditional village communities. His concern with broad questions about human nature was coupled with one of the poetic minds of anthropology. The first source of field experience (in the 1920s) which led him to the conception of the folk society showed only traces of such a way of life—the largish village of Tepoztlan, some sixty miles from Mexico

City. Redfield then went on to develop his ideas in the context of a research project involving four communities on the Yucatan peninsula: a Maya tribal village, a peasant village, a commercial town, and a city of somewhat cosmopolitan characteristics. From there on, he continued to elaborate on the contrast between folk and city, and the influence of the city in changing the folk, in writings over a period stretching into the 1950s.[1] Reading these, as well as other works of his, is an enjoyable experience to some, but evidently an irritating one to others.

It was Tusik, the tribal village, that could serve most nearly as a model for the folk society. But Redfield took care to point out that the latter was a constructed type:

> The ideal folk society could be defined through assembling, in the imagination, the characters which are logically opposite those which are to be found in the modern city, only if we had first some knowledge of non-urban people to permit us to determine what, indeed, are the characteristic features of modern city living. The complete procedure requires us to gain acquaintance with many folk societies in many parts of the world and to set down in words general enough to describe most of them those characteristics which they have in common with each other and which the modern city does not have. (Redfield 1947:294)

The typical folk society, he went on to say, would be an isolated society with minimal outside contacts. Its members are in intimate communication with one another. There is little or no physical mobility, at least of the kind which would upset relations within the society or increase external influences. Communication is only by word of mouth—no writing and no literacy to compete with oral tradition or to keep it in check. The members of the folk society are much alike. In touch only with one another they learn the same ways of thinking and doing—"habits are the same as customs." The old people find the younger generations doing what they themselves did at the same age, as there is little change. There is a strong sense of belonging together; each member has "a strong claim on the sympathies of the others." The division of labor is limited to that between man and woman, the division of knowledge likewise. The folk society is self-sufficient, as people produce what they consume and consume what they produce.

Its culture is very much of one piece. Norms, values, and beliefs are the same for everybody. What people think should be done is consistent with what they believe is done. Everything in the culture is closely connected with everything else. The round of life does not proceed from one activity to another and different one. It is one single large activity, no part of which could be separated without affecting the rest. The power of the society to act consistently and meet crises successfully is not dependent on the power of individuals or devotion to some single principle, but due to the general consistency of actions and understandings. One is not disposed toward reflecting over tradition in a critical or objective manner. There is no systematization of knowledge.

The conventions tying people to each other are tacit rather than explicit and contractual. Another person is expected to respond to situations in the same way as oneself and is dealt with as a person rather than a thing. In fact, this tendency is extended so that things are also often treated as persons. Furthermore, relations are not only personal—they are familial. It is in the terms of a universe of kinship linkages that relationships are conceptualized and categorized, creating what differences do exist among them. "The kin are the type persons for all experience."

The folk society is a society of the sacred. Notions of moral worth are attached to ways of thinking and acting. All activities are ends in themselves and express the values of the society. There is no place for the entirely secular motive of commercial gain. The distribution of goods and services is an aspect of the structure of personal relationships. Exchanges are tokens of good will.

Redfield obviously had an esthetic appreciation of the harmony of folk society. As he noted, invert the qualities of that society, and you get urbanism, in a shape much like that described by Wirth. No part of Wirth's essay is better known than his definition of the city as "a relatively large, dense, and permanent settlement of socially heterogeneous individuals." From one or another of these attributes of urbanism, he suggested, others could be derived. In fact, however, he had little specific to say about permanence, so that size, density, and heterogeneity were the factors receiving more detailed treatment.

The size of the population aggregate, in Wirth's view, has a major impact on the nature of social relationships. As soon as a community has more than a few hundred inhabitants, it becomes difficult or impossible for each individual to know all the others personally. The multitude of persons in interaction necessitates a narrowing down of contacts. Perhaps no single paragraph in "Urbanism as a Way of Life" is more significant than that devoted to this point.

> Characteristically, urbanites meet one another in highly segmental roles. They are, to be sure, dependent upon more people for the satisfactions of their life-needs than are rural people and thus are associated with a greater number of organized groups, but they are less dependent upon particular persons, and their dependence upon others is confined to a highly fractionalized aspect of the other's round of activity. This is essentially what is meant by saying that the city is characterized by secondary rather than primary contacts. The contacts of the city may indeed be face to face, but they are nevertheless impersonal, superficial, transitory, and segmental. The reserve, the indifference, and the blasé outlook which urbanites manifest in their relationships may thus be regarded as devices for immunizing themselves against the personal claims and expectations of others. (Wirth 1938:12)

Not being particularly concerned about each other as whole persons, city dwellers tend to take a thoroughly rational view of their interactions, regarding others as a means for the realization of their own goals. This could be seen as emancipation from the control of the group. At the same time, however, it entails a loss of the sense of participation which comes with a closer identification with others. It is replaced, Wirth noted (citing Durkheim), by the state of anomie, a social void.

The segmental, utilitarian character of relationships is expressed in the variety of specialized occupations. There is a constant danger that the lack of personal regard for others would involve these in predatory relationships. To check the spread of such destructive tendencies, however, urban society tends to institute professional codes and occupational etiquette. In economic life, the business corporation is another typical example of the urban ethos; its utility and efficiency results from the fact that the corporation has no soul.

The size of the population furthermore makes it impossible for each individual to be equally directly involved in the affairs of the community as a whole. Interests are articulated through delegation. What an individual says is of little importance, while the voice of the representative seems to be heard more clearly the greater the number of people he speaks for.

Among the results of density is the tendency of the urbanite to orient himself according to visual cues. Since physical contacts are close but social contacts distant, one responds to the uniform rather than the man. The crowding of people and activities can be a nuisance, and some people and activities more of a nuisance than others. So segregation takes place, and in the competition for any particular space the outcome will usually be determined by what use will offer the greater economic return. Place of residence and place of work tend to become divorced. The processes of segregation result in the urban mosaic of social worlds, yet there is enough juxtaposition of divergent modes of life to foster tolerance and a relativistic perspective by which life is secularized. The orderliness of life in the compact society is maintained through adherence to predictable routines. City people live by the clock and the traffic signal. Still, congestion may cause friction and irritation. And the very contrast between physical closeness and social distance increases reserve, giving rise to loneliness unless the individual can find more specific social outlets.

As the urbanite is exposed to the heterogeneity of the city and moves through contacts with various individuals and groups, he comes to accept instability and insecurity as normal, an experience which adds to his cosmopolitanism and sophistication. No one group has his undivided allegiance. The circles in which he participates cannot be arranged hierarchically or concentrically but touch or intersect in a variety of ways. Passing through many jobs, neighborhoods, and interests in his lifetime also keeps the city dweller from too strong a commitment to other persons. Yet for all his mobility he cannot acquire an overview of the complexity of his community as a whole. Thus he is uncertain about what is in his own best interest, and and vulnerable to the persuasive pressures of propagandists. For reasons such as this, collective behavior in the city tends to become unpredictable.

The PREVALENCE of DICHOTOMY

Wirth's analysis of urban life, and the complementary view of folk society offered by Redfield, may appeal to a contemporary urbanite on the basis of his experience, and at least as much on the basis of inherited habits of thought. We recognize as types the city slicker and his opposite part, whether he is real folk, a noble savage, or merely rural, a country bumpkin. In one form or another, the dichotomy has been with us for a long time. Caro Baroja (1963) has shown how it was a commonplace in the social commentary of classical antiquity. Coming closer to the kind of city Wirth's Chicago was, Engels (1969:58) had written, in *The Condition of the Working Class in England,* that although "this isolation of the individual, this narrow self-seeking is the fundamental principle of our society everywhere, it is nowhere so shamelessly barefaced, so self-conscious as just here in the crowding of the great city." (Yet together with Marx, in *The Communist Manifesto,* he acknowledged that this experience could rescue men from "the idiocy of rural life.") That explosive urbanization which Engels observed and which drastically changed the face of European society also inspired the growth of the discipline of sociology. In their own way the *Gemeinschaft* and *Gesellschaft* of Tönnies, and Durkheim's opposition of mechanical and organic solidarity, are thus likewise in the lineage of folk-urban contrasts. Georg Simmel, through his 1903 essay on the mental life of the metropolis, was clearly one of Wirth's closest intellectual ancestors—not least, probably, through his direct influence on Robert Park.

The fundamental influence of the big city on the human psyche, Simmel had suggested, is the "intensification of nervous stimulation." Lasting impressions, impressions varying only slightly from each other, impressions which follow from a set course and show only the predictable contrasts engage consciousness less than the crowding of rapidly changing images, discontinuities apparent at a glance, and the unexpectedness of new impressions. The latter are the experience of the city dweller. He becomes a sophisticate, reacting with his head rather than his heart, and he also becomes *blasé*. He is indifferent to all genuine individuality because the reactions and relationships which result from it cannot be dealt with fully through logical operations. He tends toward formal justice and inconsiderate hardness.

In large part, Redfield and Wirth on the folk and the city were thus merely celebrants of established wisdom. Students of human thought and social life have also continued similar dichotomizing in later years, whether or not directly inspired by these two or by earlier sources. [2] But for some time at least, a large group of sociologists and anthropologists drew their assumptions explicitly and most immediately from the Wirth-Redfield paradigm. For the sociologist, concerned mostly with his own contemporary western society, the emphasis was more on Wirth, and his contrast was probably the less dramatic one between urban and rural—the latter, within his societal context, could not be quite like the folk. Redfield's formulation would attract anthropologists more, with their interest at least partly in the most isolated, traditional societies to be found in the world. In line with the views of both authors, the dichotomy was now transformed into a continuum, in recognition of the fact that real societies or ways of life would not always show a very close fit with either of the polar types but might place themselves in between.

Notions of folk-urban or rural-urban continua became textbook social science particularly in the post-World War II period and in the United

States, reaching out unevenly to influence scholars elsewhere. Yet everything has not turned out to be well with them. The amount of new research inspired by these conceptualizations, building on them cumulatively, has been judged somewhat unimpressive. Too often they seem simply to have been frozen, passively incorporated into the quotidian belief system of social scientists. Moreover, they are vulnerable to various criticisms as they stand.[3]

WIRTH'S URBANISM:
FEATURES, ASSUMPTIONS, WEAK POINTS

We should therefore scrutinize Wirth's conceptualization, the assumptions apparently underlying it, and the criticisms aimed at it, a little more closely, hoping that this may illuminate the idea of urbanism.

Before proceeding along such lines, however, one may ask what has been, and to some extent may remain, attractive about Wirth's formulation. It is, of course, a clear and effective statement on most counts, and comprehensive enough within the limits of its two dozen pages to occupy by itself most of the central ground in its sort of thinking about urban life. To an anthropologist, its appeal may rest in large part with its emphasis on social relations and ways of thinking. It appears that "Urbanism as a Way of Life" was to some extent a reaction against the sort of ecological thinking which had become dominant among the Chicago sociologists. Wirth brought people back in. The paragraph quoted above, on the form of face-to-face relationships and the resultant definition of the person, aligns itself with a classical problematic of social anthropology. In addition, at least some of Wirth's analysis is on a level of abstraction above particular institutions and the form given to them in a certain tradition, and in part it therefore offers relief from the tendency of much social science toward more glaringly culture-bound formulations. Wirth was uneven in this respect, however; simply because of their concreteness, his well-known propositions concerning the decreasing size of the family group and the importance of voluntary associations in urban life, for example, are more immediately available to criticism based on comparative evidence. And as it turns out, some of the statements which may appear to have a wider relevance are in fact similarly limited in their cultural scope.

To this issue we will return. With regard to pinpointing the characteristics of Wirth's urbanism, a first thing to note may be that there is a strong tendency to see the city as a closed system. There are statements scattered through the essay which constitute exceptions to the tendency, but on the whole this may be Wirth's greatest fallacy. The city is necessarily an open system, or a part system, unlike the folk society. In this way the two are not comparable. Redfield later saw the point, substituting "civilization" for the city in his version of the contrast.[4] In Wirth's case, there is little more than some slight consideration of the external impact of the city. The relationship between city and society comes across as a one-way influence, the city acting upon its surroundings through a process of diffusion and thus reshaping them in its own image. Obviously the view here resembles Redfield's, identifying such influence as a major force of disorganization in folk society. But Wirth had hardly anything to say about how an urban way of life can be maintained under nonurban conditions, given the understanding that it can only originate under the circumstances found in the city itself. On the whole, the point is clear that the urban way of life is found in its most recognizable form in the city, under the direct influence of the three factors of size, density, and heterogeneity. These are seen largely as independent variables in Wirth's theory, and "the larger, the more densely populated, and the more heterogeneous a community, the more accentuated the characteristics associated with urbanism will be" (Wirth 1938:9).

In these terms, it may further be observed, Wirth's city is an ideal type—it is very large, very dense, very heterogeneous. As with other such formulations, it tends to become a practical problem what to do with real cases which are less close approximations of it. The idea of a continuum, after all, tends to be regarded as somewhat unmanageable. Almost inevitably in the ongoing study of urbanism, a threshold of discontinuity is reintroduced between what is urban and what is rural, although with little consensus as to where it should be placed. In line with the statement just quoted, one might expect the urbanness of a place to be determined by its absolute population size, density, and heterogeneity. Yet again it seems questionable if one can thus consider the urban community apart from its wider context. The apparently simple variables of size and density offer sufficient evidence of this, standing together to provide a demographic rather than strictly sociological conception of urbanism. Density may be defined as a population/space ratio. But is it really absolute density we use as a component in the definition of urbanism, or is it density relative to surrounding areas—that is, concentration? In no small part, at least, our common-sense understanding seems to be guided by the second alternative. What is an urban level of density in one context may not be so defined in a society which is more densely populated as a whole. One Indian census definition of urban density—one thousand inhabitants or more per square mile—turns out to apply to much Japanese farm country (see Tsuru 1963:44).

If one wants to argue, then, as Wirth appears to do, that a certain absolute density produces particular social effects, the communities one is concerned with may be considered urban in some places but not in others. This is one obstacle in the way of comparative urban studies. The variable of size offers similar problems. There is no universal agreement as to how populous a community must be to take on urban status. Laymen, officials, and social scientists all tend to use the variously precise ideas prevalent in their corners of the world. For people accustomed to cities with millions of inhabitants it is often surprising to hear of urban centers in other times and places, of great and indisputable importance but with population figures which under other circumstances might have made them count as mere villages.

Another problem may be noted with the idea of predicting social effects on the basis of figures of population size and density, in its own way also arising from the assumption of the city as a closed system. These figures, when they derive, for example, from official census records, usually show where people sleep. To the extent that human beings move around in their waking hours, a source of error is introduced. It is evident in the internal distribution of people in the modern western city, where the central business district is shown to be sparsely populated because few people have their residence there. It can likewise be seen in the distribution of people between town and country. Urban life also includes the part-time users of the city, the people who come to sell in the market, make a bar round, litigate in court, visit a friend in the hospital, or watch a parade. And some urban communities may have a greater share of such visitors than others. Conversely, of course, urbanites may pass city limits in order to pick firewood, buy fresh farm eggs, peddle dubious novelties to the rustics, or experience communion with Nature.

We need perhaps say no more about the variables of size and density as such at this point. In the case of the third variable, heterogeneity, a similar problem could be stated: how much heterogeneity would it take for a community to be defined as urban? But here the very referents of the term also seem less certain. Writers have indeed disagreed as to where Wirth placed the emphasis. [5]

In one sense, noted more passingly in "Urbanism as a Way of Life," a certain amount of heterogeneity could presumably be related to the size of the urban population itself—if one could imagine some sort of "generalized heterogeneity" evenly distributed among people, a larger community would encompass more of it than a smaller. What would be more likely to interest the observer of urbanism, however, is a relative concentration of heterogeneity in the city; a variety of social attributes which could somehow be measured as greater than average per unit of population. Wirth gave two major reasons why the city would be particularly heterogeneous in this sense.

One was that the city tends to recruit heterogeneity from the outside. (This was one instance in which Wirth did recognize the external contacts of the urban community.) It attracts migrants of different backgrounds, thus becoming "the melting-pot of races, peoples, and cultures." The other reason was identified as based on Darwin and Durkheim. When there is an increase in the number of organisms inhabiting a given area, differentiation and specialization occurs, since only in this way can the area support increased numbers.

There is something in this latter argument even as applied to human life. Yet here we see Wirth slipping back again into the closed-system view of the city. The dense population appears first; then an internal division of labor sets in. Although it is acknowledged that a part of the enlarged market on which specialization depends is found in the hinterland of the city, the emphasis is rather on access to the urban population itself. City people seem to be busying themselves, and making a living, taking in each other's laundry.

One may want to speculate that this tendency to see the city as if in a vacuum was one of the results of Wirth's Chicago experience. The internal division of labor in a metropolis like this is more complex than what one would find in the great majority of urban communities. Many of its inhabitants could probably experience the city subjectively in their daily lives as a self-contained universe. Its outside linkages, important as they may be to all the inhabitants, may be strongly concentrated in relatively few hands. An additional fact about early twentieth-century Chicago was that a large number of its people had come in from the outside, as migrants from Eastern Europe, Ireland, Italy, Scandinavia, or other regions. But perhaps because they had come so far from their origins, rather than from the neighboring Indiana or Illinois farmlands, Chicago to them might have been more like an isolated island in the sea.

Anyway, vague as some of Wirth's references to heterogeneity may be, he thus suggested that the city intensified heterogeneity, by bringing in external diversity and increasing internal diversity. Sometimes the two could be related, as when the city "has brought together people from the ends of the earth *because* they are different and thus useful to one another, rather than because they are homogeneous and like-minded" (Wirth 1938:10). In such ways, heterogeneity could be seen as turning into a variable itself dependent on size and density. At the same time, of course, Wirth had set out to assign separate social effects to the independent variables of size, density, and heterogeneity in turn. But there is reason to be skeptical of such a procedure. If the form of social relationships were to change in the direction of impersonality, superficiality, and segmentality, for example, as suggested in the quotation given earlier, it would not be just because of an increase in population size, but also because the population is dense enough for these many individuals to be mutually accessible. If there are processes of segregation in the city, they are due not only to density, but to density and heterogeneity combined. One cannot add the effects of size to those of density and those of heterogeneity, in other words, but the characteristics of urban life which may be due to them (disregarding other factors) may often have more to do with the ways in which they interrelate.

Furthermore, size, density, and heterogeneity need not interrelate in the same way in all cities; a fact which complicates the idea of the rural-urban or folk-urban continuum. Among the studies which exemplify the point, that by Marvin Harris (1956) on Minas Velhas, Brazil, is one. Minas Velhas was high on diversity. It had begun in the eighteenth century as a gold mining community, later turning itself into an administrative, educational, and religious center. There were sixty-nine occupational specialties, and people who were not civil servants preferred to be in business for themselves rather than be subordinate to someone else. Individualism showed itself also in disregard for the patron saint of the community and the proliferation of personal patron saints. Consciously or unconsciously, abstractly or concretely, the people of Minas Velhas endorsed and elaborated the urban character of their community. There was a love of noise, movement, crowds, and houses in the busiest streets. Education, a way with words, legal processes, suits and neckties—these were the good things in life. Yet Minas Velhas had a population of only some 1,500. As Harris noted, one could find many examples in Latin American anthropology of communities which were larger but still thought of as villages.

Size, density, and heterogeneity may thus have to be seen as constituting different continua; furthermore, the latter involves so many dimensions that finding a way of aligning them so as to be accessible to a single measurement is an extremely difficult task. Just sorting out these major variables in Wirth's model of urbanism turns into something quite complex. Yet they had been taken more or less as something given. Wirth's emphasis was rather on delineating the kind of life which corresponded to them. What this amounts to is a very generalized, and quite suggestive, picture of the experiences and responses of an average city dweller, a "man in the street." Here, expectably, many of the critiques of Wirth based on empirical evidence have concentrated.

Among the most renowned of these is that by Oscar Lewis (1951, 1965), who confronted folk-urban thinking head on, with both a restudy of Redfield's Tepoztlan and research in the metropolis of Mexico City. The differences between the two pictures of Tepoztlan, particularly of the quality of interpersonal relations, have made them together a classic case in the discussion of interpretive ethnography. In contrast to the harmonious scene presented by Redfield, Lewis found envy, distrust, and violence common. Redfield's response to the divergence seems characteristic of his humanist impulses; he acknowledged it as evidence of the personal element in anthropology. He had asked himself what were the things Tepoztecans enjoyed about life, Lewis what were their problems and sufferings. Even so, one may feel that this throws some doubt on his picture of the folk society, to the extent that it was a Tepoztlan motif.

In Mexico City, Lewis could not compare his results to any preceding local study, but asked instead whether Wirth's, Redfield's, and Simmel's conceptions of urbanism in general could serve as a description of life in the lower-class neighborhoods he knew in the city. As far as he could see, they did not. The people of these *vecindades,* migrants from the countryside, had not suffered very much from anything that could be called "disorganization," and their lives were hardly characterized by anonymity and impersonality. It seemed as if extended family ties had been strengthened and increased, rather than the opposite, even if domestic units were not as large as in the village. Another reason that Wirth's description of social relationships did not apply was that Lewis' urban acquaintances were the inhabitants not so much of the city in general as of particular neighborhoods of a village-like character. This was where they had most of their contacts, of considerable stability and intimacy. Lewis (1965:497) thus found that

> the variables of number, density, and heterogeneity as used by Wirth are not the crucial determinants of social life or of personality. There are many intervening variables. Social life is not a mass phenomenon. It occurs for the most part in small groups, within the family, within households, within neighborhoods, within the church, formal and informal groups, and so on. Any generalizations about the nature of social life in the city must be based on careful studies of these smaller universes rather than on a priori statements about the city as a whole.

Neither did these inhabitants of the *vecindad* seem to have become secularized believers in science. In fact, "religious life became more Catholic and disciplined," and village beliefs and remedies persisted. The notions of an urban mentality indeed drew some particularly sharp criticisms from Lewis. Too often were they based on outdated and inadequate theories of personality, too often was there an almost total lack of empirical evidence to support them. If the constructs of folk and city were in general a poorly understood mix of facts, guesswork, and ideology, their claims as to how city dwellers thought belonged far over to the side of the dubious and unproven.

Lewis' portrayal of the quality of social relationships in the Mexico City neighborhood points to one serious error in Wirth's reasoning. He seems to have had in mind some fixed quantity of social involvements, spread thickly over few relationships in folk society, thinly over many in the city, and rather evenly over all relationships in both cases. This is certainly not how social life is organized. There is, furthermore, the strain toward an overly generalized conception of the typical urbanite. Despite the emphasis on heterogeneity, we can discern an assumption of sameness. But there are many kinds of cities; each one of these has many kinds of inhabitants; and each one of these, in turn, has different kinds of relationships. And almost always, some of the latter are close, personal, and durable. Wirth's own study of the ghetto could show as much. Indeed, Short (1971:xxix n.), in his memoir of Chicago urban sociology, has noted that at least one of Wirth's colleagues was amused by the fact that Wirth's own relationships were far from "impersonal, superficial, transitory, and segmental."

Criticism of this conception of urban relationships has become a major

genre in comparative urban research, and Lewis was not the first to contribute to it. It includes Whyte's *Street Corner Society* (1943) and some of
its spin-off papers. Gans, we have noted, coined the term which sums up
much of the criticism with *The Urban Villagers* (1962a), writing like
Whyte about the Italian-Americans of Boston, and a number of other authors have similarly reported on the intimacy of various urban quarters
around the world. What may be said about their main point, apart from
noting that it by now has lost much of the charm of novelty, is that it runs
the risk of being overstated. If Wirth was not 100 percent correct on the
character of urban social relations, he was hardly 100 percent wrong either. It would not do to propose that relationships between city dwellers
are typically deep and wide, intimate and durable. It is the variability of
relations in the city that deserves recognition, and some more analytical attention.

One additional aspect of Wirth's depiction of the generalized urbanite
should be identified. The emphasis of the essay is, more literally than one
may at first realize, on a "way of life." A life style is described, with the
description more or less taking its point of departure in the individual submerged in that way of life. We do not, on the other hand, get a differentiated overall view of the urban social order. Perhaps the preoccupation
with a sort of "man in the street" had some relationship to the research experience of Wirth and his Chicago colleagues. With the exceptions of Zorbaugh's glimpses of the Gold Coast, as we have seen, the Chicagoans
"studied down," or occasionally sideways, as urban ethnographers have
typically continued to do. To get at "urbanism as a social order," rather
than as a "way of life," more attention would presumably have had to be
given to the higher levels of the politics and the economy of the city. Aside
from the assumption of a laissez-faire urban ecology, however, the Chicago
sociologists as a rule did not take much analytical interest in the wider
economy of the community, nor in matters of power and conflict—
remarkable for a city with events like the Haymarket Affair in its history.[6]

ETHNOCENTRISM, CULTURAL TRADITIONS, and the UNITY OF URBANISM

As we are faced with a wide range of empirical evidence, which like
Lewis' would be anomalous to a Wirthian point of view, the idea of urbanism as a fixed combination of characteristics becomes increasingly like a

mirage, moving farther away or dissolving as one tries to approach it. There is the conclusion of Reiss (1955), for example, after surveying fundamental ingredients of urban-rural contrasts, that hardly anything can be found to mark off the city against the country in universal and absolute terms. A place like Aarhus, Denmark's second largest urban center, seems less heterogeneous than was the old American frontier. Time budgets show urbanites spending as much time in close interpersonal relations as country dwellers. A sparsely settled rural region may provide conditions as favorable to anonymity as a big city. Urbanites could have no monopoly on tolerance toward deviant behavior, as witness cattle rustlers in the American West, homicide rates in rural Sicily, or the high rates of premarital pregnancy among Scandinavian peasants. Mobility is not itself an urban characteristic but a function of opportunity structures, which may be open or closed both in the city and in the country. Voluntary associations do not attract all urban people, but we can find quite a number of them in rural areas, including 4-H clubs as well as the Ku Klux Klan. Invention and creativity have been said to be concentrated in the urban center, but some innovations actually originate in the rural area and spread to the towns. There are rural people who do not farm, and urban people who do.

One might find Reiss's manner of comparison somewhat provocative. His counter-evidence is as radically decontextualized as any list of supposedly urban traits. Yet it seems advisable to look for paths out of that impasse in the sociology of urban-rural contrasts which critiques like his identify. A factor which has to be dealt with here is ethnocentrism, of that special kind afflicting researchers who generalize from their own field experience to a greater part of humanity. There may be some of this in Redfield's portrayal of the folk society as isolated and inward-turning, for the Maya of Yucatan who were perhaps his most important model could have developed some of their tendencies to closure as a reaction to outside contacts—one of those cases in world ethnography where a society implicitly or explicitly understood to be a simple, early form in some evolutionary scheme has actually been shaped either by the impingement of some more complex form of social organization or by its destruction.

We are more concerned now, however, with Wirth and the city. It may be a little unfair to charge Wirth with ethnocentrism, in that he may have taken for granted that he was communicating with American social scientists in the context of American society. Since he was not clear and consistent on this point, however, and since both followers and critics have been ready to see what he wrote as an attempt at a more general formulation, it is not unreasonable that we consider what kind of city he had closest at hand. This does not explain everything, for the evidence against some of Wirth's more exaggerated claims was available in Chicago. But the sort of place Chicago was, and the type of urban communities Wirth was familiar with in general, undoubtedly left their imprint on his conception of urbanism. This was a city growing feverishly, drawing people from many countries on several continents, a metropolis which, we have said, could seem almost like a world to itself, with business as king. It was hardly like all other towns. Not that it would necessarily be impossible to derive any general insights from it; only it might well prove treacherous to take their universal validity for granted. The appearance of transcending specific cultures in Wirth's perspective toward the city was sometimes misleading. In the words of Francisco Benet (1963b:2), it promised to Chicago a position in urban studies parallel to that of the Viennese bourgeois family in Freudian psychology.

Ethnic mixture was one aspect of this syndrome which was typical of a young city in a country of immigrants. If heterogeneity were characteristic of urban communities elsewhere as well, it would not necessarily be of this kind. "It is particularly important to call attention to the danger of confusing urbanism with industrialism and modern capitalism," Wirth also wrote, but the disentanglement of urbanism from these other major isms actually did not get much further attention in "Urbanism as a Way of Life." As Wirth went on to analyze exchange values of land as determinants of urban ecology and to take the soulless business corporation as an example of an urban emphasis on impersonal efficiency, he was hardly discussing all cities everywhere. The leveling effect of mass production to which he referred was also industrial rather than necessarily urban.

The entire imagery of urbanism in Europe and America was, of course, intertwined with industrialism and capitalism. For Engels they had been an indivisible if unholy trinity. His Manchester was like the Coketown of Dickens' Hard Times, devoted to factory production and at the same time to the destruction of the human body and spirit; generated by the mine, the factory, and the railroad (cf. Mumford 1961:446 ff.). As Upton Sinclair's reporting on its meat industry showed, Chicago was of much the same kind. Simmel had taken a particular interest in the effect of the use of money on the human mind and the social order, and in "The Metropolis and Mental Life" he thus also came close to suggesting that urbanism and capitalism were much the same thing. The *blasé* outlook could in no small part be derived from this fact:

> This mood is the faithful subjective reflection of the completely internalized money economy. By being the equivalent to all the manifold things in one and the same way, money becomes the most frightful leveler. For money expresses all qualitative differences of things in terms of "how much?" Money, with all its colorless indifference, becomes the common denominator of all values; irreparably it hollows out the core of things, their individuality, their specific value, and their incompatibility. (Simmel 1950:414)

Again, Wirth was thus part of a tradition in urban thought, but he did little to step out of it. The state of affairs has been criticized most recently again by Manuel Castells (1976, 1977:73 ff.), attempting to bring Marxism to bear on urban sociology, who suggests that an analysis of an urban way of life along Wirth's lines is mere ideology, a red herring in its misleading attribution of the facts of life under industrial capitalism to a spatial form.

At this stage one could decide to give up the search for that elusive unity of urbanism. Beginning anew, one could perhaps turn ethnocentrism into a strength. Just as Wirth constructed a model of early twentieth-century American urbanism, so each cultural tradition, old or young, could be understood to shape its own unique type of city—or a series of cities following one another, corresponding to particular periods in history. Here one would tend to give maximal exposure to cultural distinctiveness. We find such constructs in the work of culture historians, concerned with showing how a particular configuration of ideas and practices is manifested in urbanism, in *"the* Muslim town" or *"the* Latin American city." Not least, they can give adequate attention to the fact that cultural traditions may contain their own more or less explicit emic definitions of what is urbanism. The traditional Muslim town, it has been said, must have a market, a Friday mosque, and a public bath (cf. von Grunebaum 1955:141).

Among anthropologists, the point has been argued with some force by Pocock (1960), in the context of Indian society. (Not surprisingly, since there is an obvious parallel in the debate over the cross-cultural applicability of the concept of caste.) Reviewing studies in "urban" and "rural" sociology in India, Pocock was dismayed at what seemed to be an unquestioning reliance on imported ideas. Here was Wirth, whether he would have liked it or not, in the *mohallas* of old Delhi. It was assumed that religion and kinship links would weaken in the city; in fact they did not. The possibilities of friendship and neighboring would be discussed, in such publications, in terms of physical flow of bodies and the design of buildings. Whether the people involved were of the same or different castes or religions was ignored. A study of social stratification used Warner's *Yankee City* studies for a model, without much modification to suit Indian circumstances. Such a dependence on western urban thinking might have been more understandable, if not altogether acceptable, Pocock felt, if Indian cities, like many of those in Africa, had been European creations. But although a western influence was there, India had its own urban tradition, with a direct cultural continuity from village life. It was in the city that the caste system reached its fullest development. The layout of the city, like the village, was a representation of the order of the universe, rather than of the spatial needs and buying power of business and industry. There was no room for two separate sociologies, of village and city, in India.

Undoubtedly it would be an impoverished and deficient approach to urbanism in many respects that would somehow systematically disregard the way variable cultural traditions can be represented in it through ideas and institutions. Yet it seems debatable whether the parochialism of single-culture urban theory and research will offer long-term satisfaction either. Perhaps somewhere midway between the traditions of specific cultural regions and the notion of The City, one may look for broader types of urbanism. And, after all, the readiness of many writers to translate the variety of culturally specific concepts somewhat offhandedly as "urban" begs the question whether some common denominator is not there. To follow up such possibilities, we should turn to other urban theorists than those of the Chicago School.

CITIES in SOCIETY: HISTORICAL PERSPECTIVES

Saying that Chicago is a city of industrial capitalism already suggests ways of breaking urbanism down into more manageable categories. The industrial-preindustrial distinction is one. The industrial revolution gave rise to urban centers of a size unheard of before, shaped new ways of looking at human labor, and threw people together in new forms of relationships. As Manchester, Chicago, and others among its products show, it created a new urban landscape. If this was the kind of urbanism Wirth and his colleagues described, we could arguably need a view of preindustrial urbanism as a companion piece.

Explicitly a response to formulations along Wirthian lines, Gideon Sjoberg's *The Preindustrial City* (1960) is an attempt to provide just that. Sjoberg's construct is a generalized type, ranging boldly from the beginnings of urban life through medieval Europe to some of the present-day cities of Asia, North Africa, Southern Europe, and Latin America—"preindustrial cities everywhere display strikingly similar social and ecological structures, not necessarily in specific cultural content, but certainly in basic form" (Sjoberg 1960:5).

Sjoberg located the preindustrial city in what he called feudal society, a term which commentators have felt that he used quite idiosyncratically. Technology was the key variable. Feudal society, in Sjoberg's view, distinguished itself from folk society by greater agricultural surpluses, particularly of grain, arrived at through the use of plow and wheel, improved metallurgy, and large-scale irrigation works. Yet in contrast to industrial society, it was almost entirely dependent on animate (human and animal) sources of energy. These surpluses played a major part in bringing about urbanism, but an additional necessary condition was the centralization of power in the hands of a literate elite controlling the integrated complex of political, religious, and educational offices. Commerce served to a very great extent to meet the needs and desires of this ruling class.

The city was typically surrounded by a wall, needed for defense but also useful for other purposes in more peaceful times, such as controlling the influx of people, keeping undesirables out when possible, and collecting customs fees. Inside the city as well some areas were more or less closed off physically, such as quarters of ethnic minorities. Again this was partly a security arrangement. In the center of the city were the dominant buildings—palace, temple, fortress. The elite lived nearby. Their houses would not necessarily reveal all their splendor to the outside but rather turn inward, away from the teeming lower-class masses. The latter tended to live in more peripheral areas, and this was especially true of those with unclean occupations, such as butchers and tanners. Although there was frequently a market near the major buildings, such as the temple, artisans and merchants often combined their home and their place of work. [Apart from the general differentiation in space between the classes, there was a finer differentiation so that families, occupations, and ethnic groups clustered in particular streets or quarters.]

The two-class system was rigid. As the elite occupied itself with government, religion, and education, the lower class included all others. Contact between the two strata was minimal insofar as the elite limited its interactions to the necessary ones with servants, astrologers, musicians, merchants, and craftsmen. Furthermore, people tended to signal their status through dress, style of speech, and in other ways, so that appropriate understandings of deference and demeanor could be maintained. Anonymity, to the extent that it is a matter of social category rather than personal identity, was not a characteristic of the preindustrial city.

Within the lower class, of course, there were gradations of rank, but none as important as the gap between the classes. Occasionally merchants could convert wealth into influence and even make a way for themselves or their descendants into the privileged class. One reason the elite tried to keep them at a distance and to limit their influence, however, was that merchants, through their contacts with all sorts of people, including strangers, could be a threat to the existing order. Entertainers, as well, were regarded as a more or less subversive element.

Below the richer merchants were a variety of traders and craftsmen, as well as unskilled laborers—servants, messengers, load carriers, animal drivers, ditch diggers, and others. And mixed with these, of course, beggars, petty criminals, and others of indeterminate means of livelihood. The typical form of organization among these lower-class occupations (even thieves and beggars) was the guild. Depending on the requirements of the occupation, it served various purposes, such as control of business opportunities, regulation of recruitment and occupational socialization, control of internal conflict, and mutual aid. The constituent business units themselves were small. The technology hardly gave much room for economies of scale in the crafts.

Due to the circumstances of their livelihood, lower-class people could not easily maintain large households and close family ties. The poorest might even lack any family connection whatsoever. Among the elite, on the other hand, extensive networks of kin were of major importance for maintenance of group cohesion in general and for recruitment to office in particular. The offices held by the elite tended to merge with their persons, and fields of authority were vaguely defined. There was little noticeable class conflict—elite divisiveness and external threats were at times more significant. Perhaps it should be said also that the lower-class was actually even more divided. Its economic organization created little overall cohesion, it could be split by ethnic as well as sectarian diversity, and it lacked the homogenizing influence which a literate culture had on the elite. The town criers, story tellers, street singers and actors tended also to shape links of knowledge, beliefs, and values which tied lower-class people to the elite rather than to each other.

The Preindustrial City has had a large readership, considerable influence, and a number of unfavorable reviews.[7] The idea of shifting the term "feudalism" away from its customary political, legal, and social referents has not been well received, some would prefer to be more cautious on the matter of the technological underpinnings of early urbanism, and the claim that urban elites everywhere based their control on literacy is doubtful. Historians have also complained over Sjoberg's use of sources. Apart from this, what has been most controversial is the extent of his generalizations, the juxtaposition of data from widely separated times and places. Where the debate over such issues turns out to be one between sociologists and historians, overly eager to conform to their reputations as generalizers and particularizers respectively, each seldom shows much sympathy for or even perception of the other's point of view, and argument becomes fruitless. Ignoring other issues, however, the question remains how to order our understanding of major urban variations not fully accounted for by the factor of technology.

Since the modern western city is customarily described not only as industrial but also as capitalist, it seems natural to seek further illumination in the political economy of urbanism. We concern ourselves more explicitly, then, with the bases of urban existence; with the way cities make a living, or more concretely, with the way city dwellers make a living.

This takes us back to the absolute fundamentals of urbanism. When despite all our hesitation in trying to define urbanism cross-culturally we do throw the term about in a variety of contexts, we undoubtedly have in mind the common-sense notion of towns and cities as sizable dense settlements. At least since Wirth, of course, it has been a problem whether this fact of demography, space use, or even architecture could be precisely matched with facts of social relations. But in his perspective the city was already a *fait accompli*. The beginning of the line of inquiry can be pushed back a step—why do large, dense settlements occur? Why do people in societies gather to make more intensive use of some space than of other? As answers to this simple question, and follow-up questions, become increasingly complex, the end result may be more than just an anthropology of space use. Our everyday ideas about urban places being what they are, however, it seems logical to start here.[8]

A little dramatically and very generally, one might see man's use of space as an equation involving his relationships to the land and to other human beings. If men and women were self-sufficient, Robinson Crusoes without Fridays, and if they lived in an evenly and not too abundantly endowed landscape, they might perhaps scatter so as to have equally large personal environments from which to make a living, with minimal competition for their resources. But to the extent that they are dependent in various ways on one another, thus to maximize physical distance is inconvenient. It would be better always to have each other close by.

People always take this latter fact into account in some degree, by clustering, for instance, in households and villages. The city, however, from this point of view, is the maximal adjustment to human interdependency. One can see why on these grounds agriculture tends to be seen as a fundamentally non-urban pursuit. The archetypal cultivator stands in a double opposition to the city. On the one hand, agriculture is usually space-extensive, and if it is convenient to live near the land, cultivators will congregate less. On the other hand, if their livelihood makes them more or less self-sufficient, they have little business to transact with others. That is, the cultivator has no reason to be in the city, and he has reason not to be in the city.

Parenthetically, we may note that the assumptions underlying such reasoning are surely quite limiting. Modern agribusiness is as involved in interdependency as any other line of work, the space requirements of horticulture may be modest, and there are various reasons why a cultivator could choose to live in town which it takes little ethnographic knowledge to think of. His lands may be so spread out that almost any residence is equally convenient or inconvenient; his tenure of any particular piece of land may be too insecure for him to arrange for permanent settlement there; he may be only a part-time cultivator; or he may prefer urban residence for reasons other than those of his basic material provisioning—ritual, recreation, or security, for instance—so that convenience of work must be weighed against these other factors. The cultivator in town is therefore not such a contradiction in terms, as shown, for example, by the agrotowns of the Mediterranean region or of the West African Yoruba.

Nor, however, is he in the mainstream of urban development. Most urbanites are one step or more away from the relative self-sufficiency maintained by some of these cultivator townsmen, satisfying—more or less—their requirements from the land through relationships with other people.

The slightly bewildering fact, in other words, is that however much the urban mode of existence is predicated on interdependency, there cannot be room within the city for all the linkages involved. Highly schematically, we may decide that there are two major ways of solving the problem through external contacts: by giving something in exchange or by getting something for nothing. In the one case, the people on the land offer some of their produce to city people, to gain instead a share of goods and services supplied by the latter. It is a relationship more or less freely entered; in theory at least, the people on the land could decide not to become involved. In the other case, the people of the city have some sort of power over those on the land, and they can thereby make the others feed them. The clearest form would be physical coercion. But dominance may also be achieved through the control and manipulation of symbols, to which the people on the land owe such allegiance that the relationship can take on a consensual quality. The role of the city dweller in this instance involves information processing, decision making, and the application of sanctions. The man on the land may or may not feel that he is getting a square deal. There may be a gray zone here, consequently, between relationships based on power and on exchange, where participants as well as outside analysts may differ on definitions.

This simple way of representing relationships between people concentrated and people spread out, between cities and the surrounding society, allows us to consider the role of the city as a center. Until recently at least, such a point of view toward urbanism, contrasting but actually complementary to that where the city is seen as a given population concentrate, has had a greater impact among geographers and historians than among the sociologists and anthropologists of urban life. As John Friedmann (1961:92) has expressed it in an oft-cited statement, a "mere area" becomes "effective space," organized socially, politically, and economically, through the agency of urban institutions which extend their influences outward and bind the surrounding regions to the central city.

It is tempting to think of cities of power and cities of exchange as two distinct basic types. While we shall see that such a view sometimes corresponds to actual tendencies, it is somewhat too simplistic. There are obviously urban centers the varied relationships of which to the surrounding society range from those largely involving power to those involving free tangible exchange. In other cases, the typical linkage may merge elements of both kinds—an exchange of more for less rather than something for nothing, perhaps, regulated by urban power. The situation need not be stable, the evidence not unambiguous. Much of urban history, and a large part of the debate over the role of cities in society, involves the tension between the two forms of connection.

We can perhaps dignify our rough distinction by relating it to Polanyi's (1957a:47–55; 1957b:250 ff.) types of economy: householding, reciprocity, redistribution, and market exchange. Redfield's imagery makes the former two the characteristic economic forms of folk society. Producing what one consumes and consuming what one produces is householding; reciprocity is involved in those symmetrical relationships where individuals and groups present each other with the tokens of good will.[9] As we have seen that there can be elements of folk society in the city, householding and reciprocity can exist as supplementary forms in the interstices of urban social structure. They do not, however, in themselves create cities. The economic forms critical to the growth of urbanism, instead, are redistribution, the appropriation and management of goods and services by a powerful center, and market exchange, with its determination of prices by market forces. It is probably easy to see that there is some connection, although not necessarily perfect congruence, between these concepts and what we have said about power and exchange.

In recent years, the tendency has been to see the first rise of large, dense settlements in the distant past as occurring through redistributive economies. The original city fathers were evidently an elite building their existence on the collection of a surplus from the majority of the population. Such an interpretation has been stated most succinctly by Paul Wheatley in *The Pivot of the Four Quarters* (1971), dwelling particularly on emergent urbanism in North China in the Shang period but also comparing it to regions of "primary urban generation" elsewhere—the classical areas, Mesopotamia, the Nile and Indus valleys, Mesoamerica, and the Andes, but with the towns of the Yoruba added.[10] As urban centers emerged in these areas, with the transformation of relatively egalitarian societies organized largely by kinship into stratified, politically organized and territorially based states, a recurrent if not universal feature was the early interpenetration between these principles of organization, often with a growing inequality between segments within the kinship system.[11] These centers were above all foci of ceremony. Priesthoods and divine monarchs, and under them a corps of officials and guards, controlled a broad stratum of peasants in the surrounding region. During the phases of flowering, what could have begun as modest tribal shrines were elaborated as complexes of monumental architecture: temples, pyramids, palaces, terraces, and courts, "instruments for the creation of political, social, economic, and sacred space, at the same time as they were symbols of cosmic, social, and moral order" (Wheatley 1971:225). Exact and predictive sciences were developed here, as well as specialized crafts. The Yoruba towns, last of the kind to emerge independently and the only ones still existing as going concerns in a form resembling the original (and to which we will briefly return in the next chapter), while not exhibiting the complexity of architectural and other technology of the classical cases, show similarities of social form.

There may be much to argue about in an interpretation like Wheatley's. The precise degree of uniformity within that urban type of ceremonial centers which he delineates is necessarily difficult to establish, in the seven original areas or in other areas where it occurred in derivative forms.[12] The material evidence is uneven. To the extent that one must rely on archeology, one cannot be sure that places with different functions leave behind them equally rich deposits, or that the various functions in one place are evenly represented in the finds. There could thus be an overrepresentation of the remnants of ceremonial life compared to other facets of early urbanism. Moreover, the accumulated body of scholarship devoted to this evidence has followed varying theoretical and methodological paradigms. This also makes comparisons more difficult.

A question which is probably particularly important to us is what lies behind the appropriative power of the sacerdotal elite. Wheatley is reluctant to point to anything other than the symbolic resources themselves. Along with other writers, he rejects the suggestion that it is the presence of a surplus that produces a ruling elite, since there is a chicken-or-egg problem involved here.[13] It may take an elite to extract a surplus from a population otherwise satisfied with producing less. For that matter, what one may designate a surplus could also be disposed of in other, less centralizing ways. Even so, it can be held that certain material conditions could be helpful to a group intent on supporting its urban life style through the exercise of power. A productive system of cultivation and ease of communication within the territory could hardly hurt. And if the population to be controlled is relatively immobile due to a circumscribed environment, surrounded by desert as in the case of the Nile valley or perhaps by hostile nomads in the Mesopotamian case, this too could make the task simpler.[14]

What is more, redistribution in Polanyi's sense is not always only a movement from the periphery inward to the center. To the extent that the latter also reallocates goods or services to the peripheral groups or areas, it can establish itself in a key position within a division of labor recognized to offer benefits to all. Perhaps Wheatley has somewhat underestimated the importance of this in some regions of early urbanism; there may be comparatively little of it on the rather homogeneous north Chinese plain which was the area of his most intensive research. In ancient Mexico or highland Peru, on the other hand, it seems probable that ecological differentiation could have offered some basis for power to the group that could undertake to organize production and distribution within the area as a whole. A similar situation could be created also where the diversity of environments is less prominent, of course, if a differentiation of production is imposed anyway, as seems to have been the case in Egypt.

Redistribution in the first cities, that is, could include a measure of exchange. But, Polanyi and with him Wheatley emphasize strongly, this was not the same as market exchange. Only on a very modest scale might ordinary people dispose of their produce on their own, allowing prices to be influenced through haggling by factors of supply and demand. Continuous large-scale trade was politically controlled by the state apparatus, and the typical trader was a government official, fixing the terms according to state interests. The sort of relationship noted above as entailing a fusion of factors of exchange and power, then, is seen here as a part of the redistributive set-up.

Possibly this conception of administered trade has been slightly overstated. Adams (1974) has warned that the distinction between redistribution and market exchange may not have been quite as sharp in the ancient world as Polanyi made it, that the trading bureaucrat may also have had a little of the entrepreneur within him. Anyway, it can hardly be very wrong to regard these early centers as predominantly cities of power, more especially of the kind based on control of symbolism. But some centers were evidently also more engaged in military pursuits than others, and perhaps because of military crises, there was a tendency for the leadership of the ceremonial centers to become secularized with time. Warfare was also a likely significant factor behind variations in settlement patterns, between places and over time. In some instances, only a small number of people—members of the elite and their attendants—were settled in the immediate vicinity of the ceremonial plant. In the terms of a definition focusing on the size and density of population, these could be marginal cases of urbanism. As organizing centers, their urban qualities would be more obvious. For major events, greater numbers of people would gather from the surrounding region, and this entire dispersed population under the dominance of the center would also count as citizens of the community. No clear cultural dividing line was drawn between the people inhabiting the territory it governed. This was the "extended boundary town," often the form of the early city state, the *polis* (cf. Miles 1958, Finley 1977). Wheatley's volume, one may note, is dedicated to the memory of Fustel de Coulanges, who had described the beginnings of urban community in Greece and Rome in similar terms more than a century earlier in *The Ancient City*. In other instances, a more compact form of settlement appeared. Athens, it seems, took the final steps in its shift from a dispersed to a compact community on the outbreak of the second Peloponnesian war.

The pattern of politico-ceremonial urbanism thus extended into European antiquity, although in a modified form. The elite was now one of landowners and warriors in control of an enormous slave work force. Artisans and traders lived rather inconspicuously. In comparison with their other achievements, commerce and industry remained rather underdeveloped in the cities of the Graeco-Roman world; they were at heart consumer cities.

The ancient empires and their cities would decline, however, and in the Middle Ages, a new urbanism could come into being in western Europe, hardly altogether independent of old forms but under conditions sufficiently different to allow another configuration to evolve. Henri Pirenne, the author of *Medieval Cities* (1952, first published in 1925) and a number of other works, may be its foremost historical interpreter.[15] Politics, at the outset of this era, was being conducted from the manors, the affairs of intellect had their bases in the monasteries. Trade, as it picked up, was at first mobile, perhaps conducted in large part by the footloose offspring of serfs. Here, too, as in the case of ceremonial centers, greater population concentrations could be of a temporary and periodic nature, in the form of fairs. Gradually traders became more sedentary, however, clustering often at some fortification. One should not underestimate (as Pirenne perhaps sometimes did) the extent to which the regulation and protection of political rulers were felt in these commercial centers as well, at least in certain phases. But where traders in time became the strongest element, an urbanism emerged built on market exchange, on capitalism. The men in power were the middlemen and financiers of international long-distance trade, their cities often strategically located to combine different trading regions. As profits were plowed back into the enterprises, urban economies became expansive in a new way. The beginnings of relatively large-scale manufacture could be glimpsed in some places. Yet the cities also, of course, had their minor shopkeepers, artisans, day laborers, and others, often more parochially linked to the surrounding countryside.

Such centers have come to define early urbanism to many scholars whose view of the world was more or less exclusively centered on the western experience. For Pirenne, a Belgian historian rethinking the European past at about the time of World War I, the anchorage they provided for the idea of bourgeois democracy was not least of patriotic significance. To some Soviet historians, an emphasis on the role of artisans in urban growth has apparently been preferable to that on commercial middlemen.[16] Max Weber, certainly more concerned with the comparative history of civilizations than most of his contemporaries, obviously saw the medieval European town against the background of his continuing interest in the growth of rationality. His The City (1958, first published in 1921) connects well, for instance, with The Protestant Ethic.[17] In Weber's view, this sort of town was the exponent of urbanism in its most uncompromising form. It was a community built around the regular exchange of goods, where the market had become an essential component in the livelihood of the inhabitants. The market was, moreover, part of a complex of institutions which together defined the integrity of the urban community. Weber proposed that the urban settlement, to be complete, must have not only a market but also a fortification, an at least partially autonomous legal system, a form of association related to the peculiarities of urban life (the guild was an obvious example), and at least partial autonomy and autocephaly in administration. This oft-quoted formulation, surely, constituted a highly restrictive definition of urbanism. It made the most of the distinction between town and country, but its institutional expressions would not survive even in the cities of the western world in periods to come.

In these terms, Weber also contrasted occidental and oriental cities, the latter internally fragmented into separate communities and at the same time normally closely integrated into the administration of empires, often the seats of imperial courts.[18] The lack of autonomy and cohesion, in his view, made them less than complete cities. Yet they were, of course, in the shape in which Weber described them, a variety of our cities of power—symbolic, political, military, in one combination or another. It was the splendor of their palaces that impressed Marco Polo during his travels in the distant East, and it was the relationship between their fortunes and the rise and fall of dynasties which Ibn Khaldun (1969:263 ff.) discussed, as a medieval urban theorist, in the *Muqaddimah*. It is one of their forms Geertz (1967) treats with his "doctrine of the exemplary center" and the dramaturgical role of the capital in Southeast Asian states. And obviously Sjoberg had mostly them, and to a lesser extent the early ceremonial centers, in mind as he wrote *The Preindustrial City*. His view of the lowly traders under feudalism could hardly do justice to important mercantile aristocracies and bourgeoisies, sometimes maintaining urban autonomy in the face of a complex of political power external to the city—the historical realities of Flanders, Northern Italy, and the Hanseatic League.

The tendency of the distinction between oriental and occidental urbanism, cities of power and cities of exchange, Courttown and Commercetown, comes back in yet another pair of concepts with claims to classic status in the study of urbanism. Redfield's and Singer's (1954) article "The Cultural Role of Cities" represents a later stage in the evolution of Redfield's interests than most of his writings on the folk society; here the focus is on civilizations. The contrast between "orthogenetic" and "heterogenetic" cities resulted in a more differentiated view of what urban centers do to cultural traditions than that older perspective which emphasized disorganization:

> As a "central business district," the city is obviously a market-place, a place to buy and sell, "to do business"—to truck, barter and exchange with people who may be complete strangers and of different races, religions and creeds. The city here functions to work out largely impersonal relations among diverse cultural groups. As a religious and intellectual center, on the other hand, the city is a beacon for the faithful, a center for the learning and perhaps doctrine that transforms the implicit "little traditions" of the local non-urban cultures into an explicit and systematic "great tradition." (Redfield and Singer 1954:55–56)

Urbanism changed, however, with the "universal oekumene," the industrial revolution and the western expansion. Before this divide there were the administrative-cultural cities and the cities of native commerce. The former were cities of the literati and the indigenous bureaucracy; Peking, Lhasa, Uaxactun, Kyoto, and perhaps Allahabad were Redfield's and Singer's examples. The latter, the cities of the entrepreneur, were places like Bruges, Marseilles, Lübeck, early Canton, and West African market towns. In the later period there were the great metropolitan cities, "on the

main street of the world" as Park had put it, cities of a world-wide entrepreneurial and managerial class—New York, London, Shanghai, Yoko-
hama, Bombay, Singapore, as well as, on a smaller scale, lesser cities and
towns also carrying on the world's business. There were also the cities of
modern administration, the sites of the new bureaucracies, such as Washington, D.C., New Delhi, and Canberra, as well as any number of smaller
administrative towns, county seats, and seats of colonial government.

Of these four kinds of cities only the first, that of indigenous bureaucrats and literati, was a clear form of "the city of orthogenetic transformation," or, in short, the orthogenetic city. The others tended to be heterogenetic cities—the distinction is between "carrying forward into systematic
and reflective dimensions an old culture" and "the creating of original
modes of thought that have authority beyond or in conflict with old cultures and civilizations." Naturally orthogenetic and heterogenetic culture
change could occur in the same place, but many cities would tend toward
one type or the other. The first cities—the ceremonial centers—were apparently mostly orthogenetic. A folk society was transformed into a peasant
society with a correlated urban center, but a common cultural matrix
remained for both currents of social life emerging from the shared folk
heritage. A great tradition came into being in the city as its religious,
philosophical, and literary specialists reflected over traditional materials,
made new syntheses, and created forms which the common people felt
were authentic outgrowths of the old. Manifested in holy scriptures and a
geography of sacred places, the great tradition was also communicated
through stories which parents or grandparents told children, through songs
and proverbs, through professional reciters and storytellers, and through
dances and dramatic performances. It gave legitimacy to new administrative forms and kept other institutions, such as the market place, under
local cultural control. If not all places could be significant centers of orthogenetic development, at least heterogenetic tendencies could be checked.
(This, of course, was also Sjoberg's point as he noted that in the eyes of
the pre-industrial elite, merchants were a potentially subversive, culturally
impure element.) The relative faithfulness to the folk heritage also, in
Redfield's and Singer's view, limited urban-rural discord. "The wicked
city" is an idea more likely to prevail among people in the hinterland of the
heterogenetic city.

For in such a city, intellectual, esthetic, economic, and political life is freed from local moral norms. It is a meeting place of people from many backgrounds. On the one hand, conduct is governed by self-interest, expedience, and administrative convenience—reminders of Simmel and Wirth here—on the other hand there is the reaction to such urban traits in the form of humanism, ecumenicism, or nativism. The heterogenetic city is a center of heterodoxy and dissent, of rootlessness and anomie. Its intellectuals are not literati but intelligentsia; their closest kin in the orthogenetic city is the occasional heretic. The typical inhabitants of the heterogenetic city are businessmen, alien administrators, rebels and reformers, planners and plotters. Its new groups are bound together by few but powerful common interests and sentiments instead of the complexly interrelated status relationships of a long-established culture. The western metropolis is obviously this kind of city, but also the small town of nonwestern colonial society, with (at the time of Redfield's and Singer's writing) its district officer, its missionaries, and school teachers. It is rather doubtful that one can now find any urban center with a predominantly orthogenetic character. Redfield and Singer wondered whether non-western cities, once political independence was achieved, would be able to turn inward and become orthogenetic centers of a developing national culture, but they found it questionable in view of their history and their position within an international framework.

The essay by Redfield and Singer may have its main value in its suggestions concerning the cultural processes of different urbanisms, complementing the rather static and institutional view of many other writers. It is also recognizably a part, however, of a relative consensus on the main outline of the urban past which has remained rather stable for some time, and which may be discernible despite the emphases in varying traditions of historical thought on regional tradition, periodization, function, technology, and physical layout as ordering principles in the study of urbanism. We can see it again in the two more or less parallel series of urban types suggested in the European context by Robert Lopez (1963) and Fernand Braudel (1974:401 ff.). Lopez has the stockade city first; within its walls were only a temple, a fortress, and a storehouse, plus empty space. Political, religious, and military leaders were the only permanent inhabitants, with the entire population of the surrounding area coming in for festive occasions or in times of war, famine, or natural calamities. The agrarian city would come about, in Lopez' scheme, as land owners began to make their homes in the stockade for reasons of security, comfort, and prestige; they would have dependents staying on the land and working it for them. Artisans and traders would then also come to serve the city dwellers. Braudel's "open town," merging with its countryside, seems to encompass both Lopez' first types, drawing attention to the way early urbanism involved people who had one foot on the city plaza and the other on rural soil—people who viewed the urban center as a site for particular activities rather than as a place to live in.

In Lopez' market city, which is Braudel's "town closed in on itself," we join Weber and Pirenne. The merchant has become the leader, a development which Lopez suggests has drastically changed the urban mood. The superiority of the landowner eliminated, "the most successful medieval communes frankly were governments of businessmen, by businessmen, for businessmen." The captains of commerce were restlessly active, despising idleness, contemptuous of aristocrats who had lost their wealth and of craftsmen who had little chance to acquire any. To Braudel, this town was, in its autonomy, "an exclusive Lilliputian native land," with the guilds as its masters.

Although Lopez leaves us at this stage, Braudel takes us on to yet another, the subject towns, disciplined by the emergent nation states, with a court clearly in control. But Braudel also makes a point of noting that he does not want to impose a European derived scheme as a universal and inevitable sequence on the whole world. In old Russia he sees a passage from something like the open town directly to the subject town, without the closed, autonomous town engaged in frenetic commerce actually arising in its fully developed shape. In Spanish America, he sees the colonial towns as remaining centers of administration, ceremony, and recreation rather like the open towns of antiquity. In the East, from Islamic civilization to China, towns were almost always parts of kingdoms or empires, "open towns and subject towns at the same time." Braudel thus uses his types as rather provisional instruments for unfolding diversity, and he is perfectly ready to suggest alternative modes of classification—political (capitals, fortresses, administrative towns); economic (ports, caravan towns, market towns, money markets); social (rentier towns, church towns, court towns, craftsmen's towns).

There may be variations, then, but they seem like variations on a recurrent theme in the writing of urban history. About a century earlier, Marx had formulated it very similarly in his *Grundrisse:* [19]

The history of classical antiquity is the history of cities, but of cities founded on landed property and on agriculture; Asiatic history is a kind of indifferent unity of town and countryside (the really large cities must be regarded here merely as royal camps, as works of artifice . . . erected over the economic construction proper); the Middle Ages (Germanic period) begins with the land as the seat of history, whose further development then moves forward in the contradiction between town and countryside; the modern [age] is the urbanization of the countryside, not ruralization of the city as in antiquity. (Marx 1973:479)

CENTRAL PLACES and SPECIAL PLACES: GEOGRAPHICAL PERSPECTIVES

As one walks down the narrow lanes of Pirenne's Bruges or climbs the pyramids of Teotihuacan, one has come a long way from Wirth's city. Despite such tendencies toward orderliness as we may sense in the historical view of urbanism, however, we may still be looking for additional useful conceptions which can give greater rigor to the analysis of the way urban communities are put together.

In geography, also developing a perspective toward cities in the wider context, there is central place theory, pioneered by the German economic geographer Walter Christaller (1966, original edition in 1933) and including two basic varieties with obvious links to notions of urbanisms based on redistribution and market exchange.[20] We will return later to the difference between them. What they share is an interest in those asymmetrical relationships which create spatial patterns of centricity. There is one doctor, for example, to many patients; thus a multitude of relationships converge at one point. The locality where this sort of interaction occurs, through the presence of a person or set of persons who are interdependent with a large number of others, becomes a kind of cynosure within that territory where these others are scattered.

According to central place theory, couched usually in the more abstract and somewhat dehumanized language of "function" (for the part in the relationship held by one or a few) and "market" (for the number of people who at one time or other take on the other part), the distribution of the points where relationships converge can be conceptualized in the key terms of "threshold" and "range." A threshold is the minimum market necessary to make a given function viable, the range is the maximum distance over which a localized function can be effectively offered—normally, the distance a consumer is willing to travel to avail himself of it. When the use of a function within its range is less than the threshold requirement, in other words, the function cannot exist in that location. But often, naturally, the range of the function encompasses more than the threshold market size.

Some functions obviously have higher thresholds and wider ranges than others. It takes a larger market to make a living from selling furniture than from selling groceries. But people are probably also willing to travel farther for their furniture than for a loaf of bread, since they do not have to do it so frequently. Within the area served by one furniture store, consequently, there may be room for many grocery stores. On the fundamental assumption that it is practical to have different functions grouped together rather than scattered, it is likely that one of these groceries will locate as a neighbor of the furniture store.

Working on in this manner, one arrives at a hierarchy of central places. In the highest-order place, one or more functions are provided with such high thresholds that they cannot exist in any additional place in the area concerned. In second-order places those functions are located the thresholds of which are next highest, yet low enough so that more than one can be squeezed in within the area served by the highest-order place. And so forth. Apart from those functions which are most demanding as to market size and which therefore define the place of a center in the hierarchy, it also has all lower-order functions, so that central places can ideally be ordered as on a Guttman scale in terms of their arrays of functions.

Central place theory and its related methods, naturally, draw in their conventional form on the typical assumptions and ideas of geographers. The latter are concerned with the locational patterns of central places as a problem in its own right, and the empirical materials they use are usually aggregate data, somewhat divorced through their particular mode of abstraction from a conception of human beings and their person-to-person interactions. Some interdisciplinary rewriting may thus be necessary to fit central place theory into anthropological thinking. If the habit of most anthropologists and sociologists has been to think of an urban community in isolation or in relation to a perhaps vaguely defined hinterland, however, this body of theory affords a conspectus of a system of centers organizing a region. Certainly this is one reason why it has recently become a source of inspiration to anthropologists trying to find ways of dealing analytically with regions as such.[21] If our concern here, on the other hand, is still with the social order of the single urban community, we may see this as emerging in part through an interplay with its rural surroundings as well as, directly or indirectly, with other centers.

Returning to the terms of a Wirthian definition of urbanism, one might say that central place theory refers to the cumulative ordering of heterogeneity—if the different functions are seen, in a slightly different perspective, as different means of livelihood for city dwellers. That is to say, it involves specifically occupational heterogeneity, rather than heterogeneity generally. It is not in any exact sense a theory of the size and density of human settlements, since its focus is on the concentration of functions rather than of people. In these terms, the great occupational diversity of a Minas Velhas would seem to make it more decidedly a central place, even if it is marginally urban by demographic criteria alone. But we may not feel it is very difficult to bridge this conceptual gap in a general way. In an anthropological rendition, functions are served by human beings, whom we normally expect to find settled in the localities where the functions are provided. Without positing a one-to-one relationship, which would inevitably have to be qualified by a number of social organizational factors, we may at least find it probable that the more central place functions are added, the greater will be the population of the locality.

The general idea of central place theory that it may be possible to identify a series of community types with more or less elaborate constellations of livelihoods, variously powerful in shaping the centripetal tendencies of society and space, could be one which we may usefully assimilate into our stock of ideas. Any mechanistic notion of a highly predictable accretion of functions in real life, on the other hand, certainly had better be avoided. In addition, there are other assumptions in Christaller's orthodox version of the theory of which one must be wary. The geometrical patterns of central place locations which he arrived at through deductive reasoning would occur only in "pure space," hardly in an exact way in real landscapes. They require a uniform terrain where the range of a function can be calculated "as the crow flies," unaffected by rivers and mountain tops, in much the same way as Burgess' concentric circle scheme of urban ecology did. Rather more interestingly, they also assume a homogeneous rather than a socioculturally differentiated population, and a population evenly distributed over the surface of the earth.

The latter, for one thing, is unlikely partly for the very reason we have just noted: where there is a concentration of functions, there is also likely to be a concentration of people. This fact actually strengthens another important assumption of central place theory, the grouping of different functions together in the same location. If central places held only functions, no inhabitants, the former would be located together only for the convenience of that population which is spread out over the territory served. As functions are embodied by people, however, there is a partial concentration of the market in the central place itself, a core of support to which considerations of range are negligible. The possibility of a bandwagon or "multiplier" effect is there: the more functions are added to a central place, the more likely is it that the threshold market size for other functions will also be reached.

The fact that Christaller's central place theory does not in its purest form take into account these concentrations of consumers—contrasting thus with Wirth's emphasis on internal urban demand—may be one reason why his geometry often shows a closer fit with systems of periodic markets of the kind frequently found in peasant societies. Here, market places need not entail permanent population concentrations to the same extent. The rationale behind them is that where demand is poor, the population within range of a function can be made to reach the threshold level by moving the function around.

The assumption of the undifferentiated population raises other problems; more in some places than elsewhere. Here we perhaps had better take note of the difference between the two varieties of central place theory mentioned earlier. The locational pattern to which most studies inspired by central place theory have been oriented, and which is implied in much of the above, is that governed by a "market principle." The idea is that central places meet a spread-out consumer demand in a competitive, entrepreneurial spirit. The total design emerges as each provider of a function makes his own strategic choice of location. All other things equal, it makes sense for him to choose a spot as far away as possible from others in the same line, to ensure that a sufficient number of nearby consumers will find it convenient enough to take him over the threshold of survival. This location, in terms of "pure space," is likely to be midway between the nearest higher-order centers, where competitors exist.[22] But this means that the lower-order center is not unambiguously linked to any single higher-order center. Its range will overlap with that of more than one of the latter.

As long as one remains in modern western society, one may not be so badly served by the understandings which logically generate such a pattern. Here even most rural people have moved far away from self-sufficiency into an advanced division of labor. This is a large part of the "urbanization of the countryside" to which Marx and others have referred. Consumers are everywhere, and the services they require can therefore spread. Through much of human history, however, and in much of the world today, rural demand creates only a meager base for a central place system of this kind. In the words of Fernand Braudel (1977:19),

> The peasant himself, when he regularly sells a part of his harvest and buys tools and clothing, is already a part of the market. But if he comes to the market town to sell a few items—eggs or a chicken —in order to obtain a few coins with which to pay his taxes or buy a plowshare, he is merely pressing his nose against the shopwindow of the marketplace. He remains within the vast world of self-sufficiency.

Looking at central place systems only in terms of the "market principle," one would not expect them under such conditions to become well-developed. Only city dwellers would seem to be deeply entangled in the web of interdependencies which allows a greater number of specializations to reach above threshold level, and these functions could therefore not become established in any greater number of places where they would have to be more dependent on a surrounding rural market.[23]

Central place systems do not always reach out to serve people, however, but sometimes to make people serve them. The question of power comes back in here, as does Christaller's "administrative principle." When the dominant urban center maximizes effective control over a wider territory, its relationship to lower-order centers is not one of partial competition but of delegation in the interest of more certain coverage. Dependent centers are given the tasks of collecting taxes, meting out whatever passes for justice, recruiting labor, or disseminating information in their sub-areas. Considerations of the range of a function remain important (although one may now tend to think of it as a matter of getting from the center to the periphery, rather than vice versa), while the meaning of concepts like market and threshold may subtly change. This sort of central place system tolerates no ambiguity. Lower-order places must be directly under one higher-order place, and only one, for the command hierarchy to function. For this reason it may also organize the landscape in another way than do the centers of the "market principle"—the smaller places should be close to no other larger place than the one they are under.

In the comparative study of urbanism, it is obviously important not to take the "market principle" for granted in central place systems. There are now, as there have been in the past, countless instances where it and the "administrative principle" could be seen to co-exist in one fashion or another, and occasionally with some strain, within the same system. But much of the urban past, we know, has involved great inequality between city and countryside, where power of one sort or another, and the appropriation of rural resources, have been the foundation of urban affluence. And today, not least in the Third World, such relationships continue or come into existence in new shapes. The very term "administrative principle" may then frequently appear misleading, insofar as the relationships are often of a conspicuously commercial nature. Trading monopolies, with an emphasis on the extraction of local produce, are expressed through dendritic market systems where again the smaller and more peripheral market stands in a clear subordinate position with reference to one larger center, part of a new global political economy. These are the sort of structures anthropologists along with others are now dealing with in the various frameworks of "dependency theory," a lively interdisciplinary research frontier especially in Latin American studies.[24]

There is yet another fact about central place theory to be observed. It is somewhat problematically related to a view of urbanism in general, in that it takes in more, and it takes in less. If we consider only relatively large communities urban, it ignores our cut-off point. Depending on analytical convenience, the system of central places could include anything from metropolis to hamlet. On the other hand, the theory concerns only that functional makeup of communities which is affected to a notable degree by calculations of range within the potential market. It disregards functions the locations of which are determined by features of the natural environment. Entire communities may be built around these—mining towns, resorts, ports. And there may be other functions which for some reason or other find themselves located apart from the central place pattern, but whose attractiveness does not seem much impaired by considerations of cost or inconvenience of travel. Some university towns would be examples; perhaps segregated from central places on purpose because the inhabitants of the ivory tower should not be corrupted by the seekers of power and wealth.

Consequently we also need to distinguish between the urban communities with more general functions extending to a local area in which the communities are closely integrated, and those which supply specialized services to some wider societal system, not always so clearly defined in space. Even if Braudel's suggestions concerning a more varied classification of towns and cities in history show that some such differentiation has long existed, it is obvious that industrialism, with its economies of scale, and improved transport technology have increased the possibilities for such specialization. [25]

The functional classification of cities is another game geographers play more often than other urban researchers, for different purposes or sometimes perhaps (an occasional critic has remarked) as an end in itself. [26] A representative example is Chauncy Harris' (1943) well-known classification of American urban communities into eight types: retail, wholesale, manufacturing, mining, transport, resort and retirement, university, and diversified. Such a categorization may seem to be of little more than a commonsense nature, but it has still confronted urban geographers with knotty methodological problems. How dominant need a single function be for a community to be placed in a certain class? What proportion of the population must find its livelihood in that dominant function? Must it be a majority? Can it be the same for all specializations? In any case, there is no mining town where the entire working population is made up of miners, no retirement town where only old people live, no university town composed of faculty and students only. The retail town would conceivably be most closely aligned with the "market principle" of central place theory. But in any of the other cases as well, one may expect that the presence of a concentrated population would give them a head start in acquiring the sort of functions central places have in relation to surrounding areas, since in themselves they can offer at least a sizable portion of a threshold-size market. With the exception of such entities as a mining town in the wilderness, far from any other human habitation, they could even order entire central place hierarchies around themselves, and still be specialized places first and central places second. But there may also be functions turning entirely inward to serve only the urban community. Thus the distinction is drawn between the "basic" or "city forming" components of the urban economy and the "non-basic" or "city serving" components. [27] Here again one might say that it was the former that Wirth tended to disregard in emphasizing the internal division of labor in the city; the two sectors could otherwise be represented in the Chicago we have seen by Jurgis Rudkus, Upton Sinclair's immigrant meat industry worker in *The Jungle*, and by Cressey's taxi-dance girl.

DIVERSITY and ACCESSIBILITY

Towns and cities have emerged and disappeared, then appeared again somewhere else, with slightly altered characteristics. They have been assembled in various ways, from different elements. World urbanism thus exhibits many variations and exceptions, few universals or regularities. Brave attempts, such as Wirth's, to formulate a common urban pattern have in the end supplied straw men rather than lasting paradigms. Yet perhaps the *smörgåsbord* of kinds of urbanism and ways of thinking about them which we have sampled in this chapter since leaving Wirth's city may allow us to conclude with certain more general ideas concerning the conceptualization of city life, sensitizing rather than analytically rigorous, but with implications for an urban antropology partly to be further elaborated later on.

Heterogeneity was part of Wirth's definition of urbanism. Yet the city could presumably exist without variability of temperaments, hobbies, favorite dishes, senses of humor, ethnic identities, sexual predilections, notions of honor, religious cults, or patterns of speech. The one sort of heterogeneity standing in a special relationship to the size and density of settlement which characterize the city is the division of labor (if the term may occasionally be stretched to include even the relationship between laboring and leisure classes) which has created interdependencies first of all between urbanites and people on the land, but also between the urbanites themselves, in the same city or in different cities. Specializations of livelihood together constitute not only diversity, but an organization of diversity, taking some people off the land and concentrating them in the urban settlement.

Three transformations of society have played major parts in the development of such organized diversity, and we may tend to connect each one of them to a kind of urban archetype. Two of them involve principles of politico-economic order. With redistribution as a dominant principle the city of power, Courttown, arose; apparently the original city. The development of market exchange gave us Commercetown. The third transformation is technological. With industrialism, usually in combination with market exchange, Coketown came into being. One may feel the three are mere catchwords; but at times even such can be useful in a rough but quick ordering of the conceptual map.

As social complexity has developed and diffused in history, forms of urbanism have thus come in a package with such items as state organization, social inequality, the growth of literacy, and advances in the handling of energy. Some of these have, over time, drawn more and better thought than others from the interpreters of human life, and trying to identify a distinct approach to urbanism as such, one may even come to see these points of view as powerful rivals. One may be distracted by glancing over one's shoulder time and time again, to adjust one's thinking to some body of theory which is more fully developed, intricate, yet not primarily concerned with finding out what urbanism may be. If one adopts the framework of political economy, one may become engrossed with manipulating ideas concerning the forces and relationships of production, and differentiation may tend to be redefined as only inequality. Class rather than the city grasps for one's attention. If one's concern is with technology, one may choose to emphasize the impact of mass production, telecommunications, and rapid transportation on life, particularly in contemporary western society.

Obviously states of technology and political economy in the wider social system do entail an organization of centricity of which the concentration of population in the city may seem to be a mere epiphenomenon. As they do so in different ways, furthermore, we tend to shift from a Wirthian singular toward a notion of many urbanisms. But is it impossible to identify any way in which the form of settlement itself plays a more active part in determining the shape of the urban experience?

We come back to the idea of a sense of place. There are reasons why an urban anthropology could focus on the idea that life in a particular bounded space has characteristics different from those prevailing elsewhere, and use this as a meaningful frame for observation and interpretation. In whatever terms people are set apart from each other or thrown together according to other principles of organization, those who end up in the city also rub shoulders with each other and catch glimpses of each other in their localized everyday life. And this may not just be accessibility added to diversity; it may be accessibility *in* diversity, and diversity *in* accessibility. People respond not just to being close, but to being close to particular kinds of others. Conversely, when people have varied characteristics, something might happen as they get a good chance to use their eyes and ears to become aware of it. Only the division of labor may have created the city, then, but once it has come into existence, it can well serve as a catalyst for new processes exactly because it is all there, in one place. In addition, this intensively used place is not just any bare plot on the surface of the earth. It is a complicated physical environment, shaped to match its society both materially and symbolically. This environment can also go on to affect life in its own way. In a broad sense, it is a work of art.

Up to a point, anyway, we may use the ideas of geography for scaffolding in turning the facts of the division of labor into conceptions of kinds of local frames—hybrids or variations of Courttown, Commercetown, or Coketown. They clarify the distinction between central places and special places, those which make their living within the wider system by aggregating many functions and those which are rather more strictly devoted to one particular function. We are further made aware, among the former, of the different compositions of communities at the various levels of the hierarchy of centers. Using the vocabulary of central place theory, however, we can also discern how the threshold for many services may be reached within the urban population itself. This would tend to make cities within a sociocultural system more alike, regardless of their particular relationships to that system.

Yet we do not concern ourselves with matters like central place theory or functional city classification in order to turn urban anthropology into urban geography. Rather, it may be useful to think about the ways in which urban ethnography and anthropological analysis can hook up with the results or perspectives of other urban disciplines, given differences in objectives, forms of abstraction, and methodology. Here the question would be what are the implications for community life and culture of the concentrations of functions thus variously produced within wider social systems.

We will begin to grapple with it by elaborating just a little on a conceptualization of that relational point of view which we claimed in the introduction is central to anthropology. This will be a statement of orientation, and it will be taken no further in detail than is necessary for that purpose. At the same time, it is fundamental; this book is largely built around it. Which is not to say that the understandings we will thus make explicit are particularly original. They do make up a first step, however, in our anthropologizing of urbanism.

Urban social life, like any kind of social life, is made up of situations.

Individuals participate in these situations pursuing a certain range of objectives. Their shares in situations can thus be said to consist of purposive situational involvements; purposive in the sense that whether or not they got themselves into the situations intentionally, their conduct is guided by some idea of what they do or do not want to happen in them. Relationships come into being as one individual influences and/or is influenced by the behavior of one or more other individuals in the situation, and overt behavior is thus one dimension of the situational involvement. But we also want to identify two other dimensions of the latter: consciousness and resources. Consciousness (in which we would here, when it matters, include what is "below the level of consciousness") directs behavior, but the situational involvement also entails experiences which are fed back into it. More or less importantly, resources of direct or indirect utility to the individual's sustenance may also be managed through the situational involvement; some may be gained, some lost.

Such a purposive situational involvement, with its variously prominent dimensions, we will somewhat unorthodoxly refer to as a role. In recent years, it is true, role concepts have not been altogether fashionable in sociology or anthropology, since they have tended not to do full justice to the subtleties of human interaction. But we need to identify some sort of basic building blocks in our attempt to construct an overview of even quite complicated social structures, and for this purpose we will have to regard some of these subtleties as of rather secondary importance. Thus we will take the view that when different individuals' overt behavior in a kind of situation is fundamentally comparable, taking on some approximately standardized form (regardless of how this standardization comes about), they can be said to perform the same role. The comparability may be less certain with regard to consciousness and resources. You may come to a situation, that is, with other motives, and draw other experiences from it, than someone else who, on the face of it, performs the same kind of part. And within limits at least, it is what you do, rather than how much you invest or how much you profit, that defines your role. Yet all the three dimensions will be included in our omnibus concept of role, and we should immediately admit that we could get into difficulties unless we remain continuously aware of its rather complex and shifting internal structure.

Conventional anthropological practice, of course, is to employ some version of a status-role distinction, and to assume that overt behavior is matched in consciousness by normatively defined rights and obligations.

But we would prefer to avoid the consensual and static overtones of this mainstream of role analysis. We want to acknowledge that through the entities we call roles, people can negotiate, bargain, threaten, and battle with each other, interactional modes which do not quite fit with the notion of clearcut rights and duties. Such confrontations can come about because people differ in the orientations of their consciousness, or because their interests in resource management are on a collision course. We also want to be openminded about what sort of consciousness orders behavior. In what way and to what extent any standardization of overt conduct in situational involvements is normatively based is something one would ideally want to inquire into, since it could conceivably also come about in other ways (for instance, through a replicated understanding that behavior of a certain shape is most likely to be effective). And even when intentions come to be filtered through norms into action, the intentions themselves arise against a wider background of experience. The view of role which emphasizes task rather than purpose obscures much of this, not least the fact that roles are sometimes made rather than taken.

Possibly we could still work over the status-role distinction to make it express more fully our somewhat preliminary understandings of the connection between consciousness and behavior; there are times when the twin concepts could be useful in the further dissection of an individual's part in a situation. We will refrain from it, however, largely because it is convenient to have one piece of conceptual baggage less to cart around. Furthermore, there is with the term "status" that irritating ambiguity resulting from the fact that it can also refer to ranking, or even a particular type of ranking.

People have many roles; the kinds of purposive situational involvements which make up an individual's round of life we call his role repertoire. The totality of kinds of such involvements which occur among the members of some wider unit such as a community or a society we call its role inventory. As a rough breakdown of the role inventory of the modern western city, we can perhaps divide it into five domains, each containing numerous roles: (1) household and kinship, (2) provisioning, (3) recreation, (4) neighboring, and (5) traffic.

Any such categorization is necessarily somewhat arbitrary, and the boundaries between domains may oftentimes be fuzzy.[28] Yet the scheme may be sufficiently clear to be useful for heuristic purposes. One fact which it may be useful to note immediately is that some domains involve external as well as internal contracts. A housewife deals with the members of her household, but she also goes shopping for its food and clothing. When "the gang" goes out for a drink, its members take pleasure in one another's company, but they have transactions with the bartender as well. And behind the counter in the establishments supplying the consumer goods of the household and the refreshments of the peer group, there are also relationships among the co-workers. Our domain labels thus refer primarily to roles, rather than to relationships or situations, which may look different depending on one's vantage point. For the sake of clarity, however, we will use the term relationships of provisioning only for the asymmetrical relationships which regulate people's access to material resources in the wider politico-economic division of labor; in other words, the relationships in which people offer goods or services to others (primarily not of the same household), or coerce them, or manipulate their consciousness, and in these ways earn an entire livelihood or a significant part of it.[29] The relationships of provisioning thus include the external relationships connecting roles of provisioning on the one hand to roles of household or recreation on the other, but also those relationships internal to the domain of provisioning which, for instance, connect producers to middlemen. Those relationships within the latter domain which occur among people whose productive activities are coordinated into a common output, and which are thus in a way analogous to those between household or peer group members we will—not very surprisingly—call work relationships. The domains of traffic and neighboring, and the kinship part of the kin and domesticity domain, give us no trouble of this kind, since they can only involve internal relationships.

The five domains, we recognize, are relatively differentiated in urban life in the contemporary West; a role may be contained within the boundaries of one of them. In contrast to this are the societies where roles typically stretch across many domains and consequently are not so closely identified with any single one of them. Redfield's folk society is obviously of this kind. In particular, principles of kinship serve to organize so many activities that this domain tends to subsume several others.

But we do not want just the polarization of folk and city. The point is rather that the various forms of cities do not differentiate domains to the same extent. The domain of provisioning emerges gradually; its relationships of provisioning come into being particularly as the principles of redistribution and market exchange tie the livelihoods of large numbers of people together through complementarities of production and consumption, and the household can no longer be regarded as more or less self-sufficient. On the basis of what has been said before, this would seem to have occurred under all conditions of urbanism, although its forms would vary greatly.

Generalizations on the issues with which we are dealing here run a risk of being too crude. Yet it may be reasonable to suggest that the principles of redistribution and market exchange do not, on the other hand, in themselves entail a differentiation of the other part of the domain of provisioning, the work relationships, from the domain of household and kinship. The unit of production could still, relatively frequently at least, be a unit of consumption, even if one no longer produced what one consumed. As Sjoberg had it, the people of preindustrial cities may often combine home and place of work. With the coming of industrialism, one consequence is that the domain of provisioning for many becomes more fully autonomous, involving both a separate setting and a separate collection of people engaged in interaction over work.[30] Another consequence, obviously, is that provisioning relationships between consumers and at least some of those engaged in production more often become indirect, mediated by (among others) the managers and owners of the means of production.

The differentiation of the domain of recreation (even conceptually a rather tricky business, as this could tend to become a residual category of relationships) cannot be as easily related to social transformations. Even in modern western cities, it is often less than fully differentiated, as most people spend some, and some people just about all, of their "free time" in the circle of household members and kin. Others remain in the company of colleagues even after working hours are over, although the activities of work and play may be sharply distinguished. We need a theory of leisure, and perhaps a quite pluralistic theory at that, to account for the relative social separateness that leisure life sometimes achieves, and for the links between other domains and the choice of forms of recreation. Yet we cannot take on the topic here.[31]

The last two of our five domains, made up of roles and relationships of neighboring and traffic, can be seen as covering different stretches along a continuum of relationships of propinquity. The former are relationships of stable propinquity. The likely consequence of such stability is that the individuals involved extend personal recognition to one another. More substantive activities may be highly variable, with regard to both form and extent. There are places where all the people living close to one another are kin, and think of themselves as such. In that case, the domain of neighboring may not be differentiated as involving a particular kind of relationship. Otherwise, neighbor relationships would seem to be a recurrent feature of human settlements, in one shape or other. Where it is differentiated, the intensity of neighbor relationships may depend, for one thing, on the degree of exposure of people to one another, so that they would also seem to be affected by such a differentiation of settings as goes with a differentiation of domains. As a man's place of work is no longer his home, he also becomes less visible around the neighborhood where the home is situated. Like the relationships of domesticity and work, on the other hand, those of neighboring may be extended into the domain of recreation.

Traffic relationships, for their part, are involved in situations of minimal interaction and may seem to be on the borderline of being relationships at all. The participants may not even be aware that they are "taking each other into account"; they are unfocused interactions, ideally not encounters in Goffman's (1961b:7–8) sense.[32] Either one or both participants—if only two are involved—are uninterested in drawing the attention of the other. One manages a traffic relationship by avoiding sidewalk collisions; by following the rules for standing in line, taking the end position of the queue as one arrives, without crowding the individual immediately in front; by not causing offense through unnecessary claims on the other's senses, as through odor or noise (however these may be defined); by not seeking eye contact, except possibly momentarily in order to determine how more intensive forms of contact can be forestalled. One takes care in these or innumerable other ways, that is, if one wants to let the relationship pass as only a traffic relationship. But in each particular interaction, only very limited arrangements may have to be made to take one safely through it. The time period involved may vary but is generally brief—a split second for not bumping into somebody at a street crossing, a few hours with a stranger in the next seat at a concert. And as the interaction, whatever there was of it, is concluded, the participants make no assumption that they will ever meet again.

Among the five domains of roles which we have identified, two seem especially significant in making any city what it is—those of provisioning and traffic. Corresponding to any function that an urban center may have within the wider social system, there is a more or less distinctive mix of provisioning relationships, partly city forming, partly city serving. Through the former, in general terms, the city as a collectivity receives its resources, through the latter they are internally reallocated. What is primarily involved in that sense of "urbanism as a social order" which we found largely missing in Wirth's essay is an understanding of the organization of this mix. As far as traffic relationships are concerned, there is the remark by Max Weber in *The City* (1958:65), echoed by Wirth, that one could think of the urban community as "a locality and dense settlement of dwellings forming a colony so extensive that personal reciprocal acquaintance of the inhabitants is lacking." It is not, of course, lacking among all of them. But traffic relationships hardly exist where other terms are available for the definition of physical co-presence, where everybody is a kinsman or a co-worker or a neighbor or a playmate, or is present for the purpose of some recognizable interaction of provisioning. In short, they are a pure form of meetings among strangers, a result of the crowding of large numbers of people in a limited space. Although a stranger may also appear in the small and rather isolated village (and perhaps cause great excitement), he is an urban commonplace.[33]

Much of the social science research on cities is now, as it has been in most periods during the past century, concerned with the phenomena of the domain of provisioning. Given the cross-cultural scope of anthropology, one obvious question here for its urban practitioners is what functions are involved in the social and spatial organization of centricity in a society with a particular cultural tradition, and what are their social forms. In traditional Indian society, as Pocock noted, it was in the city that the caste system with its refined division of labor could be observed in its most developed constellations. Yet in this context one must also be aware that after the "universal oekumene," in the phrase used by Redfield and Singer, urban systems in different parts of the world have become in some ways more alike.

An analysis of the domain of provisioning, however, can in itself be only a part of an urban anthropology. However far the differentiation of domains has proceeded, all cities are multi-domain social structures; our position here is that an anthropology which attempts to be *of* the city rather than merely *in* the city should try to deal systematically with precisely this fact. To do justice to both the differentiation and the coherence of the urban social structure, in other words, we should investigate the forms and degrees of interrelationship among roles, not only within but also—in fact, particularly—among domains.[34]

To get a better grasp of the implications of this programmatic statement, it may be useful to consider what our overview of domains suggests with respect to the size of role inventories and role repertoires in the city. The fact of greater domain differentiation in itself would seem to entail an increase in the size of role repertoires—with each new domain that emerges, a minimum of one new role is added. But repertoires may grow further if there is internal variety within domains, and a person can be the incumbent of several roles belonging to the same domain. Role inventories, naturally, increase in size along the same lines. If different people have different roles within the same domain, however, this further enlarges the role inventory of the community.

A domain-by-domain rundown illuminates the argument further. In the domain of provisioning, the politico-economic division of labor in the city may tend to increase the role inventory significantly, since people make their living in unlike ways. If one assumes that each person has only one job, on the other hand, the contribution to the size of the role repertoire may not be so great. Variations are clearly possible here, however. Communities with central place functions might have proportionately many roles in this domain, with a minimal number of incumbents of each, while communities devoted to serving one particular function with reference to the wider society may have a great many incumbents in at least some of its roles. There is the additional possibility of occupational multiplicity, more often found in some cities than others.

In the domain of household and kinship, it does not seem probable that the number of roles performed in internal relationships would increase by much in the city. If Wirth is correct (which in this case he may be sometimes, but not always), kinship roles outside the household would rather tend to be accorded less social recognition. The household roles performed externally, in relationships of provisioning, on the other hand, probably increase in number, to some degree reflecting the variety of the provisioning domain. There is likely to be a fairly high degree of replication of repertoires in this domain, with roles occurring in a rather small number of standard clusters. Roles of recreation may come in very large numbers in urban life, but probably—as we have already implied—more in western and industrial cities than in non-western and preindustrial. Where they have their greatest impact, they can increase individual repertoires considerably (especially in the case of people content to be dilettantes), and also the variability of repertoires. With neighbor roles and traffic roles, it becomes a rather subtle question of conceptualization how many kinds there may be. Does one perform different roles, for example, sitting next to a stranger at a soccer game and in an opera house, or for that matter on a bus? On the answer to such questions depends the contribution of these domains to the size of both role repertoires and role inventory.

In general, it would seem fair to say, cities probably have comparatively large role inventories; or to put it differently, a great many different kinds of situations occur in urban life. But the size of the inventories vary between kinds of urban communities. Equally significantly, some urbanites have larger role repertoires than others—they get themselves into more different situations. Perhaps the differences between repertoire sizes are one of the notable facts of urban life. We can also see that within a repertoire, roles may be differently weighted in one way or other. We spend much more time in some of them, or get into them more often, or think they are more important than other roles. In another turn of phrase, the role repertoire can be said to have its core and its periphery.

Our suggestion, then, is that we should attend more persistently, in urban anthropological analysis, to the ways in which city people combine roles into repertoires. At the one extreme, we could imagine the case where roles would be completely segregated. Assembling a person from some wide and varied role inventory would be an act of perfect *bricolage*. This person would go on to think and behave in one situation in a way which would have nothing to do with what goes on in another, and the way he would build up resources or call upon them would establish no linkages either. At the other extreme we would find the person with a repertoire so highly integrated that no role could be exchanged for another.

We may find it a little less likely that we will find the individual with the perfectly randomized role repertoire in real life than the one with the wholly determinate repertoire. But in between we come across the great many whose lives are made up of different mixtures of determinacy and free variation. In congruity with what was said before, when we try to deal with this combinability, we would not assume that whatever departures from randomness that we find must be conceptualized in the normative terms of prescription or proscription. These may play a part, but we prefer to take into account more generally the considerations of resources and the orientations of consciousness which can order combinations even where there is a formal freedom of choice. What is of interest here is that although a person's consciousness may not be altogether one and indivisible, it is hardly quite so fully compartmentalized as absolute randomness would imply. Likewise, it is obvious that what a person can afford in one situation often depends on what he has gained in another.

This is our general perspective toward urban differentiation. As one more particular application, one could make it a working hypothesis that the makeup of the domain of provisioning has a particular influence on the formation and selection of other roles, in repertoires and in the inventory as a whole. If as a first step in the mapping of city forms, communities are categorized on the basis of their combinations of functions and the corresponding relationships within and out of the provisioning domain, knowledge of the latter should thus also aid the understanding of form and process in other relations. This might be a strategy for an anthropological analysis of urbanisms from top to bottom, bridging the conceptual divide between the biography of the urbanite and the place of the city in society.

Pursuing such a line, there would obviously be special reason to attend to the part played by resource management. There may be no *a priori* grounds for assuming that the motifs of consciousness built up in one particular role will necessarily have a dominant effect in ordering other involvements. This is a problem in the sociology of knowledge, although there is much to show that experiences in situations of provisioning can be of great importance. By definition, however, it is through the roles of provisioning that people gain the material resources (most at least) which they then proceed to draw upon, more or less extensively, in other roles as well. This gives provisioning roles a dominant position, although perhaps their influence elsewhere in the repertoire is not very specific; other roles may sometimes demand few resources, and resources can also be allocated in different ways among them.

Whatever may be the form of interrelationships within a role repertoire, we could also note here, these may be one partial explanation of the more general urban role diversity which we find also outside the division of labor in the domain of provisioning. If there is differentiation in one domain, and its component roles have a determining influence within repertoires, this would seem to draw with it differentiation in other domains as well. Provisioning roles, for example, may be linked to particular forms of recreation.

What we have just said suggests one way of thinking about urbanisms, in the plural form and as wholes. We will have an opportunity to return to this kind of analysis. At this stage, perhaps only a note of caution ought to be added. Certainly some areas of relative indeterminacy can be found in just about any urban structure. On the whole, it would seem, with this indeterminacy and rather large role inventories, urbanism allows more variability in role constellations than most social arrangements. And any urban type construct defined with precision on the assumption of chains of specific interrelations from a functional classification by way of the provisioning domain and throughout the other domains, could hardly be expected to travel well cross-culturally for related reasons. The port of Singapore, for example, is hardly in any detailed way similar to the port of Antwerp. There is no one-to-one relationship between some urban function or set of functions, defined in gross terms, and a particular set of social forms in the organization of provisioning. Furthermore, even if port cities were a unitary type as far as the organization of provisioning is concerned, other domains of life may also be exposed to other influences. There may be situations in a city where modes of thinking, behaving, and interacting are much the same as those of the society surrounding it, in itself relatively culturally homogeneous or relatively heterogeneous. Afghani urban kinship may be very Afghani, but need not be very urban.

So much, for the time being, for the need to recognize the variety of urbanisms and their internal differentiation. There is also that unity of urbanism to think of which has to do with settlement size and density.

A statement like that by Weber on the lack of personal acquaintance among city people suggests a way of translating the facts of demography and space into relational language. Where a sizable population is concentrated, an individual will have access, and be accessible, to relatively more people than in a smaller and more sparsely populated place. If, like Weber, we assume that there is some upper limit to the total amount of involvement of one individual in social relationships, however, it is uncertain to what extent these potential relationships to accessible persons will be realized. One might look at this as a species of demographic possibilism; cities and urbanites make different use of direct person-to-person accessibility through their forms of social organization. (And, of course, these latter also intervene to shape certain links between urbanites and physically somewhat less accessible people, away from the city involved.)

From the pool of potential interaction partners made up by the entire urban population, the city dweller thus draws a greater or smaller number with whom he will engage in the activities of household and kinship, provisioning, work, recreation, and neighboring. The remainder are strangers, partners in traffic relationships, if he actually meets with them. Different forms of urban organization, however, may not all produce quite the same proportion of strangers, given a certain urban population. They vary in their capacity of covering the population through other sorts of relationships. An individual enters into a great many relationships if he has a stall in the market place, probably a somewhat smaller number if he is an industrial worker on an assembly line. But both these sets of relationships may be distinct from those centered on his home, and his neighbors and friends may constitute yet other separate circles. With relationships thus spread out, there will still be strangers; but known faces may not be quite so few and far between.

This may be where we should take up again Wirth's proposition that urban social relations are typically impersonal, superficial, and segmental (words so similar in meaning that piling them on top of each other amounts to little more than rhetorical overkill). For all the valid criticisms which have been leveled at it, we may now see more clearly the grain of truth involved. The further the differentiation of domains has proceeded, and also the further the differentiation of roles within domains have proceeded, the greater is the segmentation of social relationships, almost by definition. This differentiation, to repeat, does not lead all relationships to become very narrowly defined. At least some relationships of kinship and domesticity hardly ever are; and we have noted that there is a varying tendency of relationships fundamentally defined in terms of work or neighboring as well to take on a tone of sociability, which is to say that they reach into the domain of recreation at the same time as the latter may also contain its separate relationships. (This furthermore means that links between neighbors, as they acquire content of a recreational or even quasi-domestic nature, are partially coopted into the domains based on interest as opposed to mere propinquity.)

The fact remains, however, that it is through varied involvements in relationships which are relatively segmental and concentrated in particular domains that the urbanite can make the most of the accessibility of other city dwellers, in other than traffic relationships. The kinds of linkages between domains which we discussed earlier may come back into the picture here. Quite possibly, people spread their involvements with other city dwellers most widely when relationships between domains tend toward indeterminacy. For some urbanites more determinate linkages may not only specify combinations of situational involvements, but also imply interaction with the same people in two or more domains; people who are colleagues may opt for each other as neighbors as well, and go to the same sports events during their leisure hours. They become rather like the typical urban villager, in Oscar Lewis' Mexican *vecindad* or elsewhere, who tends to recruit the same handful of people as partners in one sort of situation after another. Domain boundaries may become blurred again.[35] But in one respect at least, these people are different from a real villager. For surrounding that tiny group, as they will find if they move around the city at all, is a sea of strangers and traffic relationships.

There is hardly any way, then, in which a city dweller can avoid having *any* relationships of a segmental, impersonal, and superficial character. With his contacts spread out, some of his other relationships may even in some degree come to resemble traffic relationships, meetings between strangers. This seems particularly likely in the domain of provisioning. The greater the centricity of an individual in a certain function, the more tightly will he tend to budget his involvements among his many alters. As some of Wirth's critics have pointed out, the striving for such centricity, and the lack of personal concern between the parties to a relationship, may be accounted for more directly, for example, by the principles of market exchange than by the type of settlement. But to push speculation a step further, one might see the great city as the ideal environment of relationships focused on the cash nexus. The people engaged in them may encounter each other in no other context, and the flow of unknown people in traffic relationships provides a model for instant interactions where personalities are left out. Urbanism and market exchange may be in symbiosis, in a way similar to bureaucracy, which, with its ideals of impartiality and strict definitions of relevancy, is said to work with least distraction where the scale of social life is not too small.

Anyhow, a part of the urban anthropology to come must concern relationships between strangers, relative or absolute.[36] Anonymity is a key notion here. Wirth gave it a certain emphasis but not much in the way of analytical consideration. To many of his readers it may have seemed mostly an emotive term, but the exact role of anonymity in social relations remains problematic. One facet of it is the lack of predictability in the anonymous encounter. Not knowing anything about the biography of another individual, it is difficult to forecast his actions, whether in terms of competence or predispositions. Uncertainty thus seems to be a fairly common characteristic of urban social interaction, and one may ask what ways there could be of handling it. Another aspect of anonymity may be that the interactions of an individual who remains unidentified in a sense involve a low degree of fatefulness to him.[37] Anonymous acts are acts dissociated from his presentation of a determinate self. Knowledge of his actions is not added for future reference to the dossier which, figuratively speaking, other people keep on him. The uses of anonymity and the steps urban society may take to constrain it could be problems for investigation. One should be aware, at the same time, that anonymity is not an all-or-nothing phenomenon. If an individual cannot be personally identified, by connecting a face to a name, anonymity may at least be limited in some of its consequences by recognition of some less exact identity, such as ethnicity, class, occupation, age, or sex—Sjoberg noted this in *The Preindustrial City*. These qualities seized upon in impressing meaning on the stranger must naturally be expected to vary among societies.

The accessibility of other people in city life, however, does not only involve the handling of contacts with strangers as individuals. If for any given urbanite at any given moment the city has a surplus of people who are not part of any of his more significant relationships, they may still be relevant in other ways.

It is possible, for example, to think of people in the city as mannequins, putting a variety of meanings on show in such a way that anyone can inspect them, accept them, or reject them, without becoming heavily committed to interaction or identification with the personnel concerned. Traffic relationships may entail such a parade of impressions, in particular because they are often only a side involvement of people at the same time engaged in other activities. Walking through city streets, one may zigzag through a ball game, catch a glimpse of a craftsman putting the final touch to his products, overhear snatches of half a dozen conversations, cast a glance at assorted shop windows, and stop for a moment to evaluate the talent of some street musician. One can scarcely avoid pondering over the part played by such experiences in the urban cultural process.

It is another aspect of accessibility, of fundamental importance to the understanding of the potentialities of urban social structure, that where there were once no relationships, new contacts could come into being; relationships between strangers could change shape, becoming closer and more personal with new content. An illuminating example is the "view on the street" in Lyon in the period of the French revolution, as described by Richard Cobb (1975:125–26), an ethnographically inclined historian of everyday life. Starting out from declarations of pregnancy and seduction made before magistrates by working women, Cobb paints a picture of the possibilities for watching the street spectacle, making new acquaintances, and engaging in a furtive rendez-vous, which were inherent in a naturally peripatetic occupational practice:

> The brodeuse, the dévideuse, the coupeuse, the tailleuse, the blanchisseuse, the appreteuse, the marchande de modes, even the domestic servant, like their various masculine equivalents, are constantly walking the city, especially within the central peninsular, and bearing the handy and visible pretext of some errand—a half-finished waistcoat, a three-cornered hat awaiting its trimmings and plumes, a dress that still needs to be embroidered, a woman's hat that is still to be ironed into shape, a basket of wet linen, a bouquet containing a note, a dozen bottles of wine, a tray containing a meal prepared by a gargotier, a tray containing cakes and pastries, a brace of pheasants, a box of tools, a sack full of old clothes—the tell-tale passports to the freedom of outside during working hours.

In this particular case one can see how sorts of traffic relationships (corruptible for other purposes) depended on an organization of the provisioning domain which we may regard as largely preindustrial. The general point is that accessibility makes possible a certain fluidity in the structure of relationships. In the small community, a person could conceivably go through his entire life knowing the same people—its entire population—with birth and death the only factors of change. In the city there could be a greater turnover among one's partners in any domain of activity. The individual's total set of relationships may wax and wane; but even if it remains stable in size, new faces may join the circle while others are dropped. Or in segmental relationships old faces may appear in new contexts. Wirth's note on the transitoriness of relationships in the city could be taken to refer to the relationships which are over after as little as a single contact, such as in the bustle of public places or in the hurried exchange between a shopkeeper and a customer. It could also refer to the fact that much closer ties among urbanites may likewise come and go to a greater extent than elsewhere. On the basis of demography alone—but again it is a matter of demographic possibilism—the urban condition creates notable opportunities for achieved as opposed to ascribed social relationships. [38]

A couple of comments may be inserted here on the way such opportunities may tend to increase urban heterogeneity, even outside the organization of diversity in the domain of provisioning. One possibility is that in combination with given tendencies toward variation in the population, they may affect the evolution of subcultures. If the propensity for some mode of thought or action is scattered, only the city may hold a sufficient number of the people concerned to give them a greater chance of coming together to interact over what they share. And of all the people accessible in the city, they may choose one another as partners for the sake of this opportunity. This interaction could lead both to the stabilization of the viewpoint or type of behavior involved (since it would now enjoy group support) and to its further cumulative development. What may be latent or barely visible concerns of one or a few individuals in a smaller community, in other words, may be amplified and elaborated when many like-minded people are about. Robert Park's notion of "social contagion" shows that he was aware of the fact. It is in the bigger city, usually, that one finds not just the single pianist but a musicians' occupational culture, not one quiet political dissident but a sect or movement organized around an ideology, not a lone homosexual but gay culture.

Such an explanation of heterogeneity actually involves a variant of central place concepts. As everybody in the interacting group is simultaneously a supplier of the service concerned and part of the market for it, the members together raise themselves over the threshold for its emergence, within that convenient range of accessibility suggested by the city limits.

We may also consider what may be the advantage of the elaboration of divergent form in a situation where the possibility of a reshuffling of social alignments is always present. One might see in the quest for conspicuous individuality in a place like Minas Velhas a desire to claim the attention of others, to achieve a satisfying selection of social relationships and not to be left out when partners change.[39] Launching a new style of behavior, clothing, or other noticeable form could lead to such competitive advantage (and here we approach Wirth's Darwinian perspective toward differentiation); only if one is too successful and the innovation is adopted by many the purpose is lost, and something else has to be tried. The diversity of urban life, from this vantage point, is not stable. As Kroeber put it in his *Anthropology* (1948:283), it is characterized by "fluctuations of fashion, not only of dress but of fads, novelties, amusements, and the fleeting popularity of persons as well as things."

In these ways, then, it is possible that the greater accessibility of people to one another in the city may matter in its own right. With regard to both modes of behavior and specific individuals, the city can be a system of scanning and pickups. Asserting this much, it is also necessary to state some of the qualifications.

Accessibility, as we have said, is not always realized; it depends not least on forms of social organization. When there are determinate connections between relationships and activities in different domains, as we have exemplified above, this will constrain the choices otherwise made possible by accessibility. The material investments and the buildup of competence in certain relationships and lines of action may even otherwise be such that the cost of change would be too high. And what an individual may do, and with whom he may engage in various activities, may be so culturally regulated in other terms as well that the alternatives which may be available in the immediate habitat are simply defined away. It is quite possible for recruitment to certain relationships to be ascriptive within some smaller population (or for that matter achievable only within such a population), even if recruitment through wide-open achievement would seem to make more use of the urban situation. The effectiveness of constraints like these is worthy of consideration, as well as whatever strains may be detected between them and the temptations of a more abundant environment.

It also remains a possibility that people simply routinize their social relationships as well as their intellectual and behavioral reportoires, seeing no reason to change just because alternatives present themselves. The city may offer such a wealth of impressions and contacts that the individual is unable to cope actively with it all, and therefore becomes less receptive to each new impulse; attention slackens. This point has been argued by Milgram (1970), who by bringing in the concept of overload from systems theory seems to come closest to updating Simmel and Wirth on urban ennui.

Just because individuals are within convenient reach, furthermore, it does not mean that they always are or want to be on view, or available for interaction. Where too much accessibility is a problem, privacy becomes a value. For what activities or relationships protection is sought, however, or against whom, is also a matter of social organization. The built urban environment serves as one component in this regulation of access. Sjoberg, we remember, noted the inward-turning houses of the elite in the preindustrial city. Some kinds of activities are assigned space to which access is severely limited, other settings may be used to indicate at least conditional openness to new contacts. The urbanite may also be wary of direct approaches by strangers, while the latter may stand a better chance of being accepted if contact is made through known intermediaries. One slightly paradoxical point is that such modification of accessibility, in a situation where a large part if not all of a person's relationships may be achieved rather than ascribed, can be managed so as to make him inaccessible for significant contacts to most of the community. This is useful not least to the groups wanting to cultivate a life of their own, without having others peeping in. The fact that members may be able to earn a livelihood there through impersonal relationships contributes to making the city a sanctuary for them.

One final complication looks as if it could be the most serious one, for urbanism as such as well as for a sense of place as a frame for thought. Accessibility depends not only on the spatial factor but also on communication technology. Where cars and telephones are generally available, distance counts for less than where interaction must be face to face and where one travels on foot. In the extreme case, the physical concentration of people would no longer serve a purpose. In some ways (such as for defense) it could even be dysfunctional. Boulding (1963:143–44) points this out in an essay on "the death of the city" which the future could bring:

> We can even visualize a society in which the population is spread very evenly over the world in almost self-sufficient households, each circulating and processing everlastingly its own water supply through its own algae, each deriving all the power it needs from its own solar batteries, each in communication with anybody it wants to communicate with through its personalized television, each with immediate access to all the cultural resources of the world through channels of communications to libraries and other cultural repositories, each basking in the security of an invisible and cybernetic world state in which each man shall live under his vine and his own fig tree and none shall make him afraid.

So the conditions underlying the equation of man's use of space would have changed. Although no longer very constrained by a relationship to the land, his interdependency with other human beings could continue without much attention to distance. The city could pass away, while it might seem as if the urbanization of the countryside would continue. Indeed we may be moving in this direction, but not equally quickly in all parts of the world, or in all segments of any one society. Technology is not evenly distributed. In addition, however, one may want to comment that the attempt to have accessibility without density, whether by cars, telephones, or personalized television, can hardly recreate the full urban experience. It tends to be planned accessibility only; you reach the particular person you had in mind. Contemporary and historical urban accessibility may be partly planned, but also to some extent unintended. Running into people for whom one was not looking, or witnessing scenes for which one was not prepared, may be neither efficient nor always pleasant, but it may have its own personal, social, and cultural consequences. With this reflection we can perhaps end this preliminary inquiry into the nature of urbanism: serendipity, discovering one thing by chance when one was looking for something else, may be built into city life to a peculiar degree.

CHAPTER FOUR

The View from the Copperbelt

Apart from the work of the early Chicago School, perhaps no other single localized complex of urban ethnography can match the studies which for a number of years came out of Central Africa. This body of research was the product of the Rhodes-Livingstone Institute, set up in 1937 and transformed, in connection with the achievement of Zambian independence in 1964, into the Institute for Social Research of the new University of Zambia.[1] Taken as a whole it has so far remained the most significant excursion of British social anthropology into an urban milieu. While the studies do not offer the wealth of descriptive detail concerning a variety of groups and settings which one finds in their Chicago counterparts, they are important also for their awareness of problems of method, conceptualization, and analysis.

There is considerable variation in African urbanism, and the Rhodes-Livingstone anthropologists did not cover the entire spectrum. In chapter 3 we noted that the towns of the West African Yoruba have recently been identified as exponents of a primordial urban type, the ceremonial center. Slightly earlier, in the 1950s and 1960s, they functioned as test cases for conceptions of urbanism along Wirthian lines.[2] Even then, in Ibadan, turning itself into a metropolis with a population of close to half a million (and considerably more now), every other male was engaged in agriculture. And in other large Yoruba communities, census figures indicated that as much as 70–80 percent of the men were in this occupational category. Could one call a place a city, even if it had tens of thousands of inhabitants, if its people are tillers of the soil? Nor, for that matter, does this make much of urban heterogeneity. As far as ethnic diversity was concerned, moreover, there was hardly any in the Yoruba agrotowns. Also,

kinship was the major principle underlying the social order, again in conflict with accepted ideas of urbanism. The traditional communities consisted largely of the compounds of lineage groups, the members of which
could be counted by the hundreds or even thousands in larger settlements.
Yoruba notions of the boundaries of the urban community also seemed odd.
The Yoruba certainly distinguish between town and country, and hold the
former in higher esteem. But a cultivator who is settled in an outlying area
and spends most of his life there still "belongs" to the city (or conversely,
the city belongs to him) if he is a member of one of the kin groups with a
compound there. For ritual, political, and other purposes he is as much an
urbanite as the man who pursues a non-agricultural line of work, or the
man who returns inside the city walls from his farm every day.

   In some other ways, Yoruba towns conformed better to the expectations
of the western urban theorist. There was, after all, a fair amount of social
differentiation. They had the sacred kingship symbolizing the unity of the
community, as well as other political and ritual offices. Although traditional Yoruba society hardly had a class system in any strict sense, it was
not an egalitarian society either, but one with elaborate ideas of precedence
and deference. A number of craft specialties were at hand, as well as a
rich associational life in the form of cult groups, age sets, and occupational
guilds. In some areas of life, one could even find the instrumental, manip-
ulative approach to other persons which has been deemed characteristically
urban. Market places, centrally located in most communities near the royal
compound, were large; Bascom (1955) offers examples of sharp practices
among traders and money doublers. Wirth and Simmel would perhaps have
been particularly pleased at one feature of Yoruba urban symbolism; at
each big market, a shrine would be devoted to the trickster Esu, deity of
crossroads, commerce, quarrels, and uncertainty generally.

   The model of the ceremonial center does away with the more conspicuous anomalies of Yoruba urbanism. The institutional apparatus of sacred
kingship does constitute a point of social and spatial centricity which one
must not allow to be concealed by the presence immediately surrounding it
of a thick layer of the peasant population which it organized. And the fact
that people may be counted as citizens of the urban community whether
they live inside it or outside it makes the Yoruba town an intermediate
form between the compact settlement and the extended-boundary town,
both types represented among ceremonial centers in the past.

   Yoruba urbanism already existed as the first European visitors made their appearance in coastal West Africa, and many of the towns have continued in much the same shape into the present. Africa has had its traditional urban centers. Another of them, Timbuktu, had been the site of one of the first urban anthropological studies, as Horace Miner (1953) went there to test Redfield's ideas about the folk-urban continuum. But there were also the cities more heavily influenced by the European expansion. The best-known classification of African towns and cities remains that by Southall (1961:6ff.), in an International African Institute symposium which summarized an early phase of urban studies in this part of the world. It divided communities into type A, old established, slowly growing towns, and type B, new towns of rapid expansion.[3] The former were of indigenous origin or had at least so integrated with indigenous society that there was considerable continuity of culture and social structure between town and country. (Although this was not part of Southall's vocabulary, one might say that they were the central places of local systems.) Some inhabitants might be cultivators; apart from this, commercial and clerical occupations would dominate. One African ethnic group could be dominant, normally that in whose territory the town was located, with other groups more weakly represented if present at all. There would probably be comparatively few European residents. The type A town was characteristic of West Africa, and parts of East Africa. Yoruba urbanism would be an extreme case, and Timbuktu would also fall into this category.

Type B towns occurred particularly in Southern and Central Africa. Closely associated with European power, they were also the major industrial centers on the continent. Many of them were based on mining. There was thus a quite sharp discontinuity between them and the surrounding African society, with the towns facing rather toward an international economic system as far as their major functions were concerned. Life in them tended to be rather closely regulated by white settlers, of whom there were sizable numbers. The African inhabitants of these urban communities often represented a variety of ethnic groups, some of which had their rural base far away.

Any classification as simple as that of A and B type towns must be open to debate in some ways. Some of the former as well as all of the latter were examples of a more or less elaborate pattern of colonial urbanism which extended outside Africa as well. King (1976:71ff.), in an intriguing volume on the Indian colonial city, notes that there was some intercontinental diffusion within empires of institutions, architectural forms, and ideas of planning.[4] Clearly, wherever Europeans and indigenes shared a city, the facts of European domination tended to be inscribed into both the social structure and the physical environment. Residential segregation of the races was nearly universal. In India the Europeans were in the "civil lines" and "cantonments," in Nigeria in "government residential areas." Certainly these quarters and their institutions were always under the strict control of the dominant group, even if in type A towns one could take a more relaxed attitude to what went on in the "native town" which they had been grafted onto.

In other ways the A and B types could at the same time be too broad. Perhaps especially what went into type A was rather too varied.[5] Some years after Southall's formulation the small, administrative and commercial modern town, which he had placed with type A only as an afterthought, was defined as a separate type C, later developed more carefully by Joan Vincent (1974).[6] This town combined a wide variety of services for the surrounding area, concentrating the institutions by which it was politically and economically integrated into the wider, changing society. Although Vincent's discussion was set in an East African context, the pattern could be found to recur in much the same form elsewhere on the continent as well.[7]

As this type was broken out of type A, however, the latter would become little more than a residual category of non-B, non-C. And this would be even more conspicuous as Africa moved into independence. The typology had been in some ways overtaken by events, as new developments occurred in some old places and colonial mechanisms of regulating growth lost their force.[8] Of type A communities, some would now be stagnant places like Timbuktu and a number of the less lively Yoruba towns. Others were now capitals of new nations, engaged in an ever accelerating expansion based on the growth of commerce, industry, state bureaucracy, and, not least, high hopes on the part of migrants. These places—Dakar, Abidjan, Lagos— would join with others which had evidently been classed before with type B—Nairobi, Leopoldville turning into Kinshasa—in conforming now to another recurrent type of Third World urbanism, the primate city, drawing to themselves an overwhelmingly large part of the resources of their respective countries and leaving other centers far behind.[9]

But we need not concern ourselves more here with the problems of African city classification, as long as we can place the urban research locales of the Rhodes-Livingstone anthropologists in the general historical pattern. Their work constituted a characteristic anthropology of type B towns, a sort of colonial African Coketowns. Although several communities were involved, two mining centers became the subjects of most intensive documentation: Broken Hill (later to be renamed Kabwe) and Luanshya.[10] The former, based on zinc and lead mining, was older, regarded as a more stable community, and more diversified as it was also an important railroad junction. Luanshya was farther north, in the Copperbelt, and had come into existence only in the 1920s. But it had already experienced periods of boom and near bust, as well as serious conflict between the mine management and African workers.

DETRIBALIZATION in BROKEN HILL

The initiative to set up a research institute for social and cultural studies in what was, in the 1930s, British Central Africa came from a governor of Northern Rhodesia, who succeeded in launching the project only after a few years of wrangling with the Colonial Office in London. Both in England and in Northern Rhodesia there were those who on the one hand regarded pure research as rather a luxury, and on the other hand suspected that any policy suggestions that could come from anthropologists (who were bound to play a dominant role in such an institute) would be impractical or inopportune. Yet in the end the governor had things his way. The institute was placed under a board, chaired by the governor himself and otherwise composed of colonial civil servants and representatives of white settler interests. As the first director Godfrey Wilson was named, coming from field work, in a husband-wife team with Monica Wilson, among the East African Nyakyusa.

It was taken for granted by many observers of Northern Rhodesian society, and regarded as desirable by others, that the new institute should concentrate its interest on more or less traditional rural African life, at least partly in order to provide information useful to administrators. Wilson soon made it clear, however, that he attached great weight to the study of urbanism and urbanization, and to their influence on rural life. Originally he had hoped to do his first urban field study in the Copperbelt, but this was vetoed by the provincial commissioner who feared that an anthropologist might comment adversely on administrative arrangements. Consequently,

Wilson went to Broken Hill instead. The major resultant publication was *An Essay on the Economics of Detribalization in Northern Rhodesia,* issued in two installments (Wilson 1941, 1942).

In the first part of the study, by way of introduction, Wilson sketched the changes that had come over Central Africa in the preceding decades, and the theoretical assumptions guiding his analysis. A way of life almost wholly contained by kinship had been transformed by incorporation into a world community;

> a community in which impersonal relations are all-important; where business, law and religion make men dependent on millions of other men whom they have never met; a community articulated into races, nations and classes; in which the tribes, no longer almost worlds in themselves, now take their place as small administrative units; a world of writing, of specialized knowledge and of elaborate technical skill. (Wilson 1941:13)

To this situation Wilson brought the notion of equilibrium which was fundamental to the anthropological functionalism of his time. Equilibrium, he proposed, is the natural state of society. Its relationships, groups, and institutions make up a balanced and coherent system. They are all inextricably connected and determine one another. But Central African society around 1940 was very plainly not in such a state. Changes had been introduced into parts of the system, creating contradictions, oppositions, and a state of disequilibrium. Over time, according to Wilson's standpoint, the system would again move toward equilibrium, and strains would be resolved. Exactly what kind of equilibrium would be reached, however, was an open question.[11]

A major force of disequilibrium was obviously the introduction of an urban-based industrial economy into a rural society of simple agriculture, and this was the substantive focus of the essay. Its first part thus dwelt on the urban-rural interrelations created in particular through labor immigration, the second part was concerned with life in town itself.

Broken Hill at the time of the study had a population of some 17,000, about one-tenth of them Europeans. As on the Copperbelt, the settlement pattern related directly to the organization of the European-dominated economy, and this regulated African inhabitation. The mine and the railroad each had quarters set aside for their employees. Other Europeans—business or private persons—who employed Africans on a smaller scale could rent accommodations in the part of the town controlled by the municipality, where Africans could also rent rooms for themselves. Urban accommodation for Africans was limited, however, and therefore crowded. The basic assumption of urban policy in colonial Central Africa was that the African town population consisted of only temporary residents, able-bodied male workers who left all or most of their dependents behind in the village as they departed for the urban centers where they would themselves spend only brief periods of their lives. Thus housing was usually not planned for more than, at most, a husband and wife with a young child or two, in a single room. Wages, and the food rations which the major corporations issued to their workers, were not sufficient for a complete household either. Broken Hill in fact allowed some of its African population a rather more normal domestic life than did the Copperbelt towns, since a number of plots had been allocated to Africans who could build their own housing on them and complement their rations with some cultivation. This policy had evidently been introduced in order to compete with the Copperbelt communities where wages were higher.

People did not remain in the villages to the extent that government and business intended, however. In the earliest years of industrialization the pattern of sojourns bracketed into rural lives may have been dominant; by the time of Wilson's study a large part of the urban population spent more of their lives in town than in the country, and although as much as half of the African population of Broken Hill consisted of adult males, many of them had larger households than accommodation, wages, or rations were planned for. If the African labor force still appeared unstable, it was partly due to job changes in the towns, and to movements between different urban centers.

This situation also had conspicuous effects on life in the countryside. Large areas lost much of their population, especially men in their best years, and could not maintain their agriculture at a satisfactory level. Audrey Richards (1939), another pioneer in Central African anthropology, had already pointed out the prevalence of hunger among the Bemba, whose migrants made up large numbers of the population in the new urban communities. Since migrants returned only rather small portions of their urban earnings to their rural home areas—mostly in the form of consumer goods—the loss of manpower was not adequately compensated. The situation was least favorable to the more distant areas to which migrants had the least opportunity to return with any regularity. Nor could these areas benefit from the markets for produce provided by the urban centers. But in any case, these were of limited importance, as European-owned farms had a near-monopoly on the large-scale supply of foodstuffs to the towns.

An equilibrium of urban-rural relations, Wilson proposed, might be reached by allowing the stabilization of the African town population, of work force as well as dependents. This would not only involve making living conditions in the urban areas more secure, but by thus creating a large urban population, one could also expect that as a consequence an agricultural revolution could take place in the rural areas to feed the towns. As it was, the gap between agricultural and industrial technology was a major ingredient in the Central African disequilibrium.

In the second part of his essay, devoted more strictly to town life itself, Wilson drew a distinction between impersonal, or somewhat imprecisely, "business" relationships, and "the personally organized circles of domestic life, of kinship and of friendship." He did not push the conceptualization of the former very far in interactional terms, however, so that it is largely indirectly, through an account of the expenditures of the Africans, that one glimpses some facets of the wider social order. One major emphasis was on the importance of clothing—"the Africans of Broken Hill are not a cattle people, nor a goat people, nor a fishing people, nor a tree cutting people, they are a dressed people" (Wilson 1942:18). Some sixty percent of the Africans' cash earnings, Wilson estimated, were spent on clothes. It was true that the instrumental uses of such possessions should not be ignored. As people went home to their rural areas of origin, they brought clothing as gifts for their kinsmen and thereby maintained their positions in the communities on which ultimately they depended for their security. Clothes could also be used in exchanges with other townsmen, to get such necessities as food and accommodation if one became unemployed. Some clothing acquired by the urbanites of Broken Hill was thus not used but kept in storage, sometimes even in the shop where it had been bought. Yet the main point remained that fashionable clothing signalled a place in the urban "civilized" status system. Wilson saw the manner of dress as the most obvious way by which the Africans in town could emulate a prestigious European life style. There was no way of getting a European house. Furniture was difficult to move around for a mobile people. A new jacket or a gown, on the other hand, could be displayed on a stroll around town, when going visiting, or at the dance club which was frequented particularly by those with a greater than ordinary exposure to European ways. These clubs deserved special mention as an arena where townsmen took measure of each other's sophistication. Clubs from different towns competed against one another. Preferably one would have European visitors at the dances, to give implicit recognition to the participants' achievements. But Europeans generally seemed to care little for Africans claiming status in the idioms of European culture. White discourtesy to Africans seemed rather to increase the more "civilized" the latter appeared.

As for other African consumption patterns in Broken Hill, Wilson again noted how rapidly the economy of a household would deteriorate with the addition of more non-earning members, since wages and rations were not calculated to cover them. In the case of food as well, there was some tendency to attribute prestige to European-style items, such as white bread. African beer, on the other hand, continued to be popular. And although officially the municipal beer hall was supposed to enjoy a monopoly, home brewing was very widespread, largely for private consumption. One was used to drinking at home with friends and kinsmen, the beer hall was inconveniently located for many, and its product was rather too weak. Besides, the women in town, deprived of (or emancipated from) many of their rural tasks, had ample time for brewing.

Much the larger part of the discussion of personal relationships was devoted to a consideration of African urban marriage. There was yet no officially recognized "modern" form of civil marriage for the African townspeople; the colonial authorities claimed that "native custom" regulated marriage in urban areas as well. Wilson showed, however, that conjugal relationships of the traditional rural types did not easily fit into the urban matrix of relationships. The extended process by which a marriage was established in the village, involving continuous close economic ties with kinsmen, tended to be replaced by a union more quickly established and considerably more autonomous. Kin could be hundreds of miles away, and even if they were represented in the town itself they were of limited importance as partners in the business of gaining a livelihood, once one had entered the urban sphere of commerce and industry.

Partly because of the unbalanced sex ratio in town, Wilson believed marriage was also less stable than in the rural areas. There was some tendency for the relatively few women to circulate among the men, and thus many of the townspeople were in their second or third unions. A rather large proportion of these later unions were interethnic. It was also only to be expected that prostitution would thrive under these conditions, although not every unmarried African woman in Broken Hill was a prostitute, as the Europeans in town tended to believe, and some unions passed from prostitution by way of concubinage into stable marriage.

Wilson had relatively little to say about other personal links. He mentioned that several households tended to get together for meals, usually on the basis of propinquity. In such eating groups it was usually the men who had the closer ties with one another, while their wives went along. Mostly people of the same tribe would share meals this way. Neighboring and shared ethnic affiliation often coincided, since some housing was assigned on the latter basis and in other cases people sought accommodation close to ethnic compatriots. As another economic component in personal relationships, Wilson took note of a simple form of an arrangement often found in societies where more formal savings facilities are missing; friends would take turns in getting a larger share of their combined earnings, so that instead of squandering their money on petty purchases they would have a chance, at intervals, of getting something more substantial. What occurred in Broken Hill was apparently on a smaller scale than the "rotating credit associations" so often described from many parts of the world, but the principle was the same.

MAX GLUCKMAN and the MANCHESTER SCHOOL

In a small book published some years after the Broken Hill research, Godfrey and Monica Wilson (1945) developed further the mode of analysis of social change outlined in the earlier work, on the basis of a broader range of Central African anthropological data. The idea of equilibrium continued to be at the center of attention; in phrasing much of their discussion in terms of a concept of scale, and contrasting small-scale and large-scale society, the Wilsons came up with some formulations closely paralleling the folk-urban distinction of Wirth and Redfield. But we may have little reason to go into this here.

The study of Broken Hill turned out to be both the first and the last urban study that Godfrey Wilson would conduct under the aegis of the Rhodes-Livingstone Institute. The Empire was now at war, and it was made clear to him that it was undesirable that he, a conscientious objector, should be too closely involved with the colonial subjects. So Wilson resigned from the institute (and died a few years later). Its directorship was taken over, on an acting basis to begin with, by its second social anthropologist, Max Gluckman.

Gluckman, a South African who had come into anthropology after some training in law, had his anthropology out of Oxford, fundamentally structural-functionalist with Durkheimian emphases. He was also an equilibrium theorist of sorts.[12] But he was more sympathetic to historical points of view than some of his contemporaries, and in criticizing earlier anthropological functionalism, he emphasized the significance of conflict in social life. In this he claimed Marx as a source of inspiration. Since he often dwelt on the way the situational alignments in different conflicts cross-cut one another and thereby constrain action in each separate conflict, it can be argued whether his view of conflict did not have as much in common with Simmel.

The broad scope of Godfrey Wilson's view of Central African society and its place in the world was in important ways shared by Gluckman. In one of his publications while director of the Rhodes-Livingstone Institute, a critical review of Malinowski's rather simplistic institutional analysis of "culture contact," he insisted that colonial African society had to be seen as a "single social field," including everything from apparently traditional village life and chieftaincy to European district officers and living conditions in South African gold mining centers, and he continued to drive this point home in other writings. He also drew attention to similarities in the process of industrialization and labor migration in nineteenth-century Europe and twentieth-century Central and South Africa (Gluckman 1963a:207 ff.).

As the world was coming out of the war and could expect to return to a state of normality, Gluckman (1945) set forth a seven-year research plan for the institute based on this perspective. It was, he noted, "the first plan of the kind in the British Empire"; he also quoted a colleague as suggesting that the proposed project was "the biggest event in social anthropological history since the Rivers' Torres Straits expedition." The intention was to cover major social developments in the region, to present the widest possible range of comparative materials on both indigenous and modern social organization, and to deal with the most important social problems confronting the government of the territory. This meant the inclusion of urban as well as rural society; African groups of varying traditional cultures; rural areas differentially affected by labor migration and the expansion of various types of local cash economies; and cities of different economic bases. There were, in Central Africa as well, urban communities less involved with industry than Broken Hill and the Copperbelt communities. One should try to cover family and kinship, economy, politics, law, and religion; and (a little vaguely) European, Indian, and other groups should be "considered" in the research.

This highly ambitious program was never fully completed, and indeed was barely even under way when Gluckman left the directorship of the Rhodes-Livingstone Institute. But while Godfrey Wilson's association with the institute had been comparatively brief, Gluckman's turned out to extend beyond the years when he was its director. He returned to Oxford in 1947, but a couple of years later he took up a new professorship at the University of Manchester, and from then on a special relationship existed between the institute and the anthropology department at that university. Two of Gluckman's successors as institute directors—Elizabeth Colson and Clyde Mitchell—and a considerable number of those who during various periods conducted research under the auspices of the institute were also at one time or other connected with the Manchester department. These included John Barnes, Ian Cunnison, Victor Turner, A. L. Epstein, William Watson, M. G. Marwick, Jaap van Velsen, Norman Long, and Bruce Kapferer, all contributing through monographs as well as other publications to the mapping of Central African life. While the members of the group certainly had their individual emphases and have moved in varied directions in their later intellectual careers, their years of interaction resulted in a continuously evolving but coherent body of method and analysis, uniting both rural and urban studies. If Gluckman's seven-year plan may be reminiscent in its range of Robert Park's 1915 paper on the city, stating a Chicagoan research program, Gluckman's prefaces to several of the Central African monographs, underlining the way they contributed to the work of the group as a whole, could also be a parallel to the similar function performed by Park's prefaces to many Chicago studies. For some of the later volumes Clyde Mitchell took on a similar task. Moving from the institute directorship to the chair of African Studies at the University College of Rhodesia and Nyasaland, Mitchell for a period linked yet another institution to the network, before going on to Manchester himself. Both organizationally and intellectually, the Central African researchers thus formed the core of what became known in the world-wide community of anthropologists as "the Manchester School."

We will largely ignore the Rhodes-Livingstone rural studies here, even if the town could be seen on the horizon in several of them. As the seven-year plan indicated, for example, the effects on rural economies of urban migration, discussed by Wilson in the Broken Hill study, would be investigated further. In communities with different agricultural technology and kinship organization, it appeared, the consequences could be less deleterious than they were in the Bemba case which he had described (see Watson 1958; van Velsen 1961). In dwelling on the reporting and conceptualization of urban life as such, we will also leave aside as far as possible the concern with the migratory process and with the notion of urban stabilization, where not least Mitchell took up some of the problems noted by Godfrey Wilson. [13]

The rural studies of the postwar period were earlier to get under way, but from the early 1950s, considerable effort went into the study of the modern towns of Northern Rhodesia again, with results over approximately the ensuing ten-year period to be reviewed here. In the next chapter, the somewhat later contribution of the Manchester School to the development of network analysis will be touched upon. And we should be aware that new publications based on the research of the group in Central Africa continue to appear, although now in a fairly slow trickle, as individual members continue to work away on materials assembled in earlier years.

EXTENDED CASE STUDIES, SITUATIONAL ANALYSIS and the KALELA DANCE

Wilson was not very explicit about the methods of data gathering in the Broken Hill study. Apart from some work of a survey type, his interpretations seem based on relatively detached observation, rather than intense involvement in the life of the African townspeople. His successors in Rhodes-Livingstone urban research took a more conscious interest in matters of method, and both their methodological repertoire and the range of their substantive concerns were wide. They conducted large-scale social surveys, the resulting quantitative data of which made it possible, for example, to extend the work of the group on Central African marriage and divorce into the town context (see Mitchell 1957, 1961). For one thing, this threw some doubt on Wilson's notion that divorce was more frequent in the city, as it was also quite common in the matrilineal rural communities. Institute researchers also linked up with the growing interest, in comparative sociology, in the prestige ranking of occupations in various societies (Mitchell and Epstein 1959, Mitchell 1966a). But there was also a readiness for qualitative analysis of particular cultural manifestations. Epstein (1959) described emergent urban argot in the Copperbelt in a way which showed that a new way of life was coming into being (and, one might say, bore evidence of the cultural processes of a heterogenetic urbanism), Mitchell (1956a) developed a view of Copperbelt urban social structure out of a study of a popular dance, the Kalela.

This latter study may be seen against the background of the general innovative work of the Manchester School on the format of presentation of analyses.[14] The dominant type of account of social structure in British social anthropology had for some time been static, morphological, rather highly abstracted from real life. Gluckman and the people working with him began to use more extensive case materials as an integral part of their analyses, not merely as illustrations but to provide the reader with a better chance of scrutinizing their interpretations and perhaps coming up with alternatives. Using "cases" in one way or another may have come natural for some of them for personal reasons—Gluckman and Epstein had both had legal training, Mitchell had a background in social work.[15] But they also had intellectual and situational reasons for their more explicit use of case materials. Although they tended to be reformist rather than revolutionary in their views of how social structure should be analyzed, they felt that within an enduring structural framework, other features of social life emerged through more or less complex sequences of interaction where individuals to a certain extent could exercise some choice. In their studies of rather more traditional Central African societies, Mitchell (1956b) thus made extensive use of case materials in his monograph on the Yao, Turner (1957) in his on the Ndembu, and van Velsen (1964) in his on the Lakeside Tonga. In studies dealing more directly with the colonial situation or with life in the industrial towns, the difficulty of giving their composite and contradictory nature its due with the conventional mode of description and analysis tended to be yet more obvious.

There are, however, two relatively distinct tendencies to be found in the use of case materials in the work of the group. One of them involves a fairly narrow focus on a single event, clearly demarcated in time and space. The first example of this use was Gluckman's "Analysis of a Social Situation in Modern Zululand" (1940), based on field work conducted in South Africa before he joined the Rhodes-Livingstone Institute. Here Gluckman began by describing the ceremony of a bridge opening in Zululand, performed by a high white official. Discussing the people attending the ceremony and its various elements, he could use the description of this situation as a point of departure for a wider social and historical analysis of Zululand society. The idea, then, is to find a case which can serve as a didactic device, illuminating in a peculiarly effective way the disparate traits that go into the construction of a complex and normally rather opaque social order. The technique seems quite similar to Clifford Geertz's use, in *The Social History of an Indonesian Town* (1965:154), of a village election as a document, "a unique, individual, peculiarly eloquent actualization—an epitome," of a comprehensive pattern of social life.

The other tendency is perhaps more radical in its theoretical implications, as it more or less clearly involves a processual rather than a morphological view of social relations. This is an *extended* case study, involving some series of events, stretching over some time and perhaps not all occurring in the same physical space. It is the analyst, who, seeing that they together constitute a story, abstracts them as a unit from the endless flow of life. Here one may discern how a set of relations is shaped through the cumulative impact of various incidents, as the participants navigate through a society where principles of conduct may be in part conflicting and ambiguous.

Following two discussions by van Velsen (1964:xxiii ff.; 1967) particularly of the latter form of use of case materials, "extended case study" and "situational analysis" have been used synonymously as terms for it. This seems a little unfortunate, as in view of the title of Gluckman's Zululand study, it would have been reasonable to reserve "situational analysis" for the kind of interpretation of which that study is a paradigm—of a single, rather naturally demarcated event of compressed social significance. Be that as it may, it is on this model that *The Kalela Dance* was patterned. As Mitchell (1956a:1) described his own procedure,

> I start with a description of the *kalela* dance and then relate the dominant features of the dance to the system of relationships among Africans on the Copperbelt. In order to do this I must take into account, to some extent, the general system of Black-White relationships in Northern Rhodesia. By working outwards from a specific social situation on the Copperbelt the whole social fabric of the Territory is therefore taken in. It is only when this process has been followed to a conclusion that we can return to the dance and fully appreciate its significance.

Mitchell saw the Kalela performed several times by a group of the Bisa people in Luanshya. The team had about twenty members, mostly men in their twenties, laborers or in other relatively unskilled occupations, and it performed in a public place in the township on Sunday afternoons, in front of an ethnically heterogeneous but normally all-African audience. Most of the men wore neat singlets, well-pressed grey slacks, and well-polished shoes. One member was dressed as a "doctor," in white gown with a red cross in front; he was present to encourage the dancers. A "nursing sister," the only woman in the group and also in white, carried a mirror and a handkerchief around to the dancers to allow them to keep neat. Apart from drumming, the dancing was accompanied by songs made up by the leader of the team. Some of the songs drew the attention of the audience (and particularly the women in it) to the attractive personalities of the dancers. Others dealt with various characteristics of town life. Most, however, were concerned with ethnic diversity, praising the virtues of the dancers' own tribe and the beauty of their homeland, but also ridiculing other groups and their customs.

In Mitchell's view, the Kalela troupe and its performance cast light on the nature of "tribalism" as it occurred under urban circumstances. Here was a group of people recruited on an ethnic basis—with the exception of a lone Ngoni member—yet their dance itself could hardly be called "tribal," in the sense of deriving from the old way of life of the Bisa. The inclusion of such offices as doctor and nurse marked the Kalela as a type of dance inspired by the contact with Europeans and widespread in East and Central Africa in the first half of the twentieth century.[16] In their general preoccupation with a stylish appearance, the participants showed their adherence to the European-oriented ideas of prestige of Central African urbanites which Godfrey Wilson had already found expressed in clothing patterns in Broken Hill. So this could be one theme in Mitchell's analysis; he could weave in here the parallel finding of the studies of occupational ranking, showing that greater prestige was connected with jobs involving a higher degree of skills of a "European" type. The laborers on the team seemed to be making a symbolic statement of identification with the more "civilized" way of life of the white-collar workers. The dance was not used, he noted, to express antagonism to Europeans, or to ridicule them by mimicking their comportment.

Traditional tribal culture and social structure were yielding to the values and organizational requirements of the mining community. But the idea of the tribe, or perhaps more exactly, tribes in the plural, was still very much involved in the Kalela dance. The urban experience of migrants to the Copperbelt towns involved mingling with strangers of many ethnic backgrounds, and finding ways of dealing with them. This could be a more im-

mediate perception than that of the urban prestige system which newcomers might begin to respond to more gradually. Categorizing strangers
and acquaintances by tribe was a way of making their behavior more comprehensible and predictable, and regulating the sort of interaction one
would have with them. Some groups, of course, had already been in contact. Where peoples had previously been in conflict with one another but
now were forced to deal with one another in everyday urban life, they
tended to develop interethnic joking relationships. As Mitchell evolved a
social distance scale in tune with African life, he found that people were
more willing to allow into relatively close relationships members of groups
whose ways of life were culturally similar to their own, or at least were relatively familiar to them. Among more distant peoples they might be unable
to make finer discriminations among similar groups. To a Chewa from the
east, Bisa or Aushi or other northern peoples might all be Bemba. Some
peoples also turned out to have a higher absolute degree of acceptability
than others, and a few a lower. The former were particularly the groups
which in the turmoil of Central African history had earned a reputation for
military prowess, like the Ngoni, the Ndebele, and the Bemba. Some of
the western groups, from the areas bordering on Angola, such as the
Luvale, ranked low in acceptability. The apparent reason was that in the
urban areas they had tended to cluster in lowly and despised occupations,
such as nightsoil removal.[17]

Thus Mitchell could return to the Kalela dancers. Tribes in the new
towns did not function as cohesive groups with shared objectives and an
all-embracing formal organization. Teams such as the Bisa young men
doing the Kalela, which had parallels in other groups, were in fact the
most organized expressions of ethnicity on the Copperbelt. But these
dances were significant as statements about the interethnic encounter in
the towns, about the need to know, evaluate, and handle people in terms of
their ethnic identity. The ridicule of other tribes in the Kalela songs could
be seen as a sort of unilateral declaration of a joking relationship on the
part of the Bisa and seemed to be understood in this vein by the spectators.
The urban need to categorize people, Mitchell concluded, citing Wirth,
was what "tribalism" was about in the Copperbelt town.

TWENTY-FIVE YEARS of LUANSHYA POLITICS

Epstein's *Politics in an Urban African Community* (1958) was also based
on Luanshya and took up lines of analysis which Mitchell had touched

upon in his Kalela study. Here Luanshya as a community was more fully presented. It was really two towns in one—the mine township, centered on the Roan Antelope copper mine which was the *raison d'être* of the town a a whole, and the smaller municipal township which had grown up next to it.[18] The mine township was a company town of the purest type, where the mine management provided not only jobs but also housing and facilities for health, recreation, and welfare for its employees. For a long period, as in Broken Hill, it had issued food rations as well to its African laborers. The Africans in the mine township were under the control in all these aspects of their lives of the African Personnel Manager, who was, of course, a European. As Epstein put it, the mine township had a unitary structure. The municipal township, on the other hand, was atomistic, with a variety of offices and businesses, although African enterprise remained very restricted into the 1950s. Both mine and municipal townships were also divided by a racial cleavage, with the white components—which Epstein did not deal with—being much smaller but considerably wealthier. The administrative apparatus of the Northern Rhodesian colonial government was in control of the municipal township, while the mine management did not encourage it to meddle with mine township affairs.

Epstein described the overall development and differentiation of African life in Luanshya by focusing on changes in its administration and politics during the approximately twenty-five years of its existence which had passed when he did field work there in the early 1950s. The policy of the government with regard to the administration of the new urban areas seemed never to be based on any comprehensive strategy or aimed at a clearly defined goal, but appeared to come about as piecemeal reactions to evolving circumstances. Nor did the uncertain division of responsibility between government and mining companies help to clarify the picture. To begin with, in the first years of Luanshya's existence as an apparently rather raw and violent frontier community, the mine maintained such order as there was in its camp of migrant laborers through its own African mine police. These were very unpopular, however, evidently because of corruption and other misuse of their authority. Thus the management instituted a system of tribal elders, elected as representatives of the various tribal groups among the workers, and these were used as communication links between the latter and the mining company. Usually they were relatively senior men who would have some measure of prestige in the traditional social system, for example, through kin ties with chiefs. These elders also settled minor conflicts within their groups and advised new-comers to the mine. The system was regarded as a success and was adopted in the municipal township and in other Copperbelt mining communities as well.

In 1935, however, after the elders had been in office in the mine town-ship in Luanshya for a few years, an event occurred which hinted at a weakness in the system. African miners went on strike in two other Cop-perbelt towns. The elders in Luanshya assured the mine management that nothing would happen there. Yet the strike spread to Luanshya, the ad-ministrative office in the miners' quarters was stormed, and the tribal elders fled after failing to exercise any influence on the strikers. As the police apparently overreacted, six Africans were killed in the distur-bance. [19]

No new form of representation of the African work force resulted from the strike. It had apparently not yet developed a sufficiently cohesive orga-nization of its own. (There were hints that dance groups such as of the Kalela had played some part in the mobilization for the strike.) The tribal elders came back to handle their normal duties. But what the strike had shown was that in a labor conflict, they could not be the sort of authority figures the mine management had wanted. They were, in the vocabulary of Epstein and other Rhodes-Livingstone anthropologists who had found simi-lar phenomena elsewhere, in an intercalary role. They represented the workers to the management, but they represented the management to the workers. And to the latter, therefore, in the strike situation, they were traitors to the cause.

There were some differences of opinion in the European power struc-ture in Northern Rhodesia as to what were the implications of such unrest for urban administration. Some thought the authority of tribal chieftaincy should be extended to the towns, but this idea was not carried out in prac-tice, at least as far as local government was concerned. On the other hand an urban court was set up to administer justice according to customary law, with members which major chiefs in the rural areas sent to the town to represent them. Despite the fact that one could not really expect tribal law to cover all the situations that could come up in an urban community, the court functioned relatively well, partly because it based its work on moral principles which were flexible enough to be extended into new cir-cumstances. The members of the court also tended to be generally re-spected on the basis of their chiefly backing. One problem was that there was some overlap between the functions of the court and of the tribal elders, so that the latter sometimes expressed resentment at the greater authority of the court.

Meanwhile, new forms of political articulation started to emerge spontaneously, and these were anchored in urban rather than tribal alignments. "Boss boys' committees," made up of the heads of African work gangs in the mine, began to take their place as a channel of contact between laborers and management parallel to the tribal elders. In the town as a whole, a welfare society drew a membership of more educated Africans—clerks, teachers, and others. Similar developments occurred elsewhere in Copperbelt towns. This also led to a certain overlap of functions. Urban Advisory Councils had been introduced in the early 1940s, with a nominated African membership which should make African opinion on issues involving the town accessible to the administration. Their members were largely tribal elders, from the mine and the municipal township. But the members of the welfare society, usually poorly represented on the Urban Advisory Council, were often the more forceful in voicing an interest in civil affairs. In its more active periods, the welfare society appeared to take upon itself a quasi-official status.

This was an intermediary stage. Later yet, about the time when Epstein was in Luanshya, developments had proceeded further in the direction of an urban-based social organization. Now external stimuli played a part. The postwar Labour government in Britain had sent a union organizer to Northern Rhodesia, and as a consequence Africans had begun to unionize, with the mine workers as late starters, although quite successful when their union came about. The European mine workers were already organized in their own union. The African mine workers' union gradually tended to become the counterpart of the management, in the unitary structure of the company town, in questions outside the area of work as well. In its rise it soon overshadowed the system of tribal elders, and as it sensed that the elders could function as rivals of the union, it insisted on the abolition of the system of elders in the mine organization. The mine management, after having for some time tried to define the tribal elders less ambiguously as true representatives of the miners, finally acquiesced. To begin with, leadership in the union had rested with clerks and other more educated members of the African personnel. As time went on, however, underground workers began to assert themselves. They were suspicious of the clerks, who associated too much with Europeans and who might appease them in order to gain favors for themselves. One of the events which Epstein described in some detail was the election of a militant underground worker to the chairmanship of the Luanshya union branch, replacing a foreman. In turn, clerks later drifted away from the mine workers' union, into a new salaried staff association, and the African community in Luanshya took another step toward differentiation along lines of industrial rank.

Outside the mine, the movement toward unionization was less successful, for in other trades in Luanshya, Africans were fewer and divided among many employers. This atomistic structure of the rest of the town was also a problem which the first major political organization of the Africans in Northern Rhodesia had to deal with. The African National Congress had its origins in an association of local welfare societies. It had agitated intensively but unsuccessfully against the imposition of a white-dominated Central African Federation and then gone into some decline. As a branch was formed in Luanshya, it searched for an issue which could crystallize the interest of the public but came up against various obstacles. Taking up the cause of African hawkers who wanted to be allowed to sell in the mine township, it got nowhere; trying to organize a boycott of European butcher shops to get better treatment for African customers, it was split because the Urban Advisory Council had just conducted an apparently successful negotiation of the issue with the butchers. The Urban Advisory Council by this time included many members of the kind which used to belong to the old welfare society, now moribund. Such societies, we have just seen, also had a part in the beginnings of the African National Congress. Now the two found themselves in opposition, to the comfort of neither. The Urban Advisory Council risked getting into an intercalary position, as the tribal elders had once done on the mine, being caught between the administration and the public. The Congress might take on greater importance as the voice of the public if exactly that happened. In the mine township, there was little room for Congress activity, as the mine workers' union had monolithically preempted the space for organization. And the union and the Congress were on bad terms with one another, for reasons which had less to do with the local affairs of Luanshya.

Such were the conditions as Epstein concluded his analysis. One major tendency in his findings, to quote a later commentator, was that "trade unions transcend tribes" (Mayer 1962:581). That is, it was the Europeans who had tried but largely failed to impose an overarching tribal structure on the administration and politics of the towns. As Africans began to get their bearings in the urban-industrial milieu, they had realized that their internal tribal divisions were irrelevant in their confrontation with European miners and management, and so they had organized on a class basis instead, with lines clearly drawn instead of confounded by the ambiguities of tribal elders. An African intelligentsia of young, well-educated people took the lead in community affairs; old men whose major merit might be blood ties to a rural chief did not. Yet urban life consisted of many different situations, interdependent but not necessarily all with the same inherent logic. In a strike, tribal differences could be submerged. In a battle for union leadership, a Bemba might support another Bemba against a Lozi or Nyasalander. Sometimes, moreover, the urban occupational structure shaped ethnic conflicts. Because Christian missions had come earlier to Nyasaland than to most of Northern Rhodesia, more of the Nyasalanders were clerks. So what a Bemba thought about Nyasalanders might conceivably depend in part on what he thought about clerks. But there were also instances where the extensions of the tribe into the town were more authentic. Even a union leader, strongly opposed to tribal elders having any part in labor affairs, might acknowledge the authority of a chiefly representative in the urban court, since the latter would be concerned primarily with the kind of interpersonal morality where traditional wisdom might deserve recognition. In the municipal township with its varied structure, even the tribal elders could still find niches of prestige where they could go on unhurriedly settling petty quarrels.

"An AFRICAN TOWNSMAN is a TOWNSMAN . . ."

Max Gluckman did not personally engage in urban field work in Central Africa, but he took a strong interest in the studies conducted by other Rhodes-Livingstone researchers, and drawing on such publications as Mitchell's on the Kalela and Epstein's on Luanshya politics, he made some influential theoretical statements (Gluckman 1961b).

The dominant interest of the group, he suggested, was in "the problem of why tribalism persists." This had perhaps not really been true of Godfrey Wilson who, while using the notion of "detribalization" in the title of his Broken Hill study, did not do much to conceptualize either that or "tribalism" in the text. For the later researchers, however, this had indeed been a focus. Yet their analysis of it, Gluckman emphasized strongly, contradicted conventional wisdom among colonial administrators and an earlier generation of anthropologists in Africa. These had assumed—implicitly or explicitly, consciously or unconsciously—that detribalization was a slow, long-time process, although consistently moving in the same direction. Gradually, the social relations of the urban migrants would change, and their commitment to traditional custom become attenuated. Gluckman was not so surprised that administrators as "practical men" would take such a view for granted; they would naturally see the people flocking into the towns against the background of the village life they had just left. To an anthropologist, on the other hand, it ought to be obvious that the town must be seen as a social system in its own right. Thus the behavior of townsmen had to be understood in terms of the roles of the urban here and now, regardless of such factors as their origins and personalities. In a phrase which has since become a classic in anthropology: "An African townsman is a townsman, an African miner is a miner."

Such a point of departure would change radically the view of what really went on in African rural-urban migration. Instead of detribalization as a one-way process, far from completed as the migrant entered the town, it was an on-and-off phenomenon. (This was a view which Gluckman had already hinted at in the statement of his seven-year research plan.) The migrant was to be seen as detribalized, in one sense, as soon as he took up a position in the urban structure of social relations, and deurbanized as soon as he left town and reentered the rural social system with its set of roles. In the town, the industrial system was the dominant reality, and the primary points of orientation for a townsman were the communities of interest and the prestige system which came with it. Certainly Africans did carry a baggage of tribal culture into urban life, but this was now analytically secondary. It had to be clearly understood that it operated at this point in an urban milieu, and that it could therefore have new forms and take on another significance. Thus "tribe," as both Mitchell and Epstein had shown, did not in the urban context refer so much to an operative political unit as to a way of classifying and dealing with people whom the town dweller encountered at work, in the neighborhood, or at the beer hall. In the rural area, on the other hand, the tribal political system was still at work, firmly grounded in the system of land tenure, and most townsmen faced with the insecurities of wage work would retain a foothold there as well.

As far as African urban studies were concerned, then, Gluckman asserted, their comparative background must be in urban studies in general, and they must have their starting point in a theory of urban social systems. But these systems, he also noted, are complex, made up of loose, semi-independent, to some extent even isolated sub-systems. The urban anthropologist should not necessarily deal with all of these. The existence of some of them could merely be assumed, as the anthropologist concentrated on the major contribution he could make to the study of urbanism—the interpretation of detailed records of restricted but intricately structured social situations, of which a Kalela dance or a butchershop boycott could be examples.

CONCEPTUALIZING RELATIONSHIPS and SITUATIONS

Gluckman's 1961 paper was followed in the mid-1960s by others where members of the Rhodes-Livingstone group elaborated on the analytical framework which had grown out of their urban research. At this stage their field work in Central African towns was by and large over. They had scattered among many academic institutions, and some of them were turning to other ethnographic regions. These statements might thus be seen as marking a phase where they could take a few steps back and, looking over their experiences again, consider them within a slightly wider anthropological context. Three publications may be especially useful in delineating, together with Gluckman's paper and with some overlap between them, the Rhodes-Livingstone stance in urban theory. Two of these are by Epstein (1964, 1967), one by Mitchell (1966b).

The latter's paper was an overview of "Theoretical Orientations in African Urban Studies." One important section of it was devoted to the conceptualization of characteristic forms of urban social relations. Godfrey Wilson had already distinguished between "business" and personal relationships. Twenty-five years later, there was now a tripartite division, into structural, personal, and categorical relationships. Structural relationships had enduring patterns of interaction, relatively clearly ordered by role expectations. Personal relationships did not get a clear definition in the article, as the discussion of them shifted quickly into a sketch of the uses of network analysis. It is evident, however, that the term was intended to cover relationships where the parties had a relatively broad familiarity with one another, and where interactions were not so narrowly defined in terms of particular tasks. The categorical relationships were those where contacts were perfunctory and superficial, where the situation was not sufficiently rigidly defined in role terms to give participants a clear idea of what to expect from one another, and where they consequently seized on some characteristic readily accessible to the senses and categorized each other accordingly. Categorical and structural relationships obviously conformed each in its own way to a Wirthian notion of urban impersonality; yet the Rhodes-Livingstone anthropologists certainly also recognized the presence in urban life of more intimate links, which constituted the remaining type.

This threefold division also allowed another look at the coverage of African urban studies thus far. The obvious topic of study in the field of structural relationships, Mitchell noted, was the organization of work; but while industrial sociology had taken hold in Europe and America, it had had a slow start in Africa. (Since then, the situation has improved a little.) Voluntary associations, on the other hand, had been rather extensively studied in some parts of the continent and could be placed under this heading. A frequent focus in research on personal relationships had been the cliques of friends and acquaintances who come together in leisure life, sometimes people from the same area of origin. The field of categorical relationships, predictably, involved particularly ethnic categorizations. The Rhodes-Livingstone group's interpretation of urban tribalism came in here. It was in the context of social flux and conspicuous diversity of conduct, such as in traffic relationships and other contacts between strangers, that these designations could help chart a path through urban life.

Mitchell also returned to Gluckman's point about the notion of "detribalization" as a process—one must distinguish between the kind of change which is a slow, unidirectional sequence and which involves a transformation of the social system itself, and the kind of change where individuals make rapid adjustments of ideas and behavior as they move back and forth between situations. They might be called "historical" or "processive" versus "situational" change, or in the terminology used by Mayer (1962:579), "one-way change" versus "alternation." As Mitchell could show, the two had often been confused. He reaffirmed that it was necessary to see the urban system as having an existence in its own right, side by side with the rural system, so that the sort of change people were involved in as they circulated between the two was primarily "situational" or "alternating." This view was now developed a little further, however, since Mitchell gave more emphasis than Gluckman had done to normative and behavioral shifts between different contexts within the urban system as well. The principle was "situational selection"—one source of inspiration here was Evans-Pritchard's study of Azande witchcraft, where it had been shown how people could apply different ideas at different times without too much concern for their overall coherence. In a social system as complex as that of an urban community, such coherence was hardly any more probable. Epstein's Luanshya study had indeed shown how the traditionally inspired authority of tribal elders could serve well, for example, in settling domestic quarrels, yet was immobilized in labor conflicts. Some situations were evidently less influenced than others by the specifically urban overarching structure, and a town dweller might perhaps at least sometimes choose a more traditional line of action in these.

On the whole, Mitchell, like his colleagues, tended to give emphasis to situational rather than processive change as a matter of analytical interest. But at least parenthetically, one may note that they did not disregard processive, one-way change either, at least as it occurred on an individual level. Some townsmen could thus be understood as in a sense more urban than others. Epstein's (1959) study of the development of a new urban vocabulary bore evidence of this. There was a deep chasm between the kinds of worldly wisdom possessed by the *babuyasulo*, the country bumpkin who had just arrived (literally "came yesterday") and the "sugar boy"—raised in the town—or the "town lady." Attending to such differences at another level, Mitchell (1956c, 1969a, 1973a) added a method of measuring urban involvement to the methodological repertoire of the group, based on the proportion of his time an individual spent in town, his length of continuous stay there, his attitude to urban residence, his occupation, and the urban or rural residence of his wife. (The measurement obviously applied only to males.) The method could be used, for example, to confirm a hypothesis that migrants who could easily reach their rural areas of origin and take an active and rewarding part in their social life also entered more fully into urban life—the idea may seem paradoxical, but evidently under such circumstances the migrant could better afford to become more intimately involved with the city as well.[20]

EXTERNAL DETERMINANTS and the LIMITS of NAÏVETÉ

As Mitchell linked up with Gluckman's conception of situational change, so Epstein in his 1964 paper elaborated on another idea from Gluckman's statement of some years earlier, on the need to isolate a manageable unit of analysis. This was an aspect of the interest which Gluckman had developed in the way anthropologists generally delimit their fields of study and make assumptions about matters touching their analyses but outside their professional competence. *Closed Systems and Open Minds* (1964) was a collection of papers directed toward these issues by anthropologists with Manchester connections, under Gluckman's editorship. Epstein reviewed his Luanshya study in this context, and in the light of growing criticism of "community studies" of the sort which largely ignores the impact of external factors on community life. The Rhodes-Livingstone anthropologists, from Godfrey Wilson onwards, had consistently stated their awareness of the embeddedness of their Central African field of study in a world-wide economy and social structure. But how could they practically deal with such a complex reality? The solution which Gluckman had hinted at, and which Epstein adopted, was to concentrate his intensive analysis on a local field of social relations accessible to observation. External factors, for example of a political or economic nature, could be treated as given—that is, their presence and their general shape had to be acknowledged, insofar as they set the stage for local social life, but there would be no very elaborate or sophisticated inquiry into them. Within the local field, in addition, certain facts the derivation of which was outside the anthropologist's competence could be included in his analysis in a simplified form. One example was the "crude polarity" assumed between the unitary economic and administrative structure of the mine township and the atomistic structure of the government township, which turned out to have such important implications for the forms of political life developing in Luanshya.

It was thus justifiable, Epstein suggested in agreement with the general argument of *Closed Systems and Open Minds,* for the anthropologist to take a deliberately and measuredly naïve view of factors lying at least partially beyond his horizons of observation or outside his field of professional skill. Only in this way might he be able to develop to the fullest extent his own contribution to the division of scientific labor, in the company of economists, political scientists, and others. Admittedly, this would make it difficult for him to generalize about society at large, as some authors of community studies have been prone to do, in the erroneous belief that the local system was a microcosm of the wider whole. Yet the anthropologist's analysis of the local system could show that the impact of external forces might depend on the form of internal community structure.

A general position on how to delimit an area of study and how to deal with factors impinging on it from the outside had thus been established. Another facet of the problem was to identify which were the factors that would recurrently have to be taken into account. This was important not least for purposes of comparative research, as the factors which could be viewed as constants in the study of a single community must be recognized as independent variables when it was to be compared with others. Various formulations of "extrinsic factors," "external determinants," "external imperatives," or "contextual parameters" were thus offered, not all by Rhodes-Livingstone workers. Southall had one in the statement where the A and B urban types were delineated. Mitchell, in his 1966 paper, listed such determinants under six headings: (1) *density of settlement,* affecting in particular the range of contacts of townspeople; (2) *mobility,* including inter-urban and intra-urban movements as well as rural-urban migration and circulation, leading to a degree of impermanence in social relations; (3) *ethnic heterogeneity;* (4) *demographic disproportion* in the age and sex composition of urban populations, resulting from the selective recruitment of young males to the labor force; (5) *economic differentiation,* including occupational differentiation, differential levels of living, and social stratification; and (6) *administrative and political limitations,* in particular governmental constraints on the movements and activities of the town population (especially its African component, in the southern part of the continent). The study of these determinants in themselves, Mitchell proposed, might be the task of other disciplines. The job of the urban social anthropologist was to examine the behavior of individuals within the matrix created by these factors which, once established, could be taken for granted.

Epstein brought up this issue again in his 1967 survey article on African urban studies, more concerned with matters of substantive comparisons between city forms and less with problems of conceptualization. His categories of determinants were somewhat different from Mitchell's, mostly because he lumped some factors together, coming up with only three major categories—the industrial structure, the civic structure, and the "demographic imperative," the latter apparently covering Mitchell's first four factors. Such differences apart, the views of the two apparently coincided.

In principle, factors such as these could conceivably be manipulated as analytical variables so as to create a comprehensive typology of the forms of African urbanism. In fact, it has never been done in any very disciplined way, and possibly the results would not be in a reasonable proportion to the amount of labor it would require. For Epstein, in his essay on comparison, the three categories of determinants rather provided a vocabulary for discourse on urban variation. He could point out that the determinants need not co-vary. Rhodesian towns, for example, had had a similar civic structure as those of the colonial Copperbelt, with strict European regulation, but their industrial (i.e., economic) structure had allowed slightly greater room for African enterprise, creating a more significant class of African businessmen—a fact which could perhaps explain why the early nationalist movement there had been rather more accommodationist toward the white regime. In what used to be the Belgian Congo, the colonial administration had maintained a control over urban migration not so different from that of the Copperbelt, but it had encouraged a stabilization of the urban population and allowed more freedom for small businesses and in forms of accommodation, thus coming up with a kind of urban life which seemed in some ways to be midway between those characteristic respectively of Southern Africa and West Africa. As another variation in what Epstein somewhat loosely described as demographic factors, there were some new towns, such as East London in South Africa, that could draw a very large part of the population from neighboring rural areas, allowing a more ethnically homogeneous African community. Such possibilities of performing "natural experiments" with the variables, Epstein suggested, could be exploited further. There were new mining towns in West Africa, for example, where the industrial structure might be similar to that of the Copperbelt, while the civic structure would obviously be different. In any case, these variations also made it clear that a simple distinction such as between A and B types of African urbanism, with different regional centers of gravity on the continent, could only be a useful first approximation even in the colonial past.

The LINKAGE between TOWN and COUNTRY

This article by Epstein could be seen as defining the boundaries of the Rhodes-Livingstone view of urbanism. The effort to integrate what was largely a Copperbelt experience into an explicit comparative framework for urban studies turned out to be a somewhat isolated phenomenon, however, so that what of its rather muscular conceptualization relates to Central African peculiarities and what to African urbanism in general has perhaps not always been well understood.

The controversies which may have arisen on such grounds need not concern us for their own sake. We will see, instead, how the Rhodes-Living-stone perspective may be aligned with the view of urbanism developed in chapter 3, and use it to push ahead a little further. We are concerned again, in other words, with the part which an urban community plays in society, and with the connections between different domains of rela-tionships.

Two Copperbelt themes are of particular interest here—the autonomy of the urban system, and the persistence of tribalism. On the basis of what we have seen before, we can sense that the former is a matter of some am-biguity; an urban center always has work to do within a wider societal system—unless, like the old extended-boundary town, it assimilates its surroundings into itself—and while urbanites may have particular roles to enact, they may spring out of an underlying cultural logic shared by the entire society, as Pocock noted of Indian urbanism. One may ask, then, whether the Copperbelt towns were in such respects more than usually well marked off toward the surrounding society.

In a way, obviously, they were. They existed, above all, to perform special parts in an international economic system, linking them not with the African countryside around them but, in a leapfrog fashion, with fi-nancial and industrial centers overseas. Within the local social context, at least to begin with, they were enclaves rather than nodal points. If one as-sumes that the normal way in which town and country form a cohesive whole is through provisioning relationships in which distinct urban and rural populations face each other in complementarity, then such local cohesiveness was in this case relatively weak. Even if a place like Luan-shya could in time develop central place functions of a more general kind, these might still play a rather modest part in the general picture.

It was also a fact that at least those urban activities, in the domain of provisioning, which were most immediately involved in the city-forming sector of the economy had a culturally distinct basis compared to rural soci-ety. The technology and work organization of mining were essentially im-ports. This fact was what made Mitchell (1966b:38) point out that cities of this type were hardly a useful testing ground for the cross-cultural applica-bility of western ideas of urbanism, as they were themselves under such strong European influence.

Yet if urban communities like those on the Copperbelt in some ways maintained a separateness vis-à-vis their local surroundings, there was ob-viously a sort of backdoor integration with rural African society in another way, through the partial sharing of personnel. The migrants commuted between urban and rural ways of life, with a variously complete involvement in the different domains of activities in both. Perhaps this fact was less important in those urban domains with more rigidly predetermined structures of their own. It could be more significant where the urban circumstances still offered greater leeway for emergent adaptations, based on the fusion of received wisdom and new experience. The ideas which migrants brought to town, and the outgrowths of these ideas, could have some effect on what they did there, and with whom they did it. This is the problem of urban tribalism—or, to use a less value-laden term from here on, urban ethnicity. We will approach it here, however, in a slightly round-about way, since it is only one of a class of related problems in the analysis of urban social structure.

PERSONAL INFORMATION and PUBLIC NORMS: RETHINKING RELATIONSHIPS

To begin with, it may help widen the frame of reference to return to Mitchell's (1966b:51 ff.) outline of the three kinds of urban social relationships, structural, personal, and categorical. They are described as "three different types," and one may tend to get the impression that they are mutually exclusive—each existing relationship, that is, should fit into one or other of these types. But there would be difficulties with such a view. Is a relationship between co-workers only structural, not at all personal? An important part of industrial sociology has in fact dwelt on the modification of structural relationships by personal links. Or cannot friends who know each other well momentarily deal with each other on the categorical basis of ethnicity, as one of the factors they include among relevant knowledge? Various studies by the Rhodes-Livingstone anthropologists indeed show an awareness of such complications, and Mitchell later (1969b:9–10) made it clear that interactions in terms of structure, category, and personal acquaintance should be seen as *aspects* of relationships.

Possibly one could yet find another way of mapping social relationships which could be more explicit on the logical interconnections between the various forms of interaction (cf. figure 2).[21] This could serve our general purposes beyond a review of Rhodes-Livingstone urban studies. Personal and categorical relationships, then, seem to be conceptualized along the same dimension. It matters to the conduct of these relationships just who

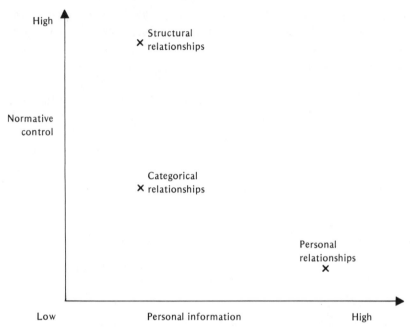

Figure 2. Personal Information and Normative Control in Social Relationships

is recruited to them, and the difference between them consists in the amount of *personal information* ego and alter have about one another, to make the basis for their lines of action. This dimension stretches, in principle, from absolute anonymity, where no socially relevant information is available, to total intimacy, where everything about the other is known. A categorical relationship has already moved a little away from the pole of complete anonymity, as at least one item of information has provided a basis for placing alter in a specific category (however superficially conceived). Personal relationships occupy a stretch along the continuum, including those where information is complex yet imperfect as well as those of greatest intimacy. Structural relationships imply another dimension, the degree of *normative control*. This refers to the influence of more or less public norms, upheld with regard to the relationship—or at least believed to be upheld—by third parties or even the society at large, and not subject to much renegotiation between particular participants. To be termed structural, relationships would have to be fairly high on this scale, closely regulated by norms. In such cases, personal information tends to be neutralized, deemed irrelevant, as far as its effect on the conduct of the relationship is concerned. A stranger and an intimate would be treated equally; alters are substitutable.[22]

Again, however, normative control and personal information are only dimensions of relationships—all relationships, even if in some particular case one dimension may be more conspicuously important than the other. As we noted in chapter 3, the role concept in anthropology has conventionally been defined in normative terms. If we look at the role instead as a purposive situational involvement, it may be easier to accept that roles differ in their relative dependence on normative control and personal information. The role of friend is in this regard obviously quite unlike that of bus conductor. Who a person is, however, as contrasted to who he could otherwise have been or who other people are, may not merely influence the course of certain kinds of ongoing relationships, to the degree that normative constraints allow it. The interplay between the two dimensions may be yet more subtle. As people come to know a thing or two about an individual, they can respond to this personal information in ways which are themselves more or less normatively standardized. These responses, moreover, can be on several levels:

(1) *role access*—the others may or may not let the individual in question get into a certain form of situational involvement at all;
(2) *relational access*—some but not all may be regarded as his appropriate alters as he enacts a certain role;
(3) *relational conduct*—if people enter into the relationships with him, the personal information involved may, as we have suggested above, affect the manner in which the relationship is conducted.

These are obviously principles of great power in the organization of social life. But what are the sorts of information on which they are based? For our purposes, it seems convenient to divide it into two kinds. One is information about what are the other purposive situational involvements of a person; in other words, the more or less complete information about his role repertoire. Where this is the type of knowledge at issue, we have a direct approach to the well-established analytical topic of role combinability. The other category of personal information is residual. It simply includes attributes of an individual other than his purposive situational involvements, yet variously relevant to these. Clumsy as the term may be, we can call them role-discriminatory attributes. These can clearly come in a great many shapes. Some of them, however, are more socially powerful than others, and it is in those we will be particularly interested here.

ETHNICITY, ROLE-DISCRIMINATORY ATTRIBUTES, and URBAN LIFE

Ethnicity is one major example of a role-discriminatory attribute, but we should not exaggerate its uniqueness. In some ways, sex and age operate in a similar fashion. Ethnicity, of course, is not equally at hand in all social units, and ethnic categorizations tend to be more manipulable. But all three—sex, age, ethnicity—are somewhat open to cultural definitions of category boundaries, and of the human qualities associated with the different categories. And in neither case will the attribute itself suffice as a definition of one's purposive involvement in a situation (with the exception of sexual activity, where male and female can in this sense be seen as roles). These attributes are, on the other hand, important in channeling involvements.[23]

Taking our conceptualization of domains as a framework, we can see, for instance, that women can have only certain roles in the household and kinship domain; they are often restricted to particular provisioning and recreational roles; and one might say that an institution such as the Muslim *purdah* is also extremely constraining in the neighboring and traffic domains. Some roles women may have, but only if they enact them toward other women rather than men—this has been the case in some kinds of medical practice. And if either sex can perform a certain role toward anybody else, the relationship may take a somewhat different shape if a woman is in it rather than a man. There are parallel but hardly equal constraints on male role acquisition and performance, and as far as age is concerned, the very young and the very old are barred from many roles but monopolize some others.

But let us get back to ethnicity and its expressions in urban Africa. In the Copperbelt town of the Rhodes-Livingstone researchers, there were examples of ethnicity functioning as a role-discriminatory attribute at all three levels noted above. Perhaps one could not find clear-cut cases of roles from which one African ethnic group was excluded while they were open to others (although in some instances something similar to such a situation may have occurred). Just outside the normal field of study of the Rhodes-Livingstone anthropologists, however, there was a glaring example of such exclusion. The "white tribe of Africa," the European settlers, did indeed reserve a number of roles for themselves for as long as colonialism remained in full force. Clearly Europeans as well as members of different African groups also had co-ethnics as preferred partners in various relationships. Africans were frequently constrained from acting on this impulse in work relationships, as they did not decide who would be employed along with them, or in neighboring relationships, in cases where they had little control over the allocation of housing. But it could steer their choice of alters particularly in domestic and recreational relationships. With regard to modifications of conduct occurring on the basis of ethnicity, an obvious case in point would be the joking relationships for instance between co-workers of different ethnic background.[24]

The power of ethnicity in Central African urban life naturally relates to the awareness of the migrants that they had brought different cultural baggage to town. One may see the preference for co-ethnics, in situations where there was a choice, in large part as a matter of trust. Where cultural background was similar or identical, people could assume, as Barth (1969:15) has put it in his analysis of ethnicity, that they were playing interactional games according to the same rules. This could matter in relationships which were partly or wholly under relatively firm normative control, with norms deriving from traditional culture. Some conjugal obligations could exemplify this. It could likewise be important in links which were relatively more ordered by personal information, since such information must necessarily include an idea of the general frame of mind of the people involved. In recreational activity, for instance, a wide range of shared understandings could play a part.[25] To pick out the right partners, then, there was the need for ethnic categorization to which Mitchell particularly, among the Rhodes-Livingstone anthropologists, drew attention. It could be a simple "in or out" dichotomy; either you are a co-ethnic or you are not. But it could also be a matter of degree, as shown by Mitchell's work on social distance scales.

If, on the Copperbelt, it was particularly in domestic, kinship, and recreational relationships that relational access was ordered by ethnicity, the latter could play a more prominent part in other domains as well elsewhere in African urban communities. Where one ethnic group controlled some sector of the economy, it could monopolize certain roles in the domain of provisioning as the Europeans did in Central Africa. Here the ethnic group could be an interest group. The most celebrated example may be the

Hausa-controlled cattle and kolanut trade in Ibadan, as described by Abner Cohen (1969). Elsewhere, co-ethnics could try to recruit one another preferentially into favorable provisioning and work relationships, without necessarily being able to achieve ethnic hegemony.[26] This is the situation to which "tribalism" most often refers, as a pejorative epithet, in the language of urban Africa today. Something like it could also be seen on the Copperbelt, for instance in the ethnic lineup in trade union elections to which Epstein referred in his monograph. Yet another sort of ethnic relational access, more often described from West Africa than from other parts of the continent, is the voluntary association in which migrants from the same area join together.[27] This is a multi-purpose organization, but embedded in mostly recreational activities there is a kind of supplementary relationship of provisioning. The shared background of the members provides not only a sense of trust but also one of solidarity. In some degree, they share a collective honor and a moral responsibility for one another's well-being. Thus members in need can count on the support of the others, through an internal redistribution of resources.

Why such associations seem to be unevenly distributed over urban Africa has been a subject of some discussion. Epstein (1967:281–82), in his review of the field, suggested that they may be weak where functional equivalents exist. In the Copperbelt towns, the institution of tribal elders may have served similar purposes for some time, without an associational form. Perhaps the paternalism of the mining companies could also to some degree obviate the need for such ethnically based security arrangements, at least for a part of the urban populations there.

We need not survey the workings of African urban ethnicity here, just make some note of its broad and variable impact on the arrangement of social relationships. On a more abstract analytical level, we may wonder what are the implications of such role-discriminatory attributes for the urban anthropological perspective sketched in the latter part of chapter 3. Connections between activities and relationships in different domains were seen there as more or less immediate linkages between varied purposive situational involvements. We also saw it as a possible strategy in the conceptualization of the social order of the city to trace the linkages from the domain of provisioning outward to the other domains.

There is a great deal in the Rhodes-Livingstone perspective to remind us of this. Epstein's and Mitchell's delineations of external determinants, the factors which they felt an urban anthropologist could treat as given, obviously suggest a framework for analysis where more varied prior information is assumed; in Epstein's terms, facts about civic and demographic structure as well as the industrial structure. We will come back to this in our concluding chapter. The tendency of Gluckman's "an African townsman is a townsman, an African miner is a miner" pronouncement, however, is to identify the urban system particularly with the domain of provisioning. The latter is seen to contain the paramount realities of town life, influencing involvements in other domains as well. Gluckman was probably more right than wrong here. If he somewhat overstated his point, it was obviously because the contrary view had so often been taken for granted. His ideas ought, of course, also to be especially congruent with the facts of life in a Copperbelt mine township, a company turned into a community, where the structure of the provisioning domain could be expected to have a pervasive influence.

Yet it must be realized that even here the roles in the various urban domains were not all constituted in the same way. In that of provisioning, certainly, there were roles under relatively strict normative control and of distinctly urban provenance. In other domains, the new urbanites were to a greater extent left to their own devices, working out an urban social system within which they might change their life styles as time went on but which at least initially would be more culturally continuous with the society from which they came.

Role-discriminatory attributes characteristically play their part in the organization of urban life as elements of such cultural continuity. It is only against the background of a particular cultural tradition, or combination of cultural traditions, that one can have a good idea of the ways an urban social order can be influenced by concepts of sex, age, and ethnicity; by notions of what men or women or elderly people can and cannot do, or by the manner in which members of an ethnic group for different purposes extend solidarity to one another and refuse trust to others. Perhaps we may say, without making ourselves guilty of too much analytical mystification, that the role-discriminatory attributes can thus be a distraction as the activities of the urbanites strain toward an overall pattern of their own, in line with what may otherwise seem to be the inherent nature of a particular kind of city. They create muddles in the model. Roles and relationships may through them be indirectly connected rather than simply unrelated or directly related. An individual may interact with the same partners in work and recreation, for example, not because it is in any way predicated by the work situation but rather more because they are co-ethnics. Even in the African company town, trade unions do not in every way transcend tribes, if we may use the expression in a metaphoric sense. In the administration of justice, in the choice of a spouse, and in the recruitment to a dance team, the specter of tribalism continues to haunt the town. And much as the "race relations cycle" of Robert Park and the Chicagoans expressed a belief that the tribalism of American cities would not persist, the one-way model of detribalization has not fared very well there either.

While role-discriminatory attributes may inject new and discrepant inclinations into the organization of urban life, however, they do not entirely bend it in their own fashion. In the end, the result may be some form of compromise, stable or unstable. By now, discussions of African urban ethnicity have resulted in an understanding that what ethnicity is in town also depends partly on what sort of town it is in. The same could be said about other role-discriminatory attributes. To be young may not mean the same in Detroit as in San Francisco, to be a woman not the same in São Paulo as in Rio de Janeiro.

As it turned out, the Rhodes-Livingstone anthropologists certainly did devote much of their attention to these interrelations between urbanism and tribalism. It may even be arguable whether, despite Gluckman's emphatic statements, they did not somewhat neglect certain phenomena in the urban system as such. The ethnography is often there; what one occasionally misses is a more intensive analytical interest, for example, in the ways people could perceive their fellow townsmen in other than ethnic terms. It may not have been altogether necessary to have only the latter focus in developing the concept of categorical relationships—Epstein's (1959) paper on linguistic innovation showed descriptively that the emergent facts of Luanshya life also provided categorizations, of sugar boys, *bakapenta* (painted young ladies, to be found around beer halls), and others. And although Epstein, Mitchell, and Gluckman rightly recognized that African mine workers would join hands across ethnic boundaries, on the alternative basis of common positions in the domain of provisioning and their contacts through work, they may have been slow to recognize the growth of divisions among Africans along the same kind of lines. By the time Peter Harries-Jones (1975:154 ff.), the last of the Rhodes-Livingstone field workers, was in Luanshya in 1963–65, discord between African strata was obvious, and there were clear developments toward class closure of social relationships. Townspeople were now *abapamulu*, "those on top," or *abapanshi,* "the lowly ones." Harries-Jones felt that his predecessors, despite the beginning signs of conflict that, for example, Epstein had observed, had leaned too heavily toward a view of the proto-elite rather as an integral, leading element in a unitary African interest bloc.

RHODES-LIVINGSTONE ANTHROPOLOGISTS and the COLONIAL SITUATION

It has been natural to concentrate here on the anthropologists of the Rhodes-Livingstone Institute as ethnographers and theoreticians of urbanism. By way of conclusion a few words may perhaps be added, however, on another perspective toward their work (where one component was other, more harshly phrased, criticisms of their interest in tribalism in town). In the years of African independence, as the parts played by intellectuals and academics under colonialism came increasingly under scrutiny, an institute which had functioned for decades under such an obviously imperialist name could hardly remain above suspicion.

One interpretation of the anthropologist's changing role in the context of the demise of empires was offered by James R. Hooker (1963), an American historian. While formulated in more general terms, it was said to be based on experiences in the Rhodesias. The Rhodes-Livingstone Institute was mentioned only briefly by name, but obviously the statement must have alluded in large part to its researchers.

In Hooker's view, there had been four phases in the anthropological exploitation of Africa. In the first, beginning after World War I, anthropologists had been the happy handmaidens of colonialism, hoping to aid efficient European administration and economic change. In phase two, they strove for greater autonomy, perhaps functioning at least in their own view as mediators between African and colonialist interests. By the time of the third phase, as the nationalist struggle had begun, the anthropologist had started seeing himself as, if not an active ally in it, at least a sympathizer with the African side. He had now become alienated from the greater part of the European community and held a very adverse view of it. Yet he could not easily escape the colonial situation, or the uniform of a white skin. The Rhodes-Livingstone Institute, Hooker suggested, during this period resembled an uneasy utopian society surrounded by hostile forces, or a determinedly multiracial cocktail party. But the anthropologist's time had run out. In phase four, as Africans neared their goal of independence, they had little use for anthropologists as partners in conversation. Perhaps anthropologists had better become sociologists, or historians like Hooker himself.

A more massive attack on Rhodes-Livingstone anthropology followed some years later. Bernard Magubane, a South African anthropologist in exile, was engaged in a series of reexaminations of European social research in colonized African societies, repeatedly provoking some heated debate (cf. Magubane 1969, 1973; van den Berghe 1970). In a first article (1968), he dwelt partly on Gluckman's "an African townsman is a townsman" paper. Later, he devoted a critique to the work of Epstein and Mitchell, but actually only to a few of their publications (Magubane 1971).

Colonial anthropologists, Magubane (1968:23) wrote, produced monographs which were "enough like reality to be credible but not enough like it to be unsafe." Generally they had avoided paying serious attention to the anatomy of colonialism. In the case of the Rhodes-Livingstone anthropologists, they ought to have focused on the colonial regulation of African rural and urban life, and of the migratory process, rather than on the issue of tribalism. Magubane also condemned what he felt was a tendency in the occupational prestige studies, in *The Kalela Dance,* and in some other works to dwell on the Africans' acceptance of European status notions, and on their preoccupation with clothing and other outward signs of European status and modernity. This focus of description and analysis, Magubane (1971:420) felt, implied a belief on the part of the anthropologists "not only in the inevitability, but also in the rightness of white conquest of the African." Under the inspiration of Frantz Fanon, he felt that one must seek an understanding of the processes of colonization on the African personality, of which the apparent aspirations to a "European way of life" were only a logical outcome. And in opposition to this, he proposed, Africans had also shown a willingness and capacity to organize in resistance to European dominance which the researchers had seriously underestimated. To dwell on such trivia of the moment as dances and fashions was at the same time to ignore wider and more significant historical processes.

In the fashion of *Current Anthropology* where the 1971 paper was published, commentators were invited, and several (including Epstein and Mitchell) were highly critical of Magubane's mode of reviewing. The picture of Rhodes-Livingstone anthropology he had presented was very selective. He quoted statements which looked worse out of context, and cited some works rather than others where complementary points were made which he instead went on to make himself. The authors subjected to this treatment had some right to express dismay.

Probably it was particularly difficult to get out of the impasse in intellectual debate because of the overtones of *ad hominem* argument. In the terms which Hooker had used, Magubane tended to depict the Rhodes-Livingstone anthropologists as colonial anthropologists of phase one, hardly a typing to which many would willingly acquiesce by 1971. And indeed, it does not seem altogether certain that they had really ever been there. While Gluckman in his seven-year plan referred to the various possibilities of cooperation with government agencies (which on such an occasion would perhaps tend to be almost ritually affirmed), there were also signs of concern for institute autonomy. Godfrey Wilson had then already prefaced the first part of his study of Broken Hill by a statement that he had tried merely to give the facts and their inevitable connections, rather than offering political opinions of his own or making "covert propaganda for any cause, or race, or party." Yet as he sketched the alternative forms of an equilibrium situation that he assumed had to come, one could hardly fail to detect that his own sympathies were with the form which was more in line with African interests. This seemed rather like phase two colonial anthropology. Later on, the political inclinations of Rhodes-Livingstone researchers may not have been entirely homogeneous, but Hooker makes it clear that at least some proceeded emphatically into the third phase. Adam Kuper (1973:148), writing the history of British anthropology, similarly notes that with few exceptions, "the Rhodes-Livingstone fellows were politically on the left, and not backward in showing it." Gluckman (1974) himself, responding to another discussion of anthropology and colonialism in a letter to the *New York Review of Books* shortly before his death, pointed out that because of his political reputation, he had been barred from entering Northern Rhodesia in the late colonial period. As for influencing colonial policy through his research, he was sure extremely few government officials were acquainted with any of it.

The Manchester connection, as a link to metropolitan academia, probably contributed to maintaining some intellectual distance between the Rhodes-Livingstone anthropologists and the prevailing ideas of their local environment. In the terms one of them (Watson 1960, 1964) coined in another context, they were "spiralists" rather than "burgesses." [28] Yet they could hardly avoid being affected in some ways by the colonial situation. As Hooker noted, they could not get out of their white skins. Wilson

(1941:28–29) mentioned anthropologists along with government officials as people who, although less prejudiced than other colonial Europeans, still find themselves "compelled in the end to observe the conventions of social distance" between the races. Perhaps as time went on they did so less. But for other reasons as well, with tensions running high between Africans and Europeans generally, intensive involvement by a white anthropologist in African activities was difficult. Locally recruited research assistants could function less obtrusively as participant observers and played a significant part in the accumulation of Central African urban ethnography. Possibly there were other ways in which a problematic field situation could be a stimulus to methodological resourcefulness.

Part of the problem, naturally, was with other Europeans, who might apply sanctions against anthropologists who in their eyes behaved like renegades and troublemakers. Epstein (1958:xviii), for example, was denied access to the mine township at Luanshya for much of his stay in the town, apparently because of his links with the mine workers' union.[29] Generally the anthropologist-settler relationship was often a tense one of antagonism and avoidance.[30] Powdermaker (1966:250), describing her own field research on the impact of mass media in Luanshya, found other anthropologists at work in Northern Rhodesia in the early 1950s conspicuously siding with the Africans; one of them mentioned having had a bar-room fight with another European because the latter had uttered a racial slur. Marginal to the local circle of researchers, Powdermaker felt somewhat alone in trying to maintain good relationships to the Europeans in the mining township, both in order to "play it safe" and because she thought they ought to be included in her research. Under such circumstances it may not be so surprising if, according to Hooker (1963:457), "the most extravagant generalisations about the manners, morals and motivations of white settlers were tossed off by anthropologists who would have raged had such things been said of Africans."

And perhaps with this we could begin a summary of what were the achievements and limitations of the Rhodes-Livingstone researchers, both as colonial anthropologists and as urban anthropologists. What they actually did may not have been quite as different from what a critic like Magubane demanded as he claimed it was. Nor, on the other hand, could it be said that they had done all that he asked for. Mostly, whatever their individual stances toward colonialism were, they did not in their professional work question one assumption which by now, a couple of decades later, is generally regarded as part of the colonial heritage of the discipline; anthropologists study "other cultures." So, ironically, despite the emphasis on the African townsman as a townsman and on the African miner as a miner, it remained fundamentally important that the African was an African. The suggestion in Gluckman's seven-year plan that Europeans should also be "considered" was in the end given a minimalist interpretation. There is no ethnography of European miners, or Europeans in Central Africa generally, in the Rhodes-Livingstone studies, and the European-dominated power structure became an "external determinant" rather than a focus of inquiry.[31] The style of writing, too, seems to show that a non-African audience was generally assumed—often an international circle of academic peers, sometimes Europeans in Central Africa. At the time, no alternative may have been perceived. By now, on the other hand, it may give an odd ring to an occasional phrase.

The choice of "tribalism" as the main topic can probably be understood in part—but not as a whole—in the context of this anthropologist-audience relationship. It was to colleagues and administrators that it was most important to explain what was the urban significance of ethnic affiliation. It seems probable, however, that relative weaknesses in other areas could also be related to the sort of anthropology that the Rhodes-Livingstone researchers carried with them to Central Africa. It was strong in the analysis of social relations as such, although they had to work on it to make it somewhat more flexible and dynamic. It did not give very much attention to the material bases of social life. The major later studies devoted to urban life actually offered less on such questions than Wilson's study of Broken Hill. And it did not attempt to probe very deeply into what went on in people's minds. Gluckman (1971) could argue rather convincingly that although there was obviously conflict in Copperbelt urban society, open rebellion against European domination tended to be muted by convergent interests in the mining economy; thus there was little or no sign of Luddite industrial sabotage. But he also recurrently asserted that anthropology was a "science of custom," and this was perhaps not the best starting point for an analysis of the complexities of ideas and emotions arising in a fluid situation. For a fuller understanding of the African view of the colonial situation generally and Copperbelt urban life specifically, it might have been possible to dig deeper into the convictions or ambivalences behind surface manifestations of a new life style.

In their own way, however, and in a way which was, of course, influenced by the particular kind of urban situation in which they worked, the Rhodes-Livingstone anthropologists dealt in the Copperbelt towns with several of the major conceptual issues of urban anthropology—with the connections and disconnections between different domains of activity, with rural-urban cultural continuities and contrasts, and with the relationship between the wider social order and a particular way of life. In the latter case, perhaps the cumulativity of their joint enterprise was such that the general setting was increasingly taken for granted. As Godfrey Wilson, and Max Gluckman particularly in his early writings, placed Central Africa and its industrialization and urbanization on the scene of world history, later writers could concern themselves with how the Bemba felt about the Luvale or with the everyday search for issues in township politics. The guidelines suggested in *Closed Systems and Open Minds,* and the notion of external determinants, could be understood as a paradigm within which a "normal science" of Central African urban research could continue and gradually fill out the picture.[32] It was this growing attentiveness to small-scale social processes, and to the methodological and analytical problems connected with them, that later led some of the Rhodes-Livingstone anthropologists to an interest in network analysis, the subject of our next chapter.

CHAPTER FIVE

Thinking with Networks

We are probably all familiar with chain letters. You receive a letter from somebody instructing you to send something—money, a picture postcard, or whatever—to the person at the top of a given list, then remove that name while adding your own at the bottom of the list, and finally pass the new list with instructions along to some number of persons whom you choose yourself. If everything worked according to plan, the chains would rapidly branch out, so that for your trouble you would in due time get a sizable number of responses from others, perhaps people personally unknown to you. But frequently, even if you choose to comply with the instructions, you get nothing at all, because somewhere along the line there are people with no wish to participate. On the other hand, it may happen that you get the same chain letter more than once, for example, if the person who sent it to you sends another letter to somebody who then again chooses you.

The problems which anthropologists deal with under the label of network analysis involve the same kinds of principles and realities which influence the sending of chain letters. In what ways are social relationships linked to each other? How does the situation where two people in direct contact know the same others compare to that where they know different others? How many people do we know, and what kinds of people? These, very generally formulated, are some of the questions asked.

The development of network analysis since the mid-1950s has already been the subject of several extensive reviews—for example, by Barnes (1972), Whitten and Wolfe (1973), Mitchell (1974b) and Wolfe (1978)—and there is no need to take on the complete task here again; nor will we review the reviews.[1] It will be enough for our purposes to remind ourselves of a handful of the better-known studies, to see what sorts of concepts have come out of them, and to give some brief consideration to their uses in anthropological thinking about urbanism.

BEGINNINGS in BREMNES

Network analysis is not only an urban research tool, although as we shall see, it has tended to grow in importance with the anthropological interest in complex societies. First to use it in a more specific sense was John Barnes (1954), in his study of Bremnes, a small Norwegian fishing and farming community. Barnes was concerned with describing the Bremnes social system. He felt that it could usefully be seen as composed of three analytically separate social fields. (Exactly how analytically separate they were need not concern us here.) One of them was the territorial system. Bremnes could be seen as a hierarchy of units with each higher level incorporating lower levels, ranging from household by way of ward and hamlet to the parish level, with the parish of Bremnes itself a part of yet wider units. This field had a quite stable structure. People did not move around much, and neighboring could become a frame of reference for organizing relationships lasting over long stretches of time. It was used for administration as well as voluntary associations. The second field was based on the fishing industry. Its units were the fishing vessels and their crews, marketing cooperatives, herring-oil factories, and so forth, organized in interdependency rather than hierarchy. The internal structure of these units tended to be rather fixed, although the personnel, and sometimes the units, could change. The third field was, for our purposes, the one of greatest interest. It was made up of kinship, friendship, and acquaintance, with continuously changing links and without stable groups or overall coordination. Each person was in touch with a number of other people, some of whom were directly in touch with one another and others of whom were not. This was the kind of field Barnes proposed to term a network:

> The image I have is of a set of points some of which are joined by lines. The points of the image are people, or sometimes groups, and the lines indicate which people interact with each other. We can of course think of the whole of social life as generating a network of this kind. For our present purposes, however, I want to consider, roughly speaking, that part of the total network that is left behind when we remove the groupings and chains of interacting which belong strictly to the territorial and industrial systems. (Barnes 1954:43)

Developing this idea, Barnes went on to suggest that between small-scale, traditional society and modern society there would be a difference in network mesh. The distance around the hole in the modern network would be greater, as people in it do not have as many friends and acquaintances in common as in the small-scale society. If they were to trace any linkage to each other at all, apart from their direct relationship, it would perhaps have to be by way of a great many others—which would probably mean that they would be unaware of the possibility.

Barnes used the network concept in his 1954 paper primarily to analyze Bremnes conceptions of class. Mostly, he noted, the people in the community interacted with relative equals—social differentiation was rather limited. Whatever status differences there might be between two people in direct contact would tend to be understated in the egalitarian idiom which governed interaction. But as people would be linked in a chain of relationships, such subtle differences could be added to each other cumulatively, so that the total difference between two people connected only indirectly over several links could be more noticeable. Thus the people of Bremnes could live in an interconnected network, mostly with a conception of three classes (those above, those below, and those on the same level), and yet interact in a generally egalitarian manner.

BOTT on NETWORK and MARRIAGE

The paper on Bremnes did not really make very much of the network concept, and the statement of ideas which would later turn out to be influential was hardly more than an aside. One of the readers who found them inspiring, however, made them a focus of a book which appeared a few years later. This was Elizabeth Bott's *Family and Social Network* (1957), and with it network analysis came to the city. Bott's work was part of an interdisciplinary study of "ordinary families" in London; more exactly, it was a study of marital relationships, as the children were only peripherally involved. Twenty families took part. Data were gathered primarily through intensive interviews with the spouses, as opportunities for observation were limited.

The "Bott hypothesis" derived from the study was that "the degree of segregation in the role-relationship of husband and wife varies directly with the connectedness of the family's social network." Some explication of its terms may be called for. Bott distinguished three kinds of organization of family activities—complementary organization, where the activities of the spouses are different and separate but fit together as one whole; independent organization, where husband and wife carry out their activities largely independently of each other; and joint organization, where the spouses engage in activities together, or where activities are interchangeable between them. The first two of these forms of organization dominate in segregated conjugal relationships, while the third is characteristic of the joint conjugal relationship. Bott's variable of connectedness was inspired by what Barnes had had to say about "mesh." The more a couple's associates also had contacts with each other, the more connected the couple's network was said to be. Without precise measures of connectedness, however, Bott couched her argument mostly in the relative terms of close-knit and loose-knit networks. According to the perspective of this study, each couple had a network of its own, consisting of the people the spouses interacted with directly. No indirect linkages were considered, except insofar as one can say that the contacts between associates are indirect from the point of view of the couple.

Only one of the twenty families really had a close-knit network, but this was also the one with the most segregated marital roles. There were more intermediate and loose-knit networks, with a few apparently in a phase of transition, and at the center of these there was an increasing degree of jointness in the conjugal relationship. What is the basis of this apparent correlation? Bott's interpretation was that close-knit networks develop where the parties to the marriage have grown up in the same local area and continue to live there, with their neighbors, friends, and relatives as stable members of the network. Each spouse then continues in his or her earlier relationships, and because these outside associates are in touch with one another, they can unite in consistent normative pressure on the spouse in question to conform to the rules already established for their respective relationships. In this situation, the spouses have less of an opportunity to become as fully involved with each other as they would in a joint conjugal relationship. Phrased more positively, they need not become as wholly dependent on one another as they would if they lacked stable outside links.

The typical loose-knit network, on the other hand, comes about because the spouses are, in one sense or another, mobile, making new contacts with people who do not know their old network partners. Here continuous outside demands are weaker, and the spouses have to rely more on each other for help, security, and other satisfactions. But mobility is not the only influence on network connectedness. The nature of neighborhoods, the forms of recruitment to work opportunities, personality characteristics, and a variety of other factors are also involved. Generally, however, it is Bott's view that a high degree of network connectedness is particularly likely to be found among working-class people. Here one will most often find the established neighborhood, with families remaining through generations, where neighbors and relatives frequently work together at a dominant industry nearby and help one another get jobs and homes. It should be inserted here, perhaps, that the generalization is most applicable to the English urban working class at a particular point in history; these conditions of life obviously may or may not apply for the working class elsewhere. The opposite complex of circumstances, where a loose-knit network generates a joint conjugal relationship, might involve socially and geographically mobile people, quite likely middle class, who have a more diverse set of neighbors and who less frequently use network contacts to find employment.

Bott's study has drawn much comment and inspired a great deal of further research.[2] It established firmly the idea of a relationship between the internal structure of the family and the pattern of its external contacts, and there seems to be a fair amount of agreement that close-knit networks go with segregated marital relationships. The evidence is rather inconclusive on the relationship between loose-knit networks and joint conjugal ties, however, and as far as conceptualization and interpretation are concerned, later commentators have pointed to a number of loose ends in Bott's presentation. One important point is that the spouses had better be viewed as two distinct units in the network analysis, rather than merged into one as in this study—it could well be a crucial question whether the parties to a conjugal relationship have separate networks or one shared network, or to what extent there is a partial overlap between the two networks. Within these networks, also, one could give further attention to internal differentiation. Is overall connectedness a sufficient measure, or should one also attend to the clustering which creates different sectors, of varying connectedness and perhaps with noticeable gaps between them? Are different categories of contacts more or less close-knit—do, for instance, kinsmen all know one another, while friends do not? And to what extent are kinsmen and friends respectively part of the overlap between the spouses' networks, or of the parts of the networks which are not shared? Under which conditions does a close-knit network really develop the normative consensus which Bott seems merely to assume, and under what conditions are existing links really used to enforce norms? These are examples of questions showing the greater intensity of network description and analysis which has developed since Bott's study. Similar greater differentiation could be noted in the conceptualization of the conjugal relationship itself. Is it sufficient to speak of jointness and segregation in the relationship as a whole, or is it necessary to consider how some couples join in some activities and separate in others? Is jointness or segregation in some activities of greater diagnostic value than others for characterizing the relationship as a whole? We need hardly go into these questions here; suffice it to conclude that *Family and Social Network* has been an unusually influential study.

RED and SCHOOL

In the decade after Bott's book, network conceptualizations of various kinds became increasingly frequent in anthropology. Choosing another couple of examples from the first generation of network writings thus becomes a little harder. Two studies by Philip Mayer and Adrian Mayer are among the best-known, however, and also point to important ways of looking at social life in network terms.

Philip Mayer's (1961, 1962, 1964) research, like that of the Rhodes-Livingstone group, centered on what we recognize as a type B African urban community, a new town under European control but with a large African population. In some ways, however, the town of East London in South Africa was rather different from those of the Copperbelt. The regulation of black life by whites was, and has remained, stricter. For example, no trade unions were allowed. East London was also ethnically less diverse than the Central African towns. The overwhelming majority of its African population was made up of Xhosa, in whose homeland East London stood, and it is with them that Mayer's study deals.[3]

The urban Xhosa could be seen, at the time of the research, as divided into several major groupings.[4] On the one hand, one could distinguish between the townspeople, born in East London and with all their social ties there, and the migrants from the rural areas. On the other hand, among the migrants there was a clear contrast between two cultural orientations called "Red" and "School." This contrast was already visible in rural life. The Red Xhosa were the conscious traditionalists, earning their designation by smearing their faces and bodies and the blankets they wore with ochre. They rejected most of the ideas and practices which the Europeans had brought, including the Christian religion and the mission education which went with it. The School Xhosa were Christian converts who, beginning many generations ago, had taken on many of the values, under-standings, and external signs spreading from the culture of the white colonizers. The proportions of Red and School varied in different parts of Xhosaland, but in large areas the two life styles coexisted, with somewhat restrained contacts between them and with only a minor trickle of new recruits from one to the other over the years.

In the countryside both Red and School were peasants, and there was no great difference in occupation among those of them who migrated to East London either. If the typical urban African on the Copperbelt was a mine worker, the ordinary Xhosa in town was a factory hand. Particularly in the domain of recreation, however, the urban lives of the Red and the School Xhosa turned out quite differently. The former made little use of what the town as such had to offer. They tried to come as close as possible to the ar-rangements they were used to from the country. Thus they engaged in beer drinks, traditional dances, and ancestor worship, and got together to reminisce and gossip about rural life and rural people. The migrants who engaged in such interactions were also those who had already known each other in the country, in more or less ascribed relations as kinsmen, age mates, or neighbors. In network terms, this meant that the characteristic Red migrant network was a unitary set of relationships, drawn from both the rural and urban ends and close-knit as a whole. The School migrant, meanwhile, was prepared through his cultural orientation to take part in a wider range of urban activities in his leisure life—education, sports, amusements, what little there might be of political activity. In some of these his partners could be long-rooted townspeople, in many others other School migrants. But there was no need for them to be people from his own rural home area. The School Xhosa could thus in effect have two networks, linked to each other only through himself; one in the country, tending to be rather tightly knit in the nature of rural society, another in the town, which could well be loosely knit as one might associate with dif-ferent people in different activities.

The East London study, Mayer observed, had a bearing on the concep-tualizations of the Rhodes-Livingstone group. What was involved in "alter-nation" between rural and urban systems was obviously different for Red and School Xhosa, and the two systems seemed more distinguishable, at least in some areas of life, for the latter than for the former. The School migrant as an individual was also rather more likely to be involved in a pro-cess of one-way change, rather than alternation. In his urban milieu, there were fewer personal pressures turning him back to his rural area of origin. In contrast, the Red migrant built into his town environment his continued commitment to the homestead in the country.

Mayer could draw on Bott's reasoning concerning the connection between network form and normative pressure. The Red Xhosa in town in a sense chose to maintain a close-knit network, because his values were such as to lead him to a set of partners known to each other and homogeneous in their way of life. Once he was in this network, however, its concerted judgments effectively limited his opportunities for future change. The School Xhosa, knowingly or not, opted for a greater continued freedom of action (within such limits as existed for any African migrant in East London) by getting into company whose hold over him was less pervasive.

BRINGING in the VOTE

The study by Adrian Mayer (1966) of an election campaign in the town of Dewas, in the Indian state of Madhya Pradesh, pushed network analysis further in another direction. Mayer was interested in the ways candidates for one ward seat in the Municipal Council used their social relationships to bring in the vote. The two main candidates in this election were those of the Congress Party and Jan Sangh. Mayer's attention centered on the Congress candidate. The ward was heterogeneous in terms of castes and occupations, and no candidate could win by appealing to one particular group only; he would have to attract a more diverse lot of supporters. Neither of the two candidates was an incumbent, although the Jan Sangh candidate had stood for election unsuccessfully before. He had also spent a longer period getting exposure to the electorate and building a wide range of contacts with it. The Congress candidate, on the other hand, started mobilizing a following rather late. His campaign took the form of creating what Mayer terms an action set of a particular form. We might regard the action set as a kind of network, although this is not in agreement with Mayer's own usage. It consists of a set of finite chains of social relationships, spreading out from an ego and created as such for some particular purpose of his, although each of the particular relationships included may have its own existence separate from this purpose. In this latter respect, they may be of quite varying character. Some may be based on kinship, others can be of a commercial character, others yet built on shared membership of an association, and so forth. It has no unity except insofar as one is infused through the direct or indirect relationship to ego.

The Congress Party candidate in this ward used an action set of quite long chains to reach into various groups. This meant that the influence wrought in each link could be of a very different nature, often more intrinsic to it than related to the influence or program of the candidate himself. Someone interested in wrestling, for example, could take the opinion of a peer at the gymnasium, who had himself perhaps been influenced by a party worker or by his shopkeeper. But whatever the nature of the relationships as such, if they could be successfully maneuvered, the result would be an inward flow of political support for ego, the candidate.

This seems very much to resemble the technique of the chain letter. At best, a snowballing effect, if everyone recruited can himself recruit several more; more modestly, perhaps on the basis of "each one, teach one," still a fairly extensive influence. Mayer suggests that the long chains of relationships are most useful in a quick, "soft" campaign designed to peak at the very point of the election. It is a mass effort of recruitment where the solidity of support is less important. The Jan Sangh candidate, in contrast, had conducted a "hard" campaign. He was himself in direct contact with many supporters, as we have noted, but may have made less use of their direct and indirect links to others. Over time his support may have been more certain than that given by the Congress supporters to their candidate. But on Election Day, it was not sufficient; the Congress candidate won.

Mayer also points out another difference between direct and indirect relationships. This involves a difference between patrons and brokers. In a transactional relationship, a patron can get what he wants from someone else only by using his own resources, and there are limits to those. A broker can deal in promises to use his influence with a patron, but it is generally understood that he cannot always come through. In a sense, then, his funds are unlimited, as he is less likely to be held responsible for broken promises. This could lead a patron to insert brokers between himself and others in the action set, and consequently make the chains in the action sets of those with patronage to dispose of longer than those where no significant patronage is involved. In India, at the time of Adrian Mayer's writing, such patronage was often under the control of the Congress Party.

NETWORK ANALYSIS, COMPLEX STRUCTURES, and NEW PERSPECTIVES

Why have anthropologists turned to network analysis? The answer cannot be simple, but looking back, one can see that a major motive has been a concern with making relational analysis more adaptable in the study of an increasingly varied set of social structures. And the greater interest in urban life, and complex societies generally, has been especially important here. It became necessary to be open-minded about the delimitation of units of study, as very often one could not rely on "natural" social boundaries. On the one hand, even the local community could be an unmanageably large and complex unit, and not necessarily relevant as a whole to the kind of analysis one had in mind. On the other hand, one could not afford to disregard linkages which went outside it, to the region, the nation, or the rest of the world. So one turned to concepts such as social field, standing for the idea of excising from a practically infinite web of relationships that particular range where the factors shaping some particular activity, or its consequences, could be traced. A field of this sort, we have seen, could encompass both the rural and urban relationships of migrants, thus stretching across the boundaries of what could alternatively be seen as separate social systems, or it could be a unit circumscribed within such a system, such as the friends, neighbors, and relatives influencing the form of a marital relationship. Network concepts have been an additional step toward the understanding of such units, insofar as they make possible a more exact specification of the nature of links within the field.[5]

The idea of networks in anthropology thus stands for abstracting for analytical purposes more or less elaborate sets of relationships from some wider system. Perhaps this should be qualified: we sometimes point out that in principle, any such system, even the world, can be seen as a "total network." Such an idea has its uses. But, in fact, what we normally do is to draw boundaries around some unit which we deem to be practical for our further scrutiny. Why these units can be so variable especially in the study of more complex social structures, and why network analysis thus turns into an exercise in flexibility, we can perhaps understand by drawing on some of our earlier conceptualization of the urban social order. In such a differentiated structure, the individual has many kinds of situational involvements, that is to say, roles, and the opportunities for making varied combinations of roles in one's repertoire may be considerable. But to each role correspond one or more relationships to other people, and thus networks are assembled with a variability which roughly matches that of the role constellations. Whether they will actually be of further analytical interest depends, naturally, on the extent to which roles also in some way impinge on one another, so that one can discern relationships between the relationships.

At this point we can perhaps see why network analysis tends to be seen as part of a complex of innovations which have entered the anthropological view of society in recent years. According to old-style structural-functionalism, society could be seen as made up of enduring groups and institutions; the personnel flowing through them perform their parts according to prescription, so that a delineation of norms may be an adequate account for social conduct. With this perspective we have now become rather dissatisfied. We have started bringing into our analyses non-institutionalized, strategic, adaptive behavior, of kinds which may occur within or parallel to the institutional framework or which may bring about changes in it. Firth (1954:10) was an early, gentle critic of the established wisdom with his distinction between social structure and social organization, the latter entailing "the processes of ordering of action and of relations in reference to given social ends, in terms of adjustments resulting from the exercise of choices by members of the society." Later, we have seen the emergence of an anthropological vocabulary of action and exchange theories, generative models, decision-making, transaction, maximization, and manipulation.

In part the new points of view developed as anthropologists moved into areas of social life which were less certainly under the normative control of society. We have seen that the Rhodes-Livingstone group began to distinguish structural from personal and categorical relationships in their studies of African urbanism. The growing interest in Mediterranean and Latin American societies, with their special characteristics, also led away from a preoccupation with enduring group structures. Some relationships were increasingly understood as fundamentally rather private affairs of cumulative exchange and personal information—for example, friendship and patron-client relationships. There was also a new awareness, however, of the latitude for choice and variation, as well as the strains, within the persistent structures. This awareness paralleled the attention to informal organization in the sociology of industry and bureaucracy.

The new analytical perspectives have not been limited to the study of more complex social structures, but there would seem to be a connection between the two. Where role repertoires and consequently also networks are varied, more or less original combinations of experiences and resources offer scope for innovative adaptations and strategies. At the same time, a society without any tightly integrative framework does not guarantee that there is a fit between the various roles an individual gets himself into, and so there are risks involved as well. One of the problems involved in social organization, as Firth (1955:2) has put it, is to "resolve conflicts between

structural principles." This kind of insight into the prevalence of contradictions, we remember, also led the Rhodes-Livingstone anthropologists to
assemble their data in new fashions. Generally, it would appear that where
role constellations are varied, individuals are also more likely to face new
and unrehearsed strains and conflicts, while, where constellations are recurrent, there may more probably be institutionalized solutions to such problems.

The reason why there are many ways of abstracting networks is thus
that there are many ways of combining roles and making something interesting out of the combinations. Looking at networks this way, we understand them partly to cut across enduring groups and institutions, partly to
cover other areas of the social landscape. In the latter there are ties which
are less regulated, constrained only by the private guidelines which the
participants have explicitly agreed to or implicitly taken for granted, relationships perhaps created in reaction to the depersonalization and un-
responsiveness of societal institutions. In the former the conduct of the individual may to some degree be shaped by normative control, but within
these limits he may also be able to draw on experiences and interests arising from the integrated totality of his relationships. And thereby the persistent structures can be seen in a different light, as the participants become
not only a rather anonymous set of personnel but entire individuals
through whom external influences may penetrate group or institutional
life. Having no great respect for conventional boundaries, network analysis
can help give a coherent view of a differentiated social structure.

Mayer's study of Indian electioneering may serve us as an example here.
In many of the relationships which made up links in the candidate's chain,
there was an institutional base which had nothing to do with politics. But
in the enactment of such relationships—between one wrestler and another, for instance—a participant could also relay a political message
which he had most likely picked up in a very different context. In this case
the long chain of indirect contacts between candidate and potential supporters indeed built on the assumption that people in complex societies
have different role constellations, since with each link in the chain new
contexts became accessible to the campaign. It is a little ironic to use an
Indian example at this point, of course, since Indian society in its traditional form can be taken as an example of quite standardized role constellations, because of the caste system.

We should perhaps note at this stage that the view of networks as cutting across groups and institutions which we adopt here is not universal in network analysis. Barnes, we have already seen, was led to adopt a concept of network in his Bremnes study to cover a residue of relationships which remained after a more conventional structural framework had been applied. This tendency to make only more personal, less persistent sets of social relationships the domain of network analysis is quite widespread, and this is where the need for it is greatest, considering the lack of analytical alternatives. At an early stage, the Rhodes-Livingstone conceptualizations of Central African urbanism similarly connected network ideas especially to personal relationships. Latter, however, Mitchell (1973b) has expressed the point of view adopted here: network analysis involves a particular kind of abstraction, rather than a particular kind of relationship.

The uses of this abstraction, then, may vary. As many have noted, there is no "network theory" in the sense of a set of logically interrelated, testable propositions—a format which seems seldom to appeal to anthropological thinkers anyway. For us, to summarize the last few paragraphs, network notions seem particularly useful as we concern ourselves with individuals using roles rather than with roles using individuals, and with the crossing and manipulation rather than the acceptance of institutional boundaries. It is in this light we see the connection of network analysis both to what may be termed anthropological action theory and to the study of urban and other complex societies.

Parenthetically, one might speculate that this connection has also involved a change in the relationship between the anthropologist and the society he studies. The urban or otherwise complex society where he does research is more often culturally similar to the society from which he comes (if indeed it is not the same society) than a small-scale, traditional society tends to be. The institutional framework may seem less intellectually problematic; for better or for worse, perhaps it is even "taken for granted," regarded as a given in his analysis. With this broad cultural affinity, on the other hand, the individual members of the society perhaps become more accessible to empathy. Their struggle to make the system work for themselves can more readily be followed and understood in all its personal, social, and cultural subtleties, and increasingly often the anthropologists may find themselves incorporated as part of the solution, or part of the problem, in the more or less sophisticated strategies of some individuals.[6] In such ways, the anthropologist as a research instrument may have become more sensitive to some phenomena in the new environment.

VARIABLES in NETWORK ANALYSIS

Overviews of network studies have often made a point of contrasting metaphorical and analytical uses of the idea of network. In most of its early occurrences, particularly in the era before Barnes's and Bott's studies, the usage was distinctly metaphorical: the term merely referred to the fact that social relationships were connected to each other. With the growth of a more intensive network analysis, those writers who are simply in search of a metaphor of this kind may have preferred more often to turn to alternatives like "web" or "fabric" in order not to imply too specific perspectives. On the other hand, "network" has become a fashionable term, applied quite generously in contexts where it may not really be needed. "It sounds smart for a few years but like many other trendy terms means all things to all men, and will drop out of use when fashions change," Barnes (1972:1) writes in his review. But perhaps the judgment is a little unfair. Even more passing references to "networks" sometimes indicate an awareness of the possibilities of a more intensive analysis, although it may not be fully carried out.

What concerns us here, however, are the studies where network concepts have been taken beyond metaphor, in a development of anthropological thinking which will hardly disappear again without a trace. The analyses by Barnes, Bott, and the two Mayers already offer some evidence of a more developed conceptual apparatus, and we may usefully give some more consideration to its major components. Unfortunately, this is a field where terminological complexity and confusion have been frequently attested to. The difficulties began to develop early. Each writer made up his own concepts to suit his own particular purposes as he went along, and until the late 1960s there was no extensive network among the network researchers themselves which might have prevented some unnecessary proliferation of terminology for more or less similar ideas. But things were hardly much improved as they began reaching for one another's ideas, only to twist them or rename them. Network, field, set, and reticulum; density, mesh, and connectedness; cluster, sector, segment, and compartment; action set, quasi-group, and coalition; all are groups of concepts of similar or overlapping meaning. Firth's (1951:29) suggestion that "any science must have a budget of terms of general application, not too closely defined" is in a peculiar way apropos here—in the vocabulary of networks, there are hardly any such terms left, as almost every conceivable term has been coopted at one time or other for a specific technical usage. And attempts to call them back into a conveniently loose usage, while sometimes just about inevitable, may then cause further difficulties.

Although close attention to obviously related concepts, and to the exchanges over them between the scholars involved, may at times reveal significant analytical distinctions, this is hardly the place to provide a dictionary of network terminology. We will try instead to see on what kinds of general attributes of networks discussions have focused. The most important systematic treatment of this field is probably Mitchell's (1969b) introduction to *Social Networks in Urban Situations,* a symposium volume drawing mostly on the Central African studies of the Manchester School during the Rhodes-Livingstone era or just after it.[7] The Manchester School was intimately linked to the development of network analysis from the beginning. Barnes, after having been with the Rhodes-Livingstone Institute, did his field work in Norway as a research fellow of the University of Manchester, and Bott (1971:316) has acknowledged the influence of Max Gluckman's seminar on her thinking. In another of the early network formulations, Epstein (1961) had used a diary of an assistant's movements and contacts to depict the complexity of Central African urban life. For the Manchester scholars, network analysis was evidently a natural development within that tradition of close reading of materials concerning particular cases which had already resulted in extended case studies and situational analyses; a development allowing yet greater descriptive rigor.

Mitchell, in his introduction, makes a distinction, also adopted by others, between interactional attributes, referring to particular links (such as intensity, durability, frequency, or content), and morphological attributes, referring to the ways in which the links fit together. While the former certainly cannot be neglected in any particular analysis, we will concentrate here on the morphological attributes, as the illumination of these is the more specific contribution of network analysis.

A first area of variation, as our examples have already shown us, involves the principles for abstracting a network from a wider social unit. This, we have said before, is not a matter of describing the intrinsic attributes of network patterns but rather one of deciding what suits one's analytical purposes. The alternatives seem to be of two major kinds, with a combination of them as a third possibility. One may define a network by anchoring it at some particular point in the structure of social relationships, such as in one individual or in both parties to a particular dyad, and move outward from there as far as it appears necessary or useful. This is what is called an ego-centered ("egocentric") or personal network; the term has been used to cover both individual and dyad anchorage, although it would seem more exact to restrict it to the former. Another alternative is to construct the network around some particular kind of content in the relationships, and thus, for example, abstract the political network from the total network—this principle of abstraction leads to what is usually called a partial network. Third, one might delimit a partial network from the point of departure of some particular ego. This latter is most obviously what is involved in the network of Adrian Mayer's campaigning politician. Somewhat less clearly this is also the nature of Bott's conjugal networks, as she takes into account only links with relatives, friends, and neighbors. Of course, Bott at the same time gives us an example of networks seen as centered on dyads, with the particular analytical problems such anchorage entails.

If a network is defined from the point of view of a center like this, the next question may be where its outer limits should be drawn. In the case of the political campaign, one is obviously interested in tracing just how far the chain of relationships can be used to mobilize political support. In many studies, on the other hand, the limits of the network are pragmatically set much closer to the center. In Bott's case, the network includes only the people with whom the couple are in direct contact. Although the lateral links between these people are supposedly also included, one might note that there *could* have been more of these than Bott knew. She had to find out about them only from interviews with the couple at the center, whose own knowledge on this point might not have been perfect. If one takes a network to consist of only the direct links from ego to other persons, one has what is termed a first-order star (cf. Barnes 1969). If one includes the lateral relationships between these others as well the resulting set of relationships is called a first-order zone. When a further step outward from these others is taken, one has a second-order star; if lateral relationships are again included, a second-order zone; and so forth (see figure 3). But the example of Bott's study shows that such network units tend quickly to become unmanageable. Looking at the network from the center, one simply may not be able to see very far. Returning once more to the chain letter—after it passes out of one's first-order star, one is likely to lose track of it.

Within the network, however delimited, the morphological characteristic which has drawn most comment is what Bott called connectedness,

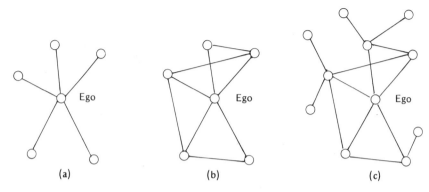

Figure 3. Networks of Relationships
(a) a first-order star; (b) a first-order zone;
(c) a second-order star

but which is now more frequently termed density. It is usually defined as the proportion of actually existing relationships out of the number which would exist among a given number of people if they were all directly linked to one another (see figure 4). We have already noted that Bott, and Philip Mayer in his Xhosa study, link density to social control. A person in a dense network is likely to be exposed to the influence of any other participant through direct as well as indirect links. But although there is most likely a measure of truth in this, several commentators have noted, there is a need for further specification of conditions. All relationships can perhaps not be used to channel influences, for instance, if communication within

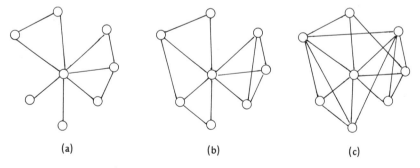

Figure 4. Networks of Varying Density:
(a) 10 actual linkages out of 28 possible among 8 persons—
density 0.36; (b) 13 actual linkages out of 28—density 0.46;
(c) 17 actual linkages out of 28—density 0.61

them flows mainly in one direction, and within the network people may be very differently placed both to exert influence and to be at the receiving end. Concepts of centrality or reachability pertaining to particular positions in the network may be used to throw light on this. Related efforts have gone into showing that density may not be at all even within networks. In some ares of a network, people may be closely tied together, with more or less every member directly linked to every other member. Between one such cluster and other parts of the network, there could be few links. It is probable that such a situation is particularly likely to be identified in ego-centered varieties of network abstractions, since otherwise the student may be less inclined to view these clusters as belonging in the same network at all. In this case, however, clustering may be highly significant. An individual involved in two distinct clusters, and exposed to the cross-fire of different influences between them, is in an entirely different position from the person in a network of more even density.

In many networks, of course, there is only one cluster of great density, and greater sparsity in the rest of the network, or a gradual decline in density from one sector to the others. Partly on the basis of this criterion, some writers have divided ego-centered networks into different parts, such as intimate, effective, and extended networks—the number of differentiated parts vary. As the labels indicate, however, network form is not the only criterion for such distinctions; interactional criteria such as intensity and content also count, and there is no certain one-to-one relationship between these and density.

A final morphological characteristic of ego-centered networks which we might note is that of range. (Sometimes, and sometimes not, this is identical with "span.") This is a measure of the number of people a person reaches through his network. It could be limited to the people who are in direct contact with ego, although one can also define it to include second-order or third-order relationships, and so forth. Stated thus, range is a baldly quantitative concept. It is also possible, however, to add a further criterion of heterogeneity. A person whose contacts includes people of more diverse kinds—as defined by age, class, ethnicity, or whatever— could thus be said to have a network of greater range than he who has the same number of contacts but with a more homogeneous assemblage of people.

USES and LIMITATIONS

We have restated very parsimoniously some important network variables. What, then, are they important for? One general answer is that they— morphological and interactional variables together—probably constitute the most extensive and widely applicable framework we have for the study of social relations. They give an idea of what is potentially knowable and what would be needed for something approaching completeness in the description of relationships. The framework may even permit some quantitative measurements of relationships and the forms which they assume together. Under the inspiration of related bodies of ideas, such as sociometry and mathematical graph theory, the practitioners of network analysis have been able to devise formulae of density, reachability, centrality, clustering, and other variables. To repeat, then, there can be a rigor about network conceptualizations which one may find admirable. It is a rigor, however, which is accompanied by practical limitations. It is extremely difficult and time-consuming to realize this potential of exactness in other than fairly small network units. A couple of well-known studies may exemplify this.

The first of them is Jeremy Boissevain's (1974:97–146) exploration of two personal networks.[8] This was conceived as a pilot study of the relationship between certain variables which need not in themselves concern us here. What we might note, instead, is the procedure and the sheer mass of data involved. The networks were those of two school teachers in Malta, one urban and one rural, and the coverage was primarily that of their first-order zones. For the rural teacher this included 1,751 persons, for the urban teacher 638—the difference seems partly related to their different environments.[9] These were persons with whom the two maintained or had had contact. A few persons were included whom they had not met face to face but yet felt they knew, spouses of close kinsmen living abroad. (There is much migration from Malta.) On the other hand, children below fourteen years of age were excluded. Certainly, since there was no way of arriving at these numbers except through eliciting identifications from the two informants, their real networks were probably somewhat larger, as they can hardly have remembered all the people who had passed through their lives. For each person—1,751 plus 638—an information sheet was completed providing data on the person's social background, number of shared role relations with the informant, frequency of contact, last contact, contents of the relationship, and acquaintances which this person and the main informant had in common. These sheets were also sorted according to the emotional importance of the various contacts for the informant. The two informants also gave extensive biographical information, including case materials on various situations involving different segments of their networks. Boissevain had originally intended to develop a larger sample of such informants. Not surprisingly, he had been able to collect the data for these two only when he apparently decided to regard the experiment as completed.

One feels less than generous uttering a word of criticism of such an effort. In line with what has been said above, however, one may note that paradoxically, the undertaking was still in a couple of ways rather limited. Like Bott in her interviews, Boissevain got the story of each network link from one side only. The information about lateral contacts between the others in the network could be unreliable if the informant himself was not well-informed. To check the information with the others as well, however, we would have needed another 2,389 interviews, some of them with people scattered over the world. Such principled methodological nitpicking is something one can indulge in when one does not have to do the work oneself. Similarly, one could note that the networks Boissevain has abstracted are shallow ones, as only first-order relationships are included. But even if links traced farther out would frequently soon lead back to many of the people already included, as people in a relatively small society such as Malta are likely to have much overlap between their networks, an extension to include second-order or third-order zones would clearly yield an even less manageable amount of data.

Boissevain made the brave attempt to include all the people in a first-order zone, rather than select some smaller set in terms of general importance, or relevance for some particular problem. He even regarded the network as cumulative, in the sense that relationships in which no interaction was currently taking place were evidently seen as still continuing, although latent. With such ambitions of extensiveness, ideal data quality can hardly be achieved. The other study we will look at moved in a different direction. This is Bruce Kapferer's (1969) analysis of a dispute within a small network of industrial workers in Kabwe—the Central African town formerly named Broken Hill, site of Godfrey Wilson's research a few decades earlier.

The scene of Kapferer's study was the Cell Room in a mining establishment, where the last stage in the preparation of zinc occurs. There were three sections in the room, and the study was concerned with the people in one of these. Fifteen workers spent all their time on the job there, while an additional eight divided their time between the sections. Most of them were employed on a task work basis, and their jobs tended to be interdependent. The work process usually moved at a steady pace, although at times a worker might be tempted to accelerate. Usually it was the younger workers who felt able to work more quickly; this was threatening to the older men who were afraid of losing their jobs if they could not keep up with the pace. In this case the dispute began when an older worker, Abraham, accused a younger man, Donald, of rate busting. The latter countered with a veiled accusation of witchcraft. The senior men are assumed to know more about witchcraft, and it is a resource a person might use if he feels his position is threatened. One might expect that this interchange would have led the other men to line up on each side according to age, but this did not happen. Instead, the other workers seemed to concentrate their attention on various side issues, and in the end Abraham found himself with strong support from young as well as old men, while Donald was rather isolated. The question, then, is this: why did some of the men take sides in a way which seems opposed to their actual interests in the normative issues of work speed and witchcraft?

Kapferer argued that the main principle underlying the participants' conduct, in this as in many kinds of situations, was to align themselves in such a way as to endanger as little as possible of their investments in the total set of relationships involved. To begin with, this would affect the men who were linked to only one of the disputants, or who had invested more in their relationship to one than to the other. Kapferer thus compared the qualities of the direct relationships linking various men to Abraham and Donald, in terms of the three interactional variables of exchange content, multiplexity, and directional flow. Exchange content could be of five kinds—conversation, joking behavior, job assistance, cash assistance, and personal service. Multiplexity referred to the number of exchange contents in a relationship. If more than one kind, the relationship was regarded as multiplex. The variable of directional flow referred to the fact that apart from conversation, the exchange contents could flow in either of two directions, or in both.

Although it is not strictly an integral part of network conceptualization, the notion of multiplexity may deserve a few additional words here, as we will continue to draw on it. Kapferer's usage was a somewhat specialized one; when Gluckman (1955:19 ff.; 1962:26 ff.) introduced the concept, he defined the multiplex relationship only as one serving many purposes. In the tribal society with which he was dealing, the great internal diversity of contents in such a relationship might be said still to be involved in it only through a single role. Relationships like these occur in urban life as well, of course, for example in the domestic domain. But especially in the more differentiated social structure, multiplexity also comes into existence as ego and alter start interacting with each other by way of two (or more) more or less distinct role sets. This we will deal with again. Kapferer's usage, meanwhile, seems rather to straddle the two kinds of multiplexity.

As he mapped exchange content, multiplexity, and directional flow in the links between the men, Kapferer found that there certainly was a tendency to line up with the disputant with whom one had the strongest ties. But this did not explain very much, for several men who had aligned themselves with Abraham had the same kind of relationships to both him and Donald, and one man, the crew boss, who seemed to have a stronger tie to Donald, still took Abraham's side. This is why Kapferer as a next step in his analysis decided to look at entire network of men from the perspective of each man in turn. This is where morphological variables (structural in Kapferer's vocabulary) came in. He employed four of these, all quantitatively measurable. Two of them related to the proportion of multiplex relationships, among a man's direct relationships to other men and among the lateral links between these respectively. The third measure was of density of lateral relationships among the men to whom ego was directly linked. The final measure was one of span, in this case defined as the proportion out of all the relationships existing among the men which is made up of direct links between ego and others together with the lateral links between these others. For each variable, the measurements were dichotomized, so that half of the men are classified as "high" and the other half "low." The four classifications for each man were regarded as a measure of the differential degree to which he was tied into the entire network of relationships. When at this stage the direct as well as the indirect relationships among the participants in the dispute were mapped, it turned out that Abraham could capture the support of many who by the nature of their direct relationships to the disputants would seem uncommitted, through his strong relationships to influential third persons.

A compressed account like this could hardly do justice to Kapferer's rich ethnography and analysis. Nor has it been possible to summarize his discussion of the relationships between the morphological criteria. It might be noted in this regard that Barnes (1972:13), while favorable toward the study as a whole, is somewhat hesitant about the formulation of the measures. What concerns us most here, however, are the field work requirements for a network analysis of this exactness. Kapferer carried out observation in the Cell Room for several months. With his field contained in an unusually small space, and involving a very limited number of people, he could get observational data on all relationships. Having no more than one or two dozen people to deal with, it was possible for him to look at the network from each individual's position, and to feel sure that every relationship within this universe was known to him in some detail. Such field situations are rare; and whatever their methodological advantages are, it is unlikely that every anthropologist would like to descend upon them.

The question, then, is where the search for rigor takes network analysis, and how anthropologists will react to it. A humanist response may be exemplified by Simon Ottenberg (1971:948) in his review of *Social Networks in Urban Situations:*

> The network view seems likely to move more and more in the direction of graph theory and the statistical manipulation of network ties. Insofar as this occurs, it will lead to greater scientific accuracy but toward a cold science. An approach which began in part as an attempt to understand how individuals operate in the urban social milieu, and how they arrive at decisions and invoke social ties, is likely to become a highly formal system of analysis in which the individual as a human being disappears in the network calculation.

There is also Anthony Leeds's (1972:5) comment, from a position generally critical of urban anthropological microstudies, that it is time to steer away from "the trivia of network methodology, street-corner studies, analyzing the rules for a fair fight, etc.," and more specifically, that "most of the African network literature seems completely bogged down in methodology because it has failed to attack important questions of broader substantive theory."

The humanist hesitancy is a matter of personal preference. There are different styles in doing anthropology. Leeds's critique appears to point to more serious practical difficulties in the development of network studies with the discipline. However admirable the intensity of their analysis may be, the entire apparatus of interactional and morphological variables and measurements is not easy to move about in the social structure.[10] There may be a danger that as one continues to strive toward maximum precision, network analysis is adapted to less and less of human life—it becomes a case of theoretical and methodological involution rather than evolution.

It hardly seems necessary, however, to proceed with network studies only in this direction. A great deal has been claimed for network analysis during its years as an anthropological growth industry (and also an inter-disciplinary one, now with a journal and an international society of its own)—that the network concept is the equal of "role" and "class" in the struggle to understand society in general, that it is to the anthropology of complex society what genealogy has been to the study of traditional kin-ship-based society. Perhaps there is something to these assertions. But possibly they may be validated most successfully by a normalization of network thinking, whereby the set of concepts involved would pass into the general vocabulary of all anthropologists, to be used with just that intensity and completeness which the occasion calls for, like the other major concepts just mentioned. For our purposes, we thus prefer to emphasize flexibility rather than rigor and exhaustiveness. As we try to find out more about how network ideas can help us throw light on urban life, methodological de-mands may at least temporarily adopt a lower profile. We may count link-ages as far as we find it useful and interesting; morphological variables (which seem to be the most important contribution of network analysis to anthropological conceptualization) will be applied in a piecemeal fashion as we find them illuminating in handling the problem at hand, rather than as an indivisible set. This is the kind of thinking with networks of which some further diverse examples may be worthwhile.

The GRAPEVINE: GOSSIP and NETWORK

Although several anthropological writers had had one thing or another to say about gossip as part of community life, they did so mostly in passing until 1963, when Max Gluckman's essay on gossip and scandal sparked a series of studies with more sharply focused interest in the subject. Despite Gluckman's position in the midst of the Manchester milieu where network analysis flowered, this essay did not make use of network concepts and generally remained within the framework of structural-functionalism. Gos-sip, in this view, serves primarily to maintain the unity of groups, espe-cially the relatively exclusive and well-bounded ones such as elites, profes-sions, or minorities. In an overt sense, of course, it is talk about people;

but more fundamentally, according to Gluckman, it is a way of expressing and affirming norms. Through gossip, one can bring injury to enemies and sanctions against defaulters within the group. One can also keep intruders out, as they do not have the accumulated knowledge about people and their past conduct which is the foundation of gossip as a noble art.

Basically the same message is restated in network terms in a brief paper by Epstein (1969), in the Manchester genre of case studies. Tapping a rather dense network including mostly white-collar workers in Ndola, another of the Copperbelt towns, he got the story of the affair of Charles and Monica from several sources. Both were members of a rather sophisticated and prestigious circle; Monica's husband Kaswende was not. Epstein was impressed with the fact that the news about the affair, and Kaswende's violent reaction to it, had spread so effectively through the network, and also with the fact that there was hardly any negative comment on the adultery involved. Most commentators seemed rather to come out on Monica's and Charles's side, taking the view that Monica was too attractive a girl for Kaswende anyway. In conclusion, Epstein suggests that the close-knit network of sophisticates used this piece of gossip to define their own norms and their separation from the mass of unskilled, uneducated urbanites. If the new urban centers of Africa have not yet formed classes acting corporately as stable groups, the flow of gossip through dense networks at least allows their members to begin defining a separate identity. (This, then, was one instance where the emergent class structure became a focus of attention in a Copperbelt study.)

Epstein still makes relatively little use of network concepts in his interpretation. He notes that it would have been interesting to trace the gossip out of the dense cluster at the center (i.e., the "effective network") toward the periphery, to see how it changes character and eventually peters out, but his data did not suffice for this. Nor does he discuss explicitly the relationship between the intensity of gossip and the form of the network. Such questions were of some concern as I myself explored the possibilities of a network analysis of gossip on the basis of field experiences in a black neighborhood in Washington, D.C. (Hannerz 1967). The question whether gossip serves to maintain cohesion was in this instance seen as a question of social control—can people, by maintaining a steady flow of information about third persons, ensure their conformity to norms?

In this case, the answer was partly negative. For one thing, in the troubled conditions of the ghetto, far from everybody was ready to indulge in gossip. One might rather not become too involved with others, particularly as these might resent intrusions into their personal lives. This, of course, has little to do with network form. Furthermore, however, such attempts at norm enforcement as might follow from gossip could fail if the network sector involved could not be sure of the allegiance of its members. The ghetto community could be seen as one interconnected network of varying density. In an existence ridden with problems, people would live according to rather variable working (as opposed to ideal) norms, and individuals would tend to be surrounded mostly by people of similar normative alignments. Yet many personal networks would evince some internal diversity in this respect, and for other individuals again the possibility existed of reconstructing the network to find support for other norms. In this situation, gossip could sometimes lead to norm enforcement; but it could also be a catalyst for cutting off or attenuating relationships to people insisting on norms to which it had become undesirable, inconvenient, or simply impossible to conform.

But gossip in the black ghetto, I also noted, was not always of the normative (and mostly invidious) kind on which Gluckman had based his argument. Much of what passed along the ghetto grapevine was simply in the character of news, and again this could be seen against the background of network form. Many ghetto dwellers, particularly young adults, accumulate fairly large networks. These are not necessarily very dense; and this would tend to limit gossip, as people are probably more likely to gossip about mutual acquaintances. What is more important here, however, is that there is often only a low frequency of interaction in links even within fairly dense network sectors. In other words, many relationships may be seen as latent. Thus long periods may pass without two acquaintances (or even "friends") running into each other. But through gossip, they may keep informed about each other at least a little more regularly, learning perhaps about changes of jobs, addresses, marital status, or life style in general. Normative judgments, which may or may not be a part of such information, may then not be very important. What is significant is that people get a map of their changing social environment which helps them to steer their course. Here, then, gossip is primarily about people, only secondarily or not at all about norms.

At this point, my interpretation came closer to the second major strand in gossip analyses, that first set forth in more general terms by Robert Paine (1967). Paine describes his view as an alternative to Gluckman's, although it may be more precise to view the perspectives as complementary.[11] This is the transactionalist view of gossip, emphasizing how individuals manipulate gossip to forward their own interests. Information management becomes the key concept. The participant in gossip wants to get information; he may also want to make the information he contributes flow in particular directions, and in a particular form. If in his first article on this theme Paine mentions networks only in passing, a later paper (1970) draws more directly on the idea, while also placing gossip in a wider context of analysis of informal communication. With this paper we return to Norwegian coast society; yet this time not to Barnes's Bremnes, but to the more northerly village of Nordbotn. It is a small community, with a generally dense network, where people generally have a good view of one another's relationships. In this situation, it is particularly the village entrepreneurs who have an interest in manipulating information, although they are not necessarily equally skilled at the game. Paine discusses the advantages and disadvantages of direct and chain messages in terms of certainty and speed (which may remind us of Mayer's distinction between "hard" and "soft" election campaigns), the occasional advantages of "unsigned" messages (rumor) over "signed" (gossip), and the difficulties in a small community of getting an "unsigned" message underway and keeping its origin unknown. The high network awareness, naturally, often makes it possible to figure out from where a piece of information started its course. Yet if there are problems involved in having information passed on, there may also be difficulties if one tries not to have it transmitted further. If one confides in someone else, others may have noticed enough of the interaction to wonder what is going on. And if one confides in more than one, it is difficult in a dense network to know where to trace a breach of confidence. Such are the problems of information management.

MAU-MAUING and FLAK CATCHING

Whether availing itself of network analysis or not, gossip has become a quite respectable research topic among anthropologists in recent times. Our next example of the possible uses of network thinking, on the other hand, does not draw on anthropological work but on an essay by Tom Wolfe, leading exponent of the New Journalism. By being coupled in book form with the celebrated "Radical Chic," the essay we are interested in here, "Mau-Mauing the Flak Catchers," has perhaps become somewhat

neglected. As a study in social organization, however, it is quite enlightening, whether or not it is overdrawn as ethnography.

This is a satire of the late 1960s poverty program in San Francisco. The
bureaucracy was expected to support community organization, but did not
know the community (and, one may suspect, had not given much thought
to in what sense there was one). It was supposed to work with the
grassroots leadership, but did not know where to find it. So, in Wolfe's interpretation, there was a wide open field for entrepreneurship:

> Going downtown to mau-mau the bureaucrats got to be the routine practice in
> San Francisco. The poverty program *encouraged* you to go in for mau-mauing.
> They wouldn't have known what to do without it. The bureaucrats at City
> Hall and in the Office of Economic Opportunity talked "ghetto" all the time,
> but they didn't know any more about what was going on in the Western Addi-
> tion, Hunters Point, Potrero Hill, the Mission, Chinatown, or south of Mar-
> ket Street than they did about Zanzibar. They didn't know where to look.
> They didn't even know who to ask. So what could they do? Well . . . they
> used the Ethnic Catering Service . . . right . . . They sat back and waited
> for you to come rolling in with your certified angry militants, your guaranteed
> frustrated ghetto youth, looking like a bunch of wild men. Then you had your
> test confrontation. If you were outrageous enough, if you could shake up the
> bureaucrats so bad that their eyes froze into iceballs and their mouths twisted
> up into smiles of sheer physical panic, into shit-eating grins, so to speak—then
> they knew you were the real goods. They knew you were the right studs to
> give the poverty grants and community organizing jobs to. Otherwise they
> wouldn't know. (Wolfe 1970:97–98)

Mau-mauing, then, is an art of network manipulation. When people in
one cluster of relationships wish to contact people in another cluster but do
not have established and time-tested links across the gap, they will honor
the demands of a broker. (A broker, of course, is a person with a particular
kind of network range, including at least two quite different kinds of people in his network and more or less monopolizing contacts between them—
direct contacts which cut him out are negligible or non-existent.) But mau-
mauing is a particular kind of brokerage, for it is really only brokerage
claimed. In the absence of any means of checking the effectiveness of
channels, at least over the short term, the party seeking contact is suscep-
tible to such claims.

So far Wolfe's reading of the mau-mauing part of the equation, restated
in more general network terms (which are certainly duller, but probably
more useful for purposes of analysis and comparison). There is some network manipulation going on from the bureaucratic side as well, however,

for the decision-making bureaucrats do not want to make themselves too accessible to mau-mauing. Hence enter the flak catcher. The job of the flak catcher in the bureaucracy is to receive people making demands, suffer hostility and humiliation, and not make commitments—to make it clear to the visitors, on the contrary, that he is in no position to commit his superiors or the bureaucracy as a whole to any line of action. In other words, to decrease reachability.

The flak catcher, too, is a kind of broker, since he stands at the nexus between the public and the real holders of power and channels contacts between them. There is probably a tendency, however, to regard a broker as someone who *facilitates* contacts among persons, groups, or institutions who are otherwise not within easy reach of one another. The flak catcher, if we may phrase it harshly, is an antibroker; his purpose in life is to *limit* contacts. Perhaps the metaphor of "gatekeeper" has the more appropriate connotations, although it is not too exact either.

We have encountered something like this before, in Adrian Mayer's analysis of the difference between patronage and brokerage. Since a patron dispenses his own limited resources while the broker deals in somewhat uncertain promises, the latter can in a way be more generous in his transactions than the former. Consequently, Mayer notes, a patron may find it useful to insert a broker as a buffer between himself and his clients, which would allow for a network of wider range and some insulation from the repercussions of failed transactions.

The flak catcher, who can take a lot of beating without swinging the gate open, and the kindly broker who is always ready to establish contacts at such a low tariff that practically anybody can afford it, are of course only two poles of a continuum (or perhaps some more complex heuristic device). To arrive at a more complete understanding of how separation is overcome in a network, or achieved where it is not automatically produced in social processes, one might construct a more elaborate array of broker forms. Broker loyalties, ability to deliver, and the objectives of the actual holder of resources in releasing them, could be some of the variables included in such conceptualization.

The structure of mau-mauing and flak catching, meanwhile, provides an example of how a network interpretation can involve both institutional and non-institutional sectors—the latter primarily serving as the background for mau-mauing, the former being the habitat of the flak catcher. It could be taken to show, too, the interplay between normative control and personal information within relationships as the smoothest role enactment of the flak catcher may entail a subtle display of conflict between personal sympathies and institutional requirements.

REACHABILITY, SMALL WORLDS, and NETWORK AWARENESS

There are instances where one can present oneself as a stranger to a chosen other and demand far-reaching attention. This, for example, is the approach of the mau-mau specialist, although its success may be modified through the insertion of a flak catcher. But often, this is not quite possible. Physical accessibility, as we noted in passing in chapter 3, does not in itself guarantee social accessibility. Information may simply be lacking about where to find the kind of person one is looking for. Or one needs to know whether the other person is trustworthy or otherwise a suitable partner before one becomes involved. Or (as a special case of the latter situation) one wants to make sure through a link to someone else that the other person will be willing to disregard public norms in some way before one enters into direct contact.

The contemporary western city has a number of institutions which specialize in managing the information gap but which otherwise hardly form significant relationships to those whom they put in touch—institutions like small-print advertising, real estate agents, or employment agencies. Under other circumstances, however, contact-making may be more personalized, and more diffused throughout society. Very generally there may be no universalistic norm guaranteeing a hearing to a stranger—or if there is in principle, it may be contravened in practice. So it becomes necessary to work through connections; to be passed along, together with personal recommendations, between people who already know each other, until one reaches one's destination. In certain societies, there is widespread agreement that little can be accomplished except through such particularistic linkages. A graphic Latin American expression is that you need a *palanca,* a lever, to move somebody. In other societies the practice may exist without gaining as much overt recognition.

Boissevain (1974:150–52) has described one instance of such network navigation from his research in Sicily. A student from Syracuse, Salvatore, needed to obtain permission from a professor at the University of Palermo to present a thesis although the registration period had already long passed.

He therefore went from Syracuse to Leone, a town where he had previously worked and where he had useful contacts—one of them was the
branch secretary of the dominant political party. This man passed Salvatore on to his cousin, who was the personal secretary of an official in
Palermo. The cousin in turn introduced him to a brother who had friends
at the university, and the brother turned out to know the professor's assistant. The assistant then put him in touch with the professor. As it turned
out, the professor was a candidate for election in a district including
Leone, which he had taken to be Salvatore's home town. He thus took a
generous view of the latter's thesis trouble, expecting to have acquired a
valuable political supporter in return. Thus Salvatore could return to Syracuse, and later submitted the thesis to fulfil requirements for a degree.
The professor, on the other hand, failed in his election bid.

A similar story of networking for a degree is told by Satish Saberwal
(1972:178–79) from a Punjab industrial town. Seth, a middle-rank bank
official, had a son who was to sit for his B. Sc. examinations. The examiners were all from colleges elsewhere. When Seth had found out who
and where they were, he started making contacts with them. One was
reached through a kinsman of Seth's who was an accountant in a bank
near the examiner's university; another through a relative who was a
neighbor of Seth's nephew; a third by way of salesman who traveled the
college circuit to take up orders; and so on. Then just before the examina-
tion was to take place, all the examiners were exchanged. Indefatigably
Seth went back to work and managed to contact the entire new set of examiners as well. It is not quite clear what part these contacts finally
played. In any case, Seth's son passed his exam.

We may have ethical questions about the use of such contacts; for our
particular purposes here, however, practical questions are more important.
Salvatore went through four intermediaries to reach the professor. Seth's
chains were shorter, but there were a greater number of them. Their efforts may also remind us of Nancy Howell Lee's (1969) study of American
women searching for abortions (at the time, usually illegal). These women
each made between one and nine starts in asking others to help locate an
acceptable abortionist. The length of the successful chain varied between
one link—when the women made direct contact with an abortionist—and
seven links. How, in cases like these, does one decide in which direction to
strike out in order to reach a target person, personally known or unknown?
How likely is it that the individual involved can at all be reached this way?

Such questions relate to a series of intriguing experiments carried out by the social psychologist Stanley Milgram and his associates (e.g., Milgram 1969; Travers and Milgram 1969). Their topic is the "small world problem," named after the widely shared experience of people who meet as strangers to each other but find out that they have unexpected mutual acquaintances. Milgram went beyond this particular linkage of only one intermediary, to ask how many links it would take to connect any two randomly chosen individuals. Of course, it is generally recognized that whether large or small, the world is only one; if one traced chains long enough, every individual could be found to link up with every other individual. But just how long is long enough, within the framework of, for example, American society?

One could look at this in terms of probability, on the basis of some calculated standard-size network of first-order links and a geometrically increasing coverage with each additional order of links included. This would hardly be a very close approximation of reality, however, as social, geographical, and other factors will create clusters of relationships which are far from randomized. Milgram instead studied the matter empirically. He selected target persons in the Boston area (where he was himself located) and then asked starting persons elsewhere in the country to try to establish contact with one specific target person, using only a chain of persons in which each two individuals directly linked would be personally known to each other. The starting persons were given the name and address of the target person and some limited information about him, and were instructed to pass along—personally or by mail—a document either directly to the target person if they themselves knew him, or failing that, to an acquaintance more likely to know him, with instructions for each intermediary to follow the same procedure until the target was reached. The document included a roster of people who had already passed it on (each participant added his own name), to prevent loops taking it back to earlier participants. Each participant also informed the researcher that the chain had reached him, so that Milgram could follow the progress (or, alternatively, the breakdown) of each chain.

This was indeed a study in chain letters, although the chains had a direction and did not snowball as ordinary chain letters are supposed to do. The first set of chains were started from Kansas, with the wife of a divinity student in Cambridge, Massachusetts, as a target person. Within a few days the first chain reached her. The starting person, a wheat farmer, had sent the document to a minister in his home town, who had sent it to another minister teaching in Cambridge, who gave it to the target person—a total of three links, or two intermediaries. This was certainly an unusually short chain, but the median number of intermediaries in completed chains was only 5.5, and chains mostly varied between three and ten intermediaries. Similar results were reached in a second study, with starting persons in Nebraska and a Boston stockbroker as a target person. It should be noted that a considerable number of chains were not completed, probably because recipients of the document did not care to cooperate.

By being able to trace each link in the chains, Milgram could make a number of observations about their patterning. He found that there was a strong tendency for men to use links to other men, women links to other women. About five-sixths of the links in the chains starting out from Kansas were between friends and acquaintances, only one-sixth between kinsmen. Possibly, cross-cultural experiments of this type could reveal variations on points such as these. Another interesting result in the study with the stockbroker as a target person was that out of sixty-two chains reaching him, sixteen had a clothing merchant in his small home town outside Boston as last intermediary. Obviously this merchant had a rather wide-range network. This study actually had three groups of starting persons: one randomly chosen group of people in Nebraska, one group of Nebraska stockholders who might have particular channels for reaching a stockbroker, and one group of randomly chosen Bostonians. The last group reached the target person with a mean number of 4.4 intermediaries, the Nebraska random group had a mean number of 5.7, and the Nebraska stockholders 5.4. The difference between the two groups of Nebraskans was not statistically significant. Evidently geographical distance does not seem to lengthen chains by very much—at the beginning of the chain, there was often a tendency to close such gaps quickly by one or two long-distance links.

Whatever interesting questions one may raise about internal patterns and variations, yet perhaps the most noteworthy finding is that the chains are so often quite short. It could be objected that these are the successful chains; the uncompleted chains would probably have turned out longer. Travers and Milgram cite a formula by which the dropout problem can be taken into account, however, and it indicates that the median length of chains if all had been completed would increase from about five to seven only. And what should also be noted is that really successful chains theoretically could be shorter, for no participant, especially in the early linkages, is likely to know what is really the shortest route between himself and the target person. He can only guess on the basis of the limited information made available about the latter. If all shortcuts were really found, perhaps the chains would again be down by a couple of links. But again, one must not underestimate the potential number of people involved in these impressively short chains. In each link, several hundred people may be scanned as possible next contacts. As Milgram puts it, the distance between the starting person and the target should be seen not only as five or six persons, but as five or six small worlds.

What is the significance of this? Perhaps hardly any. It could all be one of those things with no real existence outside the playroom of scholars. If we may stand W. I. Thomas on his head with his well-known theorem: if people fail to define a situation as real, it has no real consequences. (This would certainly not always be true.) If there are people, on the other hand, who have something like this degree of network awareness, who try to look several links down the chains in their networks and make use of what they see, their strategies and accomplishments could be very interesting.

NETWORKS of POWER

As a last example of a field of study where network ideas should be useful, it seems reasonable to mention that of power structures—this despite the fact that very little in the way of network analysis in any strict sense seems really to have been carried out on topics of this kind. A book like Floyd Hunter's classic *Community Power Structure* (1953) lends itself in some respects to network rethinking, however, as do, for example, Domhoff's (1970, 1974) more recent attempts at conceptualizing the cohesiveness of an American national ruling class. Yet Domhoff is primarily concerned with the institutions of the class, rather than the personal linkages among its members.

For a long time, the overshadowing debate on power structures in America has been between the pluralists, who see power as organized in a relatively fragmented and diffuse way with no single group dominant in influence and decision-making, and the elitists (a rather poorly chosen term, since most of them dislike what they find), who see a single, tightly knit "power elite" or "ruling class" of slightly varying definition.[12] It seems hardly advisable to try to throw light into the nooks and crannies of this debate here. One could note, however, that the two alternatives can be partly formulated in network terms. The elite view seems to entail a small network of high density—everybody knows everyone else—and probably multiplex relationships, built up as members have gone to the same schools, served on the same boards, joined the same clubs, and spent their holidays in the same resorts. One may assume that these relationships are also quite durable. In the pluralist perspective there is necessarily a wider network, as more people are sometime participants in power processes. Overall density is lower, as people with different interests may be involved in different situations, thus not getting in touch. In other words, there may be a more partial overlap of personnel between situations. Since people are of quite varying background, relationships are more likely to be single-stranded. This is not to deny, of course, that within this wider network there may be clusters of greater density, with or without more multiplex links.

The conflict between these perspectives is in some ways more apparent than real, as they may apply to different situations. To the extent that the subject is local community power structures, we have hinted before, the question is perhaps more realistically which are monolithic, which are pluralistic, and what are the reasons for such differences between communities. On the national level—who rules America?—there is a more clear-cut choice between the perspectives, although possibly there can be a resolution in a more complex theory. One of the difficulties in arriving at well-grounded conclusions, however, is obviously that of finding out something about the real maneuvers of power. It is one thing to know that persons went to the same schools, belong to the same clubs, or even actually know one another—it is a different thing to know what really passes in their interactions. Social scientists are frequently not very successful in getting close to the action in this way. In recent years, the most vivid pictures of power networks have more often come from investigative journalism. The coalitions of candidates, financiers, lawyers, undercover operators, and others are likely to appeal to the imagination of a network analyst, who could consider, for example, the ways in which links are manipulated so that they cannot be traced from the outside, or so that relatively credible claims of ignorance can be made about what goes on a link or two away in the network.

Moving to the ethnography of power in another region, we find a statement in more explicit network terms in an interpretation of Mediterranean social structure by Schneider, Schneider, and Hansen (1972). In the opinion of these authors, "noncorporate groups" will appear as important wielders of power where its distribution has not been routinized and regulated by more stable corporate institutions. In American society, this may be at the upper levels of the system—and, according to a brief footnote, at its bottom, presumably within the real (although not necessarily formal) limits imposed from above. At the middle levels, on the other hand, power is judged to be more fully structured, not least through bureaucracies.

In the European Mediterranean area, the Schneiders and Hansen note, there are regions where national power structures have not penetrated effectively—largely for historical reasons. In these regions, the entire societies remain unusually open to the strategic use of noncorporate groups, such as more or less temporary cliques and coalitions, for purposes of business, politics, or both. Within the coalition, every participant remains in control of his own resources and may withdraw at any time, just as easily as a new member may be added. This contributes to adaptability, but also to instability. To make relationships a little more solid, participants may draw on such traditional idioms as feasting and fictive kinship. Nonetheless, they are always open to new opportunities, and eagerly seeking information about them. The image one gets is of a network with clusters tightening in one moment only to be torn apart in the next, with the elements reordering themselves into new patterns.

In another article, Hansen (1974) has analyzed the bar life in a Spanish—more precisely, Catalan—town as a part of such network processes. In the past, their typical settings were the halls of various voluntary associations, but during the Franco era these were politically suspect, as havens of either radicalism or Catalan nationalism, and the more neutral bars then took their place. Here there is intense, open sociability. People are incessantly coming and going, all looking for other people. The bartender is regarded as a fount of information for the whereabouts of his customers. When one encounters whomever one has been looking for, there will be drinks and conversation—figures are named, people and activities are discussed, and plans made and remade. Far from all the verbal exchanges are about business, but such topics are part of a more general flow of news and views, about movies, the weather, or whatever else may be on one's mind.

The bar thus serves as a catalyst of network formation and transformation. It allows people to scan continuously what new linkages could be made or what old contacts could be renewed or intensified, in order to make new resources accessible. A more general lesson one might draw is that there are some institutions whose major function seems to be to facilitate individual network management. Such institutions should perhaps be sought wherever the making and maintenance of desirable linkages is problematic. Clearly institutions serving other purposes are often used for networking as well—in chapter 2 we noted the *arrivée* lady on Chicago's Gold Coast who donated to a society woman's pet charity in order to be allowed entry into the best circles. But the American upper class also has its own institutions which seem primarily to serve network needs. Retreats like the Bohemian Grove north of San Francisco, for example, the subject of one of William Domhoff's studies, through its organized sociability provides its members with a pool of potential network partners to whom direct access may be more or less assured. If it is one characteristic of power elite status that one hardly ever has to use a broker or other indirect linkages to contact someone in power, such institutions do their part to maximize density and reachability within the elite.

Both the elitist and the pluralist view of power structures tend to assume a state of "business as usual." Yet in the last decade or so, this has hardly been a very adequate description of political life in the western world, or at least not of some of its most noticeable manifestations. There has been a politics of movements—anti-war, ecology, black power, women's liberation—which has activated people in categories whose part in politics has otherwise often been passive. There is special reason to mention this current of mobilization here because one anthropological study, by Gerlach and Hine (Gerlach 1970, Gerlach and Hine 1970a, 1970b), has attempted to interpret it partly in network terms. It is hardly a matter of a particularly elaborate network analysis, and it does not link up very explicitly with anthropological network studies in general. When one is conversant with the lines of thought in these, however, it is not difficult to identify parallels in this interpretation of movements.

Gerlach and Hine emphasize the decentralized, unstable nature of the new movements. They tend to consist of relatively small, interconnected but fairly autonomous clusters—"cells" or whatever one may choose to call them. People observing them from the outside may form a negative impression of the effectiveness of this pattern of organization, which sometimes also seems torn by internal discord. Gerlach and Hine make the point (perhaps rather too one-sidedly) that on the contrary, it may be unusually well adapted for its purpose. One must not forget that these are *movements*—they are supposed to grow, to catch the allegiance of more and more people, of highly diverse backgrounds. Like the Indian political campaign described by Adrian Mayer, they use every conceivable variety of pre-existing relationship to recruit new supporters. The outcome, if these efforts meet with some success, is a crowd of people who may have little in common among themselves, who might fit poorly together in a more tightly coordinated organization, and who approach their respective environments in different ways—although perhaps each successfully in its own way. The best use such a crowd can make of itself, then, in terms of its sole shared purpose, could be to let people link up among themselves as they please, and let the resulting clusters work in unity for as long as it lasts—and then allow further segmentation on the basis of whatever new alignments emerge with time. The image is again like that of the Mediterranean power coalitions, of clusters forming, bursting, and reforming. The difference is that this time, they do so within the framework of shared, continuous commitments (which often allow some useful interlinkages to go on existing), and within a movement network undergoing overall growth.

The CITY: NETWORK of NETWORKS

From gossip and bureaucratic encounters by way of the search for an abortionist to power elites and protest movements—network thinking seems to have varied uses. Its potential for showing how, in a large population, people may combine and recombine in manifold ways for different purposes and with different consequences may well be of particular advantage in urban anthropology. Since it is a rather recent development we see little of this kind of thinking in the classic statements of the nature of urban life, but it hardly appears far removed from the relational thinking, for example, of Simmel and Wirth. When the latter proposes that urbanites are "dependent upon more people for the satisfactions of their life-needs than are rural people," one may read this as saying that multiplex relationships have dissolved into networks of single-purpose links.

Recognizing that network analysis may have some special possibilities in urban anthropology, however, we should perhaps be careful not to jump to any conclusions about the form of urban networks. It may be remembered that Barnes, in his Bremnes study, suggested that the networks of modern society would have "larger mesh"—in up-dated terminology, lower density. Frankenberg (1966:290) has also included this notion in one of the latest versions of a rural-urban continuum. There may be something to this, and in one sense there definitely is, but we had better be conscious of the assumptions. Let us give them a preliminary viewing.

Barnes and Frankenberg, like most network analysts, tend to see as links only the relatively enduring relationships between individuals who "know" each other. Thus they disregard near non-relationships such as traffic relationships, and probably also the most narrowly defined, short-term relationships to be found, for instance, in the domain of provisioning. And so, if we think of the city as a "total network," they are only saying in a new vocabulary what among others Max Weber also said: the urban population is too large for everybody to know everybody else.

Yet there may be some danger of moving on from this to a misunderstanding. We can hardly take anything for granted concerning the density, or any other characteristic, of any smaller network that we abstract from this urban totality. If, say, each urbanite would draw the people in his personal network at random, one by one, from the entire population of the city, then few of them might be likely to be in touch with one another, and a sparse network would result. But networks are not really put together this way. There could be some clusters in the total urban network where practically everybody is in direct contact with everybody else. The urban village we have repeatedly referred to is one example; the Red Xhosa appear also to approximate the pattern, although their dense networks take in their rural home communities as well. Other city people may have some dense but largely separate clusters in their networks, as well as certain relationships which appear to stand alone. We will come back to such variations in our final chapter. At this point, it may be the very fact of diversity that must above all be understood. Although one may think of the city as a total network (forgetting for the moment about its outside links), it may often be more practical to think of it, in the term suggested by Craven and Wellman (1974:80), as a network of networks. One of these, or a few of them, can make up an urban way of life. Together, they constitute the city as a social order.

CHAPTER SIX

The City as Theater: Tales of Goffman

The work of one individual holds the center of stage in this chapter. Before drawing our final conclusions in the next chapter, we also come back here to a Chicagoan influence on urban anthropology. Like his predecessors in the old Chicago School, Erving Goffman has usually been identified as a sociologist, and during most of his career his academic affiliation has been with sociology. But intellectually, this may make no great difference. His style of work might equally well be described as that of an ethnographer-anthropologist (however idiosyncratic), and he has had fairly continuous links with the discipline of anthropology.[1] Above all, however, Goffman has been his own man.

So special has been his position, since his work began appearing in the 1950s, that as one reviewer has pointed out, "we nowadays tend to think of a particular sociological space as Goffman territory" (Dawe 1973:246). New adjectives have been coined to label perspectives toward social life resembling his: Goffmanian, Goffmanic, Goffmanesque. A host of interpretive articles, and at least one book (in Danish), have been devoted to the analysis of his achievements, as well as his shortcomings.[2] As commentators search for someone to compare Goffman to, they are as likely to reach into the world of *belles lettres,* for Kafka or Proust, as to mention a name from the social sciences.[3] And his academic peers seem to take a great deal more interest in his personal views and manners than they have done in those of, say, Talcott Parsons.[4]

Erving Goffman has been particularly concerned with the analysis of face-to-face interaction and with public behavior—which means, by implication at least, that he also illuminates notions of privacy. Although in his published works he has hardly gone to great lengths in trying to identify explicitly his particular location on a map of social theory, one may sense several linkages to the classics which may at least in part be related to his own career. Born in Canada, he did graduate work at, and received a doctorate from, the University of Chicago; he spent a period at the University of Edinburgh and another at the National Institute of Mental Health, Bethesda, Maryland, both in connection with field work; and he has since then been at the University of California, Berkeley, and the University of Pennsylvania. The Chicago legacy included, since the days of Robert Park and his pupils, a commitment to naturalistic observation, to close attention to "ordinary persons doing ordinary things." On a more abstract level, there was symbolic interactionism with its concern with conceptions of self and the construction of meaning in social life, a native American strand of social thought which, under that or other names, had had a Chicago base since the times of George Herbert Mead. But the Chicago faculty which Goffman met also included Lloyd Warner, half sociologist, half anthropologist, who had been influenced not least during his research in aboriginal Australian society by the sociology of Durkheim.[5] One can perhaps trace to Warner's original mediation some Durkheimian overtones in Goffman's view of society, not least his concern with something like sacredness in relations between human beings. Similar understandings were of course strong in the British social anthropology to which Goffman was exposed in Edinburgh and for which he seems to have had a continued respect.[6] Finally, while direct channels of influence are not so obvious, one can scarcely fail to sense the affinity between Goffman's work and that of Simmel, student of intimacy, sociability, discretion, secrecy, and the stranger.[7]

The DRAMATURGICAL PERSPECTIVE

Goffman has three times conducted field work in what one may see as a relatively normal anthropological manner, for a particular period in some particular place: in a small farming community in the Shetland Islands, in a mental hospital in Washington, D.C. (and in connection with this also in the clinical center laboratory wards of the National Institute of Mental Health), and in the gambling casinos of Las Vegas. It might seem that only the last of these qualifies as urban anthropology, and it has so far been least visible in his published work. The island subsistence farmers are perhaps about as far from city life as one gets in contemporary Europe, and the study of St. Elizabeth's Hospital led to the concept of the "total institution," a closed world with characteristics almost diametrically opposed to what one may see as the peculiar possibilities of urban life. But the relevance of even these two studies to an understanding of city living must not be denied on such superficial grounds, and in another way, Goffman seems to be forever doing field work, observing human beings anywhere he finds them, and filing his facts and interpretations for future use. He also reads very widely, not always from shelves frequently visited by his fellow academics.

Perhaps partly for such reasons, most of his writings deal with no social setting in particular, and therefore run the risk of being taken to refer to social life in general. The somewhat loose connection to distinct and enduring social structures can be sensed from the introduction to a collection of his essays, where he summarizes his conception of the study of face-to-face interaction:

> . . . the analytical boundaries of the field remain unclear. Somehow, but only somehow, a brief time span is involved, a limited extension in space, and a restriction to those events that must go on to completion once they have begun. There is a close meshing with the ritual properties of persons and with the egocentric forms of territoriality.
>
> The subject matter, however, can be identified. It is that class of events which occurs during co-presence and by virtue of co-presence. The ultimate behavioral materials are the glances, gestures, positionings, and verbal statements that people continuously feed into the situation, whether intended or not. These are the external signs of orientation and involvement—states of mind and body not ordinarily examined with respect to their social organization. (Goffman 1967:1)

Goffman is thus almost always *very* microsociological, concerned with occasions and what happens between individuals in them.[8] (Characteristically, in his later writings he goes beyond the ethnographic heritage to acknowledge animal ethology as a source of inspiration for the detailed observation of human communicative conduct.) As the little interaction sequences in which he is interested seem virtually omnipresent, however, the tales of Goffman take his readers on freely roaming, yet never aimless adventures in the perception of society. And from these adventures some perhaps never really return.

What is understood to be the typical Goffman point of view is probably still best exemplified by his first book, *The Presentation of Self in Everyday Life* (1959). He starts out here from that time-worn metaphor of society as a stage; but he carries it forward systematically into a dramaturgic perspective toward social life. The book becomes a treatise of the way the individual guides and controls the ideas which others form of him. "Impression management" is the key term for this activity.

As people enter into one another's presence, they may already have some more or less well-founded ideas of who the other is and what he is like. For others, they may have to depend on whatever communication flows in the situation which they are in. Rather commonsensically, one may divide such information as an individual makes available about himself into that which is intentional and that which is unintentional—in Goffman's terms, the expression which he "gives" and the expression which he "gives off." But the distinction is too simple, for a person may intentionally offer information in a manner so as to make it seem unintentional. The advantage of doing things this way results from the fact that people often have greater confidence in information which is apparently not fully controlled by the other. For impression management, it is therefore often a more strategic resource. Goffman's interest is in detailing the ways in which people, whether they are fully aware of it or not, strive to present a picture of themselves which is to their advantage and at the same time credible to others, who presumably feel that they have been able to form their own opinion of the evidence.

The total activities of an individual during a period of continuous presence before some set of others and with some kind of effect on them are described as a "performance," and the standard expressive equipment which he uses in it constitutes his "front." The latter includes both "setting" and "personal front." The setting is more or less immovable. By appearing against the background, for example, of a particular roomful of furniture, the individual can make indications about his own qualities. Personal photographs on a wall can tell stories about pedigree or networks, a bookshelf about intellectual standing. But the most useful setting is not always at home. Goffman uses the example of the British club, a rent-a-setting arrangement by which a person can get a share in stage props which he would usually not have been able to afford on an exclusively individual basis.

The personal front, on the other hand, one can easily take along—sometimes indeed has to take along wherever one goes. It includes relatively permanent features such as sex, size, and looks, as well as more ephemeral vehicles of meaning like clothing and adornments, gestures, or facial expression. Both the personal front and the setting can, within limits, be manipulated for the purposes of impression management. The living room which seems to show off a rich family heritage may have been assembled from auctions and antique shops. One may try to bring a performance to the setting where one can appear to one's greatest advantage, and one may carefully select particular items of personal front for the occasion. There are things, of course, which one might prefer not to present to observers, and yet some of these one may be able to do nothing about, for instance defects of personal appearance. Goffman has devoted another book, *Stigma* (1963a), particularly to the handling of undesirable aspects of the self. The best an individual may be able to do in many situations is to play them down, to undercommunicate them. Other front items he may try to dramatize, to make sure that they are noticed even where there is a clutter of details competing for the observer's attention. The waiter (this example Goffman gets from Sartre) not only brings the food to your table, but while doing so, may turn his every movement into a gesture displaying his skill and conscientiousness. The baseball umpire does not only make sure that the game is played according to the rules, but, by never allowing himself as much as a split second of overt hesitation as to how or when the rules should be enforced, he also makes sure that all others experience him as fully in control.

The waiter's behavior may have changed, however, in the very moment he pushes open the swinging door from the kitchen and enters your field of vision. Immediately before, he may have been comfortably sloppy, and a bit uncertain about what should go on your plate. The physical habitat of human conduct, Goffman notes, tends to be divided into front and back regions, or frontstage and backstage. In the front region, the actual performance is put on. In the back region, to which the audience does not have access, the performer can relax and involve himself in actions which could destroy his impression management or at least distract from it. There he may keep the props for his various acts, and there he may put the performance together, experiment with it, and make mistakes without embarrassment. What is backstage and frontstage depends, naturally, on what sort of presentation is involved. But in a person's home, it is a widespread practice to use the living room as a front region, kept in order so as not to convey discrepant information. Bedrooms and closets, on the other hand, are generally backstage. The telephone (or at least *a* telephone) is kept, if practicable, where one's calls need not become part of the show. The kitchen has certainly been a part of the back region, but this is changing. It can be used, certainly, for dramatic effect. By turning a conventionally defined backstage into a frontstage, one shows that one has nothing to hide.

In part, impression management is an individual matter. At times, however, teams of people cooperate in a performance aimed at others. The successful team performance involves partners who tend to have shared access to a wider range of information concerning one or another or a combination of their selves but agree on what should be suppressed or understated, or who in any case have an at least tacit agreement on what information should be actively presented. Often the information concealed may pertain to the relationships within the team itself. Goffman uses the example from a tourist hotel in the Shetland Islands, where the young female staff members were actually a notch above the couple owning the establishment in the terms of the local social structure, but collaborated in projecting a conventional employer-employee relationship in front of the guests. Another example is that kind of political council noted also by anthropologists (e.g., Bailey 1965) which, after struggling to reach a decision, insists on presenting the outcome to others as a product of smooth consensus.

There is obviously a general, although not necessarily a precise, relationship between the frontstage-backstage distinction and the performing team-audience distinction. The members of the team tend to share a back region where they can plan the performance, argue about it, and analyze the quality of the audience.

In cases like a married couple entertaining guests, an employer and his staff attending to customers, or politicians propagating a party line, it is not very difficult for the members of the audience to sense what people make up a team. It is rather the specifics over which they cooperate that may remain mysterious to non-members. In various ways, however, performer-audience relationships are not always what they seem to be. Goffman lists several examples of what he calls "discrepant roles." The informer pretends to the performers to be a member of their team. Thus he gets access to their backstage and acquires information which he takes back to the audience, thereby undermining the credibility of the act. The shill is secretly in league with the performers, although he presents himself as a member of the audience which he influences toward the sort of response that the performing team wants. There is also a kind of audience member who is exactly that, only more so; where other audience members

tend to be amateurs, he is a professional, at hand in an often inconspicuous way to check on the standard of the performance. Theater and res-
taurant critics could serve as examples. A go-between or mediator is on two
teams who are mutually each other's audiences. Through a balancing act
where he acquires backstage information from both, he may be able to
bring them closer together. A last example of a "discrepant role" is that of
a non-person. In some situations, a non-person may become an active performer on a team, such as a personal servant helping put on the act of the
house as he moves between its back and front regions. Yet at times, those
which count here, his presence seems simply to be defined away. He is
counted neither as part of the performing team nor as audience. The taxi
driver is one sort of person who is often in this position, a complete
stranger who may become the witness of backstage behavior of the most
clearcut character.

To see social life in terms of impressions "given" and "given off," performances, settings, personal fronts, backstage and frontstage, and teams and
audiences, is also to have a particular idea of what accounts for success.
Toward the end of *The Presentation of Self in Everyday Life,* Goffman lists
three main kinds of attributes and practices needed to ensure satisfactory
impression management. There must be dramaturgical loyalty; team
members must not betray the line set forth through joint action, either in
or between performances. Those who cannot be fully trusted with a secret,
like innocent young children on a family team, must be treated with caution. Nor can the team afford members who, during the performance,
decide to put on their own show to the detriment of the joint production.
Most importantly, members must be prevented from developing such sympathy for the audience that they give the act away.

Furthermore, there must be dramaturgical discipline. A performer must
know his part and stick to it. He must be able as far as possible to avoid
disruptions, but when they occur he must be able to find his way back to
the planned performance as quickly as possible. And he should not allow
himself to become so engrossed by the act which he is presenting that he
forgets that it is an act. Again, the waiter should not only *be* a good waiter.
He must also make sure that he is understood to be one.

Third, there is the need for dramaturgical circumspection. The performer must know when the show is on and when he can afford to relax.
He must exercise judgment as to what performance to present—will it
serve his purposes if successful, and does it stand a reasonable chance of

coming off? Does he have the right team, and the right audience? To be reasonably safe, it may be better not to make the presentation too elaborate and unmanageable.

SOCIOLOGIES OF SINCERITY and DECEPTION

Reactions to Goffman's first book, and to those which have followed, have been many and varied. There has been admiration for his style of writing and for his manner of assembling ethnography; the precision in his miniatures, for example, of how people manage to make inventive use of their material environment to serve a particular dramaturgical line of action. But commentators have complained that his skills are of a kind that cannot be taught, and someone who has not got it in him cannot learn them. The result, instead, one has already had opportunities to conclude, can be vulgar Goffmanism, a cruder and trivialized view of impression management in the social arena.[9] Goffman is also a concept maker, although he prefers old words used in new ways or in new intriguing combinations over clumsy neologisms.[10] Some of the analytical vocabulary thus issued in a steady flow has entered common usage among sociologists and anthropologists. Yet occasionally a new term seems to overlap considerably with another proposed a few publications earlier, and others may seem plain unnecessary. The methodology, too, seems to be peculiarly Goffman's own, and not altogether uncontroversial. Somewhat puzzledly, Glaser and Strauss (1967:136–39), in their analysis of how theory is generated in sociology, suggest that Goffman uses data largely to illustrate theory which seems to develop mostly by a kind of internal logic. Together with such scholarly apparatus as elaborate footnoting, they serve as kinds of persuasive devices supporting ideas which might live a life of their own anyway. They never turn out to be in such conflict with one another that further theoretical work is necessitated to resolve anomalies. Glaser and Strauss are uncertain whether even Goffman himself knows exactly how his methodology works.[11]

Above all, however, interest has focused on what sort of world view is expressed in Goffman's writings. To some they have appeared to be a celebration of sham and deception, a recipe for keeping secrets and spreading lies. A certain kind of reading of *The Presentation of Self in Everyday Life* can indeed lend support to such an understanding, and in a later study, *Strategic Interaction* (1969), Goffman becomes more unambiguously involved in the study of games of misinformation, drawing many of his examples from the world of espionage and counterespionage.

But things are hardly quite this simple. *The Presentation of Self* is studded with varied qualifications to such a view of dramaturgy in daily life. There are things in life, Goffman asserts in the preface, which are real and not well rehearsed. And even if the individual is aware of making a presentation, he may be doing so in all sincerity. That is, all presentations are not misrepresentations. Furthermore, for better or for worse, interactions are often not between an active performer and a passive and unsuspecting audience, but between individual performers or teams who keep a relationship going by overtly supporting each other's acts—even if covertly they are aware of, or at least suspect, their weaknesses. Such cooperation, one would assume, might be less readily forthcoming if the interactions were nothing but zero-sum games.

A very large part of Goffman's work takes off from that passage in *The Elementary Forms of the Religious Life* where Durkheim (1961:297 ff.) discusses the idea of the soul. The soul of a particular human being is *mana* individualized, a portion of the sacredness of the group. As such it is worthy of a certain awe, to be expressed in ritual attention. And if in a secularized world the concept of soul has become a concept of self, this particular understanding of sacredness has remained. People worship each other as little gods, in countless almost imperceptible ways; they become noticeable only in their absence, when the proper rituals are not performed and when the treatment given instead is seen as symbolic violence. The expression of acceptance of presented selves, at least within limits, thus becomes part of a liturgy. What is more, others are obliged to help the sacred being along in ritual, even when he threatens his own profanation.

This view of social life, stated in alternative ways, is already apparent in two of Goffman's early papers, "On Face-Work" (1955) and "The Nature of Deference and Demeanor" (1956a).[12] In the former, "face" is defined as the positive social value claimed by a person through the line others see him as taking during a contact. (The usage here, of course, is inspired by the Chinese idea of face.) To have face, or to be in face, or to maintain face, means that the claims are unproblematic in the interaction, but if one fails to uphold them credibly, or if the claims are disputed by others, one may be found to be in wrong face. Or one may be out of face, pursuing no consistent line whatsoever. Face-work, consequently, is what has to be performed to remain in face or get back into face. One can conduct a somewhat aggressive policy of face, claiming as much as one expects the other to be prepared to offer. But often interchanges are more relaxed. One intentionally demands little, confidently assuming that one's modesty will be well rewarded as the others offer more flattering estimates of one's worth. If one should be on one's way of claiming too much, the other may politely hint at the danger before one becomes irrevocably committed to an untenable face. And if unintentionally one should slip out of face, others may pretend not to notice until one has had time to rearrange one's line.[13]

"The Nature of Deference and Demeanor" draws on Goffman's field work at the National Institute of Mental Health. The idea of deference here is somewhat wider than that usually covered by that word; it includes the symbolic activity whereby appreciation is conveyed to a person, whether the relationship is inegalitarian or not.[14] Demeanor, complementarily, is the symbolic behavior by which an individual expresses to others in his presence what are his personal qualities. There are two kinds of rituals involved in deference, avoidance rituals and presentational rituals.[15] The former are a matter of not intruding into the private reserve of another individual, such as not touching him, not using disrespectful terms of address, not entering his room unless asked to. In presentational rituals, modes of behavior are prescribed rather than proscribed. People should pay attention to one another, express their recognition, greet each other, and comment in a complimentary manner on changes in appearance, status, or repute. At the mental hospital, Goffman notes, patients of limited social competence were often not very good at the avoidance rituals. On the other hand, as we shall see, they did not necessarily receive much deference of this kind either. Similarly, their demeanor was often not such as would have been acceptable in ordinary social life. They might scratch themselves violently, masturbate openly, or let their noses run unchecked.

The distinction between deference and demeanor is often only analytical. The same act which expresses a person's own qualities may at the same time signal his regard for another person. But the relationship is not simple. At times an act of deference which would in some way be appropriate could be unacceptable to a person as a part of his demeanor. There are ideas of self which can only become a part of an interaction through demeanor, and others which must be presented through deference. Last but not least, there is a tendency for demeanor to express the qualities of an individual as such, while deference behavior is often aimed at his social position.

Through his view of interaction as ritual work, Goffman has been one of the early contributors to the growing theoretical movement toward problematizing the production of social life and social reality; a movement fragmented under many names, ethnomethodology, existential or phenomenological sociologies, and so forth, some of them clearly more explicitly philosophically inclined and methodologically exacting than Goffman. Relations between people and definitions of what goes on in them are seen as fragile things, not given by nature. Yet in Goffman's version at least, this does not mean that people can do just anything imaginable in their social contacts:

> . . . while his social face can be his most personal possession and the center of his security and pleasure, it is only on loan to him from society; it will be withdrawn unless he conducts himself in a way that is worthy of it. Approved attributes and their relation to face make of every man his own jailer; this is a fundamental social constraint even though each man may like his cell. (Goffman 1955:215)

Two substantive sociologies seem in fact to result from the Goffman perspective, a sociology of sincerity and a sociology of deception. The sociology of sincerity entails a vocabulary of poise, tact, *savoir faire,* politeness, courtesy, pride, honor, and respect; and for situations which go wrong, of embarrassment and shame.[16] The sociology of deception is one of con games. But Goffman also indicates that the analytical dividing line between the two should not be too sharply drawn. Whether or not people conduct themselves with each other's best at heart, they relate to each other by putting together a social artifact, closing out a large proportion of the diverse and often contradictory facts of their lives and thereby creating a manageable order out of relative chaos.

In this activity every man may indeed be his own jailer. At the same time, however, people tend to imprison each other, for directly, or indirectly through the self claimed, one also signals something about what the other ought to be. In the sociology of deception, this is of major importance. Through conscious but inconspicuous manipulations with one's own line of action, one attempts to constrain the other to take on a complementary part; a response which might be only superficially voluntary when the alternative is to create "a scene." Impression management as delineated in *The Presentation of Self* can have such implications for the audience. There is another example in one of Goffman's earliest essays, "On Cooling the Mark Out" (1952). The archetype of the mark is one party in a confidence game, the victim who is drawn into a gambling venture which he is made to understand has been fixed in his favor by his friends, the operators. Having won once or twice, he invests more money in the game—and then loses. The operators abscond with his money. But an angry, disappointed loser could be dangerous to them, so one of them stays behind, to cool the mark out. The latter certainly will not get his money back. What the cooler will do, instead, is to try to make the mark accept the situation as it is. And because the mark has lost not only money but also face, the cooler may be successful if he can help him redefine the situation and his own self so that the ritual loss is minimized. The mark should be prevented, that is, from going to the police, or from going after the con men himself, or making a nuisance of himself in some other way.

Cooling marks out, Goffman notes, is a social process which goes on all the time, in the most varied contexts all over society. Wherever an individual has invested an important part of his self in some role or relation and then loses it, people who have been involved in bringing about his failure or passing that judgment on it which results in his disengagement may prefer to ease him out as smoothly as possible. So institutionalized mechanisms are created. An inefficient manager is "kicked upstairs," a priest helps the dying patient reconstruct his self into a soul for the life hereafter.

It is significant that a con game serves as Goffman's model for the managed disengagement ritual. His sociology of sincerity seems to have its natural home among an old bourgeoisie which can at least sometimes afford exquisite manners without ulterior motives; a world governed, as it appears, by etiquette manuals, as on Zorbaugh's Chicago Gold Coast. The sociology of deception, on the other hand, has tended to draw both Goffman and other students toward underworld ethnography. Not so much, probably, because it is not practiced elsewhere as well, but because it may be in the underworld that one finds some of the purest examples of strategies based on no other resources than an ability to manage impressions. It is there, in other words, that people often begin in business with two empty hands, and an engaging smile.[17]

Yet there is also the analogy between the con man and the priest to remind us that the difference between sociologies of sincerity and deception should not be exaggerated. The latter seems to invade the former; once one has tried to make the distinction between them, this may be what one could find objectionable about Goffman's perspective. Ritual sharp practices seem to be everywhere in interactions. It is possible to see this as a very cynical view of society, with *The Presentation of Self* as a do-it-your-self manual.[18] But it is an understanding which can be turned upside down. The cynic then becomes an outraged moralist warning us that the ritual means we have for caring for each other while still keeping the wheels of society turning also lend themselves to misuse; a misuse of the public funds of personal symbolism. The same book then becomes a guide to the unmasking of the villains.[19] Both interpretations have their advocates—and that is the way it may remain, for Goffman does not seem to care to make his readers too comfortable.

TOTAL INSTITUTIONS

In much of Goffman's work the exchange of messages about self and other appears to occur in a sort of isolation. As he occupies himself with the ground rules of the ritual order in everyday life, one may not be told much about what people hope to get out of their interactions apart from deference, or about who wins if the consensus of ritual should break down. It may be in his abstracting of situations from structures and his separating communicative activities from material life that Goffman comes especially close to Simmel's "formal sociology."[20] There can be little doubt that this has produced new insights into recurrent features of social interaction. Even a largely favorable commentator (Collins 1973:142), however, can express concern over a concentration on microproperties of face-to-face behavior, making "Goffman territory" less than it might have been—"from a revolutionary theorist in the grand tradition, he has become the baron of a prospering but remote province."

For some purposes, one may clearly want to know what are the mutual influences between people's particular positions and movements in the social structure and their participation in the ritual order. It is in one of the earlier of Goffman's published works that such an analysis has so far been most evident, in that the distribution of power within a specific institutional setting figures very conspicuously in it.[21] This is *Asylums* (1961a), a collection of essays based on his research at St. Elizabeth's Hospital. The mental hospital, Goffman proposes, belongs to a wider class that can be termed total institutions. Other instances are prisons, boarding schools, army barracks, and monasteries. (More recently, it has been commented that the slave plantation is yet another example.[22]) Obviously they are not alike in every way, but as a type the total institution is characterized in particular by its barriers to contacts between inhabitants and the world outside. It contrasts with the predominant tendency in modern urban society where the individual sleeps, plays, and works in different settings, with different people, under no obvious overall plan. In the total institution members do all these things more or less together, in a tightly regimented way where as a rule they are all treated alike. But what we have just called members, and could as well call inmates, are only one of the two major categories of people involved. There is a basic dichotomy between inmates and staff. For the latter, control of the lives of the inmates is work only, eight hours a day. Sleep and play for them belong in the outside society. The relationship between staff and inmates is one of extreme inequality and great social distance. There is reciprocal stereotyping and a regime of one-sided bureaucratic surveillance. As Goffman (1961a:9) puts it, "two different social and cultural worlds develop, jogging alongside each other with points of official contact but little mutual penetration."

Total institutions, he goes on to say, are natural experiments on what can be done to the self. The inmate may arrive with a sense of who he is which has up to this point had its rather stable underpinnings in his normal daily round of activities. In the case of mental hospital patients, this sense of self may already have become problematic, so that sometimes they have themselves sought hospitalization. Subcultures in American society apparently differ in the amount of imagery and encouragement they offer for such self-analysis. Goffman notes that it seems to be one of the doubtful cultural privileges of the upper classes. Anyhow, with the entry of the inmate into the total institution, some radical shifts begin to occur in his "moral career," the sequence of changes in his beliefs concerning himself and significant others. Not only is his old context of life lost to him, but he is under the almost total power of the staff, which tends to ignore any differences between him and other inmates, particularly those deriving from their previous existences outside, now defined as irrelevant. There is an admission procedure, including taking a life history, photographing, weighing, fingerprinting, assigning numbers, searching, listing personal possessions to be placed in storage, undressing, bathing, disinfecting, haircutting, issuing institutional clothing, instructing concerning rules, and assigning to quarters which seems to be both a farewell to an old identity and shock treatment when compared to normal interaction ritual. In the language of *The Presentation of Self,* the inmate seems no longer entitled to his own personal front, to a setting or to a backstage. In the interest of efficient administrative procedure, inmates are to be treated as identical modular units. They owe deference to the staff; in principle, the staff owes no deference to them. In the mental hospital, we have noted before, there are some patients who are incapable of maintaining normal interpersonal proprieties. Others lose such capabilities while they are there, because they are there. But offenses against the ordinary rules of interaction ritual are committed routinely and on a large scale by the staff, who can get away with it because of the utterly uneven distribution of sanctioning power.

In general, while in the total institution, the inmate has little control over his own activities. There is a continuous lack of privacy. He may be assigned tasks which seem absolutely meaningless, and he thus realizes that his time and effort, and consequently he himself, are worth nothing. Relations between inmates are ignored or discouraged by the staff, as they could interfere with processing. As the inmate adjusts to the system, he learns that if he behaves well according to the rules of the regime, he may be rewarded with certain privileges, and to some extent be able to reassemble a distinct self which is in line with these rules. Offenses against the rules, on the other hand, will meet with punishment.

Even inmates of total institutions sometimes manage to slip away, however, inside the institution but out of staff control. Goffman calls this "the underlife," not a phenomenon unique to the total institution but a more general one of people in an organization getting around its rules and assumptions. Characteristically, it is the lowly placed members of the organization who become most engaged in the underlife, since they get fewer rewards from the official rules. This is obviously true of total institution inmates, although some staff members are also involved in underlife activities of their own. There is a great variety of little ways in which the system can be beaten; ways of getting extras of desirable food, ways of altering institutional clothing to something just a bit more stylish, ways of getting an extra nap. The underlife also has its microgeography of places where one can disregard the rules of the regime, either alone or with other inmates, or even with staff members who in these settings can allow certain liberties. There are storage places—"stashes" in Goffman's terminology—where inmates keep possessions to which they can have no official claim. Informal communication systems are invented, to carry messages between inmates and to the outside world, or from it. An underlife economy is in operation, however modest, alongside institutional lines of provisioning. And inmates do relate to one another personally in other ways as well. One should perhaps beware of taking too romantic a view of these relationships, for some of them are simply coercive. But in others, people manage to go some way toward balancing the profanation of their selves in the institutional relationships, by exchanging symbolic tokens of esteem and self-respect.

Dealing with the power differentials of the total institution, Goffman takes on the perspective of the underdog, as he also does, without sentimentality, in dealing with spoiled identities in *Stigma*. His interest in the underlife of the institution is at the same time a part of his generally sceptical view of social life. Things are not necessarily quite what they appear to be, or what they should be according to proclaimed rules. All over society, organizations are trying to determine for people what they ought to do and who they ought to be in order to serve their purposes, and just about all over people respond in part, collectively or individually, by creating an underlife. This is to the organization, Goffman suggests, what the underworld is to a city. So one returns, we see, to the locale of the sociology of deception.

MINGLING: NORMALITY and ALARM

To reiterate, however, the greater part of Goffman's work does not center on relationships where one party is under the more or less strict long-term control of the other. Above all it deals with the ways in which people who are strangers or at most acquaintances handle matters of personal integrity during co-presences by exchanging signals with each other. Mostly it has been a question of symbolic integrity. At times, physical integrity also becomes involved, and Goffman is keenly aware of the connection between the two.

This is particularly evident in one of his later books, *Relations in Public* (1971), where he elaborates on some earlier concerns as well as strikes out in certain new directions. We may perhaps feel that his analytical field of "public life" remains rather indistinctly demarcated, but the individual's ability to read his environment is clearly an important concern. There is an extended discussion here of the ways in which one can tell who is with whom. Through "tie-signs" people claim anchorage in each other and intentionally or unwittingly inform others about it. Some of the signs are simple and conspicuous, like holding hands. Others are perhaps not so obvious. People who stand in a queue may be densely packed together whether they are in company or not, but if one person frees his hands temporarily by passing a package to another, almost or wholly without comment, then bystanders may assume that these two are together. Sometimes a tie can even be recognized without the people involved appearing together at all. In one of his characteristic footnotes, Goffman offers the example of people coming out of the swimming pool at different times to use the same bottle of skin lotion. Just as people may be intent on proclaiming their links or may do so more or less accidentally, they may also wish to conceal existing relationships—deceptive interaction again, with spies providing examples. In another variation, they may feign a link where none exists, as children sometimes do where they can enter only in the company of an adult, and the adult is in fact unaware of the company.

Tie-signs are often of greater interest to others when the individuals who appear linked are not all absolute strangers to them. One may be attentive to cues of familiarity or even intimacy between one's friend and some person one has not encountered before, or between two people whom one knows well as individuals although one is uncertain about their relationship to each other. But even in the presence of only strangers it may be useful to know if two or more of them together constitute a "with." For in contacts with withs, particular rules may apply. A with may be entitled to continuous space, so a non-member does not place himself between its members unless there are special provisions for it. Or if one should want to strike up a conversation with a stranger, or merely ask a question, it may be more acceptable to do so with a single person than with a with, the members of which have a prior claim to each other's attention. On the other hand, the with may be counted as safer in interaction than a single individual. At least the members accept being in each other's company, so they are probably not completely unpredictable.

Here, as occasionally elsewhere in his work, Goffman becomes concerned with what we have called traffic relationships, where the purposive involvement mostly entails giving an acceptable form to physical closeness. Much of *Relations in Public* is devoted to this theme. In physical traffic, he notes, the "vehicular units" are sometimes hard shells, controlled from within, such as cars, and at other times the rather softer shells of the human beings themselves. In the former case, there is a risk of considerable damage should a collision occur, and partly for reasons of speed, people may be in less than complete control of their vehicles. If they collide, they may not be able to extricate themselves from each other very readily, and they may hold up other passers-by as well. At the same time, there is little need for subtlety. This kind of traffic relationship need rarely be transformed, without as much as a moment's notice, into something else. Such traffic may indeed best be governed by formal laws. Where human beings are their own vehicles, on the other hand, they may feel confident of their ability to handle even the most microscopic bodily maneuvers, and even if at times they unintentionally fail, the consequences of, say, bumping into somebody are usually not serious. There is, however, a chance that one will want to turn a co-presence into something more than just that. Traffic relationships of such qualities require a wider range of informal skills.

Yet people are often not much aware of using them. To study traffic relationships is often to study how people deal with one another while they are doing something else—looking in shop windows, talking to someone in their with, or simply thinking hard. Under most conditions, one does not expect everything that happens to be within one's field of vision, whether things or other people, to be coordinated with one's own business or even relevant to it. So as long as they seem to be in a normal state—which can cover a great deal of variation—one largely ignores them. Unknown individuals within the field, with whom one does not engage in focused interaction, very nearly turn into non-persons. It is when the individual reads something out of the ordinary in his environment that he takes conscious notice. The strangers in one's surroundings should not break certain rules. One senses when a person intrudes into one's personal space, coming up closer than the situation warrants. The physical setting may contain "stalls," well-bounded spaces which one occupies on an all-or-none basis, such as telephone booths or waiting-room seats; here one expects signaled claims to them to be respected, even in some cases when one is not continuously present at the stall. There is the expectation of "use space," as in the instance of the art gallery visitor who is annoyed if another person inserts himself between him and a painting. And there are other infractions of the rules for mingling which may similarly cause some concern: people who do not wait for their turn, people who stare uninhibitedly at you, or people who unexpectedly start talking to you.

So the thin line between a state of normality and one of alarm may be crossed. A sort of preparedness for the crossing, however, may always be with us. We know that the non-persons whom we see or do not see can abruptly turn into persons, and as such interfere with our business and our lives, They are a possible threat, and so our monitoring of the environment, whether conscious or unconscious, is an important component in our management of danger. We are more acutely involved in it in some situations than in others, and there are some people who are habitually more engaged in it than others. Alone on a dark street rather than with a group in broad daylight, for example, in the former case; in the latter case, people who have good reason to believe that others may object to their doings if they are discovered, such as pickpockets at work in a crowd. If one conducts one's business in a group, the division of labor may even include a person who specializes in keeping a watchful eye on normality: a sentry. And in some part, we may structure our perception of the surroundings in terms of possible sources of alarm. Goffman draws our attention to "access points," like doors, windows, or more fanciful varieties like hidden tunnels, from which new persons may more or less suddenly enter our field of vision, and to "lurk lines," where dangers may be hiding behind a bush or a street corner.

We may try, then, to be prepared. But if others, already in our field of vision or waiting just outside it, are intent on entering our lives suddenly and without invitation, they certainly prefer to have us as unprepared as possible. They stay concealed until the moment of truth arrives, or they for their part appeal to our sense of normality. The mugger looks like nobody in particular behaving like everybody else, the burglar investigating future prospects poses as a delivery man. "Stocked characters," the types of people who by servicing a particular setting have a particular right of normal presence there, are often appropriated as fake identities by people who would otherwise be a cause of alarm. Electricians, plumbers, bug exterminators, and meter readers have access to territories from which unidentified strangers are usually closed out.

The question of preparedness, thus, like so much in Goffman's work, turns into a battle of wits—but only as an initial stage. For in this treatment of alarm in traffic relationships, there is also the ugly element of physical terror. Violence is stage two, as the unknown other turns out to be a mugger, a rapist, or a sniper. Not only a face may be lost, but a life. In *Relations in Public,* as reviewers have concluded, Goffman has come a long way, from the drawing-room niceties of deference and demeanor to the dramaturgy of "crime in the streets."

GOFFMAN, URBANISM, and the SELF

One can react to Goffman's perspective on many levels. In the most general terms, it could be seen as an ontology of the human existence. Or one may prefer to regard it as for the most part only a detailed analysis of interactional trivia. But we need hardly get into such arguments here. Even if our inclination is to see him as a theorist of wider significance, the question here is where Goffman fits into urban anthropology. For if there is any special connection between his perspective and urbanism, it is hardly made explicit in his writings. There is a brief discussion of what sort of society he assumes in *Relations in Public* (Goffman 1971:xiv–xv). Generally speaking, he has in mind his own society—but what is it? The American middle classes, the English-speaking world, Protestant countries, the West? Goffman makes his awareness of the problem clear, but has no simple solution to offer. A reference unit like "American society," he notes, is "something of a conceptual scandal." And things do not become simpler if one wants to pinpoint smaller units within this fuzzily demarcated whole as the carriers of particular modes of conduct. Classes, regions, age grades, and ethnic groups may be difficult enough, entities like "epochs" make us even more wary. Moreover, even if Goffman does draw mostly on Euro-American culture for his materials, there is also an occasional, unsystematic use of more exotic ethnography to hint that his concepts of small-scale everyday ceremony may apply more widely.

If Goffman himself seems reluctant to take any very definite position, either modest or immodest, on the boundaries of Goffmanland, we will have to draw together an argument more of our own making. But we are less interested in matters of geographic region than in relational arrangements, even if the former may also be worth discussing. We will try to point to some reasons, in other words, why a perspective of this kind may have a particular relevance as one tries to understand urban life and the urban experience, although it need not be confined to such concerns. Our reasoning has two main parts, but they are more like the sides of one coin.

There is, to begin with, the sense of self as a construct of human consciousness—the construct which Goffman in a Durkheimian mood shapes into a little deity. Under what conditions are people most likely to become preoccupied with such entities—are they variables, or are they constants? A statement by another of Goffman's ancestral figures, George Herbert Mead (1967:140), can perhaps serve as a lead here: "The self, as that which can be an object to itself, is essentially a social structure, and it arises in social experience." This is a central tenet of symbolic interactionism, and although Goffman's view of the formation of the self is perhaps just a little elusive, we will trust that it is sufficiently similar to fit reasonably well into our argument. An individual's conception of who he is or what he is like, although hardly wholly determined by his contacts with others, is thus born in interactions and continues to feed on them. To some degree, conceivably, an awareness of self is always there, but often it exists quietly, causing no problems. Its creation and maintenance can be a routine process. Then under particular circumstances, this awareness can be heightened, the self calling for more conscious attention and reflection.

We can try to identify such circumstances, it seems, in terms of a "contrast model" and a "deprivation model." Both are relevant to our thinking about urbanism. The contrast model relates to the experience of diversity in urban life. City dwellers can be put together in a great many different ways, from the multitude of activities, alignments, and perspectives which can serve as construction materials. They fashion their conceptions of self from these; but in their meetings with others composed in a different way, their self-awareness may be intensified by the observation of the difference between self and other. Not that the full range of differences is necessarily put on display—often there is rather a tendency to play them down—but intentionally or unintentionally, some of them are necessarily revealed. There is the further fact that the individual's social involvements in the highly differentiated urban structure may vary somewhat unpredictably over time, so that he may also be more likely to ponder the difference between past and present selves. The contrast model, that is, may work both internally and externally, resulting in a sense of individuality much like that which Simmel (1955) described when he wrote about each individual standing at his own unique "intersection of social circles" (in "The Web of Group-Affiliations").

The argument as a whole is rather speculative. If one wants to place the contrast model on a comparative footing, nevertheless, one finds bits and pieces of evidence for it in anthropologists' reporting on their encounters with societies of less complex structure. Barth (1975:255), writing about the small, isolated, and simply organized Baktaman people of New Guinea (perhaps as close as one can get to a Redfieldian folk society), suggests that since there are few external contacts and thus no known systematic alternative to their own way of life, they have no need to question their own customs and assumptions, and have an incomplete and unfocused collective self-image as a people. Moreover, situational involvements within Baktaman society are little differentiated. People participate as "whole persons" in most interactions, and there are not many ways of being a whole person. So on an individual basis, the contrastive road to a sharply delineated sense of self is not very passable either.

In the rather more complexly constituted community of Fox Indians described by Gearing (1970:133 ff.), people can indeed differentiate situations and tend to think of themselves and each other in something like role terms. But these roles are not put together so as to make up any great variety of individuals, and as their lives go on, people move between roles in much the same way. So the Fox, according to Gearing, do not tend toward introspection concerning their life histories. They take for granted that one life is like another, and that experiences are shared. This is also emphasized by Paul Riesman (1977:148 ff.) in his personal ethnography of the herding and farming Fulani of the West African savanna. The Fulani could fully understand one another, and toward the end of his stay Riesman as well, to the extent that they shared exposure to the same conditions. At the beginning of that stay, on the other hand, they seemed to find him by definition unknowable and unpredictable, a total stranger of whose experiences they had no idea.

Where self and other are not habitually in clear contrast, it would seem, empathy comes naturally. Where again and again they are understood to be different, however, another empathy may result; a preparedness not only to see what is unique about one's own situation, but also to take on a different person's experience vicariously, and perhaps under some conditions even to be actively curious about it. With the contrastive self, to rephrase, goes an awareness of the contrastive other. This, evidently, is the "mobile sensibility" with which Lerner was preoccupied in his well-known version of modernization theory in *The Passing of Traditional Society* (1958). Whether its significance for "modernization" itself is as great as he suggested is another matter.

The development of a definite sense of self, for its part, has been registered in various more complex settings. Some have noted it as an achievement of the classic city states, others find it characteristic of the renaissance. The historian Colin Morris (1973) finds it flowering in medieval Europe and, in line with our contrast model, suggests that an awareness of alternatives was among its critically important bases; not least did this grow in the emergent urban centers, the towns to which Pirenne and Weber devoted their attention. But the characteristic European form of social organization, based on personal links and loyalties, may also have played a part in "the discovery of the individual" of the twelfth century. Be that as it may, the sense of self in this period found its own associated social and cultural forms—in confession, in autobiography, in the portrait, in romantic love, and in satire.

The vocabularies of writers such as those just cited differ, but the notion that the self is less of a concern where it is similar to other people's, and more so when it entails its own different story, appears to be recurrent. From our point of view, it is natural to think of the city as one sort of place where such a diversity of selves can come about; admittedly more probably in some cities than in others, and quite likely with socially ordered variations in individual awareness of self within a city as well.[23] Perhaps something about European culture could indeed have played a part when self concepts evolved successively in antiquity, in the middle ages, and in the renaissance. Yet expressions rather like those identified by Colin Morris for medieval Europe also make their appearance in contemporary non-western life, partly through diffusion, partly being invented anew, and most likely serve similar purposes as people, shaped in new complex structures, find themselves with new and original selves. Personalized photo albums, requests for pen pals, nicknames from the movies, and a Horatio Alger mentality of self-help seem like familiar ingredients of Third World urban life in the twentieth century.

If an interpretation like Morris' suggests that the contrast model of self-awareness works at least from Commercetown onwards, and perhaps from Courttowns of the ancient past as well, the deprivation model seems most intimately linked to Coketown urbanism. It is perhaps the more widely cited model, proposing in essence that some kinds of activities and relationships, even though their primary purpose may well be a quite different one, are also more intrinsically satisfying to the sense of self, which can thus remain unreflectively at rest. It is when people find themselves engaged for much of the time in "soulless" pursuits and contacts giving no comfort to the self that a feeling of deprivation sets in, and people begin to strive more acutely for other experiences to compensate the loss.

This is obviously a sort of alienation perspective which comes back again and again in discussions of modern urbanism and mass society. The dullness of industrial and bureaucratic work, and the impersonality and substitutability in social relations, are conspicuous referents. Simmel hinted at this interpretation as well, in his remarks on lacking recognition of individuality in the metropolis. As Robert Park discussed the weakness of the moral order under urbanism he was also raising such issues. In anthropology, Sapir (1924) stated the point of view in his essay on genuine and spurious cultures. A more recent variety is Peter Berger's (Luckmann and Berger 1964; Berger 1965, 1970, 1973; Berger, Berger and Kellner 1973). There is a touch of the contrast model in Berger's view, not least in his analysis of social mobility, but above all he is concerned with what industrialism and bureaucracy do to the self. Under more traditional social systems, Berger suggests, there could be a satisfying congruence between roles, as defined through public normative control, and the subjectively experienced self. The individual could identify himself primarily through the roles which placed him in the social order. Bureaucratic and industrial roles, however, are often too limited in their scope to contain the self, and consequently there is a disjunction between self and role (or at least some roles). Phrased differently again, there is a sense of a split between the public and the private self, where the latter is the only "real" self.

To constitute and validate this "real" self, the individual in modern society must engage in a variety of activities in which self-definition becomes a primary purpose. Family life certainly plays a major part here. But a new industry has also arisen, supported by mass media, to supply the props for "the search for identity" in recreational activities. An institution like psychoanalysis also fits peculiarly well into the needs of individuals whose selves risk being underdefined.[24]

On the whole, there is a new ideology of the self. Berger argues that the old concept of honor, through which the individual claimed esteem in terms of his roles and role performance, has become obsolescent. Its replacement is a notion of human dignity, the personal worth of any individual irrespective of role placement and enactment.[25] Parallel to this there is the decline of what can be seen as the sincerity of the past, and the celebration of a new understanding of authenticity.[26] Sincerity, again, is the mark of the individual identifying with his roles. Authenticity is marked by the refusal to be constrained. It is present in the cult of informality and of "letting it all hang out." The unfettered, full involvement of people with each other as whole personalities is idealized.

Berger identifies American society as that where the new tendencies have gone farthest, although he is concerned with a type of society rather than a particular cultural tradition. Even in America, however, the process has not yet come to completion. One may see honor and dignity, sincerity and authenticity as simultaneously present, sometimes in different arenas, occasionally in a conflict which is not necessarily sharply defined.

There need not be any conflict between the contrast model and the deprivation model. The sets of circumstances which they identify as leading, possibly, to a heightened self-consciousness may be simultaneously present, and in part they overlap. But we ought to note that the idea of the authentic self, unmediated by role definitions, which Berger and others see arising out of the sense of deprivation, stands in a somewhat uneasy relationship to the Goffman perspective toward interaction ritual. Its particular application in *Asylums*, showing the suppression of the inmate self and its reemergence in the underlife of the institution, seems like an almost perfect application of the deprivation model. Yet there are problems elsewhere. We have already used the term "sociology of sincerity" for a part of this perspective. The fit with that concept of sincerity which contrasts with authenticity may not be perfect, but the affinity is there. The man who is willingly his own jailer is not in search of the authentic self. Probably this is why many of Goffman's examples of interaction as well-intentioned ritual, although revealing, seem a little dated. Their bourgeoisie live in a social world where backstage and frontstage are clearly marked out, where social hierarchies are closely matched by differentiated deference patterns, and where people can go out of their way to conduct themselves ceremonially in forms which have little to do with the material practicalities of life. Norbert Elias (1978)—a writer who is like Goffman concerned with the social significance of etiquette, whose writing antedates his although it has only more recently been discovered by most of English-speaking academia, and who has more definite historical concerns—suggests that the codification of bourgeois manners was part of the transition from medieval times to the renaissance, toward a society characterized by greater openness but not by equality.[27] In our times, a higher degree of egalitarianism must at least simplify deference, and from the point of view of an ideology of authenticity, any stylization of interpersonal relations, even if based on the noblest of motives, is fundamentally misguided. It is not difficult to discern that this is currently one important source of unhappiness with Goffman's perspective toward society.

Undoubtedly there is a danger in our becoming too self-congratulatory with respect to the achievement of authenticity. Some of the changes going on may simply involve alterations in the boundaries of sincerity. Yesterday's etiquette may now seem affected. If today there are new rules—but still rules—for being suitably informal, they may perhaps more easily elude us. Only when confronted with some of the more aberrant inmates of the asylum, in their very unpredictable relations with each other and with staff, do we perhaps sense what deference and demeanor still count for in ordinary life.

If the "authenticity critique" aims at letting the prisoners of social structure loose, we may thus sense that a counter-critique is possible. The idea that in any interaction one should allow free play to one's sentiments and be generous in exhibiting one's biography may be nice psychology but terrible sociology. No reasonably complex society could get its work done if every interaction between its members would involve such almost infinite individual complexity. If one party is thus self-indulgent, it could place an intolerable burden on the other. By now there are other writers—such as Richard Sennett in *The Fall of Public Man* (1977)—suggesting that contemporary social life is suffering as people have forgotten the forms for treating each other civilly without intimacy.

The proper bargain between ceremony and authentic self-revelation, serving well the purposes of both individual and collectivity, may not be easy to strike. One must be aware, however, that it need not be the same for each relationship. We return here to the manner of mapping social relations, along the dimensions of personal information and normative control, which was outlined in chapter 4.

Goffman's habitat tends to be somewhere along the middle of the continuum of personal information, or at least not at its end points. Many of the relationships he deals with may be rather high on normative control, although there is sufficient room for the little rituals of deference and demeanor lubricating the machinery of society so that the individual can have his worth and his right to participation recognized. The use of personal information here does not do much to change relationships but rather maintains them in a given form. There are other relationships where revelations of self are used partially and tactically—and sincerely or deceptively—to draw new responses from the other, and thereby move the interaction onto new paths. But at least for as long as Goffman retains an interest in the relationships, impressions are managed rather than abandoned.

The deprivation model, for its part, posits that important relationships in the social order are so high on normative control and so low on openings for personal information that people feel a pain of personal obliteration, driving them into other relationships where they can compensate by expressing their selves more fully. Ideally, on the continuum of relationships formed by personal information, these are at the pole of intimacy; specimens, it seems, of the total openness of I and Thou in the communitas delineated by Victor Turner (1969).

What, then, is accomplished for the conception of self in these different relationships? To begin to answer this question, one may have to take on more directly the problem of the construction of the self (as opposed to the presentation of self) through interaction. Goffman tends not to make much of the issue of where the individual picks up his own idea of himself, as he is or as he wants to be. That idea is simply there, and he wants it acknowledged by others. And in the Goffmanian sociology of deception, this can hardly itself be a goal. It would presuppose a noteworthy measure of self-deception to assume that other people's acceptance of a self falsely presented can feed directly into the individual's own concept of self; at most, he could take pride in being a skilled liar. Fundamentally, however, the sociology of deception deals with a more open system of transactions, where the pretenses to a certain self are converted into resources of quite different kinds, such as more tangible services or material goods.

But one may wonder whether even Goffman's sociology of sincerity quite covers the construction of the self, in approximately the sense which George Herbert Mead suggested. No doubt the construction and maintenance of the self can be to some extent aided by routine interaction rituals. Yet often these involve others to whom the individual does not attach much significance, and the relationships involved are frequently segmental in a Wirthian sense. There is a relatively small frontstage, and a sizeable backstage. If the individual's interactionally based construction of self can be merely the sum of segmental selves, there need be no further problem. If their integration should also be anchored in interaction, on the other hand, this construction of self seems to be most importantly accomplished through the openness of relationships rather more like communitas.

A number of writers have contributed to the delineation of such relationships in recent years.[28] Denzin (1970a:262–63) touches on the issue with his concept of "self-lodging," explicitly contrasted to Goffman's "presentation of self." The individual's conception of self is seen as lodged most securely in certain relationships, and to return with some frequency to these relationships would thus be one of the motives underlying human conduct. In an essay with Kellner, Peter Berger has analyzed the role of marriage in the social construction of reality. Through the long conversation which makes up much of their relationship, the spouses keep on building a shared view of the world around them which becomes stabilized precisely because it is shared, externalized. It is a world-building activity which draws on the round of experiences outside the relationships as well, importing, in other words, elements to be reworked and built into a common and relatively coherent culture. These can stretch back to childhood experiences, and they also include the day's events at the office. The world-building activity also in a sense exports its products, as the spouses are likely to take the perspective into outside activities too. In general terms, such a relationship entails an important "nomic process," contrasting to the possible anomie in the world view of the isolated individual. In the more particular terms immediately relevant to our discussion, however, this process also gives the participants a stronger and more integrated sense of who they are than is available in most other relationships. "Marriage in our society is a *dramatic* act in which two strangers come together and redefine themselves" (Berger and Kellner 1964:5).

Berger and Kellner, obviously, are not describing just any kind of marriage. It is a contemporary western companionship marriage, and even as such perhaps somewhat idealized. The meeting of the minds seems to work out better than may always be the case, and the reality construction work going on in the relationship apparently has little outside competition. In the terms of Elizabeth Bott's study of couples and networks, this is a joint conjugal relationship between people whose external links are rather loose—American middle-class rather than British working-class. Yet the important point is not so much whether marriage has this particular part in the construction of self or of reality in general. It is rather that some relationships, somewhere, may be somewhat specialized in performing such a service, although they are not necessarily the same for all individuals and almost certainly not the same for all social structures.[29] One can see parallels here also with Robert Paine's analysis of middle-class friendship in modern society. The notion of friendship, Paine observes, is not the same in all societies, and thus anthropologists, moving between levels of emics and comparative study, have had trouble dealing with it. In modern middle-class society, however, the basic meaning and value of friendship is a sense of worth; not least, "the friend is someone who understands one, who can explain one to oneself" (Paine 1969:507). And it is an "explanation" which is made reasonably credible as the friend is understood to be knowledgeable about the subject, for friends also communicate openly about themselves to each other.[30] Again, it is a relationship strong on personal information and weak on normative control.

Possibly we can conclude this part of our discussion by agreeing that the self may well become a more important focus of consciousness in the sort of social complexity more or less strongly associated with urbanism. In other words, the individual may be aware of being "someone special," in a descriptive if not always evaluative sense. There can be an awareness of self in the form of a recognition of distinctiveness when fewer people are seen to lead very similar lives, and the consciousness of both roles and self as distinct entities may increase if there are roles under strong normative control which are somehow felt to be intrinsically unsatisfactory to the incumbent. It need not be altogether surprising if the individual becomes a preoccupation of symbolic activity under such conditions, or if an opposition between the "real" self and the social structure becomes an important motif in the rhetoric of individuality. Of the latter idea, however, we can perhaps usefully be just a little sceptical. It is difficult to think of a self set wholly apart from its social involvements. While the individual need not be just the sum of his roles, he is at least in large part a particular way of joining them together and performing them, with pleasure in some cases, perhaps distaste in others.

Some relationships, we have also seen, appear to play a greater part in the production of this perhaps more elaborate imaginative artifact of a self, and others a greater part in the display of the finished product, although many relationships are clearly involved in both. The Goffman perspective toward the presentation of self must have as its counterpart a viewpoint toward the self undergoing social construction. This implies that the dimension of personal information in social relationships which we have made note of before is rather more complex than we might at first have thought. It is not just a matter of one party offering information about himself to the other party, for use in the conduct of the relationship. It can also happen that one individual is influenced by the other's indications about him. We could as well recognize at this stage, too, that there are further possible variations. The conceptual working-out of the idea of awareness contexts by Glaser and Strauss (1964) shows some alternatives. One party may make greater disclosures about himself, or more truthful disclosures, or simply different sorts of disclosures about himself than the other party does, or he may use personal information concerning the other which may have been collected in other relationships and which the other does not know that he has. To stretch the framework a little and speak figuratively, in the manner of symbolic interactionism, an individual in a relationship may disclose things about himself only to himself—out of one relationship into another, for example—while withholding it from the other party. And, of course, if more than two people are involved, as in the team performances of *The Presentation of Self*, more intricate patterns yet can be seen in the distribution of personal information within a situation.

SEGMENTALITY AND SELF-PRESENTATION

Here we seem to get to the second part of our argument concerning the usefulness of Goffman's perspective to the understanding of urban life. Our concern is now the more centrally Goffmanian one, how the self appears to alter rather than how it takes hold in ego's own consciousness. The way social relations are put together in the city, establishing one's image to others can be a rather different matter there compared to other kinds of social formations.

Robert Park's remark on "skating on thin surfaces" and the "scrupulous study of style and manners" in urban relations fits in here. But we can also start out from another statement by Max Gluckman (1962:35–36), in his analysis of the prevalence of ritual in general, and *rites de passage* in particular, in tribal society:

. . . in the very conditions of a large city, looked at in contrast with tribal society, the various roles of most individuals are segregated from one another since they are played on different stages. Thus as a child matures he moves out of the home to infant school, primary school, and secondary school, and within each of these phases he moves from class to class. Each year of his growth is marked by this progress; and each time he advances a step, he moves, within a distinctive educational building, from one to another. Then in one stream he progresses through higher educational institutions, housed in their own buildings, to work as a salary-earner; or, in another stream, he goes through apprenticeship, or as a juvenile employee, into his role as a wage-earner. Work goes on in offices and factories, in quite distinctive buildings from those in which most people live, worship, and seek their recreation, or participate in political life. Religious worship takes place in permanently sanctified buildings. And these various activities associate individuals with quite different fellows: at school twins are likely to be the only members of a family in the same class; factories assemble people drawn from large areas; and so do most religious congregations. How a child behaves at school, or a man as a worker in his factory, does not immediately and directly affect familial relations, although it may well do so in the end; there is segregation of roles, and segregation of moral judgments.

This is a variety of the folk-urban contrast, and another way of expressing the idea of segmentality in urban relationships. What most obviously connects the statement to Goffman is the use of dramaturgic metaphor. Under urban conditions, according to Gluckman, life takes place on a multiplicity of separate stages; a little more cautiously, we may admit that this is at least the general tendency. And audiences are different each time. We may say that under such circumstances, the difference between what is made known about the self in a particular situation and what could be known involves the parts which the individual plays in all other situations. The latter are in a sense backstage; with respect to any one situation, the city would thus seem to have a high backstage/frontstage ratio. If on the other hand one could think of a society which is only one single stage—a most extreme type of folk society, or, for inmates, a total institution without an underlife—the difference between the presented self and the self that could be known would have to center on an "inner" self, not normally revealed in overt behavior. This is a rather problematic notion. It seems clear that in the mode of impression management involving the greater number of separate stages, there is more room for maneuver, and greater possibilities also for a dramaturgic analysis grounded in observable facts. The contrast is a coarse one, but it hints that *Homo goffmani* is more townsman than tribesman.

The city, in other words, is an environment where there are many and varied ways of making oneself known to others, and one where a great deal of manipulation of backstage information is possible. The opportunities are there, in the social structure. What people do with them, and how consciously they seize upon them, can vary considerably. In the remainder of this chapter, we will point to some of the possibilities.

One of the things an urbanite may do is to disconnect performances. Nels Anderson's Chicago hoboes, we may remember, told each other nothing about their backgrounds, although presumably what was thus held back largely pertained to their past. It is also possible to switch back and forth between performances; an extreme case in point is the life of Ronnie Kray, partly of the London underworld, as summarized by Raban (1974:67):

Ronnie's behaviour was gloriously inconsistent. He was a thug, a respectable businessman, a philanthropist, a socialite, a mother's boy, a patriot, a strong-man-with-a-heart-of-marshmallow, a gunman, an animal lover, a queen, at the end, a tweedy country squire with his own estate in Suffolk. Caught at any one moment, his identity had a perverse dramatic perfection. An astonishing number of people never doubted that he was what he seemed. For every audi-ence, he had a different voice and face, and people who saw him performing in one role did not guess the existence of others. His repertoire would have been the envy of many versatile professional actors, and he could effortlessly slip from part to part during the course of a single day. The secret lay in keeping his audiences separated; it was only when he was in the dock that they came together, and then it was to destroy him.

Another variant is to introduce in one performance information of doubt-ful validity concerning another performance. This is apparently what hap-pened in the mau-mauing of the flak catchers, according to Tom Wolfe's in-terpretation cited in the previous chapter. The bureaucrats had no way of telling whether the wild men turning up in their offices were real ghetto leaders or not. They could only be more or less taken in with the claims made.

The city may thus offer rich opportunities for presentations of self which would seem more or less consciously deceptive. From a slightly different angle, it also provides chances of escaping in some relationships from a self which cannot be avoided in others. We· may think here of Berreman's (1978:231) suggestion that the city is not an ideal environment for the In-dian caste system, since it can allow people at least situationally to slip out of that place in the hierarchy which in principle should define their entire social existence.[31] But risks could be involved in seizing such apparent op-portunities. If one is aware of what people are in one's various audiences, one would presumably be careful enough not to make contradictory presen-tations where one knows that audiences overlap. One might not have suf-ficient network awareness, however, to realize that separate audiences can be in contact in their back regions. Not only the separation of stages but also sparse networks are a prerequisite for the kind of presentational ma-neuvers we are looking at here. Where gossip comes in, impression man-agement may have to go out. A notable example of what may come out of a failure to keep audiences well apart is blackmail, a species of crime which clearly feeds on a differentiated structure of relationships like that of the city.[32]

There are other more specific ways in which variations in an individual's presentation of self may be affected by, and may themselves influence, the way networks are put together, and there are thus advantages in integrating the dramaturgical perspective with network analysis. One set of examples may be found in those relationships of provisioning where the service rendered by one party consists of receiving and acting upon personal information disclosed by the other party about himself—the relationship between doctor and patient, for example, or lawyer and client. This kind of information could often be damaging to the latter party if it were allowed to spread, and he would rarely use it in other presentations. A professional code is therefore introduced which is assumed to constrain the use of such knowledge. The question is, to what extent does the client, patient, or someone else in an equivalent role, place his faith in such purely normative restrictions? It could be that he prefers making a new contact for such a relationship, rather than going to someone he already knows in another capacity (thus making the relationship multiplex). The latter could entail switching from one presentation of self to another in front of the same person, probably not a comfortable undertaking. Furthermore, the individual might prefer that the new link be isolated from the rest of his personal network, rather than deeply embedded in it. This would be double insurance, just in case normative constraint on outside disclosures on the part of his alter should not suffice. And, of course, such a precautionary measure may appear even more reasonable in establishing implicitly or explicitly information-processing relationships where no professional code of discretion exists. Even shopping habits may be regarded as containing sensitive revelations of one's personal life. An anonymous supermarket clerk may not think twice about one's purchases, however, while Mr. Brown in the corner store who chats with all one's neighbors would perhaps never forget.

At this point, we should probably consider again the habit of network analysts to think only of more enduring, personal relationships as significant network components. Particularly when it comes to information processing, this practice may have its limitations. The strangers whom the city dweller meets in traffic relationships, and in some relationships of provisioning like that to the supermarket clerk, are, we have said, at least very nearly non-persons in Goffman's sense. At times this may mean that one is not particularly careful with what self one projects in the interactions concerned. As we also noted in chapter 3, they are assumed not to be fateful. In a way, we may take for granted that there is safety among strangers. But there is a problem of dramaturgical circumspection here. If the show is not on, perhaps it should have been, for although you may not recognize the other person, he may recognize you. Intentionally or by chance, the seemingly innocent co-presence may actually be a case of surveillance, where significant personal information flows in one direction only. And although our network awareness with respect to strangers is by definition near nil (we may, of course, note their withs in a co-presence), they may be, and may know that they are, only two or three links away from us through more tangible relationships. As another possibility, such an indirect linkage could be discovered only later by both parties, after one or both have made appearances out of line with their presentations of self within that linkage. Either way, a credibility gap may result.

We need not take our tracing of the connections between dramaturgy and networks any further for the time being. Certainly there are great opportunities for daring impression management in the city, as well as for disastrous occasions where contradictions are found out. It is important, however, that we do not think of the connection between urban social structure and the management of impressions only as a matter of the chances city people have of concealing what outlandish things they may have done. For one thing, presentational manipulations are not typically of the magnitude of those of Ronnie Kray (whom prison psychiatrists later judged schizophrenic). What people try to restrict to back regions are less often likely to be really dark secrets than secrets which are light or medium grey; not spectacular deviance, but minor sources of embarrassment. Or it may simply be information held irrelevant to the performance in progress.

For another thing, people may be as interested in revealing as in concealing, and if there is anything interesting about the rather humdrum activity which impression management often can be, it is perhaps the complexity and uncertainty which may go into the interplay between these two tendencies in the presentation of even quite an ordinary urban self. Here we come back from yet another angle to our continuous interest in the organizational and cultural implications of urban role diversity, and the network diversity which goes with it. Again we assume, for the sake of argument at least, that the diversity of roles is considerable, and allows great freedom of combination. We can also make the usual assumption that when an individual is concerned at all with what becomes of his image in a certain relationship, he has at least some vague idea of how he wants or does not want to be seen, and of what information might lead to either view. There are times when the presentation can be unproblematically made up entirely through those activities which are, so to speak, intrinsic to the relationship; through compliance or noncompliance with relevant norms, and through attention to personal style. Occasionally some special effort goes into such presentation as well, as in the instance of Goffman's Sartrean waiter. Perhaps in some cases this may also be related to the diversity of urban living. Where many alternative social situations are possible, a skilled performance may be needed to define which one is intended.

In other instances, however, the individual defines himself at least partially by allowing information (or disinformation) from his other involvements to filter through situational boundaries. And thus the question arises with what degree of elaboration and fidelity to the facts that entire self is presented which can be made up from the individual's repertoire of social involvements.

The problem may be what kind of consistency one expects from an individual, and how one feels that it should be reflected in his round of life. Anthropologists are by now well aware of the importance of situational selection in the ordering of behavior, and at least in an implicit and imperfect way, the principle is no doubt also understood by laymen. Few might really expect absolute consistency, for example, between a person's behavior at home and at work. Yet there is surely some sense of the propriety of various combinations of involvements, in both ego's and alter's minds. It is for this sense of what goes with what that the diversity of an urbanite's involvements could sometimes cause difficulties.

In principle, we may have learned to expect, an individual's selection of roles should express a unitary self. As a matter of minimal required fit between them, they should consequently not imply sharply contradictory personal values and beliefs. To be both a member of a strict religious sect and an eager gambler is probably in the eyes of most people to overstep the limits of acceptable inconsistency. Ronnie Kray's way of life was in this sense more than a combination of roles. It suggested multiple selves. And from this dark secrets may be made. But when will diversity be interpreted as contradiction, and what can one do about that information about one's doings which seems to strike a jarring note?

In the city with its relatively opaque structure, even the shared and precise sense of what goes with what may not be so strongly developed. So many different kinds of social involvements occur that nobody has a clear map of them all, and an individual does not carry his entire repertoire of roles on his sleeve, the way he does with conspicuous role-discriminatory attributes like race or sex. Thus it is not only that society cannot easily make sure that everybody conforms with whatever may be given standards of combinability. Just deciding what could be such standards is less simple insofar as ego and his alters lack a mutual overview of each other's stages. There is the further complication that an individual may be drawn into roles due to circumstances beyond his control rather than to his personal volition. Whether this is always clear to others trying to gauge his self, however, is an altogether different question.

With respect to networks the situation is similar. One may be judged by others not merely by one's activities but also according to the company one keeps. Thus to an alter, the characteristics of ego's other alters on other stages may be a matter of some interest. Here again, we might think first of the withholding of information about linkages to well-known villains and fools. But such reticence as there may be about revealing the qualities of one's associates is really rather more likely to concern lesser mismatches with what is at any one time one's frontstage behavior. The people in one network link or segment may just seem too dull, too unserious, too conservative, too radical, too pious, too naïve, too anarchic, too flighty, or too much of a number of other things to seem even indirectly presentable to the people elsewhere in one's network. Again, however, the limits of tolerance may be hazy.

The many forms of impression management in everyday urban life can perhaps often be related to factors of roles and networks such as those just mentioned. There may be occasions which one would prefer to keep well insulated from one another because of the contradictory demands they make on the self, but which impinge on each other so that at least certain of its accoutrements must be made to match them all. At worst, the experience may be like that of a chameleon on multicolor patchwork. The situation of Barbara Lamont (1975:5), a New York radio and TV reporter, at the beginning of a day is an illuminating example: "I stand naked in front of the mirror asking myself, what can I wear to a funeral that I can also wear on an undercover investigation of a housing project that I can also wear to my analyst that I can also wear in front of my station manager that I can also wear to dinner at the One Hundred Sixteenth Street Mosque?"

We can also identify different tactics of willful disclosure, through which an ego attempts to round out an alter's picture of him in some desirable way. Factual information concerning other involvements may be introduced; or at times, not least if alter has already received such information through some other channel (such as gossip), the emphasis may be on supplying an interpretation which in some way or other clarifies its relation to the self.

Yet another of Goffman's essays, that on role distance (1961b:85 ff.), provides insights into one way of doing this with roles. It is not just that you either have them or you do not. You can communicate to others, explicitly or in less obvious ways, whether a role is "really you" or something peripheral, perhaps accidental or forced, by showing attachment or distance to it. Goffman's example is the child on the merry-go-round who signals to onlookers that he is getting too old to really care. Somewhat similarly, there are what Scott and Lyman (1968) have called "accounts," verbal devices used to bridge the gap between actions and expectations. There are two major categories of these: excuses and justifications. The former can be used, in the situations of disclosure we are now discussing, to suggest that a certain kind of involvement may be disregarded as a part of the self. Ego acknowledges that it is inconsistent with the understanding of his character that he wants alter to accept, but he denies responsibility in some way or other. In justifications responsibility is accepted, and an attempt is made to show how the involvement does fit into the self being promoted.

Needless to say, there are many revelations which can be made routinely and unproblematically, as no inconsistency is understood to be involved. Different segments of urban society, however, may be variously demanding in this respect. There are circles where an awareness of contradictions in city life fosters a degree of tolerance so that excuses seldom appear to be called for. It may even be one form of urban sophistication to define a desirable self in terms of its ability to cope with, perhaps derive pleasure from, involvements which would seem to stand in opposition to one another. Here what could appear to be probable materials for dark secrets may instead be merrily paraded in the presentation of self, and every inconsistency becomes its own justification.

It is likewise possible that the sort of accounts accepted in one part of urban society will be rejected in an another. They, and other ways of guiding disclosures about what happens on one's other stages, could perhaps be seen, then, as cultural forms with some more or less specific distribution. Because urban role constellations and networks can be so varied, however,

there will often be something tentative and innovative about the way revelations are made. One cannot always be sure whether they will be met
with approval or censure, and some new thought may occasionally have to
go into pulling an act together. As we noted briefly in discussing network
differences in the preceding chapter, there may be a contrast here to the
sort of social arrangement where role constellations are small and standardized, and where discrepancies are thus also of recurrent form. Where the
urbanite may have to experiment with an original presentation of self, the
traditional small-scale society may have instituted an avoidance relationship, routinely anchored in the collective consciousness.[33]

Why, then, disclosures? Few questions may be more important for the
understanding of urban life, and it brings us back to issues raised toward
the end of chapter 3. If we take the Wirthian view of urbanism too literally, we may be stuck with an overly static picture of relationships among
strangers. It is one of the useful ideas of Max Gluckman's interpretation of
ritual, as cited above, that through communicative work, people can
change those definitions of persons which seem to be inherent in a type of
social structure. In his case, the *rite de passage* is used to make an adult,
and thus a new person, out of a child. Although relationships between the
same individuals of flesh and blood will continue both before and after the
initiation on the same stage, a threshold of discontinuity in their form has
been marked. Similarly, in tribal society people may interact with the same
others in multiplex relationships over a wide range of activities; but
through ritual, whole persons can to some degree be fragmented into roles,
so that what happens in one kind of involvement need not affect all other
facets of a relationship. With disclosures in the presentation of self in
urban life, it is the other way around. People who are only directly observable segmentally can turn themselves into more or less entire persons.

In the city, that is, some of people's most important relationships may
have to be made. Urbanites do not willy-nilly find themselves familiar with
all the people they would want to have in their more durable networks, the
way someone conceivably could as a by-product of growing up in a small
community. Instead some close relationships may have to be built from
scratch, beginning in contexts which need not hold out any great promise
for the purpose, where people could equally well remain quite remote from
one another. To get anywhere soon in establishing oneself as a person
under such conditions, one may have to "come on strong."

Anthropologists have indeed sometimes commented on the special ways in which city people may seek each other's recognition. We remember Harris' emphasis on the quest for individuality in Minas Velhas. Rivière (1967:577–78) briefly suggests a related variant in a reanalysis of Oscar Lewis' *The Children of Sanchez*, in terms of honor and shame. Because in the city, one's background may not be known to others, the individual search for demonstrable honor becomes more intensive. In Mexico, Rivière concludes, its conspicuous form is *machismo*. Perhaps more directly to our point, Lewis (1965:498) has himself commented, on the topic of classic folk-urban contrasts of social relationships, that "in modern Western cities, there may be more give and take about one's private, intimate life at a single 'sophisticated' cocktail party than would occur in years in a peasant village."

Some of these exchanges may merely offer entertainment for a brief encounter, and other things can go into catching an alter's attention apart from disclosures brought in from the back region. But certainly filling out the picture of oneself by revealing something about one's other involvements is one major way of personalizing a relationship. It is in the process of making a friend out of a neighbor that we tell him of our work and our family. And it is a part of the definition of closeness in ongoing relationships, for example within the household, that disclosures about outside involvements are continuously made. Normal procedure in building such a relationship, of course, is hardly to turn oneself inside out in one sitting. There may well be critical points in the process, connected with decisions to disclose information to which unusual symbolic importance is for some reason attached. But on the whole, it is likely to be a gradual process, where ego, before proceeding further, may wait for alter to react to revelations and to respond in kind. The process may be halted if the relationship in its new and expanded form turns out to be a disappointment. On the other hand, as it proceeds, alter's demands for completeness in ego's disclosures may grow stronger, so that at some point ego begins to lose control over his presentation. Finally, indirect knowledge of ego's wider role repertoire and network, made available largely through his verbal revelations, may no longer be enough, and alter begins to appear in person on the other stages as well. At this point, old divisions between frontstage and backstage have broken down; and if ego has been aware of the possibility, this has presumably for some time constrained any tendencies toward fancifulness in his presentations.

Here, too, as we can glimpse the demise of impression management, we may have moved out of the range of relationships of primary interest to Erving Goffman. We can see, however, that it is through one tactic or another in the presentation of self that city dwellers often make their escape from anonymity and segmentality in social relations. Personal disclosures, more or less artfully constructed, are a dynamic element in urban life. Goffman has heightened our awareness of their forms and processes, and this is one reason why we may see him not least as a major contributor to urban anthropological thought. He has furthermore shown us a way of thinking about the dangers as well as the opportunities that an uneven distribution of personal information may entail. There is also in his work a penetration of the modest rituals through which selves are worshipped which can inspire further analysis of symbolic activity in a city life where the pantheon in question may be richly diversified. A consciousness of self and the management of personal information, of course (as Goffman would certainly agree), is not all there is to life, in the city or anywhere else. But perhaps we are not consistently aware of them because they are, in one way or another, almost always with us. If this is so, Goffman has proven himself a master of "the exoticization of the familiar," which we have earlier pointed out as one of the valuable products of the anthropological imagination. He has the ability, as Bennett Berger (1973:361) has noted, of "rendering strange and problematic the very assumptions and routines which make ordinary social life possible and worthwhile." Our remarks in the latter part of this chapter may have gone some way toward clarifying some of the connections of this perspective to ideas we may think of as central in urban anthropology.

CHAPTER SEVEN

Conclusion:
The Construction of Cities
and Urban Lives

Let us now retrace our steps. The analytical ideas and the interpretations of urbanism which we have sampled are quite diverse. To the extent that we are merely suggesting that there are a few things an urban anthropologist should know there may be nothing wrong in this, since a liberal education is not necessarily distinguished by its tight logic. Yet we would prefer to draw from them also some reasonably organized set of understandings, commensurable with the emphasis on ethnography and a relational point of view stated by way of introduction, which could serve as a basis for the orderly growth of an urban anthropology.

We began in Chicago, with Robert Park and his students. Park could at the same time think on a large scale about urbanism and observe it in detail. He was aware that some relationships in the city, at least, had rather peculiar qualities; he saw the possibilities of cultural process in the urban environment; and he drew attention to the variety of "social worlds" contained in it. He noted the profound importance of the division of labor in shaping life styles and community structure, and through his ideas of ecology he anchored his analysis of urban variation in a certain sense of place. Other Chicagoans contributed pieces to Park's plan, in a series of pioneer ethnographies of youth gangs, ghetto dwellers, hoboes, and others. If they did not achieve anything like full coverage of their city, they at least showed how much there is to be learned about the ways people live in a place like Chicago. And they demonstrated—some, admittedly, a little more persuasively than others—the importance of field work in the learning process.

One might discern some lack of analytical precision in their ethnographic work, however, and an important reason for this may be that Chicago social theory, as it evolved, paid less attention to relations between people than to relations between the latter and space. As we got to Wirth's "Urbanism as a Way of Life," we could see that in part, he restated Park's views, and in part, he lingered on issues of social organization. But he was less than cautious in his generalizations about the nature of urban relationships. The city seemed to be one and indivisible, and perhaps rather more like Chicago than any other place. Moreover, Wirth was more concerned with what the city did to people and their contacts than with why people made cities at all, and his city thus appears as a given fact and as more or less a closed system.

Without rejecting everything that Wirth had to say, we thus went to seek remedies for ethnocentrism and other weaknesses through a tour of historical and geographical perspectives toward urbanism. We saw that cities could be seen as centers of societies rather than as isolates, and that different systems of power and exchange created their own varieties of such centers. Taking an extreme view, one might thus say that even if the city everywhere can be defined as a sizable, dense settlement, the basis for its existence as well as its form can be understood only with reference to the centripetal tendencies of the particular social system where it is found, and to its cultural forms. Yet a thoroughgoing relativism along such lines has rather limited support, and students of urbanism have instead tended to think comparatively in rather broad terms of political economy and technology. Courttown, Commercetown, and Coketown were the designations we came to use for three major types in the history of urbanism. Behind such a label, however, any one community can hide quite a complex structure of activities. We took note of the geographers' central place theory as one way of thinking about how cities and systems of cities may thus be put together, but we realized also that its locational concerns are not always equally relevant. There are central places, such as market towns, and there are special places, such as mining towns, resorts, or university towns.

This tour of points of view, then, left us with two major understandings. Cities have in common the fact that they make people more physically accessible to one another, in more or less shared, limited space. They differ, first of all, in their livelihoods, which had the major part in making them as the settlements they are. But there is more to urban living than merely making a living. Just how differentiated the kinds of roles are in which people engage themselves varies between types of cities, but it seems to be of some practical utility to divide them into some limited number of domains. Here we have chosen five which we have called household and kinship, provisioning, recreation, neighboring, and traffic. If some such differentiation is a recurrent fact of life in cities, so that people have separate social contacts more or less in each of the domains, this is a major factor behind the narrowness of relations on which both Park and Wirth remarked. Distinguishing between domains, however, we also see that generalizations need to be held in check. The "typically urban" relationships may be prevalent in connection with roles in the domains of traffic and provisioning, and may be quite atypical in relationships within those of domesticity and recreation.

Yet domain distinctions are not just a tool for more adequate conceptualization. They also help us see the analytical task of finding out with what degree of orderliness or variation the different involvements fit together. To what extent do roles of distinct domains impinge on one another? Since cities tend to be typified on the basis of what goes on in the domain of provisioning, does this domain significantly order the contents of other domains as well? We have no more than raised such questions.

Of the domains, it is that of traffic roles and relationships which relates most directly to sheer physical accessibility as a quality of urban life. These are contacts (however minimal) between strangers, and handling them, both in real life and analytically, is a problem in its own right. On the other hand, the fact that the city, from the viewpoint of any one of its inhabitants, contains a surplus of people whom he does not know and does not have anything in particular to do with, does not necessarily mean that they will forever remain strangers. They may constitute instead a pool of potential alters, accessible to be drawn into relationships at some later point. This, we have said, could have interesting implications for urban social organization as well.

We then examined the studies by the Rhodes-Livingstone anthropologists of Central African mining towns, one variety of African and colonial urbanism. Here we again confronted the issue of the relationship between urbanism and cultural tradition, defined in terms of "tribalism" and "detribalization." Urban communities such as Luanshya and Kabwe were not, as far as their major functions were concerned, well integrated into the surrounding Central African society, and their domains of provisioning had their own dynamics. In other domains, one could see how peculiarly urban tendencies became more obviously interlaced with African cultural tradition. The latter had a further impact on overall social organization because a number of ethnic groups were involved, creating alignments which could be at some variance with those intrinsic to the urban system (although sometimes they could also coincide with these). This could be identified as the major problematic in the study of urban ethnicity; here it led us to formulate a notion of "role-discriminatory attributes," which without themselves being defined (like roles) in terms of particular situational involvements, could play a similar part in ordering an individual's participation in social life. Ethnicity is one such attribute, sex and age are others. Depending on how these are culturally defined, they may determine what roles an individual can take on, toward whom he may perform them, and in what way they will be performed. As studies in role combinability have shown us, some roles can have a similar influence in organizing role repertoires, while in themselves being situationally specified as the role-discriminatory attributes are not.

At this point we may perhaps say something about our treatment of the role concept itself, and we can do so in connection with the Rhodes-Livingstone point of view toward the character of urban social relations. The anthropologists of Central African urbanism, like the sociologists of the Chicago School, noted that some of the significant contacts in the towns were between strangers. But rather than generalizing across the board about what urban relations are like, they cautiously divided them into three major forms: structural, personal, and categorical. As we reviewed this conceptualization, we suggested that the aspect of consciousness organizing social relationships has two major components: a degree of personal information, and a degree of normative control. To assume, as anthropologists have tended to do in their use of the role concept, that situational involvements can all be defined in normative terms, consistently and with equal precision, is to take for granted something which may well be made a topic of study. Defining role simply as a purposive situational involvement, with dimensions of consciousness and resource management, may be somewhat unconventional and not always tidy, but it may leave us with more open minds.

The Rhodes-Livingstone anthropologists also raised the problem of the limits of anthropological competence, an important one not least in the study of such complex systems as cities are in themselves, or constitute parts of. Their conclusion, we saw, was that anthropologists ought not to trespass on fields outside their specialization, but rather draw on findings based on other expertise as boundaries and points of departure for the specifically anthropological analysis. As far as urban studies were concerned, the practical consequence of this argument was the identification of the contextual parameters of what was, for anthropological purposes, the social system of the city.

In the chapter which followed, we considered the uses of network analysis. We found a rather elaborate framework for describing, and to some extent even measuring, the patterns of connection between social linkages. The possibilities for rigor in research procedure could thus in themselves appear attractive. As this rigor could sometimes seem to come at a high price, however, it was more important for our purposes to stress the flexibility of network thinking. With ideas of density, reachability, network awareness, and so forth, it could help us transcend some limitations of group, institutional, and local analysis, in a way which might be especially useful in the study of societies pieced together from many kinds of units.

Finally, we discussed the communication of selves and the microsociology of public order, as interpreted by Erving Goffman, and tried to specify their relationship to urban life. Goffman, we could easily see, rather disregards the overarching frameworks of social structure. Within them, however, he does the detailed ethnography and analysis of what people claim to be and what they understand others to be; and he does so with a fine attention to symbolic forms and the uses of microenvironments. If personal information is a problem in city living, as we have been told since the times of the sociological classics, Goffman seems to be our foremost guide in the naturalistic observation of how it is handled.

With the help of the ideas we have thus broached, then, we hope to get a clearer sense of what would be an urban anthropology that does justice to both anthropology and urbanism. In this final chapter, they will be worked into a series of comments on topics which would seem to be of fundamental conceptual importance as anthropologists grapple with the complexities of city life: the shapes which urban lives as wholes can take, in role and network terms; the embeddedness of domain ethnography; the fluidity of life, and the uses of career analysis; the conditions for role innovation; the implications of urban social organization for cultural analysis; the study of entire cities; and, briefly, some possible consequences of our perspective for urban anthropological method. Before we set out on this path, however, we might have a quick look for background at what appears to have been a dominant practice in ethnographies of city life in recent times.

DOMAIN ANTHROPOLOGIES, the SOFT CITY, and MODES of URBAN EXISTENCE

Rather predictably, the greater number of ethnographically inclined studies carried out in urban contexts can be more or less readily identified with one or another of the role domains we have delineated. In the domain of kinship and domesticity, Elizabeth Bott's work has been followed in England by Colin Bell's (1968) study of middle-class families in Swansea and the London study by Firth, Hubert, and Forge (1969). Third World studies in the same domain include Vatuk's *Kinship and Urbanization* (1972) from Meerut, India, and Pauw's *The Second Generation* (1963) from East London, South Africa, a companion piece of Philip Mayer's study of the Red and the School in the "Xhosa in Town" trilogy. Representing the domain of provisioning there are a number of occupational ethnographies— Pilcher's (1972) on the longshoremen of Portland, Rubinstein's (1973) on the Philadelphia police, Klockars' (1974) on the professional fence, and *The Cocktail Waitress* by Spradley and Mann (1975), with an emphasis on one occupation although involving a wider role complex rather like that of Cressey's old taxi-dance halls in Chicago. Studies of somewhat larger-scale work organizations include, from urban Africa, Kapferer's (1972) on a Zambian clothing factory and Grillo's (1973) on railwaymen in Kampala. There is also the growing interest in the "informal sector" of small-scale enterprise; Gould's (1965) paper on the ricksha drivers of Lucknow is a rather early representative. We may regard a number of studies of youth life as belonging primarily to the ethnography of the recreation domain—on hippies, such as Cavan's (1972) view from San Francisco, or on gangs, many by Thrasher's American successors and some from other countries like Patrick's *A Glasgow Gang Observed* (1973). Rather out-of-the-ordinary adult amusements are also reported, for instance by Bartell (1971) on the phenomenon of swinging, while it is perhaps surprising how few focus on more conventional pastimes. Jackson's (1968) series of vignettes from England's industrial North, with its workingmen's clubs, brass bands, and bowling greens, would be one example. Non-western studies in this domain could be represented by Meillassoux (1968) on associational life in Bamako, Mali, and by Plath's *The After Hours* (1964), on "the search for

enjoyment" among Japanese urbanites. There is no dearth of studies dealing, more or less concentratedly, with neighborhood relationships. Such
diverse items could be included as the many studies of suburbia, inner-city
studies like Suttles' on *The Social Order of the Slum* (1968), and a number
of Skid Row studies, and Johnson's *Idle Haven* (1971), an account of life in
a mobile-home park. The literature on Third World squatter settlements
could also to some extent be counted here, a fairly substantial component.
As far as traffic relationships are concerned, with Goffman as their master
theorist, it is mostly a genre of American urban ethnography, although Lyn
Lofland has made some attempt to develop a comparative viewpoint in *A
World of Strangers* (1973).

The tendency may be to regard the topic as somewhat luxurious, and to
choose rather more tangible problems in societies where researchers are as
yet less abundant. It is also most likely true that some of the subtleties of
traffic relationships, remaining on a low level of awareness and rarely ver-
balized by the participants, will elude an ethnographer who is only a temporary immigrant in a foreign society and whose cultural competence is
less than perfect. As one example of research in this area, however, there
is Berreman's (1972) report on the categorization of strangers in public settings in an Indian city. Perhaps because traffic relationships are ephemeral
things, writings on them are mostly brief papers rather than lengthy monographs. In publications of the former kind, we have recently begun to see
accounts of life on the sidewalks and in the subways and elevators of urban
America.

There is obviously nothing wrong in principle with domain ethnographies of the kinds we have exemplified here. Ethnography must begin
somewhere and end somewhere, and the institutions, groups, or more
loosely constituted networks which fall within domain boundaries are often
natural foci. We come back here, however, to the question whether they
are anthropology of the city, or only in the city. The study of traffic relationships can perhaps hardly help belonging in the former category, to the
extent that one is ready to regard these as just about intrinsically urban
phenomena. As far as the others are concerned, we may feel that they are
only urban anthropology in the strict sense when they give a reasonable
measure of attention to the fact that they deal with entities which are
somehow integrated parts of a differentiated urban social system; when
they are not "blind to overlap and connection," as we may remember that a
critic of the early Chicago studies put it, but contribute to an understanding of the ways this system both segments and coheres.

We have aimed here at drawing together the sort of general and flexible conceptualizations which could be useful in clarifying such an integrated view of the construction of cities and urban lives. The city, for our purposes, is (like other human communities) a collection of individuals who exist as social beings primarily through their roles, setting up relations to one another through these. Urban lives, then, are shaped as people join a number of roles together in a role repertoire and probably to some degree adjust them to each other. The social structure of the city consists of the relationships by which people are linked through various components of their role repertoires.

One may choose to begin analysis with the city as a whole, or with the individual urbanite; both perspectives have their uses. Let us first take what as anthropologists we call the ego-centered perspective. In his engaging book *Soft City,* the British essayist Jonathan Raban (1974:1–2) has some lines which can perhaps define a spirit of inquiry:

> . . . the city goes soft; it awaits the imprint of an identity. For better or worse, it invites you to remake it, to consolidate it into a shape you can live in. You, too. Decide who you are, and the city will again assume a fixed form round you. Decide what it is, and your own identity will be revealed, like a posiiton on a map fixed by triangulation. Cities, unlike villages and small towns, are plastic by nature. We mould them in our images: they, in their turn, shape us by the resistance they offer when we try to impose our own personal form on them.

Softness, as we conceptualize things here, is indeterminacy; the urbanite deciding who he is makes his choice of roles freely. Think, for a moment, of roles as entities in themselves. So the entire role inventory of the city is there, exhibited as in a supermarket, for the shopper putting together his repertoire. The shelves are full of goods of many kinds, and you have a large shopping cart. The variations in what can go into it seem almost endless.

Not quite; we can in fact work out all the combinations which are theoretically possible. (It would be the kind of task which is nowadays almost effortless, since we simply ask a computer to do it for us.) As we inspect the results, however, we see that some of the combinations will not occur in practice, while we would have questions to ask about the feasibility of others. The city, after all, offers some resistance.

As students of urban lives begin to ask what combinations can or cannot be made, and how combinations are managed, a large field of subtle analysis is opened. Only a few variations in reasoning can be suggested here, giving some further idea of the ways in which our core conceptualizations can be put to work.

At times, we have seen, the sources of restriction on role combinability lie outside what is strictly speaking the role inventory itself. You enter the supermarket with one or two role-discriminatory attributes, and hence you are allowed to shop around for certain items only. You are a young girl of Italian immigrant stock, on the threshold of adulthood, in the Chicago of the 1920s—your most important role is likely to be within the household, while you may have no role of your own in the provisioning domain. Perhaps your recreation outside the household is severely constrained as well. You may, possibly, have a fair amount of interaction with neighbors in your quarter of Little Sicily, but you should not be moving about on distant streets, at least not after dark or, as Goffman would put it, without a "with." If your family had been Eastern European instead, your involvements could have been more spread out. It is a little more likely one would have found you among the factory workers or the taxi-dance girls, but not among the Gold Coast debutantes. If you are a middle-aged Anglo-Saxon male instead, you may be an office manager in the Loop, or quite possibly a hobo in Bughouse Square. Were the former to be the case, you may spend a reasonably large part of your time in household and kinship roles, and a bare minimum in traffic roles. But if you were a hobo, it would probably be the other way around. If you are a Xhosa male in East London, you may be in unskilled industrial work whether you are "School" or "Red," but your recreational roles would be noticeably different.

Examining the organizational effects of role-discriminatory attributes, we see clearly that the city is softer to some people than to others. They draw their repertoires from varying proportions of the role inventory. As we can also see, however, the role-discriminatory attributes entail for some people only a first rough sorting of roles. One or a few components of a repertoire may be assigned in this manner, or more or less stringent limits on choice may be set. For the rest, the role repertoire orders itself. The hobo spent much of his time on the sidewalks of Chicago not because he was a white Anglo-Saxon but because he was a migrant casual worker. We may only briefly remind ourselves what goes into such ordering of roles. An individual draws the state of his consciousness—knowledge, beliefs, values, interests—from his experience in roles, and in these roles (particularly in the domain of provisioning, to some extent perhaps in others) he may also build up resources. What he has thus gained guides him in deciding what further roles he may seek. Certain roles may seem more attractive than others, certain roles more within reach than others.

But we must not make the creation of role repertoires sound like a wholly solitary activity. It cannot be, for there is the further complication that a role, as we usually see it, entails a relationship. One cannot have it unless one can find an alter, or sometimes many, to perform a matching role—an alter whose readiness to do so may depend on what personal information he has about ego, not least on what he can discern of his roles and role-discriminatory attributes. At this point, a requirement of some minimal consensus can come into defining what is a suitable role combination. If nobody is prepared to be ego's partner in a relationship where he would perform a certain role, he has (in the terms suggested in chapter 4) no role access at all. If only some category of people, also defined in terms of a role or role-discriminatory attribute, offer themselves as potential partners, he has what we have called relational access. But there may be some room for maneuver here, in the form of impression management. Alters may insist on relevant personal information before entering a certain relationship, or they may enter a relationship which they had refused had they been better informed. It could be up to ego to present his role repertoire more or less fully and correctly, or to place some particular interpretation on it.

Assuming that a role repertoire has thus been assembled, there is still some further organizing involved in turning it into a whole. In some way or another, one must distribute one's finite resources, time, and concern among the roles. Their requirements sometimes come into conflict, more or less conspicuously. Overtime at work, for instance, is at the expense of household or recreational activities. But roles can also support one another. The channeling of resources from the provisioning role to others is one example, using skills in one's work which one has learned in the household or in recreation is another.

These internal tinkerings within the role repertoire are also in no small part relational phenomena, as it may be a matter of some interest to alter how ego portions himself out. Scheduling, resource investment, and other aspects of role performance may thus be subject to negotiation. It is a question of obvious interest, however, what the limits of negotiability for various roles are. Briefly, we may suggest at least two kinds of situations where roles will tend to become fixed. One is where they are part of a tightly integrated, often large structure, and where renegotiation of one relationship would set off undesirable chain reactions more or less throughout the structure. The other involves the type of role through which ego will deal with some relatively rapid succession of alters, in contacts where it would be highly impractical to change the terms of interaction each time. We can see that the former situation is likely to obtain frequently, for example, in the internal workings of bureaucracies or industrial organizations, the latter in provisioning relationships involving some service of considerable centricity.

In such instances, then, relationships are ordered more by normative control than by personal information, and there is a great substitutability of participants. They are of kinds which often occur in cities. The "deprivation theory" of self-consciousness referred to in the preceding chapter relates to these situations, as they can bring about a disjunction of role and self concepts.

There are also roles, on the other hand, which more often take the squeeze from repertoire adjustments, or which in another phrasing could be described as more permeable. Some of these are simply part of relationships which demand rather little coordination between ego and alter, and therefore little negotiation. Contacts between neighbors are often of this type. In consequence with what we have said, we would furthermore expect such roles more often to entail relationships in dyads or small groups, not so difficult to rearrange, and relationships where there is no constant flow of alters. Domestic relationships and friendships may count here. We should set forth arguments such as these only with some caution, however. What is negotiable and what is not may be decided not only by social organizational logic but also by personal priorities.

There may be room here for a reflection on what may be a difference in the standardization of roles between two kinds of role structures. Where role repertoires are to a higher degree replicated, the adjustments to be made between roles may not be so varied either. Roles are permeated in standardized ways by influences from other parts of the repertoire. Where repertoires are varied, standardization is achieved instead by making roles impermeable. The contrast is a gross one, obviously, and would need to be qualified.

On to a slightly different matter. As ego and alter meet, the demands involved in holding together a role repertoire may well affect their performances toward one another; this they may or may not point out. There are other ways as well, however, in which the wider role constellation can be made relevant in an ongoing relationship. The discussion of disclosures in the preceding chapter can be taken a little further here.

When a relationship involves relatively frequent interactions of some duration, it is likely that some further personalization will occur, in the form of disclosures concerning other parts of the participants' repertoires. In this case, one may picture them as occurring alongside the activity on which the relationship is centered, rather than as an integral part of it. This, at least, seems to be a clear enough conception, for example, as colleagues tell each other what they did during the weekend. (We may just keep in mind that some relationships may be so ill-defined in terms of intrinsic content that they continuously have to sponge off disclosures from outside involvements. Some kin relationships are like this—we are normatively enjoined from treating kinsmen as strangers or nonpersons, but we have to look around for the materials with which to express recognition, since nothing else may be prescribed.)

It may be argued that acts of disclosure per se can constitute an establishment of multiplexity in a relationship; whatever the latter was before, they entail a sociability which, however minimal or fleeting, takes it into the domain of recreation as well. Yet the greater significance of personal revelations for the growth of multiplexity would seem to be in their capacity to suggest distinct new contexts of interaction between ego and alter. They offer a map of actual or potential compatibility, which allows the parties either to reject each other tacitly or explicitly as partners beyond the minimal interaction in and around their single shared activity (sometimes even in that) or to expand their relationship into new areas.

One may toy, as we have done before, with a notion of randomness in urban social relations. If a person with a certain role repertoire would draw for each role the necessary number of alters at random from the pool of individuals with the matching role, it would be relatively unlikely that he would come up with the same alters in many relationships, so that multiplex linkages would result. (At least it would be improbable if none of the roles involve great centricity.) In reality, such linkages might be somewhat more common insofar as choices made in one role constrain choices in another—if two people choose to work in the same factory, for example, their desire to live nearby may also make them neighbors. Such mechanisms aside, it would appear that the intentional multiplexity based on disclosures is the most important kind of multiplexity in an urban social structure, the minimal units of which are more narrowly defined roles and the relations connected to them.

It is a kind of multiplexity which sometimes comes about merely as a matter of convenience. Ego has an empty slot for an alter with whom he could engage in a particular sort of relationship, and in another relationship he finds someone who can thus serve double duty. The two matched role pairs, in a way, can be said already to exist, but there is one role pair in search of a relationship. Alternatively it is possible that ego has a preference for alter as an individual—a preference which may be unilateral or reciprocal. Here the management of multiplexity can take on new forms. Ego may maximize togetherness for its own sake by thinking up new things to interact over—that is, there may be an active search of alter's role repertoire for additional opportunities for interaction, and ego may even expand his own role repertoire with something to match a role in alter's constellation. For such a preferential relationship (sometimes called "friendship" or "love," the Martian ethnographer may scribble in his notebook) some contexts are better suited than others, allowing more complete expression of the individual qualities and interpersonal sentiments involved. The expansion into multiplexity under such conditions is thus likely to occur in areas under limited normative control. One changes from a single-stranded relationship in the context of factory work to a multiplex one including also shared recreation, for example, but probably not so often in the opposite direction.

Some limitations on intentional multiplexity may be recognized. Even where ego and alter are able to identify further matching roles, these may entail limited numbers of relationships. If these are already tied up with other partners, ego or alter or both may be unwilling or unable to cut these off. A further complication results from the fact that in contexts other than isolated dyads, ego may not be alone in determining what alter is to be recruited. Expansions into multiplexity may thus most often occur through roles entailing a flexible number of relationships, or where there is some turnover of alters, so that vacancies are created, and through roles where ego is in sole control of the recruitment of alters.

Further effects of personal disclosures may be described in network terms. Without such revelations on the part of his alters, ego's network awareness may be largely limited to his first-order star, plus those lateral links among his alters which are directly observable to him. His perception of the density of his network involves only the visibly tight clusters of role relationships in which he is himself a participant, and the range of his network through higher than first-order links remains more or less unknown to him. No doubt urban life is often rather like this, not least because alter's disclosures concerning his network to ego are frequently very partial. When revelations occur about who are alter's alters, however, the new information may take on significance in various ways. Ego may find that there is only a single intermediary between himself and somebody else with whom he is not personally acquainted, who is best approached through a pre-existing link but whom he would like to influence in one way or another. He may then ask this intermediary alter of his to intervene on his behalf. Disclosures may also show that ego's personal network is more dense than he knew, as alters perhaps in different domains of his life turn out to be directly connected to each other.

Disclosures may lead not only to identification of existing linkages, however, but could also be the basis of the formation of new ones. Ego in finding his alter linked to a useful third person may ask alter for an introduction; this increases ego's network range and alter's network density. On the other hand, he might find even an indirect connection with a certain third person undesirable and therefore cut his own contact with the intermediate alter. By drawing alter into a multiplex relationship, ego also often condenses his own network, to the extent that it entails forming direct links between previously separate network segments.

The variety of ways in which urban lives can be put together may seem bewildering. If city dwellers can put roles together in different ways in their repertoires, can select among alternative alters, can make or not make disclosures, can expand or not expand links into multiplexity, can put their various network partners in touch with each other or keep them apart, can anything illuminating be said about entire rounds of life unless one is prepared to treat each one as a wholly unique creation?

Perhaps there is a little need to try. In social anthropology, ego-centered perspectives have mostly been used to throw light on particular situations in which individuals make use of some specific segments of their networks or role repertoires, analytically excised from the whole. The construction of whole lives may seem to be biography rather than ethnography.

Still, it may be interesting to have some idea of alternative outcomes as totalities—as something in the way of an answer to the question what it is like to be an urbanite, a little more differentiated than the portrait (or caricature) sketched by Wirth. The possibilities for variation being what they are, we can seize on only a few broad types as a beginning toward such conceptualization. We will identify these modes of urban existence tentatively as *encapsulation, segregativity, integrativity,* and *solitude.* Real lives, of course, may be crosses between these.

Encapsulation so far looks like the darling of urban anthropologists—urban villagers, Red Xhosa, and the people of Oscar Lewis' *vecindad* in Mexico City belong here. The defining characteristic of encapsulation is that ego has one dense network sector, connected to one or more of his roles, in which he invests a very high proportion of his time and interest. At the extreme point, little of his network is left outside. In a pure form of encapsulation, also, all alters have a similarly intensive involvement in the network they make up together. The highest degree of encapsulation can obviously be reached if relationships from the greatest possible number of domains are combined into multiplex relationships, or if the smaller number of relationships from one or more domains are contained within the larger number of another domain. Since one can hardly expect traffic and provisioning relationships to be contained within these boundaries (the traffic relationships could not very well be there), maximal encapsulation might involve people who live, work, and play together, and who also find their kin among one another. Since this may be brought about most readily through a relative standardization of role repertoires and relational access to roles, it is hardly surprising if it frequently has an ethnic base. But although it has less often been observed by anthropologists, this can be an upper-class mode of existence as well. The "elitist" analysis of community power structures referred to in chapter 5 emphasizes that members of a privileged stratum may bring about closure by choosing mostly each other as spouses, neighbors, and partners in recreation as well.

In other groups, if such multiplexity is too much to ask for, one may at least find a strong tendency toward attenuation of links outside the "capsule," and the elaboration of links inside. Ethnic groupings may obviously be involved here also (see, for instance, Wirth's description of Jewish ghetto life as quoted in chapter 2), but the core could well be a shared role rather than a role-discriminatory attribute. The work on "occupational communities," such as that by Becker (1963:95 ff.) on jazz musicians and that by Salaman (1971, 1974) on architects and railway workers, offers examples of different degrees of encapsulation here. Since recreational relationships are those most certainly under individual control, one is not likely to find anything that could be called encapsulation which does not include a great part of ego's leisure life, but what else is involved is less certain. Disclosures will probably be made in ego's encapsulated relationships about his experiences outside rather than vice versa, but there may be some variation in this—some sets of encapsulated relationships may be very self-sufficient in content.

The encapsulated urbanite may appear to make very limited use of the opportunities of the city. He has not picked out a set of alters uniquely his own, and if his role repertoire is not quite standardized he gets little out of what is original about it. Influences emanating outside his dense network do not easily reach him, and conversely his ability to reach out to unknown others through his network when this could be advantageous is not great, since his alters tend to be of little use as intermediaries—they are people much like himself.[1] (This obviously applies less to an elite.) In a couple of ways, however, there can be something characteristically urban about encapsulation, as Robert Park understood when he described the city as "a mosaic of little worlds which touch but do not interpenetrate." We touched on this in chapter 3; a person can encapsulate himself only with others of his kind where there are a number of such others, and a larger community is likely to have more people of more kinds. Moreover, to the extent that encapsulation depends on keeping outside links weak and disclosing little about what goes on inside, boundary maintenance should be simplified by the fact that ego's alters in outside relationships have other relationships in which they can immerse themselves, and need not be very curious about ego.

One might add a note here on the existence of a sort of unilateral encapsulation, of individuals whose round of life is to a high degree taken up by relationships to some small number of interconnected alters who are not equally encapsulated. The relationship between inmates and staff in Goffman's total institutions would serve acceptably well as an example. Coser has also touched on this in his *Greedy Institutions* (1974), where he is concerned with various "patterns of undivided commitment." One such pattern allows ego quite varied contacts, but only as a completely loyal extension of some personal or institutional master; eunuchs and royal mistresses of modest ancestry are historical examples.[2] Another pattern is shown by certain religious sects and political revolutionary groups; these are more or less like the form of encapsulation already discussed above.[3] The third pattern of undivided commitment, and that which is of interest here, Coser finds with housewives and domestic servants such as live-in maids. If this is regarded as marginally similar to encapsulation, in some cases at least, what was said before about encapsulated people's limited access to others through intermediaries is less likely to hold. Both directly and by way of vicarious participation through disclosures, a housewife may well be intensively involved in her alters' outside relationships, while she may have fewer external links of her own.

Segregativity and integrativity are our two perhaps rather unfortunate neologisms. Under the description "double life," the former is a mode of existence which has a strong hold on our imagination. Janus with his two faces, Dr. Jekyll and Mr. Hyde, Clark Kent and Superman, and Park's continued comment on the urban mosaic that "encourages the fascinating but dangerous experiment of living at the same time in several different contiguous, but otherwise widely separated, worlds" are expressions of the theme. Ronnie Kray, the London gangster whose life was described in a quotation in the preceding chapter, is an example. So, evidently, were the taxi-dance girls in Chicago. We use the new term instead of "double life" because the separate involvements can be more than two, and because it is the counterpart of integrativity, for which no familiar term seems to be available.

The individual engaged in segregativity, then, in principle has two or more segments in his network which are kept well separated. Typically, one may assume that this is intentionally so. Ideally ego is the only individual involved in both (or whatever the number is). If he is not alone in such multiple involvement, an implicit or explicit pact is likely to exist among those who share it to the effect that disclosures to others should be withheld or restricted. The line between encapsulation and segregativity may at times be a thin one, as a largely encapsulated individual may still have some outside links which he strives to keep segregated from the central arena of his life. "Real" segregativity could be said to make more evenly weighted investments in different network segments. It does not seem necessary to posit anything about the degree of density in any of the segments. The only important thing is that at least two of them are held not to mix in any way, as it would reveal inconsistency in ego's presentation of self. A marginal case would be ego's intensive involvement in some solitary activity which, while not generating any relationships of its own, yet constitutes a sort of role which is not revealed to his network. (Fantasies à la Walter Mitty may also belong here.) It is possible for a segregated network segment to consist of fleeting relationships—various minority sexual expressions provide examples, with an ethnographic account in Humphreys' *Tea Room Trade* (1970). In its central sense, however, segregativity should perhaps be seen as consisting of more durable sets of relationships, each of which is understood to show ego as he really is. Segregativity is, more than any other, the mode of urban existence of someone living with a "dark secret."

Integrativity is probably the most ordinary way of life in the city, and it may be for precisely this reason that we can find no reasonably informative label for it in common use. In integrativity one individual's network is spread among domains without very strong tendencies to concentration in any one. Network segments related to roles may vary in size and density depending on the nature of the activities concerned, but if it were not for ego's mode of management of his entire network, links between them would probably be few or non-existent. In this case, however, ego has no policy of network segregation. Even if he does not insist on bringing everybody together with everybody else, and pragmatically feels that some of his alters may as well be left apart, the general tendency is to create encounters between previously unacquainted alters rather offhandedly, and similarly to make disclosures in one relationship about other roles and relationships. In integrativity, ego does not exclude the possibility that quite various relations can serve as a basis for expansions into multiplexity. On the whole, then, his personal network develops toward greater density over time, with less pronounced tendencies toward clustering, even if links between the erstwhile clusters often remain comparatively weak. But of course, his network range may vary. Some people in integrativity have a rather routinized round of relationships and do little to develop new links out of occasional encounters. Others may incessantly seek out new people mostly for rather non-committal leisure relationships, while probably at the same time letting other relationships sink back into latency or oblivion. Subject to such range variations, ego in integrativity may serve well as an intermediary, unlike an individual in encapsulation, who cannot, or one in segregativity, who will not. Segregativity and integrativity could both be said to make real use of the size and diversity of the city. While segregativity depends on maintaining distances as they are between different people and activities, however, integrativity could (perhaps perversely) be seen as a corrupting influence on urbanism as a way of life—creating links where none existed and making unknown faces known.

Turning to solitude, one might think of "loneliness" as a convenient alternative term. But solitude is a social condition and loneliness a psychological one, and they need not always go together. No urbanite, surely, is likely to be without interactions and few without any durable relationships, so solitude is relative. Conceivably, the lone urbanite can be one with a small role repertoire, at least in the domains where enduring relationships are normally formed; it is likely that his network is small, or at least that few alters are conveniently available; but what is perhaps most important is that few personal disclosures are made in his relationships, and that they do not tend to expand into the recreational domain, which in relational terms is more or less an empty space. Solitude in the city may seem paradoxical, but one is not with other people merely by being among them. The underlying fact, naturally, is that urban relationships in large part may have to be actively achieved, and actively maintained. Usually solitude is likely to be a temporary state, before new relationships have been formed (by newcomers to the city, such as some inhabitants of Zorbaugh's "world of furnished rooms"), or after an old network has come apart. But for some it becomes a long-term state of affairs which they have not desired, if they lack the social assets around which relationships are created—a job, a place to call home, an outgoing personality. This is where most often one may find attempts to make and seek disclosures in relationships where they are otherwise unlikely: the willingness to engage strangers in interaction, the eagerness to become personal with the sales clerks where one does one's shopping.[4] Such ouvertures, however, may well fail. To quote Raban (1974:140) again, "you crave recognition; all you receive is treatment." Yet others again may have solitude without loneliness, perhaps finding satisfaction in activities which entail no relationships and carefully cultivating opportunities for these.

In summary, solitude is a mode of existence by and large without significant relationships; encapsulation one with a single set of them; segregativity one with more sets, kept apart; integrativity one with more sets, brought together. One may think of various ways of arranging them into patterns. In time, the life of an individual may encompass all of them. Childhood is usually a sort of encapsulation, partly mutual, partly one-sided. In adolescence tendencies toward segregativity are often strong. Adulthood for many may be a phase of integrativity. Solitude may come with old age. But clearly there is no such simple pattern to which everyone conforms.

People of different modes of existence may relate to one another with varying degrees of ease. Someone coming out of solitude, and willing to give it up, may be quite adaptable in the sense of being able to commit as much of himself to a relationship as his alter requests; he can go straight into encapsulation, for example. A problem could possibly arise if he is ready to commit more than alters can cope with. Anybody with more varied involvements, on the other hand, either integrativity or segregativity, might find the demands of a set of people tending toward shared encapsulation too great, and friction might result. Segregativity and integrativity may go fairly well together, as neither finds anything unusual about alter dividing his time between ego and various others. Those pursuing integrativity as a way of life may be slow to notice the reticence of the segregator and assume rather that he is one of them.

We can now return to our domain anthropologies. It is true, as Oscar Lewis pointed out in his critique of Wirthian thinking, that urban life in large measure takes place within smaller universes—family, neighborhood, firm, sect, gang, or whatever—and that we need careful studies of these. But we must forever be aware of their openness to other areas of urban life, at least until we have convinced ourselves that they have in some way become closed. There should be full recognition of the fact that the arena momentarily in focus is, in most cases, only one out of many for the individuals concerned, a part-time engagement. Out of the four modes of urban existence just outlined, only encapsulation gives rise to well-bounded groups where people are members more or less as whole persons rather than by virtue of incumbency of particular roles. Even then, the group is in certain senses embedded in the wider urban system, but attention to the other modes of existence as well gives us further opportunities of seeing how activities within the smaller unit are affected by the ways participating individuals handle their roles and networks.

A whole range of questions can be raised with this aim. What is the intrinsic activity content of the unit under analysis? Is there any tendency toward standardized role recruitment, so that all or many participants also have other roles or role-discriminatory attributes in common? How is this unit influenced by the participants' internal repertoire management—are its roles more or less permeable? To what extent are the individuals who are directly linked here also indirectly linked through relationships in one or more other domains (or through other units within the same domain)? Are any disclosures made within this unit concerning the participants' outside lives, and in what ways may such disclosures order its activity content and internal relationships? Does it serve as an arena where previously existing relationships are made multiplex, or is it a pickup area for recruitment into other relationships?

An EXAMPLE: the ETHNOGRAPHY of NEIGHBORING

Studies like Elizabeth Bott's on the way marriage relationships are influenced by wider networks, or Adrian Mayer's of how an election campaign may feed politics into relationships of all kinds, have given examples of the way partial ethnographies can be carried out so as to contribute to an understanding of the coherence within urban differentiation, and so as to be informed by it. It may yet be useful to demonstrate the perspective a little more fully within one domain. We will do so by drawing on materials relating to neighboring from a handful of studies.

First of all, intrinsic content: who is a neighbor, and what is neighboring in itself? Sometimes, and for some purposes, the answer to both questions may be quite unambiguous. The clearest instance may be where a governmental body uses territorial divisions within towns and cities as organizational frameworks within which inhabitants are induced into various activities together. Inhabitants are thus instructed what to do and with whom to do it; neighboring is tightly interlocked with the overarching structure of provisioning. The ward system of urban Japan, waxing and waning over the years, is one example (cf. Dore 1958:267 ff.; Nakamura 1968). "Neighborhood committees" and similar organs of present-day mobilization regimes likewise tend to give a standard shape to some neighborhood relations. Douglas Butterworth's (1974) study of the Committees for the Defense of the Revolution in Havana concerns such phenomena, but otherwise there is little on them in anthropological writings.

In contemporary western cities, on the other hand, and in a great many others, there is usually little involvement from the top in such small-scale territorial organization, and neighborly contacts are rather more indirectly influenced by a number of other circumstances. We had some brief remarks on this in chapter 3. Neighbors, to elaborate now, are people whose places of residence (or work, as we will point out) are close to each other; this is the obvious minimum. Furthermore, normally, they become aware of each other's recurrent presence in the surrounding more or less public space, and consequently of the special relationship they have to it. They are also likely to signal this awareness by extending recognition to each other as they meet, which makes this something other than a relationship between strangers.

The commonsensical definition implies some of the possibilities for variation in neighboring. The nature of the physical setting is one source.

Where people are more exposed to one another, they will be quicker to learn to recognize one another. If they can see one another entering or leaving houses, or spending time in private or semi-private but visible spaces around the houses, this obviously helps. If there is some common focus or sense of boundaries to prevent definitions of neighborhoods from becoming altogether ego-centered and thus only partially overlapping, neighbor relations can also more easily take off. Hills or rivers may provide such boundaries, but they can also be man-made, such as parks, railway tracks, or highways. Where fewer outsiders pass through the area and distract perceptions, residents may have a surer sense of who actually belongs.

Glimpses of such influences are occasionally offered in ethnographies, but they have had more extensive and systematic attention in the context of western cities than elsewhere. In a case like Whyte's (1965:365 ff.) analysis of suburban neighboring in *The Organization Man,* quite far-reaching claims have been made for them.[5] More comparable studies in non-western urban communities would be of interest, as their layout and architecture is so often quite different.

The opportunity to learn to recognize neighbors and become involved with them, however, is also often inversely related to the intensity of one's involvement in roles enacted in other arenas. Where husbands are household breadwinners and have their places of work elsewhere, they often get much of their knowledge about the neighborhood, and the contacts they have there, through the disclosures and mediation of their wives or children. Elderly and retired people may similarly have a more intensive neighborhood involvement. Johnson's *Idle Haven* gives some indication of this, and Reina's (1973:91) study of Paraná in Argentina mentions the elderly men who "police" the *vecindad* and converse with whomever is available at the same time as they watch their grandchildren. In areas where few household members remain at home during the day, and where residents are of a kind who spend much of their free time as well in dispersed activities, it follows that neighboring may be very limited—"children are the real neighbors, and it is a childless world," we remember that Zorbaugh wrote about the rooming-house zone in Chicago.

Neighborhood life may thus center on people who are intensively involved there but participate less in other domains of urban life. A starring part, however, may also come to the individual who performs a provisioning role in what is an arena of neighboring to others, a role through which he manages neighborhood space or caters to the inhabitants in some other way. Bittner (1967) has a revealing study here on the policeman as a keeper of the peace on Skid Row. The French *concierge* is another obvious example, as is the shopkeeper whose establishment may be one of the type of nodal points which make understandings of neighborhood boundaries less ego-centered. While neighbors' involvements with each other may be uneven and lacking in overall coordination, in other words, some organization may come about through replicated provisioning relationships.

A couple of further variations in the work-neighboring connection may be given due recognition here. It should be noted that someone who is durably present in a neighborhood because of his work is in a sense also in a neighbor role, as not every encounter between him and the others there need involve a work task on his part. The habitual assumption (even accepted in these pages in several contexts) that neighboring is exclusively tied to residence may in fact be understood as open to doubt as soon as it is made explicit. Of course, the separation of residence and work place is itself a tendency which has been taken further in large western industrial cities than in many other places, and where it is not so pronounced neighboring is likely to take other forms. But where it has occurred, neighboring may well be seen as taking place at least potentially in both contexts, although perhaps with different degrees of elaboration. Thus one finds neighborhoods with mixed recruitment by way of work and residence, as exemplified above; here one may ask whether relationships linking residence-neighbors with work-neighbors (in links conceptually separate from the provisioning relationships which may run parallel to all or some of them) differ in their role definitions from neighboring relationships within either category. One also finds neighborhoods more or less wholly recruited on a work basis, such as shopping streets with shopkeepers and their employees as daytime neighbors. Of their kind of neighboring there is hardly any ethnography.

We need say no more about who is a neighbor, or about the fact that some are more neighborly than others. The content of neighboring may entail only such rituals of deference and demeanor as is contained in the exchange of greetings, and the expression of regard also through minimizing annoyances in shared space—no noise, no odor, no obstacles placed on streets or sidewalks or in the yards, corridors, and staircases of multi-household dwellings. The latter component shows neighboring to be in one way much like a traffic relationship, in that the principle is for neighbors to interfere with each other as little as possible; "strong fences make good neighbors."

The relationship, however, may grow to be something more than this. On a more positive note, there can be a certain exchange of goods and services, such as giving away small quantities of household staples on request in a sort of generalized reciprocity, lending out tools, watching children or a neighbor's house if he or she has to go out. The principle is clearly that what is a relatively modest prestation from a neighbor would entail considerably greater inconvenience if the same assistance had to be sought from another source, perhaps socially closer but physically more distant. The best neighbor is therefore, strictly speaking, the next-door neighbor.

The contents and extent of this reciprocity may vary. If the mere amount of time one has for neighboring is one thing that depends on what one's role repertoire is like, one's needs for neighborly exchanges is another. If kin or friends are within easy access, one may not have so much use for the occasional services of one's immediate neighbors. The intensive neighborly interaction of the suburbanites in Park Forest, Illinois, described by Whyte in *The Organization Man,* conversely, could be characteristic of a community of interurban migrants with few other useful local ties. In order to come to mutually satisfactory arrangements, however, neighbors must then have congruent needs. Bell's (1968:135) Swansea study shows this. The housing estate he studied contained both families rather like those of Park Forest, spiralists moving from one town to another, and local residents of longer standing. The spiralists were in need of new multi-purpose links, while the locals already had more varied networks and had no place in them for such demanding new linkages. The two categories therefore tended to coalesce in separate clusters of neighborly relationships.

As we have suggested before, it is most likely with rather standardized role repertoires that people come to specific types of relationship with similar negotiating positions, and arrive at results in which the optimal adjustment would take the form of roles of recurrent definition. As far as neighboring is concerned, this would also be where relative propinquity would have the greatest effect on the actual formation of relationships. Where neighbors are really substitutable for each other, one becomes involved with those most conveniently accessible.

Jeremy Seabrook's (1967:50 ff.) personal recollections of a British working-class neighborhood, where he emphasizes the underlying homoge-

neity, seem to fit well into such an argument. Seabrook notes that relationships between neighbors were "based upon observance of a rigid and
complex system of rules and conventions," that "the closest links were generally established with immediate neighbours," and that "those a few doors
distant were treated with a cordiality which diminished progressively as
their dwelling-place became farther removed, until those at the end of the
street had to be content with a cursory nod and the briefest glance of recognition." Bryan Roberts (1973:187), observing the great heterogeneity of
lives among the low-income inhabitants of two Guatemala City neighborhoods, appears to come up with the opposite form of this relationship
between repertoire diversity and role standardization as he notes that
"there is a recurrent theme in the description of the various personal relationships found within the neighborhoods: most relationships are essentially dyadic, and what is exchanged is specific to the pair interacting."

We move on to ask in what ways neighboring can be influenced by the
channeling of personal information between it and other roles and relationships. There is one special problem in this area: that of controlling the
flow of information between the domestic and neighboring domains. Since
they are physically so close, it is not always easy to keep the former safely
backstage to the latter. Disclosures may begin to run wild across the somewhat ineffectively marked boundary, and as soon as a person is physically
present in domestic space, neighbors could at worst have practically uncon-
trollable access to him.

This is obviously quite widely regarded as a problem, and one tries to
solve it through some degree of reserve. Reina (1973:86) notes it in his
Paraná study:

> Each household maintains a strong sense of familial intimacy—there is an un-
> disclosed life within one's own walls. In contrast to the constant public gather-
> ings in the *zona central,* in the vecindad the rule of etiquette is that "each one
> should be in his own home." Toleration and calculated avoidance protect each
> family style. Neighbors seldom discuss differences openly, but guess at them.
> Differences are glossed over as long as one keeps "to oneself."

Goffman's analysis of the consensual maintenance of public selves in interaction ritual seems very much to the point here. Similarly, La Fontaine
(1970:130) found in her study of Kinshasa, Zaire (then still named
Léopoldville), that neighbors often appeared to agree tacitly to maintain a
fictive ignorance of one another's lives, as showing too much knowledge
would be considered impertinent. To outsiders, neighbors would claim not

to know a man's ethnic origin, or even how many children were living with him; and this despite the fact that their living arrangements, as so often in Third World cities, made them highly visible to one another.

Further microstudies of such settings could be undertaken. What division into private, semi-private, and public spaces for domestic and neighborly activities arises where the households of a compound share kitchen, laundry, and toilet facilities in or adjoining an open court yard, and use the latter for other purposes in their daily life as well? What are they supposed to know or not to know about each other? And what, in the end, do neighboring and domesticity, frontstage and backstage, amount to when a Calcutta family makes its home on the sidewalk, as in Lelyveld's (1970) sketch?

But there are other kinds of disclosures with social consequences to be concerned about—two kinds basically, in this case disclosures made in the contexts of other domains which lead to neighboring, and disclosures between neighbors which change the relationship they have to one another. In one form considerable attention has been devoted to the first of these: the process called chain migration, where individuals who already have some other relationship gradually recruit one another so that they come to inhabit the same territory. Ethnic neighborhoods such as those formed in American cities in the heyday of immigration are obvious examples of chain migration, and the concept actually has been in only limited use outside the fields of ethnicity and long-distance migration. In these instances chain migration can appear as the typical first stage in that process of neighborhood evolution where a later stage is an "urban village" encapsulation in multiplex relationships lasting from the cradle to the grave. Where ethnicity is the apparent criterion of recruitment to a neighborhood, however, it is yet likely that particular roles and relationships constrained by this role-discriminatory attribute have been the effective factors in each particular recruitment, so that the ethnic aspect becomes conspicuous only in the aggregate, and perhaps on the basis of a non-member's perception of categories (cf. MacDonald and MacDonald 1962, 1964). And naturally these other factors may be similarly at work where there is no ethnicity to catch our attention. This also means that quite diverse neighborhoods can be formed through the same process. Each pre-existing link could presumably be of a different kind—kinship, friendship, contacts at work, even provisioning relationships—so that a variety of multiplexities exist in the neighborhood, without any overall homogeneity. Obviously, too, there are neighborhoods only partially populated by chains (long or short), and for the rest through other kinds of recruitment.

With regard to personal revelations between people who have already become neighbors, there is an illuminating example in Herbert Gans's *The Levittowners* (1967:46–47), describing the presentations as they occurred soon after people had settled in the new development:

> They described where they had come from, and their—or their husbands'—occupations, and went on to cover childrearing methods and plans for fixing the house (women), the lawn, cars and work (men). Every topic served either to bring people closer together or to pull them apart, by indicating where differences existed and what topics were taboo. For example, one of my neighbors was an Army pilot, and on our initial meeting—produced by a washout on our front lawns—we exchanged occupations. After I mentioned being a professor, he made a crack about another neighbor, a blue collar worker, to indicate that, although he referred to himself as "a glorified truck driver" he was, nevertheless, a white collar worker like me. He went on by talking about a relative who was studying for his Ph.D., but, aware that most professors were liberal and agnostic, he also let me know that he shared Southern race attitudes and was a fundamentalist Baptist. Disagreements would surely come up about race and religion, and if we were to be good neighbors, these subjects should not be discussed.

Neighborly disclosures, we can see, do not always establish compatibility. This does not mean that they are insignificant. Pure neighboring, we may feel, is one of that sort of relationships which have little content of their own; they benefit from importing some from the outside. Even their ritual aspect of showing appropriate personal regard to an alter with whom ego has little in common may be enhanced by the occasional reference to his work or to his recreational interests. Gans's example also suggests that information about outside roles can play a part in establishing the prestige order of a neighborhood.

But there may also be more tangible results. Someone can turn out to have particular skills or network connections which make him a rather special neighbor for all or some of those around him. Or people can find that they may usefully become each other's partners in other kinds of ties as well. Sometimes one may recruit a business associate this way. More often it will be someone to share leisure activities with.

Where one finds a neighborhood intensively and reasonably harmoniously involved in its own internal relationships, this usually seems to be due to its particular chemistry of inside and outside roles of neighbors. At least some of its people have time over for neighborliness; people know enough about each other to understand each other's behavior fairly well without disapproving too much; and there is some potential for complementary and multiplex relationships. Here, also, one may perhaps most readily achieve an overall neighborhood organization, resembling that which a government may somewhere else introduce from above. Often it is an organization for external conflict. Government becomes the adversary, in a protest against local planning, or strangers become suspects and neighbors vigilantes when the orderliness of traffic relationships threatens to break down.

But urban neighborhoods are not always like this. Various writers—Dennis (1958) in a short but well-known paper, Roberts in his Guatemala City study—have commented on the problems of neighborhood organizing where people have mostly single-stranded relationships, little knowledge about each other and little trust, no shared past and no common future.

The FLUIDITY of URBAN LIFE

This last consideration brings us to a facet of the organization of role repertoires and networks which we have undercommunicated so far, although in another form it got some attention toward the end of chapter 3. Remaining within a synchronic frame of analysis, one might think of Wirth's notion of "transitory" contacts as referring only to the fleetingness of traffic relationships or brief encounters of provisioning. Monitoring somewhat longer intervals, however, one becomes increasingly aware that the description may also apply to links which we may think of as durable, but which may be so only within limits. New movements and meetings in the social structure result from the maneuvering with roles and relations. Take note of a city dweller's repertoire and network at one point in time, and come back to it a few years later. He may have changed jobs, moved to another place, and taken up a new hobby. Not even in the kinship and household domain are things quite the same, for he has divorced and remarried. (This may be where change of relationships is actually least characteristically urban, since there are traditional rural societies with high frequencies of divorce; not least the Rhodes-Livingstone anthropologists have told us this.) The potential for personal change in the city, then, may hardly be rivaled in other community forms. We may call this the fluidity of urban life.

Systematic and concerted efforts by anthropologists to study the temporal dimension of social relations have mostly been devoted to the domestic developmental cycle and to the social reflections of maturation. In a small-scale society, this may cover much of what is involved. If we look at urban society in role terms, on the other hand, we could consider the theoretical possibility that the variability which can be observed between individual repertoires at one time could occur within one repertoire over time. Here the changes in kin roles may be the most predictable ones, as in the analytically quite well-conceptualized developmental cycles. The passage through provisioning roles has also been a focus of research, although mostly in the sociology or more or less bureaucratic organizations. About change and stability in recreational and neighboring roles less seems to be known, and also about the ways roles out of different domains are linked in change.

Fluidity is not just change between roles, however; it is also change in relationships and networks. New alters may appear in old roles, others are dropped. Some remain or return. As single-stranded relationships become multiplex and vice versa, a co-worker becomes a co-worker and a friend, then changes jobs but remains—sometimes—a friend. In one phase of his life, ego has a lot of varied contacts with alters who do not know each other. In another phase, the density of his network may have become much higher; its range may or may not have changed at the same time.

One should not exaggerate such variations over time. Total flux may be rare, for more people it is partial, and for some city dwellers nothing much may seem to have changed over a lifetime, or at least not since they arrived at adulthood. But the full diversity of urban lives is hardly completely understood unless one also has an idea of the varied ways in which they change as time passes. The key concept in our perspective toward fluidity in social life is career; not in the everyday sense of more or less rapid, more or less linear upward occupational change, which is only one kind, but, to try a general definition, the sequential organization of life situations.[6] As examples show, one could limit a career analysis to the roles of a single domain. As the definition implies, one may also try to think holistically about the way all the domains are made to fit together in a way of life through time.

We certainly do not expect careers to be wholly unpredictable. Determinacy in the construction of role repertoires actually tends to imply sequentiality. At no point, it would seem, is the individual able to make a fresh start in assembling an entire new repertoire, but he is always constrained by the roles he already has and the relationships connected with them. The degree of predictability, however, and the amount of personal control exercised, are variable. One may describe as a "careerist" an individual who is preoccupied with career management, with the direction and timing of phase changes in his future. If he is successful, each phase would be entered because it was chosen over that preceding it, in whatever domain would be involved. (But, of course, an unsuccessful careerist is still a careerist, while not all with successful careers need be careerists to any great extent.) Such a career could come in different versions. Let us look at a couple from the domain of provisioning. One of them could be seen as an orderly progression through phases ABCDE. This would be the normal sequence, so that to get from A to E, one would at least be likely to pass through B, C, and D. When the careerist is aware of this, his major motive for entering B or C might be that unsatisfactory as these could be in themselves—perhaps worse than A—they must be passed on the road to the more desirable D and E. (But one could risk getting stuck in them.)

Planning many phases ahead like this may be possible where there is an acceptably reliable organizational chart open to inspection, as in a bureaucracy. This career could perhaps also be laid out within the provisioning domain alone, so that each phase consists more or less of one role, and performance in it is the criterion for further phase change. Our second form of career management is a little more complex. In one of the better-known anthropological career studies, Anthony Leeds (1964) depicts the movements of individuals through the expanding opportunity structures of urban Brazil. Under strong international influence, new roles open up before there is an organized supply of people to fill them. To be able to make the best use of such a situation, one should be well-informed, well-connected, and prepared to pick up the relevant skills as one goes along. Often, the result will be that one juggles a number of provisioning roles at the same time. As one embarks on a career, one needs a *trampolim,* a springboard. This could take many forms: making the right marriage, minor but preferably flamboyant political activity, conspicuous involvements in journalism or sports. The important part is to begin to establish a reputation, in circles as wide as possible. The careerist spends a lot of time seeking information, and spreading information about himself. News media and kin connections are important here. He also spends time simply *futing,* promenading with his ears open, running into people in coffee houses or book stores. In this manner he makes his way into various roles, but continues looking around all the same, also using these roles as vantage points. At some stage he begins joining cliques made up of people with complementary roles who can help look after one another's interests. For the successful careerist there are different such cliques at progressively higher points on the ladder, finally perhaps of national scope.

This is no simple ABCDE pattern. Each phase apparently involves nursing simultaneously a number of chances for onward movement, and only in the next phase, stochastically, it may be revealed where the career might lead to thereafter.[7] There is furthermore an active management of roles and relations back and forth among domains, kinship, recreation, and provisioning. Although for career analysis one needs a phase concept, trying to demarcate a phase in a tangle of fits, spurts, and false starts like this may be no simple matter.

Springboard jumping and open-eared promenading, however, are as much the work of a careerist as the quest for merit of a lieutenant intending to become captain, colonel, and general. Other careers take form without much planning, and phase changes may not proceed from worse to better. People may be pushed out of roles when the resource base melts away, or when alters no longer offer themselves to keep certain kinds of relationships going (which is sometimes the same thing). Careers may haphazardly take alternative forms—ACEDB, AEBDC, CEBDA. These are the unfolding fates of people not in control, like Nels Anderson's hoboes. For Jurgis Rudkus in *The Jungle*, again, slaughterhouse worker—jail inmate—steelworker—tramp—robber—political crook. For Cressey's taxidance girl, short-term gains interspersed with long-term decline as the young woman shifted among categories of customers, establishments, and roles. Where the careerist strives for ABCDE, the taxi-dance girl got EDCBA.

Career analysis may offer some of the most poignant insights into the different ways that urban lives can be shaped. It can show with some particular clarity what happens as a phase change in one domain reflects on others; how different segments of a person's role repertoire and network can be "out of phase" with each other, for instance, and make contradictory demands which are only to be dealt with through more or less radical rearrangements. The model case is that of occupational success destroying old kinship and friendship links. The spotlight on adjustments of such kinds occurring as people make their way through a fluid society also shows, however, that career analysis need not be a wholly ego-centered perspective. Sometimes, the unit in focus may be a particular relationship, analyzed for the interplay with a wider network surrounding it. What we have described before as unilateral encapsulation offers one example— something one could call a "dependent career" can result if one person's life is to a high degree under the continuous influence of what happens to a certain other person. A spouse, children for some time, and perhaps a private secretary may find themselves in this position, and may turn into vicarious careerists as a consequence. *"Cherchez la femme"* has become a standard plot for careers in western society.

We should also ask of our larger, conventional units in the anthropology of particular domains how they are affected by career facts. In neighboring, fluidity varies a great deal. There are urban villages, spiralist quarters like Whyte's Park Forest and Bell's housing estate in Swansea, and Zorbaugh's Chicago "world of furnished rooms," all marked by their particular rates of mobility. Changes of residence may be generated by phase changes in another domain, as in the spiralist case, or the reason may be found in the neighborhood itself. Janowitz (1952) has coined the concept of "communities of limited liability"—when they are not to one's liking, one can withdraw from them. This was in a study of American suburbia, and it may be questioned whether they are as prevalent in urban life elsewhere. Probably not, but on the other hand there may be some danger that we underestimate the fluidity of preindustrial or non-western cities. Work by Robert Smith (1973) on historical data from wards in two Japanese urban communities shows remarkable residential instability in the eighteenth and nineteenth centuries, and La Fontaine (1970:133) also makes a point of it in her study of contemporary Kinshasa. When conflicts between neighbors flare up, she states, they are often resolved by the departure of one of the parties from the housing unit. For this reason, probably, hostilities and suspicions in this arena seldom take the form of witchcraft or sorcery accusations. A survey showed that few people had lived in the same place throughout their stay in the city, and whatever might have been the reasons for these movements, many Kinshasa people thought of it as an attractive aspect of urban freedom.

Career conceptions can be taken further yet, to show in more general terms what fluidity can do to urban life. This touches again on that difference between two anthropological perspectives referred to in chapter 5, interpreting the growth of interest in network analysis—the difference between seeing people as anonymous and conformist personnel, dutifully enacting one role at a time, and seeing them as individuals with minds of their own, trying to bend social organization to suit their own circumstances and purposes. In this particular context, the latter point of view suggests that it does matter to the social order who the incumbents of roles are, where they have been before, and where they may be at some later time, because they are people with memories and plans.

A somewhat abstract example of this is the long-term effect that the career organization of lives may have on network morphology. If ego moves through many roles, he will pick up a great many alters over time. If links do not altogether lapse (and this is clearly an important condition), the ego-centered network in the fluid society will be cumulative; it will increase its range over time. Friendship developed out of some other relationship, we noted at one point before, may remain after that other link is broken. Under a social arrangement where all people remain in all strands of their multiplex relationships continuously, there would be greater general multiplexity. In the fluid society, single-stranded and multiplex ties alternate over time. Surely old relationships may be retained in only a minimal way. They may shrink into largely latent acquaintance, or mere recognition. But as long as there is no return to mutual ignorance, the link could be said to exist in some way as a social fact. With this increasing range in personal network ought to go, theoretically, a greater density in the total network of society. In the fluid society as compared to an equally complex society where "everyone stays in his place," to rephrase, we would find at any one time a relatively low multiplexity combined with higher density, although perhaps with many latent links. [8]

The social consequences of this state of affairs could include a special kind of particularism in the fluid society, as people act with some attention to relationships formed in previous phases of their lives, or residues of such links. If two persons, identically located in the role structure as synchronically perceived, compete for the favor of a third person, he who has had another kind of contact with this third person in an earlier phase may receive preferential treatment (or its opposite). The particularistic criterion of the fluid society is "Haven't I seen this person somewhere before?"

Such network consequences of changing role repertoires would not come about, it is true, if people marched perfectly in step through their interconnected careers, so that actual relationships could continue, however redefined. But this would seem like a very hypothetical situation. A rather more reasonable qualification to the proposition that changing careers leads to wider-range networks would be that people might develop fewer and narrower links in roles where they do not remain long (and do not expect to remain long), so that the number of links which accrue from each phase in the career becomes smaller. This takes us to another fact of life in a fluid society. Personal disclosure by ego, and an interest in it on the part of alter, may take time and a sense of commitment which may be absent when a relationship is part of a career. An example of how this could affect society may be found in those provisioning relationships which are often held to function best when they are extended beyond the fleeting relationship—involving medical attention, social welfare, education, law enforcement, for example—but which in fact are often limited to one or a few encounters because the individual in the provisioning role thereafter moves into another career phase. Less conspicuously, one may expect that there are many other contexts as well, of a more or less institutional nature, where the individual's degree of involvement is related to tacit notions of phase duration, and where this influences overall functioning.

While his involvement in a current career phase may be somewhat limited, the individual in a fluid society may at any one time have some concern for the possibility of changing his situation and thus continuously scans his environment for new opportunities in roles and relationships. Usually he may do so at a low level of awareness, as an unplanned and unrecognized part of ongoing life, but this scanning can also have some forms more or less its own. In different contexts we have mentioned some of them—the bar in Hansen's town in Catalonia, *futing* in Leeds's Brazilian cities, small-print advertising (jobs, accommodations, personal). We could add singles bars in urban America to the list. These, then, are institutions of the fluid society. It may also have its peculiar idioms, called into use when a change is about to take place, or is at least to be tested. There are times when it is appropriate to send out feelers while preserving anonymity; some advertising is like this. There are circumstances where one wants to reject invitations to join one relationship, but not so brusquely as to hurt another one which is already a going concern. There are occasions when someone has to be shifted delicately from one role to another, in a change of phase to which he might object, as in Goffman's "cooling the mark out." In general, these actual or potential phase changes may be critical moments, situations where much can depend on the successful presentation of self or mutually supportive ritual exchanges. But they can also be confirmed by more relaxed rites of passage, like send-off parties for departing spiralists.

Fluidity can thus have its own social and cultural forms, lubrication for the machinery of careers. It may have its states of feeling—nostalgia can be typical of personal as well as social change. Another aspect of fluidity is that ideas derived from the perception of careers can become part of culture, available for more general use. An obvious example is the way they are interpreted as indices of individual character and competence. Occupational careers are especially important as carriers of such meaning. Someone who moves rapidly upwards is bright, someone who moves slowly may be dull but still trustworthy. He who moves rapidly sideways is unstable, and moving downwards is a sign of personal inadequacy. Such judgments may be correct or incorrect. They may be given to disregarding conditions which may make it difficult to control careers at all. The interesting fact is that they can be imported from one domain into another, where such indices may not exist, although the information is held relevant.

One additional point may be made about time and social organization. As long as we are not dealing with social change in itself, we tend routinely to assume that surrounding the individuals working toward their own goals, there is still a relatively stable institutional framework. This understanding may be useful enough, but there are times when the organizations themselves are set up on a temporary basis, both on a small and a large scale. The contemporary western city is a prominent habitat for such outfits. Toffler (1970:112 ff.) has coined the concept of adhocracy for tendencies of this sort in modern bureaucracies, McIntosh (1975:42 ff.) notes the importance of project organization in contemporary professional crime, and we may remember the "ganging process" in Thrasher's Chicago. This adds yet another reason for taking an interest in the fluidity of urban life.

MAKING ROLES

Thus far we have largely stuck with the idea that roles can be seen as more or less ready-made things in themselves; available, as it were, for inspection and acquisition in the great supermarket of society. As we take on one of them, we may be able, perhaps, to modify it slightly from a standard or average form in order to make it fit snugly into the rest of our repertoire, but in essence it remains the same role which we see recurrently modeled in the life around us.

This point of view seems useful enough for many purposes. There are even occasions when a role can exist as an idea within a society even before anybody has taken it upon himself to enact it. In the case of Leeds's Brazilian careers, in a society borrowing heavily from external models, it could be merely a gleam in the eye of an expansive captain of industry, commerce, or bureaucracy, a role looking for an incumbent.

We should not disregard the fact, however, that the city dweller sometimes does not pick a role off the shelf but produces it in his own workshop; and this opportunity to innovate within the role inventory may in one way or another be related to the nature of urbanism. It appears possible to distinguish at least three factors underlying such role making.

The relative rigidity of definition on the part of certain other roles, coupled with an assumption of the substitutability of incumbents, is one of them. These roles may be so discomforting to the people recruited into them that they must be balanced with other roles which can offer a greater sense of satisfaction. And if roles of the latter kind do not already exist, they are created. This is the argument of the deprivation model of self-consciousness discussed briefly in chapter 6, and suggested as an explanation particularly for the growth of new recreational roles in contemporary industrial-bureaucratic urban society. But roles of the first kind can also sometimes in a way "lose touch with reality." They may look fine on a chart without actually doing the job they are supposed to do, and so cannot stand alone in the long run. So additional roles grow up around them as a support structure.

When we speak of "informal structures," we very often have in mind roles of these kinds, and the relationships formed among them. "The anthropologist has a professional license to study such interstitial, supplementary, and parallel structures in complex society and to expose their relation to the major strategic, overarching institutions," Eric Wolf (1966:2) has proposed. We have indeed come upon them repeatedly. Thrasher's interpretation of the emergence of youth gangs, quoted in chapter 2, resembles Wolf's characterization even in the choice of wording. The most obvious instance otherwise is the "underlife" in Goffman's total institutions. We may see these structures as basically defensive devices by which people try to ward off the damages which could be inflicted upon them by a social setup which they cannot control. As Wolf points out, that setup is logically, if not temporally, prior to them. It is, of course, possible that the roles which come about in this way themselves will stabilize and become part of an available role inventory. But it seems as if, in no small part, they are again and again generated anew.

If some role making is defensive, not all of it need be. The second factor of which we may usefully be aware is that the variability of role repertoires can itself be a mother of invention. The more there is of such relatively free variability, the more likely would it seem to be that an individual can combine his diverse experiences and resources in unique ways and place them in new contexts, thus taking a lead part in creating situations which have not occurred before. The imagery of entrepreneurship seems to be the point here. Think of each situation, as it more normally occurs, as a sphere of its own, with a rather routinized flow of resources and experiences. The person who can combine situations and break down the barriers between his respective involvements in them in a novel way may find a new role taking form at the confluence.

Such original combinations can also be made from elements drawn together over time in a zigzagging career. Bryan Roberts' (1976) account of economic change in the provincial Peruvian city of Huancayo can be read to exemplify processes of this kind. In the face of increasing metropolitan dominance, Huancayo's own relatively large-scale textile industry declined and finally closed down. Overall, the domain of provisioning became more fragmented. Yet the city did not really seem to be doing worse than before. New small businesses proliferated, set up frequently by people who had originally come in from the countryside to work in mines and factories. In some such businesses, Roberts notes, "a whole migration career is reflected in contemporary activities." A clothing workshop can take over machinery from the bankrupt factory where the owner was once employed and at the same time use village contacts to "put out" work, recruit other workers to the town, and distribute products.

One tends to find a great deal of such combinative innovation in the "informal sector" of Third World urban communities. Perhaps as a more out-of-the-way instance of turning old experiences into a new role, we could remember the notorious Manson gang of the late 1960s California. Charles Manson was another of those individuals with a career following no discernible pattern, unless one is retrospectively read into the disastrous form of group leadership which he developed. According to Sanders (1972), one of the chroniclers of the gang, Manson had been in and out of corrective institutions since his early teens. A decade or so later, he had acquired a rather complete jailhouse education. By the late 1950s, one could follow him jumping from one means of livelihood to another: busboy, bartender, freezer salesman, service-station attendant, TV producer, pimp. "Pimp talk," about the means used in controlling prostitutes, had indeed been a

large part of what he could absorb in the prison where he had recently
been. Now he was in practice, in a rather ordinary version. What one
might argue is that later, in the world of new countercultural amalgama-
tions in Southern California in the 1960s, the former juvenile delinquent,
thief, and panderer had some of his temporary successes in winning
friends, influencing people, and living off the land by giving original symbolic shape to some of his old skills; among people, it could furthermore be
noted, who often did not have comparable and thus competitive experience
themselves.

Role innovation in the city would seem to be favored, thirdly, by the
possibility of pushing the division of labor forever further. There is, of
course, the idea which Wirth took up from Darwin and Durkheim that the
concentration of people, like other organisms, increases competition and
encourages specialization as a way out of it. But perhaps rather more simply, among the large number of people conveniently accessible, one can
also find sufficiently many who can be enticed into desiring the most
esoteric or minuscule service, thus raising it above the threshold of feasibility.

A visitor to a Third World city may again marvel at the kinds of things
that can be turned into an enterprise in the "informal sector." In a
Nigerian beer bar, free-lance nail cutters hover around the hands and feet
of customers. Outside a Colombian amusement park, a teenage boy with a
bathroom scale offers to weigh the passers-by. In an Indian street, a *bahuru-
piya*, "man of many disguises," uses the very heterogeneity of the city as a
dramatic resource, impersonating one urban type after another, and finally
claiming his reward from an amused and astonished audience (cf. Berreman 1972:577). If, on the other hand, a shantytown dweller from Africa
or Asia should come to London or New York, another set of specializations
which he had never imagined would undoubtedly seem equally remarkable—pet fashions, interior decoration consultancies.

Exactly when a role is new or just a variation of an old one may naturally be rather ambiguous, although we may not need to go into such questions of conceptual practice here. What seems more significant is that urbanites can go on feeding new items into the role inventory where, in
principle, others can then also draw upon them for their own repertoires.
Once the prototype has been made, mass production may commence. And
the process could be self-perpetuating. As one new role is instituted, an informal structure may grow around it. As an original combination is suc-

cessful and draws more people into it, someone sees a different slice to cut out of it and breaks away with yet another specialization. Some cities, of course, may have a greater potential for such ongoing development than others. "The fox knows many things, but the hedgehog knows one big thing," the Greek poet Archilochus had it; there are urbanisms which are more like foxes and other which are more like hedgehogs.[9] The former seize on variety, play around with it, and thus create more of it. The latter invest heavily in one single line and push on with that. Jane Jacobs' book *The Economy of Cities* (1969) is an argument in favor of fox-like urbanism, with small enterprises which keep combining and segmenting.[10] The contrast between Birmingham and Manchester is one of her illustrative cases—the former with small, changing establishments, the latter with large ones which find it difficult to adapt to new circumstances and which therefore decline. The company town in this sense becomes the ultimate urban hedgehog, planned from the beginning with a role structure devoted to one purpose and thereafter unwilling to be distracted by others. Perhaps the orthogenetic city of Redfield and Singer was also more like a hedgehog, the heterogenetic city a fox.

The SOCIAL ORGANIZATION of MEANING

Hitherto, as we forecast in the introduction, we have been mostly concerned with the ordering of social relations in urban life. The combination and recombination of roles and the arrangement and rearrangement of networks are first of all themes in a relational rendition of the city. But anthropology is also centrally concerned with culture. In the end, we ought to give some thought to what kind of cultural analysis urban anthropology needs.[11] It is now quite a widespread fashion, outside anthropological and sociological circles as well, to describe life in a complex society as made up of a variety of cultures. They are generational, such as youth culture; ethnic, like black culture; occupational, as the culture of dance musicians; institutional, exemplified by the culture of bureaucracy or even "the culture of the White House" during a particular administration; class cultures, like the culture of poverty; deviant cultures, like that of transvestites or tramps; or countercultures, as in the case of the hippies. And surrounding such islands of the culturally different are entities with designations like mass culture, popular culture, or mainstream culture. Much ethnography has come out of this concern with diversity. Rather fewer writers have tried to deal systematically with cultural complexity as an analytical problem. Some of those who seem to contribute significantly to such an analysis, furthermore, do not define their work in these terms, and write with little or no reference to one another.

We are concerned here with meaning; something that can be perplexingly subtle, not quite tangible, almost imperceptibly shifting, perhaps never easy to handle in an analytical argument. To try to grasp the problems involved, we may begin with the old anthropological conception of human beings as both thinkers, occupied with moral and intellectual affairs, and doers, solving practical problems. In the latter aspect, they are fundamentally acting on meanings to deal adaptively with their environment. In the former aspect, they try to understand and evaluate, and here they are concerned with the opinions of their fellows. More often than not, anyway, they prefer approval to censure, and they are somewhat anxious that their ideas should not be entirely quixotic. So they draw on social intercourse to establish meaning. The two aspects of human life continuously interrelate, of course. But they interrelate in more problematic ways in some social contexts than in others.

A last visit, at this point, to the ideal-type folk society. Meaning tends to be unusually transparent there. The array of situations with which people have to deal is small, and the same people in time become involved in most of them. In other words, the role inventory is quite limited. At the very least, it may be differentiated only by age and sex, and roles assigned to males or females on the basis of age will then be assumed by everyone of the appropriate sex as the life cycle moves on. As people face much the same situations, they could even independently come to similar understandings. But, in addition, they see and hear each other dealing with them. This is of practical use to people as doers, since they can thus pick up ready-made solutions to problems. At the same time, they get proof that others regard these solutions as realistic and morally acceptable, since these others are indeed themselves drawing on them.

Meanwhile, back in the city as we have seen it, things can get much more complicated. In the highly differentiated and yet coherent social system, it would seem, meanings drawn from the individual's own situational experience and meanings taken over from others in communication stand a greater chance of drifting apart.

Faced with the problem of how the individual extracts meaning from the complex world surrounding him, we may try to arrive at an answer by counterpoint. On the one hand, there is the favorite theme of the sociology of knowledge—a person's conception of reality depends on his place in society.[12] Familiar versions emphasize particular sorts of placement, such as class position or occupation. But these are usually overall judgments which can be qualified in various ways. Here we take it that the individual draws experience from all the situations he is involved in; there is an intake, big or small, into his consciousness through each of his roles. To push this "sociology of knowledge" theme to its logical limits, however, one may have to see him as having the experiences characteristic of his situational involvement, and pondering their interpretation, in intellectual solitude. Only thus would it seem possible to guarantee the pure form of this positional determination of perspective toward life.

A society could possibly exist on the basis of such meaning only. In his polemic against too facile an assumption of a total sharing of motivations and cognitions within a social system, Wallace (1961:29 ff.) has argued that orderly interactions can indeed take place without this replication of uniformity. They turn out to be rather like silent trade, workable as long as ego finds alter's behavior sufficiently predictable—never mind why alter acts the way he does. Wallace continues to propose that a complex society could never function with a very high degree of uniformity in individual systems of meanings. There must be a division of knowledge in order to operate it.

That may be. But there are times when we really try, and believe that we have some success, in collating with one another our experiences and interpretations. On the other hand, that is to say, there is the more centrally cultural theme of a traffic in meanings. Communicating with each other in this way, people may have vicarious experiences, and standardize the way experiences will be implanted in their minds. Meanings arising more immediately from the qualities of the individual's situational involvements may thereby be "corrupted." What develops is what we call culture: a collective system of meanings. And when we describe it as collective, this is not just to say that the individual systems of persons A and B (and perhaps C, D, E . . .) in fact show a degree of overlap. The point is that such replication is both promoted through communication and assumed as a basis of a relationship. A takes for granted that B at least in part has the same system of meanings, and he likewise takes for granted that B is aware that A also has it, and vice versa.[13] In this way he can sense that the collective system of meanings has an existence of its own, independent of himself, as his purely individual system of meanings could not. In the phrase made popular by Berger and Luckmann (1966), there is a "social construction of reality."

We are interested in the interplay between these two themes, then; between the differentiation of perspectives through the social structure and the homogenizing effects of culture. In the process of examining it, we may be testing the limits of traditional anthropological thinking about what the culture concept refers to. John Fischer (1975) has suggested that phenomena may have degrees of culturality, along different dimensions. Perhaps the dimension of extent is that which is most often recognized. Phenomena of a high degree of culturality are widely shared, those of a low degree less widely. Here the old "one society-one culture" assumption comes in, while the subculture concept has been popularized as a label for less extensively shared systems of meanings. Another dimension is that of time—we tend to think of culture as long-lived meaning. Further dimensions could presumably be added. The degree of commitment people have to an idea would be one example.

The problem of the first dimension—how widely throughout society is a certain system of meanings shared?—seems like a good point of entry into further discussions, however. By our definition as a collective system of meanings, a culture can involve no less than two people. We could take a different position. There may be areas of an individual's consciousness which he understands to be more fully shared with other people with whom he interacts, and other areas which may not be so shared. Since they are unlikely to exist strictly compartmentalized in the individual's mind, one might have preferred not to emphasize the distinction, but perhaps to describe the entire inclusive pattern of individual systems of meanings— call them "mazeways," as Wallace has done, or "propriospects" with Goodenough (1971)—of the members of a society as making up its culture. Surely what is collective and what is merely individual would be hard to disentangle fully. The perfect meeting of minds (no less than a merging of minds) may never take place. Yet only for a brief while in infancy is the individual's consciousness significantly autonomous, before symbolic communication with other human beings sets in. After that, to the extent that his system of meanings is actually systematic, this results largely from its cumulativity. It grows over time not simply through addition but as meanings, sometimes at least, act upon each other. The more common situation is probably that where the individual selectively attends to phenomena and interprets them in terms of previously accepted meanings, perhaps with a feedback effect on the latter. Extant consciousness thus continuously structures new experience which then itself sediments as a part of the system. (The opposite situation, where an established system of meanings is overhauled on the basis of new experience, seems more rare. In a radical form, it constitutes a conversion.) Consequently, after an individual has started communicating with others, he may never experience anything wholly alone any more, insofar as he perceives it against a background of previous communication.

Our focus for cultural analysis, however, is on the way various constellations of people work away at developing or maintaining common perspectives, involving more immediately shared meanings. According to this view, the dyad becomes the minimal unit for the study of cultural process. If understandings are shared no more widely, this would indeed be a miniculture. But let us wait for a moment with further linkages, and see what insights the smallest unit offers; if not literally a dyad, in any case a combination of people not significantly different.

Collective systems of meanings are created as individuals reveal their individual understandings to one another. It is through the input into the shared perspective from individual experience that culture as an open system mines reality. The collective system of meanings is also cumulative, like the individual consciousness. It expands as individuals face new experiences together, inform each other of individual perceptions against the background of what they already have in common, or discover additional facets of their individual systems of meanings to be shared. The debate of sorts which anthropologists have been conducting concerning what should be taken to be the locus of culture—inside people's heads, or "out there," inscribed in observable things and events—from this point of view seems best resolved by recognizing that it is in both places. Nobody (anthropologist or otherwise) can get hold of another individual's ideas until they have been given some external form; most often talk, talk, talk. But neither can we get around the fact that if we try to read external realities as an "assemblage of texts," as Geertz (1972:26) has put it, some of them may be read differently by different people, and some will be comprehensible to some people but largely meaningless to others. A little finger stretched upwards could mean "only one," or it could be an obscene gesture. A wink is a meaningful wink to you, but perhaps just a random twitch to me.

Most basically, we may perhaps distinguish two types of relationships in which collective systems of meanings are made. In the first and simpler of these, people are involved in the same situation in the same way, that is, through the same role, and communicate with each other about this involvement. Here, possibly, the meaning of messages could be much the same in each direction, of equal strength, and coinciding with that which the recipient derives directly from his situational experience. Consciousness is confirmed and amplified in becoming collective, through the social construction of reality.

This is the sort of cultural process which Albert Cohen (1955:60–61) has made the subject of a well-known analysis, focusing on the cultures of juvenile delinquents. The crucial condition for the growth of new cultural forms, Cohen suggests, is the effective interaction of a number of individuals faced with a need to adapt to similar circumstances. In the case of the delinquent youths, the problem is one of finding mutual acceptance for new lines of action. Every move therefore becomes an "exploratory gesture":

> . . . each response of the other to what the actor says and does is a clue to the directions in which change may proceed further in a way congenial to the other and to the direction in which change will lack social support. And if the probing gesture is motivated by tensions common to other participants it is likely to initiate a process of *mutual* exploration and *joint* elaboration of a new solution. My exploratory gesture functions as a cue to you; your exploratory gesture as a cue to me. By a casual, semi-serious, non-committal or tangential remark I may stick my neck out just a little way, but I will quickly withdraw it unless you, by some sign of affirmation, stick *yours* out.

The second type of situation is one where people create some sort of shared consciousness from the perspectives of unlike involvements and is already more complicated, as attempts to evolve a collective system of meaning could come into conflict with understandings specific to a role. The outcomes of such cultural process can conceivably vary. A compromise collective consciousness might be hammered out, sufficiently similar to the various role perspectives to be credible; this would seem simpler if perspectives are not too divergent to begin with. Participants may inform each other about their individual understandings, so that these all become mutually known and thus in a sense collective, although people remain more convinced by their own—"he knows that I know that he (mistakenly) believes . . ." or something more or less closely resembling one of the particular perspectives becomes the dominant system of meaning in the situation, while other perspectives are drowned in it altogether or retained in some degree or other as private reservations. In these situations, then, there may be a social construction of reality, but there is also a social destruction of reality insofar as the validity of an individual system of meanings is tacitly or outrightly denied.

After the very microsociological tone of Cohen's analysis of symmetry in cultural process, an equally highly macrosociological interpretation can exemplify what may become of collective consciousness as it emerges under assymmetry, with the domination of one party over others; Marx's pronouncement that "the ideas of the ruling class are, in every age, the ruling ideas." In other words, power tends to count in determining what definitions are to be sustained. For an underdog, it can be very difficult to have his own version of reality institutionalized in a situation. Sometimes, if he insists, he may find himself institutionalized instead.

Marx's statement, one might say, makes society as a whole—a society of inequality—a setting for our second type of cultural process, writ large. In a similar way, folk society would be somewhat like the first type. As we are concerned with cultural variation within one social structure, however, we would want a more detailed picture of the ways cultural processes in different relationships fit together. If, in the total social network of the city, each relationship were fully open to the importation and efficient transmission of understandings derived from the participants' other involvements, the same meanings might possibly in the end flow in all of them. Culture would be homogeneous, and the theme from the sociology of knowledge would barely be audible. This, however, does not happen. Neither does each relationship develop culture in itself, for itself, by itself. Some relationships do more cultural work than others, and meanings transfer more easily between some than between others.

It is in the nature of many segmental, transitory connections that little active construction of shared meaning goes on within them. Interaction, indeed, becomes rather like silent trade, or draws on assumptions of certain minimal understandings originally built up in other situations, each participant with other alters. Rather rarely, such relationships also suddenly transform themselves for energetic culture building; what sociologists describe as "collective behavior," such as crowd phenomena, could well be seen as the formation of instant, ephemeral cultures. (Although this would not involve a high degree of culturality along the second dimension mentioned before.) But other relationships are more likely to be the hothouses of cultural process. We saw in chapter 6 that Berger and Kellner used a certain kind of marriage for a case study of the social construction not only of the self but of reality more generally, and that friendship could be another example of such relationship. Here shared interpretations can be evolved not only, perhaps not even primarily, from experiences intrinsic to the relationship. The experiences can be brought in from all the participants' involvements to be given a working over. The understanding thus validated can then in its turn be exported to influence participation in other situations.

It is one part of urban anthropological cultural analysis to map where, in the various social structures of cities, such intensive generation of shared meanings occurs. (Think of a diagram of the total urban network; color the more culturally active relationships in shades of red, the more passive ones blue.) At one time, a characteristic institutional form for the development of one particular genre of ideas may have been the salon; at another time and in another city, the coffee house (see Coser 1970:11–25). The gang, the cult group, or the university department may serve similar purposes. A further problem for analysis is the way meanings flow through the network, and sometimes perhaps clash. We have dealt before with the particular case of introduction of personal information into a relationship through disclosures of external involvements. Now the point is the general one that we can see the individual as standing at an intersection of several situations, managing more or less skillfully the traffic signals by which the movements of ideas between them are directed. How do meanings spill over from one context into another, and what are the consequences if more or less adjacent relationships construct contradictory realities?

In a statement in much the same vein as Albert Cohen's above, Everett Hughes (1961:28) has succinctly summed up some conditions of cultural development in complex society: "Wherever some group of people have a bit of common life with a modicum of isolation from other people, a common corner in society, common problems and perhaps a couple of common enemies, there culture grows."

Anthropology has long had a concept of "cultural drift" referring to such a divergent cultural process, although it appears not to have figured in urban studies; the writings on it also give some emphasis to isolation (see Herskovits 1951:500 ff.; Berreman 1960:787 ff.). But isolation, under the circumstances of city life, is a problematic notion. Since it can hardly be a matter of physical isolation, we must understand it to entail intellectual isolation, and tenuous social links. When meaning passes through a series of relationships, evidently, cultural drift can proceed in a given direction with the least distraction if the people interacting most intensely with each other to establish a collective consciousness have relatively standardized role repertoires, and outside relationships which are weaker and do not entail understandings in conflict with those of the internal linkages. In this way the microevolutionary cultural process can adapt the shared meanings to the experience of a finite number of kinds of situational involvement. People stand a greater chance of recognizing themselves in each other's experiences of situations. Certain roles and relationships, then, can be understood to form more or less homogeneous and coherent cultural clusters within the entire differentiated social system.

In part this is a matter of the collective system of meanings in one relationship linking up with that in another and to a considerable extent replicating it. We may see them as intercommunicating vessels, containing more or less the same culture. Yet meanings which are shared in one relationship can also interconnect through a participant's role repertoire with those which made up the perspective of his role in a more definitely asymmetric relationship elsewhere. People may in fact have a special need to immerse themselves in cultural process over those congruent experiences of outside involvements in which their individual perspectives are not satisfactorily incorporated into a collective system of meanings—where no such system worth mentioning exists, or where some other participant's perspective is dominant. In other words, the relationships where this type of culture building occurs can mediate and serve as a safety valve in the contradiction between culture and positional experience. The common reality construction can be of the form described by Cohen, but in a way at one remove.

Such relationships can come into existence by chance, or they may be purposively set up for cultural work. There is the spontaneous gush of shop talk which follows when two people discover an opportunity to commune over more esoteric and rarely discussed perceptions of their trade, and there is the group organized for "consciousness raising," to fortify perspectives which tend to be suppressed elsewhere.

The more encapsulated people are within a cluster of roles and relationships such as just described, the less likely would a notable discrepancy between individual experience and communicated culture seem to be. Clusters, however, can come in different sizes and constellations. They may involve small groups, cutting themselves off from their surroundings as best they can. The point has been made before about the importance of urban numbers: as differentiated as the urban social system may be, the city usually allows people to find at least some others of a similar placing, thus making possible the development of a culture adapted to it.[14] Cultural clusters can also be conceptualized on a larger scale, on the other hand. The idea of class cultures is an illuminating example. People connect similarly to the wider social system through provisioning roles, and have similar experiences and relate to one another at work and through a rather restricted range of probable involvements in the domains of recreation, kinship, and neighboring. Through this more than randomly dense network, shared understandings may be able to accumulate and circulate without great difficulty.

Within clusters of such a wider extent, surely, one may find smaller units nesting, made up of individuals interacting particularly intensively over more restricted experiences. But they can then do so against the background of meanings shared in the wider cluster. Students of contemporary British cultures have made the point that recent youth cultures— like those of mods, rockers, and skinheads—have not been the cultures of just any youths, but have rather clearcut links to class cultures (see Clarke et al. 1975; Mungham and Pearson 1976). According to Keniston (1971:395–96), something similar has been observable in American countercultures: children of parents who are in the world of mass media, advertising, and the like have tended to enter wings of the countercultural complex preoccupied with a rebellion of expressive style, children of people in the older professions have leaned toward concerns with political ideology and action.

Class, however, does not always encapsulate people. A body of writings with a bearing on what we have said, on varieties of class consciousness, has also grown up especially in British sociology since Lockwood's (1966; cf. Bulmer 1975) essay on the impact of different work situations. A proletarian cultural tradition seems to wax strong especially in industries like mining, docking, and shipbuilding, where workers have close relationships to one another and extend them into leisure life.[15] At the same time, their interactions with superiors and outsiders are rather distant and infrequent. The development of shared consciousness can draw without much interference on the worker's own experience. The image of society opposes "us" and "them." Conversely, a deferential tradition becomes dominant among workers who get to relate little to one another but on a more personal and frequent basis to superiors, rather in the manner of client to patron. They see those of higher status as their "betters," and they attribute greater legitimacy to the values held by these others without striving to realize them for themselves. The deferential workers in the city may be in service occupations or in small enterprises, so that peers in a similar situation are not within quite so easy reach. But their prototype in British society is evidently the farm worker.

We may let the deferential workers of Britain illustrate a characteristic cultural form of categories of people who lack sufficient autonomy and cohesion to develop a shared system of meanings in line with their own location in the social structure, and instead become the rather passive partners in maintaining another cultural complex.[16] If they and the carriers of the proletarian tradition stand approximately as opposites, one can identify cases in between where groups are not isolated enough to construct a strong culture of their own, yet are not so fragmented either that they are wholly exposed to systems of meanings developed by other people under other circumstances. Cultural processes à la Cohen and à la Marx are both present, destabilizing one another.[17]

The realities which have come under analysis and debate under "the culture of poverty" and related labels fit in here.[18] The list of characteristics compiled by Oscar Lewis (1966:vliv ff.) and others primarily reveals underprivileged people as doers, adapting as best they can to difficult situations; in line with the nature of things, not always particularly well. But the poor as doers and the poor as thinkers in a way have trouble with each other. Their "assemblage of texts," the facts of life, may be in part unclear and contradictory. They can see people in their immediate surroundings behaving in ways which look practical enough under the circumstances, and they can learn something of the technicalities of getting by from these observations. They might also assume that if they become doers in the same way, these others could hardly condemn·them. On occasion, they even hear the rightfulness of such adaptations asserted. But at the same time, other definitions and values are also beamed at them, so powerfully that their credibility cannot be discounted although their immediate relevance to the problems at hand is actually somewhat questionable. In the United States—and most of the culture of poverty debate has concerned deprivation in American society—one can hardly avoid the meanings of what is largely middle-class culture, even deep in the ghetto. The consequence, to take the text metaphor a bit further, seems to be that the poor acquire somewhat different reading habits. Some attended more closely to one set of meanings, others to another; many keep up, after all, with both.

The problem of the urban co-existence of systems of meanings, with greater or lesser ease, has come to the fore with attempts to understand the ways of life carved out by the poor, but it is not unique to this context. The old Chicago School dealt with it, not particularly successfully, as "disorganization." The Rhodes-Livingstone anthropologists handled an aspect of it as "situational selection." A latter-day critic of theirs might discern in the Copperbelt towns a tension rather like that facing the American poor, between colonial values of external derivation and homegrown understandings from the bottom of the heap. Goffman's frontstage-backstage division sometimes turns out to be yet another way of looking at the conflict in meaning between situations. But generally, the problem is taken on only in a piecemeal way. Work is needed in putting the pieces together, and conceptualizing more fully the urban social organization of meaning. It may be useful to think of the consciousness of the individual as made up, in part, of a repertoire of cultures, relating (although not necessarily in any very simple fashion) to different roles in the role repertoire. As role combinations vary, so also can cultural repertoires be different.

We have seen that city dwellers can at times encapsulate themselves rather fully in relationships where one system of meaning reigns, with limited internal variations. Nevertheless, as we have remarked before apropos encapsulated groups, their members in the urban community may still be exposed in a marginal way to outsiders, simply because of physical accessibility; and this could entail similarly peripheral exposure to other cultures. Some of the possible consequences of the opportunities for such passing acquaintance were touched upon toward the end of chapter 3. In his *Understanding Media,* Marshall McLuhan (1965:5) proposed that the electronic age has brought about a cultural "implosion," as life styles which were previously distant press themselves against each other through the television screen and in other ways. We might see urbanism as an earlier implosive form, possibly less effective, perhaps more truthful, similarly bringing people to a greater awareness that alternatives exist and giving just some limited idea of what they amount to.

An urbanite, however, may be more intensively engaged than this in situations under the auspices of different systems of meanings. No problem, perhaps, if these are—in Ralph Linton's (1936:272–73) half-forgotten

terms of cultural analysis—"specialties" rather than "alternatives," peculiar to a certain situation. But when meanings emerging out of situational
experiences make more expansive claims to moral and intellectual validity,
questions arise. "That dangerous experiment of living at the same time in
different worlds," as Park put it—how does it affect the individual system
of meanings, and how do contradictory allegiances look to others?

It could be that we should not try to ride too far with the notion of situational selection, valid as it undoubtedly is to a certain extent. The sense of
contradiction may at times be heightened. Undoubtedly this can in itself
slow down and call to a halt the process of cultural drift. The "immanent
meaning" of a situational experience, as it were, is neutralized by the variety of other ideas crowding consciousness.[19] In other instances, however,
an individual with a varied repertoire may land himself in a conflict of
commitments to separate systems of meanings which is less readily resolved. Cultural ambivalence can become a common affliction of people
with varied repertoires.

As far as public exposure of inconsistency is concerned, we have dealt
with relevant considerations particularly in chapter 6. A person engaging
in segregativity as a way of life may escape the problem, switching cultures
without an image problem. One who condenses his network of relationships, in integrativity, may have to resort to what we described as "accounts," and similar devices. For people troubled by similar inconsisten-
cies, such constructs can even evolve into little bridging cultures in
themselves, synthesizing understandings from both arenas and smoothing
out difficulties. "Marginal men" may handle some of their problems this
way; young people, for example, with one foot among the oldtimers of an
encapsulated immigrant population and another in the more open networks
surrounding it.

A varied cultural repertoire, it may be added, need not involve only
problems. Role making such as Charles Manson's, apparently grasping one
system of meanings with the help of another, hints at one source of profit-
able innovations. One may see a play on the word "conversion" here, drawing on its meanings in both belief and economics. In the former sense,
conversion in the cultural career of an individual is a matter of discarding
one system of meanings for another; in the latter sense, one can ask if the
assets of consciousness in one sphere can be advantageously exchanged into
another.

The possible permutations within the point of view toward cultural complexity suggested here seem practically endless. It may be objected that it pushes things rather too far. The shared meanings of a dyad are of a degree of culturality hardly worthy of the attention of scholars who have been used to concerning themselves with weighty matters like the cultures of entire societies. There is enough more extensive cultural sharing in the city as well not to have to be bothered with such miniatures, and moreover, the culture is really pretty stable. All our concern with cultural construction as a process is, from this perspective, much ado about rather little.

Certainly one may not always be interested in working at this level of analytical intensity. But even if one does not, it may be useful to be aware of what intricacies of development and transmission are summarized and glossed over in more general statements. With respect to the width of sharing of meanings as a criterion of culturality, we have begun perhaps with the opposite assumption to that conventionally made by anthropologists. The "one society-one culture" notion implies that individuals in a society start out from a common cultural baseline, a structure of meanings of much the same form inside every head, never mind how it got there. Cultural differentiation then tends to be seen as a deviant pattern to be problematized. Possibly it is sensed as being accomplished by stretching, compressing, or twisting this original structure according to the individuals' placement in the structure of social relations. While the imagery may be enlightening in some ways, we have not assumed such a common baseline here. The human brain may impose certain forms, or allow variations only within limits, in cognitive systems. What we have been concerned with here, however, are the processes by which its working materials are delivered. Considering the variety of experiences which different people have, and the uncertainties of communication which have to do with misunderstandings and unevenness of contacts, one may as well feel that it is no small wonder if meanings come to be widely held in common.

With this in mind, we have avoided the casual bandying about of concepts like "mainstream culture" or "the dominant culture" which are so convenient (and sometimes even inevitable) in discussing cultural differentiation. The entities which they refer to are not just there, to be taken for granted. Even the most widespread understandings must be constructed from something and actively propagated, with greater or lesser success. We tend to use these terms least hesitantly when talking about what they exclude; the poor, the young, the deviants, the immigrants. Once we start scratching on the surface of what is supposedly the dominant culture, we often have to report back that it dissolved in front of our eyes, turning again into a number of smaller and subtly interlinked units.

We should thus ask what are the conditions which could create anything like a mainstream culture. In the picture we have drawn so far of rather decentralized cultural processes, in the context mostly of face-to-face interaction, the answer would have to be that it comes about in part when a large proportion of the population is in a relatively open network, as opposed to being encapsulated in many small ones, and is reasonably generous about spreading the same ideas through most of its relationships.

Then, however, we have left out a collection of relationships of varying significance in different social structures. These are the relationships which establish centricity in the social system and which are sometimes l´ ḻhly active culturally. In Redfield's and Singer's orthogenetic city, it was the sacred complex which was interpreted to the public by priests and story tellers, largely in one-way communication. In the modern western city, this centralized cultural apparatus has some obvious components like mass media and schools; institutions like courts and social services also play a part in it, and we should not forget the distribution of standardized meanings by way of artifacts in an economy oriented toward mass consumption. This is culture which we do not necessarily pick up from people in our immediate vicinity, but we can be quite sure that we learn it with them.

The culturally homogenizing impact of relationships of centricity cannot be assumed to be of the same form and intensity in all kinds of urbanism. The connection between the meanings distributed through such channels and those of people's ordinary face-to-face contacts, furthermore, is not obvious. The participants in the mass culture debate, which was so intensive in the United States in the 1950s and then waned, had interesting ideas in this area, but those were seldom tested through ethnography. Undoubtedly the meanings derive more from some face-to-face cultures than from others; this may or may not make the former "mainstream." Who takes these meanings most to heart, feeding them into other situations, is another problem. At times they perhaps simply maintain, in a circular fashion, the culture of that segment of society where they originated. At other times, they may be among the influences interfering with culture built more directly from personal experience, for better or for worse.

If we have been somewhat wary of superculture concepts, then, we have also avoided the term subculture. In part because the two go together, as the latter to most of us implies the former. But one may also do well to use it only after one has fully understood how inexact a term it is. If a class culture is a subculture, for example, there are also subsubcultures, like the youth culture within it, and certainly subsubsubcultures as well. Other systems of meanings may overlap or tie together such units, or what we refer to as subculture and mainstream. If we need a vocabulary to distinguish between types of units in the analysis of the social organization of meanings (not only for classificatory games but to think with), we may need more than two terms.

Something more may be said about time and culturality as well; it relates to our view of fluidity in urban life. Social relationships may indeed be variously active in cultural construction in different phases. To begin with, as the first understandings are collectivized, there may have to be a high degree of explicitness about what I want you to know that I know. In the terms of Basil Bernstein's (1971) sociolinguistics, communication has to be in an elaborated rather than restricted code. This is true whether a relationship entails the mutuality of Albert Cohen's model of cultural process or the entry of one party into a system of meanings which is already an ongoing concern, under the dominance of those who have been around longer. In the latter case, of course, one finds oneself being socialized into an existing culture, directly in the relationship which draws on it or anticipatorily for expected career movements. Anyway, later on, as things settle down, we may be able to communicate in shorthand, in a restricted code. As with the wink, the explicit messages which are exchanged are then only the top of an iceberg, and to raise its hidden parts to the surface can be a frustrating business. Garfinkel's (1967:38 ff.) ethnomethodological analyses of everyday speech are revealing here. There is the record of a natural conversation between man and wife, so familiar with each other's habits and circumstances that a large proportion of what needs to be communicated comes across without being said, while what is said may seem incomprehensible to anybody else. There are also the interchanges where one party, on an experimental basis, tries to force the other to make all statements and assumptions explicit and crystal clear, and which therefore quickly develop into situations of discomfort and confrontation, events of cultural sabotage.

Clearly there is much of this cultural routine in the most fluid structure of social relationships as well. It may be worthwhile to devote an occasional thought also to the underpinnings of this routine. Even as a system of meaning stabilizes, it is not just there, solidly, without further human help, but has to be maintained, we may go so far as to say continuously recreated, just to stay put. But moreover, the prevalence of fluidity in urban life means that more active cultural processes get under way again and again. Some reach widely through society. Just as crowd behavior may have something cultural to it, we should not forget the short-duration shared meanings which become fads and fashions, and are then disowned. Other cultural processes are of more limited range, going on somewhere in a personal network as people change place, with possible repercussions in other relationships. It may involve merely an individual's arrival at another existing cultural edifice, and no change for anybody but himself; since the newcomer brings experiences of his own, however, the beginning of his involvement may also precipitate a reconstruction. These things keep happening in offices, neighborhoods, associations, and elsewhere.

CITIES as WHOLES

Hurriedly rather than exhaustively, we have dealt with some of what could be detail issues in urban anthropological theory. For the most part, the kind of analysis of the formation and use of role repertoires, networks, and cultures which has been outlined may seem to be set in rather limited assemblages of social relationships—neighborhoods, gangs, public places, ego-centered networks, and so forth. In this we have not differed much from most anthropological research in cities: the difference is rather in trying to find a unified way of handling them.

In the debate over what urban anthropology is and should be, however, some have argued that the study of such small units is not enough. And so we finally come back to the question of units of study in urban anthropology.

The critique of the prevalent interest in the lesser units within the city is that it is microsociological in the extreme, and turns urban anthropology into a "street anthropology" of the most pedestrian kind. In a couple of publications, for example, Richard Fox (1972, 1977) has argued for an alternative perspective. In the city, he suggests, anthropologists find themselves in a situation where their discipline in a way comes apart. The majority of them have so far opted for remaining true to one part of the heritage: participant observation, the romantic approach to the culturally alien. Thus we get the portraits of the life styles of the poor, the deviants, and the recent migrants. The city itself, however, recedes into the background. The other position is to take the holistic aspirations of anthropology seriously even as one deals with the most complex and large-scale form of society. If this is one's choice, the city as a whole is the unit in focus, to be understood as a social form in its interplay with the surrounding society. This would be a superior basis for a truly comparative urban anthropology, as it would give concentrated attention to the way different societies make different cities. Such a perspective should also take in history, to reach a full awareness of urban variation and to show how cities also go through careers. With a time depth like this, the large-scale anthropology of urbanism would divorce itself further from the tradition of field work anthropology, with its built-in bias toward synchrony. On the whole, it would seem to be the difference between an urban anthropology from above and an urban anthropology from within.

We had a quick overview of urbanism along lines rather like those advocated by Fox in chapter 3; writers like Weber, Pirenne, Sjoberg, and Redfield and Singer also inspire his anthropology of cities. Some questions of a related nature involving the links between the urban community and the larger society were raised in chapter 4. At the time, however, we also saw hints that a study of urbanism concerned with the part performed by the city in the wider setting was not quite likely to become a complete urban anthropology either. It has a way of concentrating on the struggle for livelihood and power, of the city in its context as well as internally between urbanites. The people in the city-forming sector of the urban economy are cast in the starring roles: in Courttown priests and warriors, in Commercetown the merchants, in Coketown industrialists and workers.

This is no bad choice for a study of a segment of urban life, but arguably it is still only a segment. To really study a city as a whole, one would have to take into account all its people—city fathers, urban villagers, spiralists, street people, whatever kinds one may recognize. And one would have to follow them through all domains of activities, not only as they make a living but also as they run their households, deal with neighbors, brush against each other in the city square, or simply relax. Moreover, one would want to require of such a study not only that the ethnography is all there but that one would get a reasonably clear idea of how it all hangs together. Some of the brave attempts that have been made to draw together the anthropology of entire cities have unfortunately seemed rather like catalogs of descriptive domain anthropologies, without much analysis of the relations between them.

Obviously all this is more easily said than done. At some point there has to be a trade-off between extensive and intensive coverage. Perhaps it could yet be of some interest to sketch the principles of an anthropology of a city as a whole, in line with the views set forth in the preceding pages. Where should one begin in trying to build an acceptably systematic picture of how it all fits together?

The Rhodes-Livingstone anthropologists emphasized that an urban anthropologist might preferably treat some sorts of facts as given—"external determinants," or "contextual parameters." Mitchell's more elaborate list of such categories of facts included density, mobility, ethnic and demographic composition, economic differentiation, and political and administrative constraints. Epstein's compact version covered much the same ground under the labels of industrial, civic, and demographic structures.

Obviously the Rhodes-Livingstone framework is based on much research experience. In its relatively great detail it may offer the chance of rather quick progress toward analytical precision. Against this advantage, however, may be posed the value of parsimony in the analytical apparatus. One might prefer to introduce new variables more gradually and try to get as much analytical mileage as possible from them before adding others. To assume that a certain phenomenon should be seen as an external determinant seems equivalent to saying that within the framework of other available facts, it remains an imponderable. But the qustion which factors must be regarded as in some measure analytically independent can hardly be answered on the basis of first principles. True, it may be that if the civic structure differed between mining towns in what used to be British and Belgian territories in Africa, the reason must be found, as Epstein suggests, in variant colonial policies which the anthropologist can only take for what they are. If politics and administration of a less formal kind are also to be seen as a part of civic structure, however, we will shortly note that they may themselves be seen as emergent, out of the very structure of social relations which they then proceed to influence on their own. To move a step further, if it is known that a town makes its living largely from mining, and that the influx of migrants is controlled so as to have as few townspeople as possible other than recruits to the labor force, it is rather predictable that a demographic disproportion in age and sex terms will result, with a further impact on the character of urban life. At times, then, one may be tempted to ask if urban anthropologists must always be so modest in giving up the ambition of finding out certain things for themselves as a lengthier listing of external determinants might imply.

Our analytical strategy here, tentatively suggested in chapter 3, is to make the domain of provisioning our point of departure in the study of the urban totality, and see how far we can get by working out the wider implications of its composition. As it turns out, this more or less amounts to singling out the variable which Mitchell calls economic differentiation, and Epstein industrial structure, for primary attention. Some sketchy remarks may at least give an idea of what would be the general procedure.

First of all, there are those external relationships through which the urban community—with the possible exception of an occasional ancient agriculturally based city state—draws together a collective resource base; the external linkages, that is, of the city-forming sector of the economy, with the countryside as well as within a system of cities. Any city-forming sector has its own array of provisioning roles. They differ, for one thing, in their linkages to one another and to the society surrounding the city. At one extreme we find places where a large proportion of these roles entail direct external provisioning relationships, without mediation. One may think of them along the lines of central place theory as collections of little centricities in the social structure, standing shoulder to shoulder or back to back but facing outward; they may be more or less successful, but their fate depends more on their external dealings than on transactions within the community. At times they may be in an indirect relationship through competition, trying to draw the attention of the same outside alters. On the other hand, their involvements with the outside may be largely complementary, and each may be of support to the other as together they build up the relative centricity of the community as a whole.

The opposite of such a multicentric city-forming sector would be one where the immediate external relationships are in relatively few hands. A town or city devoted mostly to serving one particular function within a wider economy would more often have this type of outside connection. In a Copperbelt town like Luanshya, for instance, the provisioning of thousands of miners would all be channeled through the hands of a rather small number of people at the upper management levels; this is one aspect of what Epstein called the "unitary structure" of the mine. Here, then, the allocation of resources through relationships internal to the city-forming sector take on greater importance.

Between such multicentric and oligocentric or even unicentric types of city-forming sector are any number of intermediate forms. The city-serving sector, for its part, may occasionally be said to overlap considerably with the city-forming sector. In the sort of multicentricity just hinted at, the urbanites could draw by and large on the same services as people outside the urban population. Where it does have a more recognizably separate existence, however, with another number of provisioning roles, resources must again flow through provisioning relationships within the city, from incumbents of roles in the city-forming sector to those with roles in the city-serving sector. The structure of the latter appears more often to be relatively multicentric, with a range of separately organized services offered side by side. The Luanshya example seems illuminating here as well, if somewhat extreme. While the mine was city-forming and "unitary," the municipal township was to a great extent city-serving and, in Epstein's view, "atomistic." There is another flow of resources, of course, between people in the city-serving sector.

Much of the drama of urban life certainly revolves around the maneuvering with roles and relationships in the provisioning domain. People in the same role, as we just said, can compete for scarce alters and the resources which may come from them; alternatively or at the same time they may collaborate with one another in a unified bargaining position vis-à-vis these alters to get the best possible rate of exchange for their services; they may, moreover, try to restrict access of others to the same role, so that they can themselves be of a scarce sort and therefore at an advantage in negotiations. Because finite resources are involved, conflict, whether open or muted, tends to seem near at hand in relationships of provisioning. Yet this, at the same time, suggests bases for alliances.

Only with an intimate knowledge of the particular mix of provisioning roles in a city, and the distribution of the population over these roles, is it likely that one can reach an understanding of alignments in urban conflict, and the sheer amount of it. We have touched before on the study of community power structures, where separate interests can be pursued not just in a diffused manner within varied and more isolated contexts but also through a machinery where decisions are made which are binding on the whole community. In some ways, this machinery may have its own form, not the creation of the city itself as it was in Weberian urbanism but a construction imposed on it by agencies of the wider society, as in the case of the colonial forms of urbanism referred to by the Rhodes-Livingstone an-

thropologists. But in other ways, those which have been of greater interest
to political sociologists, community power structures are emergent phenomena. It could be true as skeptics have it that some of the variations
found among such structures are simply artifacts of the differences between the methodologies used to investigate them, but there are surely
more real differences as well.[20] To note only one of the more obvious, if an
urban community has a unicentric or oligocentric city-forming sector, it is
likely that community politics again and again comes to focus on control of
the provisioning relationships through which the center distributes resources on which the entire community depends. The incumbents of roles
at the center may use their control of resources to try to maximize their
power over community life in general, and might at times be largely un-
challenged. In other instances, the response may be the creation of a long
battleline between the roles of the center and much of the rest of the community, recurrently drawn in largely the same way. Where both city-forming and city-serving sectors are more fragmented, another pattern may
emerge, and a less stable one. As no single person or interest group is in
secure command of particularly great resources, an observer may even
come to wonder whether anyone wields community power. Its structure
seems forever shifting as different people push different issues, try to coalesce strategically with others, and evaluate the implications of each outcome in their environment for their own position—an "ecology of games"
in Norton Long's (1958) sense.

From the analysis of the domain of provisioning, our study of one city
would move out into other domains. In thus encompassing urban life, for
one thing, we can get some sense of the extent to which the organization of
diversity in provisioning breeds further diversity in other situational involvements. As far as resources are concerned, the particular nature of
people's participation in the former domain can set the more or less constraining framework for their doings in other contexts as well (and for
those of any persons materially dependent on them in their households).
But provisioning roles can also have other influences on the way roles are
put together and adjusted to each other in role repertoires. Experiences
may shape general orientations, other roles may have to be scheduled in
time around those of provisioning, and one's input into roles and relations
elsewhere may depend on a calculated feedback into the provisioning domain. In the domain of household and kin relationships, to take a few examples mostly from contemporary western urban society, the nature of

domestic life may depend on whether the domain of provisioning offers employment for both sexes and a wide range of ages. The prevalence of strong extended kin ties may be connected to the role in the urban economy of know-how and property devolved along them. In the domain of recreation, a manual worker is unlikely to be able to afford breeding race horses for a hobby; people with his background of worldly experience often simply prefer football games to poetry readings. If he works on shift, he may spend much of his leisure time in rather solitary activities such as gardening, because few others may be around to interact with when he is free.[21] Hoping in one way or another to change the structure of the domain of provisioning as a whole, or at least his own position in it, he may draw on time available for recreation as well to further such objectives, by engaging in movement politics or taking adult education courses. In what kind of neighborhood a person will find himself depends significantly on those particular relationships of provisioning through which urban space is allocated. The sort of relationships he may have with neighbors may vary, we have seen, with the time at his disposal for being around and with that need for minor reciprocities which may be both a direct and an indirect result of his involvement in making a living. Traffic roles are in no small part a matter of timing, of distance between home and work (if the two are in separate places), and of choice of vehicle. They may entail a walk down dark streets, hanging on to a strap in a crowded train, or a ride in the back of a limousine at the time of one's convenience.

But, to repeat, the city may be in part soft. Having tried to make out as far as possible in what ways and to what degrees people's activities, ideas, and relationships throughout are influenced by the way their city and they themselves make a living, we would turn to those areas of their lives which stand in a more indeterminate relationship to what happens in the provisioning domain. Here are the ties which do not align themselves with those of provisioning and work, and which may even entail crosscutting loyalties. Here we detect the systems of meanings which arise and spread through other situations, and which can simply co-exist with those in the provisioning domain or come into conflict with them. To be just a little more specific, here, for example, are games of leisure which one pursues in the company of people whom one does not know from work, who might in fact be "on the other side," although for the moment this is neither here nor there. Here we find those neighborhoods where inhabitants may be friendly or distant, but where the people who go off to work in the morning all head in different directions. Here are the consuming interests which keep creeping into a person's mind perhaps even as he is performing a boring job—interests to which he may even try to accommodate his work obligations.

In the soft spots of the social structure, one is likely to find the more original role combinations, the more unpredictable careers, the less routine confluences of meanings. Where the stricter determination of role repertoires and relationships by the provisioning roles tends to create large gaps in the total urban network, between rather dense clusters, the more loosely structured areas of life build bridges, although partly by inserting clusters of other tendencies. But precisely because they allow experimentation and innovation in people's constellations of involvements, they may allow the development of new ways of linking these together optimally with provisioning roles. In this way, we had better understand that what is soft and hard in urban life do not only shade into each other but can be dynamically interrelated.

Thus perhaps we can gradually build up a picture of the entire urban social order, its rigidity and flexibility, its sources of cohesion and fragmentation. To bring it a step nearer to completion, we should take note that its inhabitants can have connections across city boundaries not only in the provisioning domain. The Copperbelt mining towns have been our most prominent examples here of places where a large number of migrants combine both urban and rural involvements in their role repertoires. The people called spiralists can similarly, through their careers, accumulate relationships between cities. And we find the people who, due to work or recreational interests of somewhat specialized types, maintain a variety of external links through travel or correspondence; participating in what Melvin Webber (1964:108 ff.), with a possibly not very appealing term, has described as "nonplace urban realms." These varied external contacts continue to make the total network of the city an open-ended one. For one thing, the passage of meanings which goes on within them prevents the city as a whole from going off too effectively on a process of cultural drift of its own, maintaining instead what cultural unity there is between city and society.

Can the total urban ethnography, along the lines sketched here, ever be done? Perhaps not, in any particularly exhaustive way. It would take an enormous amount of work, and would be of enormous length. To cover the entire variety of ways in which urban lives can be constructed the ethnography might turn literally into personal information, a monograph that is a *Who's Who* in network form.

It is one possibility to use the understanding of the task which we have reached as an instrument of guidance instead for more limited efforts. Some familiarity with a given urban community may make it possible for us to work out in our minds at least a rough outline of the total ethnography. We would know rather well what is the city-forming sector of its economy and what the provisioning domain looks like in general. We would have some idea of the spread of roles in different other domains and of notable cultural clusters. Certain connections between roles might seem obvious; others would have to be worked out. We might find out soon enough what the consequences are where the structuring of life is hard. What happens where it is soft may never cease to surprise us.

Such a general image of the city can be useful in studies of smaller segments of urban life, and might with advantage be incorporated into them more consciously. The question has sometimes been raised how anthropologists might best deal with "the city as context" when their actual focus is on such entities as an occupation, a neighborhood, or an ethnic group within it (see Rollwagen 1972, 1975). If group X is represented in cities A and B, are there differences between its ways of life in them, and how does one account for it? Our interpretation would be that the more distinctive the city-forming sector of A or B is, the more directly the urbanites which a study deals with are involved in this sector, and the closer the connection between provisioning roles and any other activity is, the more useful is it to see this activity as a phenomenon related to the specific character of the city as a whole.

If an idea of the whole city may be useful as a background image in this way, however, we may still be reluctant to give up the notion of a more inclusive urban portrait; "portrait" in the sense of an art form rather than that of absolute and exhaustive likeness. To work out a more intellectually—and esthetically—satisfying anthropological mode of dealing with entire urban communities we will undoubtedly have to engage in some experimentation, with regard to both research and reporting. Historians have occasionally come some way toward such synthesizing presentations of cities as one might aim for, gradually drawing on a wider range of topics and materials, but usually with no explicit criteria for their selection and organization. In the sociology and anthropology of complex societies, we have in community studies a genre which has also attempted the ethnography of whole places with some success, although again without much concern for the codification of procedure. Without entirely sacrificing the humanistic elements of these kinds of studies, the framework for the anthropology of a city suggested before may prompt a little more systematic thinking about what ought to go into such ethnography; something that could be helpful especially in dealing with urban forms rather larger and more complicated than those most frequently dealt with in the community studies. On the basis of an overview of the whole urban social structure, one would select for more intensive coverage zones within it which together would give the most adequate sense of the entire thing. The units of ethnography to be brought into the synthesis should be illustrative of differentiation, while at the same time overlapping or connecting in some way or other to depict coherence as well. The "network of networks" phrasing may put us on the right path: we would want to include significant clusters of relationships, yet also the links which connect them. Units would be of different kinds: council meetings, shop floors, family interiors, street life, major events, individual careers. Since presumably, for reporting purposes at least, we would want some of them to cover much ground and suggest many leads, situational analyses like that of the Kalela dance in Luanshya would come in as useful devices; in this case, a focus on a particular pastime which is also a comment on both provisioning and traffic relationships. Ideally, the urban portrait could include both insights into characteristic fluidity in social organization and samples of cultural process. And it might acquaint one with some of the people who draw on the materials of the city for both construction and presentation of self.

In this picture of life in a city the use of space in urban culture and social organization may also be brought out vividly. The city is a piece of territory where much human interaction is crammed in. In one way or another, whatever remains of what it once was as natural landscape may be used in organizing it as a human community—the Left Bank, Capitol Hill—but to a great extent, it is the cityscape we have to attend to, an environment which urbanites have created for themselves and each other. This is also as assemblage of texts. The reading Burgess and others gave Chicago was rather too lopsided (too much attention to dollar signs, especially) to serve as a model for the exegesis of urban settings generally. One would need to be more openminded about what considerations influence the way land is parceled out, and what ways are used to appropriate it, in a manner which takes into account State Street as well as the cosmography of ceremonial centers, real estate agents as well as squatter invasions. But, in addition, we should try to get a sense of how the cityscape spells out society in general and their own community in particular to the people inhabiting it, and how it facilitates some contacts and obstructs others.[22] What the imposing walls and towers of the Kremlin mean to Muscovites, and Piccadilly Circus to Londoners, what the Mall and the "civil lines" stand for in an Indian city with a colonial past, and tall factory chimneys without smoke in a declining industrial town. How a busy market place, a temple, or a cool shady park may bring about unexpected meetings; how public places like bars or libraries sometimes really are that, while at other times they have been taken over as home territories by groups which select themselves and resent intrusions. The way different degrees and kinds of encapsulation in the social structure correspond in the physical layout to "across the tracks," ghettos, and turfs. What are, for different purposes, the backstage and frontstage of urban life, and the significant props of the frontstage. How change and stability in the public face of the city— monuments, buildings, street pattern—affect what there is of an awareness of the past among its people. All this, again, brings the sense of place to urban anthropology.

It is features like these that we usually pick when as laymen we try to catch the essence of a city. Whether they mean the same to the native as to the outside observer is only a problem as old as anthropology itself, and one for the anthropologist to solve. But we also have other ways of summarizing the distinctiveness of a community, notions in which the scene may be important but where attention is really centered on the style of actors. Finally, we may want to draw these as well into the anthropology of cities. A configurational approach we may call this; as anthropologists have been drawn to it in other contexts, they have taken to terms like ethos, personality, temper, genius. It sometimes meets with scepticism, not being very analytical. Yet in the experiment of trying to show what a city is like, its integrative capacity can perhaps usefully complement the rather particularizing point of view toward roles and relations which we have otherwise taken here.

The character of the city is often thought of as one of indivisible, recurrent in much the same form wherever urban life is found, a rather amorphous quality pervading many if not all activities. This was a part of Wirth's and Simmel's message. Nevertheless, at a closer look and in part anyway, those conspicuous motifs which seem to cut across much of the culture and social structure of the city and give it the peculiar quality of urbanness may turn out to be differently and contradictorily defined in different places, depending on how cities, and centricity in social structures, are brought about. Although urban communities of a different nature may occur within the matrix of one society, often one pattern is so dominant that it becomes the sole source of urban imagery within a cultural tradition.

If we try to become rather more comparative and more precise about what goes into an urban configuration, another Brazilian study by Anthony Leeds (1968:37–38), a thumb-nail sketch of the stylistic difference between Rio de Janeiro and São Paulo, provides an example. The privileged, patrimonial governing elite of Rio, Leeds suggests, occupies positions which must continuously have symbolic validation in order for it to maintain power and prestige. Its sensuality is a display of both availability for new alliances and status exclusiveness. But all sectors of the *carioca* community are permeated by the resort atmosphere of the carnival and the beaches. Members of the elite set the pace of Rio life for the people of other strata as well, who emulate them in their commitment to festivity. In contrast, São Paulo is a nexus of private commercial and industrial elites, most of whose activities are also enhanced by privacy rather than display. The ethos of Rio is that of a Courttown, that of São Paulo a Coketown ethos.

The tale of the two cities, it seems, begins again in the domain of provisioning, in the city-forming sector. From here, however, the special style of Rio (which is the one of greater interest, the style of São Paulo seeming rather an anti-style) extends particularly into the recreational domain; here, being so very visible in its forms of ritual interaction, it just spreads and spreads and spreads. It has its high points, but anyone can come to Rio at any time and see it around him. Mere traffic relationships, in other words, suffice for exposure. Some of the mini-environments most widely understood to symbolize Rio as a whole are also settings of stylistic performance *par preference*.

If a city can be summed up with any justice, then (which may or may not be the case), in terms like a dominant ethos, we may reasonably seek the roots of this ethos in the functions which make the city. Directly or indirectly from these roots must spring, at the same time, highly observable forms of frequently repeated behavior, frontstage to almost anybody much of the time, often linked to characteristic built-up forms as well. In the

Central Italian town of Montecastello in Silverman's *Three Bells of Civilization* (1975), the urban ideology of *civiltà* seems to be connected to the concerns of a land-owning, town-living elite—courtesy, generosity, and genteel behavior, an etiquette of responsibility and benevolence partly serving to smooth over rough spots in relationships to people in lower stations and to conceal more crassly exploitative facets; and a claim of access to higher places as well as civic pride, expressing both hierarchical and laterally competitive relationships in a wider system of urban places. This seems still to be more the ethos of a Courttown than of a Commercetown, even if Montecastello is only a miniature city of power. Compare this to the spirit of Gopher Prairie, the typical American small town of Sinclair Lewis' novels, dominated by the hustling small businessmen along Main Street, pulsating with the internal and external competitiveness of a relatively low-level commercial central place.

AFTERTHOUGHTS: In the FIELD in the CITY

We have made our attempt to formulate what an urban anthropology could be about. Throughout this volume, the emphasis has been on distilling from various more or less important works a feeling for what are, if not uniquely, at least rather characteristically urban phenomena, and on conceptualizing them in a reasonably economical way which should also be in line with anthropological thought in general, while at times possibly giving it some slight extension. Particularly as we touch on ways of portraying cities as wholes, however, and stress the desirability of innovative formats of ethnography, it may be in place to add some afterthoughts on what our conceptualization of urban life implies in methodological terms. There is certainly no one single recipe for doing urban anthropology, but what has been said could perhaps throw some new light on old practices.

No really strong reason seems to have emerged for evicting participant observation from its central position in anthropological methodology. There may be differences of opinion on this point. Those who have long felt that the advantages of anthropological field work have come at a high price may indeed consider its cost in the maze of urban society prohibitive. We must be aware of the difficulties of access, the limited range over which participant observation is possible, and the consequent problems of representativeness and macroscopic relevance. Replicability, reliability, verifiability are items of a vocabulary of scientific values by way of which objections have been phrased to traditional anthropological method.

Undoubtedly anthropologists have reason to be cautious about generalizations based on data from the restricted social field within which intensive work usually occurs. If anthropologists should turn out to remain rather unresponsive to proposals of alternative methodologies, however, it is not because they deny that their approach has its drawbacks, but because they feel that it may still serve their particular purposes better than anything else available. In fact, there may be some special advantages to observational, unobtrusive data collection in urban life as we have depicted it here. The need for exploration is still present. Among the diversity of cultures in the city some may be conspicuous, others hardly noticeable to the outside and not usually identified. Any instrument but the highest possible degree of immersion in these cultures may be too insensitive. It would be unlikely to catch the subtle nuances which make up much of the cultural variation, for instance, in contemporary European or American cities. There is, in addition, the fact that with the cultural implosion of the city, people who would rather not want a culture of theirs to be open to anyone's glances are quite sophisticated enough to choose another culture out of their repertoires for interaction with strangers; in conventional terms, something "mainstream" rather than "deviant." The greater chances of getting beyond such a façade of impression management is one part of the case for urban participant observation. Clearly, in some such instances participant observation raises important moral problems. Without going into these, let us conclude that it is often an effective way of finding facts.

There are other advantages, perhaps more familiar from field work elsewhere. One can get insights through participant observation into behavior which people do not readily verbalize about, and one's data can focus better on relations and their context, rather on abstracted individuals. The critics of anthropological method thus too often seem simply unaware that they propose to throw out a baby with the bath water. If criteria for a more systematic evaluation of data quality are needed, they must be sensitive to the nature and uses of the data. As a matter of basics, our main concern with the practice of participant observation in urban anthropology should perhaps not be that it is unsuitable, but that it may sometimes be taken too lightly. Occasionally, one suspects that some urban research involves merely a tenuous contact with a "field" on the other side of town, to be maintained on a spare-time basis in competition with family, friends, and a full-time job. This could be better than nothing at all, but it is far from the intensity of involvement which anthropologists normally expect in field work. One may fear that poor ethnography will sometimes be the result, and hope that this will not be the dominant practice in urban anthropology. An around-the-clock commitment to field work may at times be impracticable in an urban study, since some units of study are themselves only part-time phenomena. But in principle, it is their own timing, rather than the anthropologist's convenience, that should determine his work schedule.

Yet for all that may be said in favor of participant observation, there is no reason to espouse a purism of anthropological method as a matter of principle. In fact, although participant observation is widely understood to be central to it, anthropological field approaches have always been characterized by a fair amount of eclecticism. The watch word is "triangulation"; loosely speaking, the strategy of putting together data arrived at in different ways, sometimes finding several routes to the same fact.[23] A good working knowledge of existing methodology for data production in the human sciences is obviously very beneficial for one's readiness for dealing with the unfolding peculiarities of a field situation. But what also deserves emphasis, and does not always receive it even as anthropologists become more self-conscious about their ways of doing field work, is the need for inventiveness. There is not just one finite set of authorized methods of getting at reality. Field methodology is better seen as protean, forever changing shape, as established procedures are modified to fit another context and as new tools are fashioned under the inspiration of the field situation, without obvious earlier counterparts. One may discover that the photo album of an acquaintance is a revealing source of network information, and begin a systematic search of such documentation; one may find that with barely literate informants, the ranking of occupations is more easily accomplished in something that looks like a card game than with a bureaucratic form to fill in.[24]

"Be prepared", however, is a motto for anthropological field work anywhere, as well as for scouting. Perhaps urban life, by its very nature, implies a demand for an even higher degree of such general methodological flexibility on the part of the researcher. But there may also be reason to look for the consequences of our conception of the city along a couple of particular methodological dimensions. One of these involves time. In discussing fluidity in social organization, we have suggested that even disregarding cumulative change in the social system, urbanism may allow notable transformations in people's life situations as, over the years, they fit differently into networks and the role inventory. Urban historians, time specialists among the students of the city, have often been critical of the neglect, or poor understanding, of such change in other disciplines (see Thernstrom 1965, 1973:2 ff.; Chudacoff 1972:5 ff.). With a conventional field period of a year or maybe two, the anthropologist may certainly be on the spot to observe some such changes as they occur. He is less likely, as field work has normally been practiced, to get a firsthand view of careers and their intermeshing over a longer time span.

Some of the writers we have referred to have tried to build diachrony into their ethnography and analysis. The Chicagoans were concerned with process in several ways; the Rhodes-Livingstone group developed the idea of extended case studies. But the build-up of a systematic urban anthropology would appear to require that yet more attention be devoted to ways of reporting on fluidity.

One possibility is certainly to extend field work in time—not necessarily through continuous presence, which is not often feasible, but through recurrent periods in the same field. As usual, one may need a longer tour as a first phase, to get deeply into the field, while later sojourns can perhaps be shorter and still useful as one can pick up threads not so far from where one left them. Apart from such timing of the field work itself, the development of urban anthropological method would seem to include further attention to the instruments of retrospective (and perhaps also prospective) study. Some skill in handling documents and archival data is increasingly recognized as a part of professional competence in anthropology generally. In its urban branch, it would seem at least as useful as anywhere else. The growth in recent years of an urban history centered on the lives of ordinary people has shown how much knowledge can sometimes be retrieved from such sources alone. Yet this is certainly also an area where urban anthropologists may try to triangulate. Oral history can often come out in a way which complements the evidence of registers and archives. Since in talking of fluidity we have the organization of personal rather than social change uppermost in mind, life histories would be particularly significant. So far, publishing life histories has probably usually been seen as a rather soft part of the anthropological enterprise—they have been left in print much as they were offered by the informant, without much serious attempt at analysis. Systematizing the study of careers, one would tend to work with the life histories more actively, and evolve criteria for comprehensiveness in collection to which little thought has been given so far. One would also worry over biases and gaps which retrospective accounts of lives almost inevitably contain, and see if they can be dealt with (for instance, by finding collateral information from another source).

The other methodological dimension on which some brief comments ought to be made relates to the size and complexity of the city. The uncertain or blurred boundaries of many units of study is not only a characteristic conceptual problem of urban anthropology but can also be a source of practical difficulties in the field worker's daily life. Network chains run on without a visible end, new faces keep showing up while others drift out of the picture unpredictably. One way of handling this problem, as we have seen, has been to avoid it as far as possible. By concentrating on the encapsulated groups of the city, urban anthropologists have tried to shut out such noise from the systems of information they are building. This has also meant that the anthropologists themselves, as participant observers, have tended toward encapsulation as a mode of field existence. (Possibly having another, non-field existence alongside, in a kind of double life.)

In the end, however, the problem must be confronted if we are ever to have a more complete picture of urban life. Once we begin to take more interest in the varied ways of being an urbanite, or in the study of urban wholes, we may also involve ourselves as field workers with the networks of the city in other ways. At times we may become network integrators; probably there are other times when we prefer to leave our various alters' networks as they are, largely unconnected with each other, so that field work entails a segregativity in which we parcel ourselves out among several distinct field contexts. The only mode of urban existence that would seem to fit ill with the goals of the field researcher is that of solitude.

But even as he takes on the task of dealing with less comfortably manageable units, an anthropologist cannot be everywhere in the city at the same time, and cannot know each of its inhabitants. He may still want to find out about what goes on out of reach of his individual field of direct and intensive observation.

One part of the solution to this kind of problem may lie in a qualitative-quantitative mix; perhaps the most obvious form of triangulation. Forever a topic of debate in urban anthropology, it has its type advantages and its type uncertainties. While subtle forms of thinking and acting may themselves hardly be accessible to extensive modes of data formation, one may hope to get some sense of their distribution obliquely through survey questions about related matters. Similarly we may wish to get some understanding of the aggregate effects of certain modes of action which we have been able to observe at close quarters. And we may indeed feel, after acquiring some measure of cultural competence, that it is possible to formulate intelligent questions on certain issues and get valid responses to them even from utter strangers. But we are aware at the same time of the difficulties that may arise. There may be gaps in the reasoning which tries to connect data of different types, the field worker who tries to be both a reasonably unobtrusive participant observer and a survey data collector may have troubles with his presentation of self, or it may simply be hard to find the time to gather data both wide and deep.

Since these difficulties vary with field situations and definitions of problems, generalizations are often not very illuminating. Leaving the topic aside with these few comments, we may approach the issue of extensive coverage from another angle, that of the social organization of research. The qualitative-quantitative mix by definition entails an uneven coverage. By simply involving more people in the research activities, more intensive coverage of some sort can be given to a greater portion of urban life. But how to do so is perhaps a question to which urban anthropologists could profitably give more systematic attention.

On the one hand there are the urban anthropologist's more intensive relationships with specific inhabitants of the field, on the other hand there is the collaboration between professional researchers. With regard to the former, to begin with, are there any special considerations involved in working with informants in urban studies?

Possibly, in a more homogeneous community these individuals tend to be chosen more on the basis of personality characteristics: they should be observant, somewhat inclined toward introspection and at the same time reasonably verbal, and they should have a good rapport with the field worker. In a complex structure such as that of the city, one may also become more acutely concerned with the need to choose them strategically to provide complementary perspectives toward social life, along its various axes of differentiation. Perhaps in order to extend coverage, urban anthropologists furthermore tend to use informants more in lieu of observation, rather than parallel to observation. So far, however, there has been little discussion in urban anthropology of the ways such informant panels are recruited (see Hannerz 1976:81 ff.). One might wish as well for more analysis of the further development of informant-anthropologist relationships, in their personal as well as professional aspects. For one thing, to what extent do the perspectives of regular informants become anthropologized, as they establish a collective system of meanings with the field worker?

From regular informants it may be only a short step to locally recruited research assistants. At first sight the difference could seem to be that the latter are paid and give more of their time than the former; as far as the character of research activities is concerned, it may be more important that the research assistants go out of their way to find out things they might not otherwise have known so much about, in settings where they might not normally find themselves. One may wonder about the fit between the research assistant and these situations, in terms of his entire role repertoire and his role-discriminatory attributes. What are the effects, furthermore, of the interposition of assistants between the anthropologist and parts of the field which ultimately he regards as his? The urban anthropological research establishment may turn out to have its own brokers and flak catchers. The socialization of the research assistant as a paraprofessional could also rate more attention in the discussion of field methodology.

The Copperbelt studies of the Rhodes-Livingstone Institute offer some examples, but little discussion, of the use of local research assistants. At the same time, its cluster of anthropologists, as the Chicagoans earlier, give us some idea of what can be accomplished in the way of large-scale urban ethnography when there is some coordination of the efforts of a number of professional researchers. No doubt we will continue to have the anthropologist as lone wolf in the city as well, with no more than an assistant or two to aid him in his project. Some research problems can be so circumscribed as to be rather easily manageable for a single investigator, and it is quite conceivable that one kind of anthropologist may even want to undertake some form of whole-city anthropology singlehandedly, perhaps as a long-term labor of love. Simply for organizational and financial reasons, for that matter, no alternative way of doing research is available for many of the people wanting to do urban anthropology. But it is unfortunate that, except for those of Chicago and the Copperbelt, there are as yet hardly any examples of larger-scale professional team ethnography in urban communities, although it has been suggested as an appropriate form for urban anthropological work (see Price 1973). Not least would this seem to be the more promising basis for taking on the study of entire cities, along the lines sketched earlier.

There is one more variety of research organization for urban studies to make note of, by way of conclusion: interdisciplinary research. Occasionally, the form may be suitable simply for the same purpose as the other organizational types just mentioned, to extend coverage of a large and complex social structure. At other times, the aim may be to combine methodologies and active conceptual integration as well. There are, naturally, advantages to such cooperation. If we are to follow the arguments of Gluckman and his colleagues concerning the limits of naïveté, neither anthropologists nor their peers in other disciplines should become too involved in issues with which others can deal more competently. And active interdisciplinary collaboration would seem to be the highest form of a scientific division of labor.

Even so, one may want to qualify one's enthusiasm. Quite frequently, it appears as if the pioneering interdisciplinary work is done by some brave individual who has ignored the demarcations of normal science and put things together in new ways through the internal conversations in his own mind. In anthropology, there may have been rather more of such openness in recent years than there used to be. It might appear that Gluckman wrote within the context of a more consolidated and sharply bounded discipline than that which we have now. The actual working together between specialists across discipline boundaries, on the other hand, is not easy. Interdisciplinary team work sometimes seems to be celebrated as a panacea for all problems of intellectual complexity; often prescribed, more seldom actually used in a successful cure.

Be that as it may. The problems of interdisciplinary linkages are not really ours here, conceptually or methodologically. Unless we have an understanding of urbanism which is recognizably anthropological, however, our input into such cooperation within this field may be slight. We have tried in the past pages to take some steps toward such an understanding. It seems that what we have come up with also has some implications for the way the urban anthropologist might practically handle his field, in some ways different from traditional field work. A great deal more could be said about this, but again the continuities are probably more significant. The anthropologist in the city may become a time-conscious team member (sometimes), but he is still a participant and an observer, taking an instrumental and eclectic view of complementary ways of finding facts. In method as in concepts, there can well be something distinctly anthropological about urban anthropology.

Appendix:
Analytical Concepts
in Exploring the City

One reader of the manuscript of this book has suggested that others might find it useful to have somewhere a summary statement of the basic analytical apparatus used in it, preferably in a diagrammatic form, since concepts are introduced in a sort of steady flow through many chapters. What follows, then, is an attempt to visualize, in a reasonably uncomplicated way, the understanding of how urban society is constructed, in terms of roles and relations, which has been stated in a more roundabout way in the main body of the book.

Social life consists, perhaps most concretely, of situations. People involve themselves in these through relatively standardized modes of purposive behavior (and also with parts of their consciousness and material resources) which we call roles. The total array of such modes of behavior known within some major social unit, such as an urban community, may be described as its *role inventory*. The particular series of modes of behavior in which one individual is involved is a *role repertoire*. It seems practical to see both these kinds of role collections as divided into *domains* (household and kinship; provisioning; recreation; neighboring; traffic) containing greater or smaller numbers of roles. (These concepts are discussed on pp. 100–5.)

People are recruited into situations, and into particular roles in these, in no small part on the basis of what we call *role-discriminatory attributes*, culturally defined characteristics of individuals which exist apart from particular situations. Such major attributes are sex, age, and (in social units which are heterogeneous in this regard) ethnicity or race. (The notion of

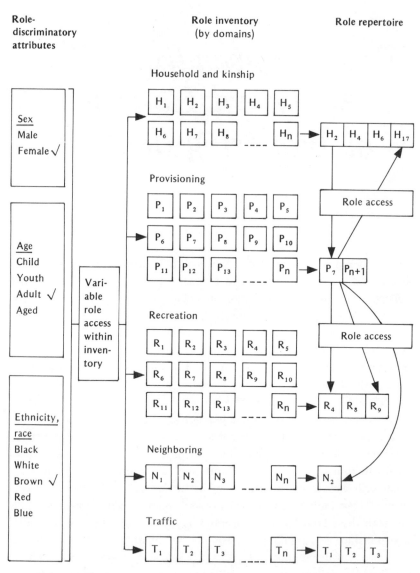

Figure 5. The Construction of a Role Repertoire in Urban Society

role-discriminatory attributes is discussed on pp. 151–56.) We may say that they are among the factors determining *role access* (see p. 151).

In figure 5 we can thus see, in a highly simplified manner, how a role repertoire is assembled in these terms, in an ethnically heterogeneous community with a more or less complete domain differentiation. An individual who is a brown adult woman, as opposed to say an aged blue man (the color terms stand here for any kind of ethnic designation), may be regarded in the community as fitting into certain roles within the role inventory but not others. (It is, of course, often a combination of role-discriminatory attributes, rather than a single one of them, that influences such access.) From among the roles still accessible, a role repertoire is put together, as indicated by the arrows between the inventory and repertoire columns. But further problems of role access may enter in here. The inclusion of specific roles in the repertoire may have a determining influence on what other roles the individual may or may not take on, simultaneously or at a later point in time. In this figure it is suggested that the household/kinship role H_2 has been important in the recruitment of this individual to provisioning role P_7. Being in this role, in turn, has allowed her to enter household/kinship role H_{17}, recreational roles R_4 and R_9, and neighbor role N_2, from which she would otherwise have been restricted. With regard to her other roles, e.g., H_6, R_8 and T_2, it seems that her role-discriminatory attributes and the remainder of her role repertoire, insofar as they are known to others, at least have not disqualified her from them. One role in her repertoire, P_{n+1}, is somewhat mysteriously included there but not in the role inventory. This could possibly serve as one way of denoting some basically new mode of behavior, in this case in the provisioning domain—an example of "role making" as discussed on pp. 276–80. But of course, as soon as it makes its first appearance in an individual role repertoire, one might see it as also making its way into the wider inventory.

It should perhaps be added that the number of roles enumerated in the role repertoire in this diagram is severely limited for the sake of convenience, although possibly the approximate proportions of the repertoire indicated as falling into the different domains may not be quite so unrealistic; see on this point the discussion on pp. 107–8.

In figure 6, we have taken the additional step of showing how a part of the personal network is constituted for the person (ego) with the role repertoire shown in figure 5. Her relationships to 13 alters are shown; to 3 of these (11, 12, 13) she is connected only minimally through traffic relationships, and since network analyses usually do not include such links they are marked here with broken lines. But note that of these no. 11 is linked through a more tangible relationship to no. 10, so that ego's traffic relationship to her may be of further significance—see the discussion of such connections on pp. 234–35.

As for ego's relationships to 1–10, this sketch of them may be related to

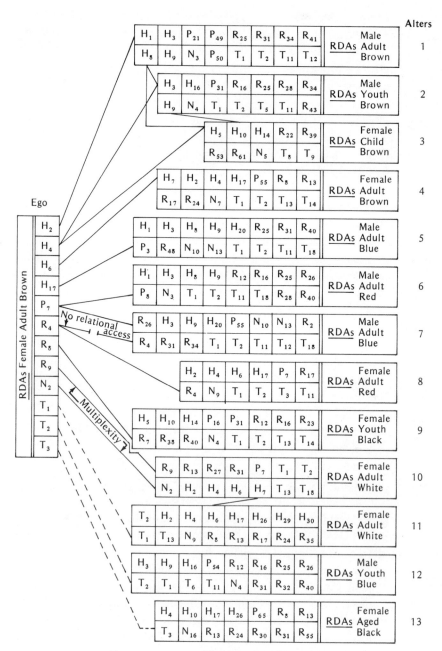

Figure 6. A Part of the Personal Network

the network concepts discussed in chapter 5, and compared to the more usual kind of network diagrams as exemplified in figures 3–4, p. 179. In such diagrams, of course, the entire role repertoires are collapsed into single points. If one wants to show how personal networks are put together as each role entails its own relationships, some such manner of portraying it as in figure 6 seems necessary. It may have the virtue of showing, at least, how quickly networks may ramify. Within the network segment made up of ego and alters 1–3 (which may be made out to consist of ego, her husband and two children) lateral relationships are also shown. In other words, this segment has the quality of a "first-order zone" (see p. 178). In the rest of the diagram, no relationships between alters (except that just mentioned between 10 and 11) have been included, nor between alters and other persons; this part of the diagram, that is, is a "first-order star" (see p. 178). But through each role shown in their repertories, these alters will have at least one relationship, and often many more, so that already the "second-order star" could be expected to be very large. We have only shown through ego's links to 6 and 7 that an individual could link up through one role both to more than one other individual and to more than one other role (role P_7 to P_8 and R_{26}). Between ego and 7 we also make a point of noting one non-relationship, that between one R_4 and another R_4. This is an example of an absence of *relational access* (see p. 151); although ego can take on role R_4, she is for some reason constrained from performing it vis-à-vis someone like 7. One may suspect that it is regarded as unsuitable for a brown woman and a blue man to have a recreational role relationship of this sort. It is, on the other hand, quite in order for ego to have such a relationship to a red woman (no. 8). And in all other relationships shown, of course, a person of ego's characteristics obviously has relational access through the roles concerned to people like these alters. With no. 10, ego has relationships through two distinct role pairs, one recreational and one neighborly. This is a multiplex relationship—see discussions on pp. 183–84 and pp. 253–54.

In figure 7, finally, we focus on one of the relationships included in figure 6, that between ego and alter no. 8 which they have both entered through their respective roles R_4. What we are concerned with is what governs the conduct of this relationship. Some relationships, we have argued, are under stronger *normative control* than others, so that whoever ego and alter are, apart from the roles they are in for the moment, is largely irrelevant—prescriptions for behavior are relatively precise (see pp.

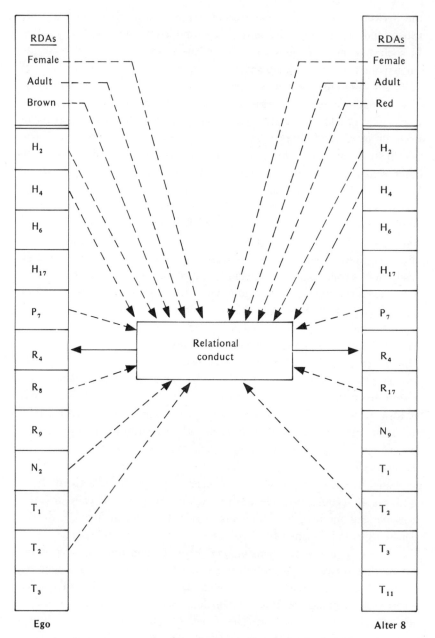

Figure 7. Relationship between Ego and Alter No. 8

150–51, 251–52). There are other relationships where ego and alter can pay more attention in their contacts to *personal information* about other attributes and involvements. In this way these can influence not only role access and relational access, as discussed above, but also *relational conduct* (see p. 151). In figure 7, we see that the relationship $R_4 - R_4$, a recreational relationship, is rather strongly influenced by personal information—the broken-line arrows from role-discriminatory attributes as well as other roles show that the conduct of the relationship is partly shaped by considerations involving these. It may be noted here that not all attributes and roles need affect any particular relationship, even if it is as permeable to external influences as this one. As far as ego is concerned, a couple of her household/kinship roles, one other recreational role, and two traffic roles are not "brought into" this relationship. We may also point out that there need not always be symmetry in what the parties to a relationship feed into it concerning other involvements. Ego may make disclosures about her neighbor role (N_2), but this alter does not make her role N_9 relevant to the relationship.

This, then, is one way of trying to conceptualize, verbally and diagrammatically, how a complex social structure coheres as roles are combined by individuals and as the individuals combine in relationships. No doubt it can readily be further elaborated; no doubt the present relative simplicity of the conceptual framework may make some ambiguity inevitable. But it may give us some sense of how to deal systematically with urban life in both some of its essentials and in its great variability.

Notes

1. The Education of an Urban Anthropologist

1. Certainly it was also a not altogether negligible fact that in an increasing number of Third World countries, foreign researchers were no longer particularly welcome. Moreover, funding for long periods of field work abroad seemed increasingly difficult to come by, perhaps especially for young American anthropologists. Urban anthropology at home could thus be a way out.

2. The first volume with this title is Eddy's (1968); the others are by Southall (1973a), Gutkind (1974), Uzzell and Provencher (1976), Fox (1977), and Basham (1978). Similar enough are the books of Weaver and White (1972), Foster and Kemper (1974), and Eames and Goode (1977).

3. I am obliged to Henning Siverts for this formulation, in a seminar in the Department of Social Anthropology, University of Bergen, in 1971.

4. This neglected volume has been presented slightly more fully elsewhere (Hannerz 1973).

5. An unofficial organ of this latter trend is the journal *Urban Life,* which began publication in 1972.

6. A first report on this project, centering on methodology, is contained in Hannerz (1976).

2. Chicago Ethnographers

1. I have chosen not to clutter the text which follows with references but to reserve them for specific points which have seemed to require exact documentation. Instead, this note may be seen as a bibliographic mini-essay on sources which I have found useful in developing my own understanding of the Chicago sociologists. Since this is a group of scholars who have drawn much comment through the years, I certainly make no claims to offering a complete picture of the literature.

Of the works of the Chicagoans themselves a number of the monographs are cited or summarized in the text. Much of the important work of Thomas and Park, however, took other forms, and has been collected in book form only in later years. The Heritage of Sociology series from the University of Chicago Press is particularly useful here. Of W. I. Thomas it contains a volume on *Social Organization and*

Social Personality (1966), edited and introduced by Janowitz. Ralph H. Turner has done a similar collection of Park's work *On Social Control and Collective Behavior* (1967), and in the series are also a 1967 reissue of *The City,* a collection of articles by Park, Burgess, and McKenzie, first published in 1925, and Park's German doctoral dissertation *The Crowd and the Public,* translated and published with some other essays under the editorship of Henry Elsner, Jr., in 1972. The collections of Louis Wirth *On Cities and Social Life* (1964a), edited and introduced by Reiss, and Roderick McKenzie *On Human Ecology* (1968), with similar services by Hawley, are in the same format as the first two volumes on Thomas and Park. Other useful volumes in the Heritage of Sociobiology series include Robert Faris' brief memoir *Chicago Sociology 1920–1932* (1970) as well as *The Social Fabric of the Metropolis* (1971), where the editor, James F. Short, Jr., gives a lucid overview of Chicago urban sociology as an introduction to a sample of texts by its practitioners. Outside this series there are the three volumes of Park's collected papers, *Race and Culture* (1950), *Human Communities* (1952), and *Society* (1955), under the general editorship of Everett C. Hughes. The second of these contains the papers most directly focused on urbanism, and my page references in the text are to this easily accessible volume, rather than to the original dispersed publications. Of course, there is considerable overlap between these three volumes and those in the Heritage series. There is an earlier collection of writings by Thomas in *Social Behavior and Personality,* edited by Volkart and published 1951 by the Social Science Research Council.

Among the many general comments on the Chicagoans two recent full-length books, Carey's *Sociology and Public Affairs: The Chicago School* (1975) and Matthew's *Quest for an American Sociology: Robert E. Park and the Chicago School* (1977) deserve first mention; the latter makes especially enjoyable reading. A chapter by Stein in *The Eclipse of Community* (1960) and one by Madge in *The Origins of Scientific Sociology* (1962) are also noteworthy. The latter has an additional chapter on Thomas's and Znaniecki's *The Polish Peasant in Europe and America.* The chapter by Burgess and Bogue (1967) is inside retrospective. There is an emphasis on Park in Burnet's (1964) article on Chicago sociology; Park has also been briefly portrayed by Hughes in an article which first appeared in the weekly *New Society* and then was reprinted in Raison's *The Founding Fathers of Social Science* (1969) as well as in Hughes' own *The Sociological Eye* (1971), where other articles also provide glimpses of Chicago urban studies. The discussion of Park by the Whites (1962) seems to me to exaggerate his anti-urban tendencies. There is a two-installment article on Thomas by Young (1962–63) and one on the Thomas-Znaniecki collaboration on *The Polish Peasant* by Symmons-Symonolewicz (1968). The appraisal of that study by Blumer (1939) is well known. Baker published autobiographical sketches by Thomas and Park in 1973. On Wirth's ideas there is a general paper by Bendix (1954) and a critique of his ghetto study by Etzioni (1959). The almost endless debate over his "Urbanism as a way of Life" will be dealt with in the next chapter; for bibliography, see chapter 3, note 3.

2. The concept of "moral order" was more often used than defined in Park's writings, and one may suspect that its boundaries were not sharply drawn. One

discussion which I draw on here and which I find rather enlightening was first published in 1925 in the paper then entitled "The Concept of Position in Sociology," later reprinted in *Human Communities* (1952:165–77).

3. The literature of comment on determinants of urban land use, as initially inspired by the Burgess scheme, has become very extensive. Schnore (1965) and London and Flanagan (1976) are among the writers offering useful comparative overviews.

4. There is, however, one autobiography by a female hobo, "Box Car Bertha," *Sister of the Road,* published as told to Dr. Ben L. Reitman (1975; first edition in 1937). Reitman, who gets some mention in Anderson's book, was himself a colorful person. Deserted at an early age by his parents, he ran errands for prostitutes at the age of eight and went to sea a few years later. While working as a janitor in the Chicago Polyclinic, he caught the attention of doctors and was helped to a medical education. He involved himself intensively with the world of the hoboes, not least with their educational activities, but also was a well-known character in Chicago's Bohemia, not least the Dill Pickle Club which Zorbaugh mentioned in *The Gold Coast and the Slum.* For a long period he was the lover of Emma Goldman, the anarchist; he also reputedly had an affair with the politically active widow of Albert Parsons, one of the radical labor leaders who were hung for their alleged part in the Haymarket Affair (see Adelman 1976:109–14).

5. The life history by Shaw, *The Jack-Roller* (1930), is a useful complement to Thrasher's work in providing one extensive and coherent case study of a gang boy's life.

6. The "four wishes" were for new experience, security, response, and recognition (see Volkart 1951:111 ff.; Thomas 1966:117 ff.).

7. There is some similarity between the *Mensch-Allrightnick* contrast and Paine's (1963) distinction between "freeholders" and "free enterprisers."

8. It should be noted here that the scheme of the "race relations cycle" was itself ecologically inspired.

9. Thrasher (1963:81–82) notes similar ethnic name changes among boxers.

3. The Search for the City

1. Among Redfield's relevant works here are his 1930, 1941, 1953, and 1955 books. A 1947 paper has been the basis of the summary of his folk society concept here and the recently renewed attempts to define "the great divide" between styles of time. Other related papers, previously published or unpublished, appear in his collected works (1962).

2. There are obvious similarities, for example, between the dichotomies cited here and the recently renewed attempts to define "the big divide" between styles of thought. One may be reminded of Redfield in Horton's (1967) emphasis on the lacking awareness of alternatives, or in Gellner's (1974:158 ff.) delineation of the vision of normality and the pervasiveness of entrenched clauses in traditional thought. Yet here, of course, the emphasis is not on an urban-rural contrast as

such. The work of Goody (Goody and Watt 1963; Goody 1977) has contributed to giving the achievement of literacy a more central place in the debate.

3. The debate on folk-urban or rural-urban contrasts includes comments by Benet (1963a), Dewey (1960), Duncan (1957), Fischer (1972), Foster (1953), Gans (1962b), Hauser (1965), Lewis (1951, 1965), Lupri (1967), McGee (1964), Miner (1952, 1953), Mintz (1953, 1954), Morris (1968), Pahl (1966, 1967), Paine (1966), Reiss (1955), Sjoberg (1952, 1959, 1964, 1965), Steward (1950), Stewart (1958), Tax (1939, 1941) and Wheatley (1972). A later, posthumously published paper by Wirth (1964b) is also relevant. The continued comments here can only partially cover the issues raised in this debate.

4. See, for example, the paper "Civilizations as Things Thought About" (Redfield 1962:364–75, especially page 370).

5. Wirth's vagueness on this point has led Oscar Lewis (1965:496), for example, to assert that "by 'socially heterogeneous' he had in mind primarily distinctive ethnic groups rather than class differences" and Paul Wheatley (1972:608) to feel that "he was more concerned with class differentiation than with ethnic diversity."

6. Just as in Redfield's notion of folk society such matters get little attention. When in the 1947 presentation "the chiefs, the men who decide disputes and lead in warfare" put in an appearance, it is in the context of a sacred festival, with the emphasis on their doing their traditional duty.

7. For some of the reviews of Sjoberg's study see Thrupp (1961), Wheatley (1963), Fava (1966), Cox (1969), and Burke (1975).

8. For a rather more elaborate treatment of preindustrial urbanism in this vein see Trigger (1972).

9. The parallel between Redfield's brief formulation and Mauss's (1967) classical treatment of reciprocity is obvious.

10. The particular case of the Yoruba is further discussed by Wheatley in a separate article (1970).

11. This transformation is discussed in some detail by Adams (1966:79 ff.).

12. One should perhaps be cautious about the labeling of early urbanisms as "original" and "derivative," as it may change with new archeological discoveries; the settlements of Mesopotamia and the Indus valley, for example, could have a common ancestor (see Service 1975:240).

13. A rather extensive literature on the notion of surplus bears on this problem; see, e.g., Pearson (1957), Harris (1959), Dalton (1960), Orans (1966), Wheatley (1971:268 ff.), and Harvey (1973:216 ff.).

14. Harvey (1973:206 ff.), who develops a stimulating Marxian analysis of forms of urbanisms within the framework of Polanyi's categories, also comments on these factors. For further discussion of the role of circumscribed environments see especially Carneiro (1970).

15. But the literature on medieval urbanism is, of course, very large. Lopez (1976) and Rörig (1971) are among the useful summaries.

16. See, for instance, Gutnova (1968).

17. Weber's *The City* first made its way into print in German after the author's death, in *Archiv für Sozialwissenschaft und Sozialpolitik,* and was later incorporated into *Wirtschaft und Gesellschaft*. Bendix (1960:92) believes it was originally written

in 1911–13; Mommsen (1977:13) also suggests around 1911. Sennett (1969:5) is thus evidently in error in claiming that it first appeared in 1905.

18. The contrast between occidental and oriental urbanism has continued to interest scholars. For recent discussions see, e.g., Murphey (1954), Murvar (1969), and Bryan Turner (1974:93 ff.).

19. The notebook in which Marx made this comment has been dated December 1857–January 1858.

20. For geographers' overviews of central place theory, see, e.g., Berry (1967), Berry and Harris (1968), Johnson (1970), and Carter (1972:69 ff.).

21. The pioneering work here is Skinner's (1964–65) on markets and social structure in China. For more recent developments see, e.g., Carol A. Smith (1974, 1975, 1976), Blanton (1976), and Oliver-Smith (1977).

22. According to the ideal "market pattern," a lower-order center would place itself midway between three higher-order centers in order for space to be covered with maximal efficiency. A "transport pattern" places the lower-order center midway on a straight line between two higher-order centers. This is still a pattern of competitive relations, but it connects centers more easily to each other by road or rail. It may be added here that later central place theorists have worked with more flexible mathematical models as substitutes for Christaller's geometry. The realities of travel and consumer behavior can thus more easily be dealt with.

23. There is further comment on this in connection with the discussion of the "primate city" concept in ch. 4, n. 9.

24. For some recent writings in this vein see, e.g., Cornelius and Trueblood (1975), Walton (1976a), and Portes and Browning (1976). There is here, of course, a reaction against the idea that urban centers bring economic growth to their rural surroundings. Clearly, sometimes they do, sometimes they do not. Hoselitz's (1955) early article on this question also relates to what has been said above on historical urban patterns, partly by comparing his concepts of "generative" and "parasitic" cities to Redfield's and Singer's "heterogenetic" and "orthogenetic" cities.

25. This view is expressed by Sjoberg (1960:91).

26. For critical reviews of the functional city classifications of geographers, see Robert H. T. Smith (1965) and Carter (1972:45 ff.).

27. The various conceptualizations of this distinction are reviewed by Carter (1972:54 ff.).

28. Southall (1959, 1973b) has an alternative classification of domains—kinship and ethnic; economic and occupational; political; ritual or religious; recreational, leisure time, or voluntary. It coincides partially with that suggested here, but for the purposes of urban study one may feel that Southall's schema obscures certain similarities and variations and disregards some kinds of interaction altogether. Some political and religious roles involve provisioning and work; others may be only a little different from recreational roles. Neighboring and traffic interactions would tend to be more significant as relatively autonomous phenomena in the city then elsewhere.

29. It should be noted here that we include in the domain of provisioning also interactions of a type analogous to the consumption of services even when the prestation by which resources are gained involves some more or less clear form of con-

trol of the "customer" (e.g., judge-defendant, case worker-client, policeman-pedestrian) rather than a service strictly defined, and when resources in recognition of the prestation are allocated indirectly.

30. It is undoubtedly wise to treat this contrast between working lives before and after industrialization with some caution, even if it is reasonably valid; see the critique by Pleck (1976).

31. But there is an extensive, more or less analytical body of work on leisure to draw upon for the task, such as some of the contributions to the volume edited by Smigel (1963).

32. Further contributions by Goffman to the study of traffic relationships will be discussed in ch. 6.

33. The prevalence of strangers may even be regarded as a defining feature of urbanism. Lyn Lofland (1973:3) comes close to such a viewpoint, and Gulick (1963:447) takes a related approach in his early programmatic discussion of urban anthropology; he proposes that the cutting point between urban and non-urban communities could be placed where the most prominent inhabitants of a community know and are known personally by only a minority of the inhabitants.

34. The perspective developed here is inspired in a general way by Barth's (1972) view of the construction of social organizations.

35. Yet this need not be the consequence, insofar as people may interact with the same others while defining the situations as distinct.

36. Lofland's A World of Strangers (1973) is one contribution to this.

37. There are some comments on this aspect of urban life in a paper by Jacobson (1971).

38. The threshold at which the population size is sufficient to allow a considerable circulation of partners in relationships admittedly need not be very high, so there is no very precise relationship between such circulation and urbanism. But it seems likely that a large population is conducive to it—partly because of the increased possibilities of successfully attenuating links to past partners.

39. See on this point also Rainwater's (1966) interpretation of the cultivation of a dramatic self under the unstable circumstances of social life among lower-class Afro-Americans.

4. The View from the Copperbelt

1. There is no sizeable body of commentary on the Rhodes-Livingstone Institute, or the Manchester School in social anthropology, such as there is on the Chicago School. Apart from the writings referred to elsewhere in this chapter, attention should be drawn to the somewhat ambiguous collection of memoirs by former institute directors, including Richards (1977), Wilson (1977), Colson (1977a, b), Mitchell (1977), Fosbrooke (1977) and White (1977), in an anniversary issue of *African Social Research,* to the study by Brown (1973) of the early years of the institute, to the brief retrospective paper by Frankenberg (1968), and to the critique of the work of the "Manchester School" in Central Africa and Israel by van Teeffelen

(1978). I have also benefited from a seminar talk on the topic by Clyde Mitchell in the Department of Social Anthropology of the University of Stockholm in 1971. I am grateful to John Comaroff for inviting me to discuss the urban studies of the Manchester School in two sessions of his Central Africa course while I was a research fellow at the University of Manchester in 1976, as it helped me formulate my overview of this body of work.

2. Apart from Wheatley's (1970) interpretation of the Yoruba town as a ceremonial center referred to before, writings on Yoruba urbanism include Bascom (1955, 1958, 1959, 1962), Krapf-Askari (1969), Lloyd (1973), Mabogunje (1962), and Schwab (1965).

3. The classification included only the urban communities of Africa south of the Sahara.

4. For further comments on colonial urbanism generally see, e.g., Horvath (1969) and McGee (1971:50 ff.).

5. Rayfield (1974), narrowing his field of study to West African urbanism and making only passing reference to Southall's classification, delineates three types in this area, largely in historical terms—the cities of the western Sudan, founded as far back as the ninth century, centers of the trans-Saharan trade, such as Gao and Timbuktu; the cities of the Guinea coast, beginning about 1600 and engaging in the transatlantic slave trade (and some other commerce); and the modern colonial cities, dating from the late nineteenth or early twentieth centuries. Some towns of the former two types have gained new leases on life in the colonial era, but Rayfield sees others engaged in a cycle of rise, florescence, and decline. This set of types (shall we call them A_1, A_2, A_3?) draws attention to the considerable development of historical and anthropological research concerning, for example, the Niger Delta city states in recent years, communities which flowered during the years when European expansion was mostly commercial but which by the middle of the twentieth century were often little more than ghost towns (cf. Dike 1956, Jones 1963, Nair 1972, Plotnicov 1964, and others). Yet Rayfield's typology may not be exhaustive; there is no obvious place in it for Yoruba urbanism.

6. The suggestion that a type C should be distinguished seems first to have been made by Middleton (1966:33).

7. In my own research in Kafanchan, a relatively new Nigerian town, I could identify many of the characteristics mentioned by Vincent.

8. The recent growth of squatter settlements in Lusaka, the Zambian capital, has, for example, been described recently by van Velsen (1975).

9. For a recent overview of these developments in West Africa see Gugler and Flanagan (1977). The "primate city" concept was coined in 1939 by Mark Jefferson, a geographer, who stated as "the law of the primate city" that "a country's leading city is always disproportionately large and exceptionally expressive of national capacity and feeling." Jefferson quickly went on to note exceptions to this law, and his article contained further dubious propositions. It is therefore rather the concept than a theory of the primate city that has survived from it. Yet the conspicuous fact that in many areas one city has grown far larger and in other ways more important than others demands explanation, and it has consequences which

in their turn deserve interpretation. Linsky (1965), in one attempt at explanation, finds that there is no single unambiguous pattern of emergence of primate cities. When in a country one urban center has a much larger population than any other, however, it is most often in a small country, or at least one where the densely populated area is small. Furthermore, primate cities are particularly likely to occur in countries with a colonial past, a low per capita income, an export-oriented agricultural economy, and a rapid population growth. Linsky's interpretation of these relationships is that only where the area to be served is rather small can a single center provide all large city services. A poorer population will create lesser demands for such services than a wealthier one, so that there will be little need for many centers of parallel functions. The export-oriented economy would tend to concentrate this population in the city, minimizing the problem of distributing the services. Countries with such characteristics tend to be or to have been colonial; but colonialism contributes to the pattern of primacy by its centralization of political and administrative functions. A more multicentric pattern could emerge if there were greater industrialization, in which case smaller centers might arise close to the sources of raw materials (as exemplified, of course, by the Copperbelt towns discussed in this chapter); if the economy is agricultural this is less likely. The quick population growth, finally, might result in large scale urban migration from a countryside no longer able to support its population—or no longer willing, in cases of change away from labor-intensive forms of agriculture.

We might note that Linsky's ideas concerning the service functions of the primate city could be rather readily formulated in the "threshold" and "range" terminology of central place theory, although the assumption of population homogeneity in Christaller's original models obviously does not hold here; there is a strong concentration of the kind of people who consume particular services in the primate city itself. As far as Jefferson's original formulation of the primate city is concerned, the prevalence of such cities in the Third World clearly falsifies the notion he seemed to entertain in his "law" that primate cities are orthogenetic rather than heterogenetic in their cultural characteristics. But this error was perhaps made evident enough already by one of his own examples—New York. It may have attracted some of the best and the brightest, people from all over the United States who feel they have outgrown their local circumstances. It is, or at least has been, "the Big Apple." But do Americans feel that it is a concentrate of the American character? Hardly.

10. After Wilson's (1941, 1942) study of Broken Hill, the town was later the locale of Kapferer's (1966, 1969, 1972, 1976) studies in urban and industrial anthropology. The publications on Luanshya include three full-length anthropological monographs—Epstein (1958), Powdermaker (1962), and Harries-Jones (1975)—as well as Mitchell's (1956a) Kalela dance study, an article by Harries-Jones (1977), and an early account by a mine administrator (Spearpoint 1937).

11. In the second installment, Wilson (1942:81) quoted the reaction of a District Officer to this assumption: " 'I liked your paper (Part ı)' he said, 'because it was so damned optimistic; all we have to do is to sit back and wait for equilibrium!' "

12. For a presentation of his developed views on the subject see Gluckman (1968a).

13. See, for instance, Mitchell (1956c, 1969a).

14. The relevant bibliography here includes Gluckman (1940, 1961a), Mitchell (1956a, 1964:xi ff.), van Velsen (1964, 1967), Garbett (1970) and Johnsen (1970).

15. The contribution of the Rhodes-Livingstone group to the development of legal anthropology, including Gluckman's (1955, 1965) work on Barotse law and Epstein's (1953) on urban courts, need be noted only in passing here, but obviously it was related to this personal background.

16. The more recent study of these dances and their part in colonial African social life by Ranger (1975) deserves to be read alongside The Kalela Dance.

17. Mitchell has developed his analysis of Copperbelt ideas of social distance and their foundations in a later publication (1974a).

18. Harries-Jones (1975:231–32) voices some dissent here. Despite the administrative cleavage with its implications for political life, he says, the townships of Luanshya functioned as one community in most ways.

19. For two more recent studies of the early instances of industrial conflict on the Copperbelt, see Henderson (1975) and Perrings (1977).

20. Mitchell describes the hypothesis as originating in Philip Mayer's (1962, 1964) study of the urban Xhosa in South Africa. Gulick (1969:150) appears to show a similar relationship between urban and rural involvements in Lebanon, but his few data are not unambiguous.

21. I am indebted to John L. Comaroff for leading me to this reformulation. Readers may detect some resemblance to Bernstein's (1971) sociolinguistic ideas, and more distantly to Mary Douglas' (1970, 1978) scheme of "group" and "grid," with inspiration from Bernstein.

22. It should be noted that the distinction between the dimensions of normative control and personal information suggested here is a rough one which can be complicated further. One problem is that of the locus of normative control. Sometimes the consensus on norms may be society-wide, but not always. A thief may not be generally understood to have rights and duties; but there may be honor among thieves, and in the relationship between a thief and a fence both are perhaps well aware of conventional expectations in their circles. Another cluster of further analytical problems involves the various ways in which personal information can be at hand in a relationship. We will return to this in ch. 6.

23. Defining sex as a role-discriminatory attribute, we do not accept the loose notion of "sex roles" for analytical usage. Here we differ from Banton (1965:33 ff.; 1973:50 ff.), who describes "sex roles" as "basic roles," although he shows awareness of the view adopted here. Southall (1973b:76–77), on the other hand, appears to share our view.

It could be argued that "class" is an attribute of much the same diffuse nature as ethnicity in ordering involvements, and that it should thus be treated as a role-discriminatory attribute. Admittedly this is a border case. Here, however, we prefer to see it rather as anchored in specific roles in the domain of provisioning; when a person is in such a role, or indirectly connected to it through another member of his or her household, this can exercise a determining influence on recruitment to other roles as well. "Class" thus becomes a summarizing term for a cluster of roles, with provisioning roles at its core. There is some further discussion of this in the context of class cultures in ch. 7.

24. For an extended discussion see Handelman and Kapferer (1972:497 ff.).

25. Nor, of course, should one ignore the importance of a shared first language in such relationships.

26. I have discussed such variations in ethnic arrangements with respect to resources elsewhere, on the basis of American materials (Hannerz 1974b).

27. In a book Epstein (1978) published too late to be fully considered here, there is some information on Copperbelt ethnic and regional associations, as well as on other topics of Copperbelt ethnicity. With respect to West Africa, see, for instance, Little (1965).

28. Or "cosmopolitans" instead of "locals" in Merton's (1957:387 ff.) rather better-known but more or less parallel terms. Brown (1973:196–97) also emphasizes the significance of this external link and reports that when the colonial government at one time expressed a desire for information of a more practical kind from the Rhodes-Livingstone Institute, it was advised to go out and get itself a government anthropologist instead.

29. Cf. Powdermaker (1966:250–51): "Advice on how to make initial contact with the Africans differed. In England, an anthropologist had told me that the only way was through the African Mine Workers' Union. But in Lusaka I had heard enough gossip to make it clear that management was suspicious of anthropologists working closely with the union and I knew that management rather than the union had the final authority to decide who could do research on their private property."

30. For an example of a "white establishment" view of anthropology, see the *Central African Post* leader from 1953 reprinted as an appendix of Mitchell (1977). In the *Northern Rhodesia Journal,* an anonymous writer published a "Battle Hymn of the Research Experts" which may deserve being quoted in full (Anonymous 1956–1959:472)—I am indebted to Elinor Kelly for locating this item for me: (To be sung to the tune of the *British Grenadiers,* accompanied on Melanesian reed-pipes)

> *Con brio Americano, prejudissimo, Unescissimo*
> Some talk of race relations, and some of politics,
> Of labour and migrations, of hist'ry, lice and ticks,
> Investments, trends of amity
> And patterns of behaviour
> Let none treat us with levity
> For we are out to save 'yer.
>
> When seated in our library-chairs
> We're filled with righteous thought'ho,
> We shoulder continental cares
> Tell settlers what they ought to,
> We'll jargonise and analyse
> Frustrations and fixations,

Neuroses, Angst and stereotypes
In structured integration.

Strange cultures rise from notes and graphs
Through Freud's and Jung's perception
Despite your Egos' dirty laughs
We'll change you to perfection,
We've read Bukharin, Kant and Marx
And even Toynbee's stories
And our dialect'cal sparks
Will make explode the Tories.

Rhodesians hear our sage advice
On cross-acculturation,
On inter-racial kinship ties
And folk-way elongation,
On new conceptual frame works high
We'll bake your cakes of custom,
And with a socialising sigh
We'll then proceed to bust 'em.

Our research tools are sharp and gleam
With verified statistics,
Our intellectual combat team
Has practiced its heuristics
From value judgements we are free,
We only work scientific
For all-round global liberty
and Ph.D.s pontific.

31. Turning to other sources, however, one may catch a glimpse of what the Rhodes-Livingstone group did not cover. On white mine workers see Holleman and Biesheuvel (1973); on the mining industry in southern Africa as a supranational system, see Wolfe (1963).

32. There is no reference to Kuhn's (1962) concepts of scientific paradigms and normal science in *Closed Systems and Open Minds*, but similar ideas are implied especially in the concluding chapter by Devons and Gluckman (1964:259–60): "Throughout the introduction and the conclusion we have emphasised the need to simplify, to circumscribe, to be naive, and so on, in analysis in the social sciences. We have argued that these procedures are necessary, but that out of this necessity comes limitation to the problems and questions that can be answered. This implies caution and modesty in research . . . For the great revolutionary innovator in the social sciences there are no rules . . . But what we have written is for ordinary mortals, not for the revolutionary geniuses."

5. Thinking with Networks

1. Other central works in the network literature thus far include Mitchell (1969b), Aronson (1970), Boissevain and Mitchell (1973), and Boissevain (1974).

2. Bott has reviewed much of this research herself in a new chapter added to the second edition of *Family and Social Network* (1971), which also includes an extensive bibliography. In addition, one might note the papers by Cubitt (1973) and Kapferer (1973).

3. Bernard Magubane, whose criticisms of Rhodes-Livingstone anthropology were noted in the preceding chapter, has also given a polemical treatment to Mayer's Xhosa research (Magubane 1973).

4. We ignore here the traditional ethnic subdivisions. Since Mayer's study, we may also note, the South African *apartheid* policy has altered the position of Africans in towns, attempting as far as possible to deny that there is a population with strong urban roots.

5. In more recent years, it would seem that this particular concept of field has played a lesser role in anthropological writings. Network terminology appears to have made it superfluous.

6. This is certainly not to say that the members of other kinds of societies have not tried to draw advantages from their association with an anthropologist; but perhaps because in a complex society he is more often seen as a useful "connection," a channel to jobs, education, and other socially mediated resources, he increasingly frequently has to see himself as a manipulable component in a social system. Probably a great many field workers have experiences of this kind. Among examples which have found their way into print are Whitten's (1970) discussion of the different ways in which he was incorporated into networks in two field situations, Goldkind's (1970) account of the accumulation of power by a Chan Kom man who was the dominant local contact for visiting scholars from Redfield and onwards, and Gutkind's (1969) notes on an encounter with unemployed Nigerians outside a Lagos labor exchange.

7. While I draw mostly on Mitchell (1969b) in the account of network concepts which follows, it may be noted that there is a similar overview in Boissevain (1974).

8. A briefer version of the study was published earlier in Boissevain and Mitchell (1973).

9. Boissevain's interpretation is that the villager, who meets the same people again and again and is aware of this, uses simple co-presences to become acquainted with a larger number of people than does the urbanite, who does not run into the same people repeatedly, or if he does so does not notice it. Network analysts, as we shall note again below, hardly ever include strangers in networks. Traffic relationships are thus left out, as are, for example, many kinds of provisioning relationships.

10. In his later important contribution to African industrial anthropology, *Strategy and Transaction in an African Factory* (1972), Kapferer provides quite extensive background data on the people involved in the events occurring on the floor of a small clothing factory, and on the wider societal context of these events. Yet the network analysis which forms a part of this study as well is again limited to the shop floor, so that the field situation resembles that of the Cell Room.

11. For further clarification of the relationship between them, see Gluckman (1968b) and Paine (1968).

CITY AS THEATER: TALES OF GOFFMAN

337

12. It need hardly be pointed out that what is involved here is the political science concept of pluralism, rather than the anthropological one. For a comment on the differences see Kuper (1969).

6. The City as Theater: Tales of Goffman

1. At the University of Edinburgh, in the early 1950s, he was in the Department of Social Anthropology, and currently, he is the Benjamin Franklin Professor of Anthropology and Sociology at the University of Pennsylvania.

2. The book is a collection of essays edited by Gregersen (1975). A list of other writings on aspects of Goffman's work would include, e.g., Messinger et al. (1962), Taylor (1968), Gouldner (1970:378 ff.), Lofland (1970a), Young (1971), Berman (1972), Blumer (1972), Aronoff (1973), Bennett Berger (1973), Boltanski (1973), Collins (1973, 1975:161 ff.), Dawe (1973), Lyman (1973), Manning (1973, 1976), Perinbanayagam (1974), Davis (1975), Gamson (1975), Jameson (1976), Bogart (1977), Hall (1977), and Gonos (1977).

3. See, for such comparisons, Berman (1972), Birenbaum and Sagarin (1973:3–4), and Hall (1977).

4. A conspicuous example is Bennett Berger's brilliant "Fan Letter on Erving Goffman" (1973).

5. Collins (1973:139) suggests that "Goffman is the major inheritor of the Durkheimian tradition in its pure form" and emphasizes Warner's mediation, as others have also done. Possibly another Chicagoan, Edward Shils, should also be noted as a source of related ideas in approximately the same period; see one of the volumes of his collected essays (Shils 1975).

6. *Relations in Public* is rather remarkably "dedicated to the memory of A. R. Radcliffe-Brown whom on his visit to the University of Edinburgh in 1950 I almost met." Manning's (1973:137) opinion is that Goffman "springs from a British tradition of social anthropology with its Africa-derived concern for ritual, symbols, and deference."

7. But as we know, Simmel's influence had been brought to Chicago by Robert Park. In Goffman's time, it was apparently propagated there particularly by Everett Hughes.

8. His argument for the study of situations as such is also stated briefly in Goffman (1964).

9. See the comment on this by Bennett Berger (1973:359–60).

10. Lofland (1970b:38) has proposed that Goffman became "the champion inventor of the mini-concept" in response to the barren conceptual landscape of interactionist sociology as he found it at Chicago. He also quotes the ironic comment that "Goffman has more concepts than there are referents."

11. This may or may not be so; anyway, perhaps the fundamental Goffmanian methodological stance seems well expressed in the introductory remark in *Behavior in Public Places* that "a loose speculative approach to a fundamental area of conduct is better than a rigorous blindness to it" (Goffman 1963b:4).

12. Both are reprinted in *Interaction Ritual* (1967).

13. Goffman returns to this topic in discussing "remedial interchanges" in *Relations in Public* (1971:95 ff.).

14. To be precise, we should note that Goffman points out that the recipient of deference need not be a person. One example is the meeting of two ships, greeting each other with their whistles. This qualification need not concern us here.

15. The distinction is Durkheimian. Goffman returns to it in *Relations in Public* (1971:62 ff.).

16. There is a special treatment of embarrassment in another paper (Goffman 1956b).

17. The reference in ch. 3, n. 39, is relevant here as well.

18. This is approximately the view taken by Gouldner (1970:378 ff.).

19. Young (1971) prefers this interpretation, while Bennett Berger (1973:355) warns that Goffman just does not lend himself to easy political labeling.

20. Note here Tenbruck's (1965:93) interpretation of Simmel: "The forms of sociation stand in their own right and must be studied in their right; they have independent force and meaning in and of themselves, even though their observable effect may be obscured by limitations inherent in the composite character of society."

21. But cf. Bogart (1977:520): "Nowhere in the corpus of Goffman's entire work, for instance, can there be found a sustained discussion of power as a phenomenon of a social structure, as a result of the control of vital economic resources, or as the outcome of socio-cultural processes which bestow authority on those who are perceived as involved symbolically in the ordering or control of the social cosmos."

22. Early inspiration for such a view comes from Elkins' (1959) controversial comparison of the plantation to a modern concentration camp. For later comments see, e.g., Raymond Smith (1967:229 ff.), Bryce-Laporte (1971), and Beckford (1972:61 ff.).

23. An intriguing essay by Wright (1971) is also relevant here.

24. Here one might argue that it is not among the categories with the dullest working lives that psychoanalysts find most of their patients. Goffman's remark in *Asylums* about the analysis of self as an upper-class cultural privilege again seems to the point. For a further contemporary interpretation of the preoccupation with self, see Tom Wolfe's (1976) essay "The Me Decade and the Third Great Awakening."

25. This concept of dignity seems to resemble the egalitarian ideology of Guyanese plantation workers analyzed by Jayawardena (1968), as well as certain aspects of the black American concept of "soul" (cf. Hannerz 1968; 1969:156 ff.). In both instances, obviously, formal role placements have tended to leave something to be desired.

26. See on this point Lionel Trilling's *Sincerity and Authenticity* (1972:10 ff.), as well as Hall (1977).

27. For further comments on the significance of Goffman's relationship to the changing order of interpersonal ritual see Collins (1973:141; 1975:163 ff.) and Manning (1976).

28. Apart from those discussed here, see also, e.g., Watson and Potter (1962) with their distinction between "presenting" and "sharing," much in line with what we have in mind.

29. Elsewhere I have argued that male peer groups are in such a position in the black American ghetto community (Hannerz 1969:105 ff.; 1971).

30. See also Suttles' (1970) analysis of friendship.

31. One might feel there is some paradox in this; in ch. 3 we noted that it was also in the traditional Indian city that the caste system reached its fullest development.

32. Goffman has some brief comments on blackmail in *Stigma* (1963a:75 ff.). There is a more elaborate treatment by Hepworth (1975), although it does not relate closely to our framework.

33. Barth's (1971) analysis of father-son relationships in two Middle Eastern societies, with its inspiration from Goffman, is an illuminating example here.

7. Conclusion: The Construction of Cities and Urban Lives

1. See on this point Granovetter's (1973) well-known paper on "the strength of weak ties."

2. Such roles may be considered in the context of an array of brokerage roles, as hinted at in the discussion of "flak catchers" in chapter 5.

3. Further evidence on the tendency to encapsulation on the part of radical groups is supplied by Kornhauser (1962) and Bittner (1963). It may be wise, however, not to take this for granted as a permanent characteristic. In another period, it may be the expansive network strategy, described by Gerlach and Hine and discussed in chapter 5, which characterizes radicalism.

4. Cf. Stone's (1954) profile of the "personalizing consumer."

5. For other discussions of the impact of the man-made environment on social relationships see, e.g., the classic study by Festinger, Schachter, and Back (1950), parts of Jacobs' *The Death and Life of Great American Cities* (1961), and Suttles' *The Social Order of the Slum* (1968:13 ff.).

6. While Hughes (1958), from his central position in occupational sociology, has done much to stimulate career analysis, Becker (1963), with his studies of careers in deviance, may have played the major part in bringing it out of the study of occupations into the analysis of social organization as a whole. Note also Barth's (1972:208) comment on the lack of attention to careers in anthropological study. The remarks on the subject here draw on a seminar on career analysis in the Department of Social Anthropology, University of Stockholm, held during the spring and fall terms of 1973. I am indebted to the participants in the seminar for their comments on several of the issues touched upon in this section.

7. For a notably similar account of careers which unfold gradually as new opportunities are channeled through old relationships, see Lemann's essay "Survival Networks: Staying in Washington" (1978).

8. Assuming that everyone remains in the same matrix of relationships.

9. Admittedly I would have been unaware of Archilochus if it had not been for the essay in which Isaiah Berlin discusses literary foxes and hedgehogs in Russia; reprinted in Berlin (1978).

10. Jacobs, of course, deals particularly with innovation within the provisioning domain, but similar processes could be seen to be at work elsewhere as well.

11. An earlier discussion of this topic—first presented in 1973—can be found in Hannerz (1978).

12. Among the ancestors are Marx and Engels, beginning with *The German Ideology* (1970:47): "In direct contrast to German Philosophy which descends from heaven to earth, here we ascend from earth to heaven. That is to say, we do not set out from what men say, imagine, conceive, nor from men as narrated, thought of, imagined, conceived, in order to arrive at men in the flesh. We set out from real, active men, and on the basis of their real life-process we demonstrate the development of the ideological reflexes and echoes of this life-process. The phantoms formed in the human brain are also, necessarily, sublimates of their material life-process, which is empirically verifiable and bound to material premises . . . . Life is not determined by consciousness, but consciousness by life." The best-known pioneering work in the sociology of knowledge may yet be Mannheim's *Ideology and Utopia* (1936); for a study in the sociology of knowledge which emphasizes occupational rather than class perspectives and is of considerable urban anthropological interest, see Bensman and Lilienfeld (1973). Our postulation of "intellectual solitude" as a basis for positional determination of consciousness is not necessarily in line with the classics of the field, but seems required to ensure the contrast to the cultural diffusion of ideas.

13. This conception of a collective system of meanings is inspired by Scheff (1967).

14. For a theoretical elaboration of this point see also Claude Fischer (1975).

15. It should be noted here that this "proletarian cultural tradition" need not be opposition to a dominant culture in any very clearcut sense. Frank Parkin (1972:79 ff.), in a succinct statement, has suggested that it is fundamentally a subordinate, accommodative value system. His view, which should be set in the framework of the debate on the role of intellectuals and political parties in the development of class consciousness, is that such an oppositional system of meanings tends to come from the outside. Perhaps one might see such a system as more strictly counter-cultural, developed by individuals with a more immediate experience of the dominant system, and at the same time as an attempt to develop vicariously the sociology of knowledge perspective toward the world as it ought to be from the place in the social structure where the workers are.

Pilcher's (1972) ethnography of American longshoremen, it may be added, does not link up explicitly with the British analytical writings on the proletarian cultural tradition but seems to offer additional supporting evidence.

16. There is a connection here to the "category" and "frame" concepts used by Nakane (1970) to analyze Japanese society. The "proletarian tradition" is developed and maintained among workers who link up with others of the same category; for

the "deferential traditionalists" there is a frame around relationships linking them to people of another category.

17. A paragraph in Gramsci's *Prison Notebooks* (1971:326–27) seems to the point here: ". . . the co-existence of two conceptions of the world, one affirmed in words and the other displayed in effective action, is not simply a product of self-deception. Self-deception can be an adequate explanation for a few individuals taken separately, or even for groups a certain size, but it is not adequate when the contrast occurs in the life of great masses. In these cases the contrast between thought and action cannot but be the expression of profounder contrasts of a social historical order. It signifies that the social group in question may indeed have its own conception of the world, even if only embryonic; a conception which manifests itself in action, but occasionally and in flashes—when, that is, the group is acting as an organic totality. But this same group has, for reasons of submission and intellectual subordination, adopted a conception which is not its own but is borrowed from another group; and it affirms this conception verbally and believes itself to be following it, because this is the conception which it follows in "normal times"—that is when its conduct is not independent and autonomous, but submissive and subordinate."

18. References to this debate are given in chapter 1; the point of view set forth here is basically that developed further in Hannerz (1971). See also the illuminating discussion by Suttles (1976).

19. For some brief comments on this issue see Bennett Berger (1966:151 ff.) and Arnold (1970a, b).

20. For further discussions of variations in community power structure which are relevant here see, e.g., Rossi (1960), Fisher (1962), and Walton (1976b).

21. The example is from Salaman's (1971:398–99) study of railroad workers.

22. Gulick (1963:455), in an early paper on the contribution of anthropology to urban studies emphasizes the anthropologist's "inclination to visualize and to portray," but for the sort of interpretation we have in mind here there is certainly also inspiration to be had elsewhere—see, for instance, Lynch (1960) and Strauss (1961). For a brief discussion of spatial symbolism in one specific urban setting see Gerholm's (1977:160 ff.) study of a Yemeni town.

23. For an illuminating discussion of triangulation see Denzin (1970b:297 ff.).

24. The example of the photo album as network evidence is from Plotnicov (1967:24); it may be added that the point of view toward urban field work set forth here is also closely related to Plotnicov's (1973). The example of occupational ranking through a card game is from Hannerz (1976), but inspired initially by Silverman (1966).

References

Adams, Robert McC. 1966. *The Evolution of Urban Society*. Chicago: Aldine.
—— 1974. "Anthropological Perspectives on Ancient Trade." *Current Anthropology*, 15:239–49.
Adelman, William J. 1976. *Haymarket Revisited*. Chicago: Illinois Labor History Society.
Anderson, Nels. 1961. *The Hobo*. Chicago: University of Chicago Press. (Originally published 1923.)
Anonymous. 1956/1959. "The Battle Hymn of the Research Experts." *Northern Rhodesia Journal*, 3:472.
Arnold, David O. 1970a. "Subculture Marginality." In David O. Arnold, ed., *The Sociology of Subcultures*. Berkeley, Calif.: Glendessary Press.
—— 1970b. "A Process Model of Subcultures." In David O. Arnold, ed., *The Sociology of Subcultures*. Berkeley, Calif.: Glendessary Press.
Aronoff, Joel. 1973. "Review of Relations in Public." *Sociological Quarterly*, 14:142–43.
Aronson, Dan R., ed. 1970. "Social Networks." *Canadian Review of Sociology and Anthropology*, 7(4).
Bailey, F. G. 1965. "Decisions by Consensus in Councils and Committees." In Michael Banton, ed., *Political Systems and the Distribution of Power* (ASA 2). London: Tavistock.
Baker, Paul J. 1973. "The Life Histories of W. I. Thomas and Robert E. Park." *American Journal of Sociology*, 79:243–60.
Banton, Michael. 1965. *Roles*. London: Tavistock.
—— 1973. "Urbanization and Role Analysis." In Aidan Southall, ed., *Urban Anthropology*. New York: Oxford University Press.
Barnes, J. A. 1954. "Class and Committees in a Norwegian Island Parish." *Human Relations*, 7:39–58.
—— 1969. "Networks and Political Process." In J. Clyde Mitchell, ed., *Social Networks in Urban Situations*. Manchester: Manchester University Press.
—— 1972. *Social Networks*. Reading, Mass.: Addison-Wesley.
Bartell, Gilbert D. 1971. *Group Sex*. New York: Signet.
Barth, Fredrik. 1969. "Introduction." In Fredrik Barth, ed., *Ethnic Groups and Boundaries*. Bergen and Oslo: Universitetsforlaget.
—— 1971. "Role Dilemmas and Father-Son Dominance in Middle Eastern Kinship Systems." In Francis L. K. Hsu, ed., *Kinship and Culture*. Chicago: Aldine.

—— 1972. "Analytical Dimensions in the Comparison of Social Organizations." *American Anthropologist*, 74:207–20.

—— 1975. *Ritual and Knowledge Among the Baktaman of New Guinea*. New Haven, Conn.: Yale University Press.

Bascom, William R. 1955. "Urbanization among the Yoruba." *American Journal of Sociology*, 60:446–54.

—— 1958. "Yoruba Urbanism: A Summary." *Man*, 58:190–91.

—— 1959. "Urbanism as a Traditional African Pattern." *Sociological Review*, 7:29–43.

—— 1962. "Some Aspects of Yoruba Urbanism." *American Anthropologist*, 64:699–709.

Basham, Richard. 1978. *Urban Anthropology*. Palo Alto, Calif.: Mayfield.

Beals, Ralph L. 1951. "Urbanism, Urbanization, and Acculturation." *American Anthropologist*, 53:1–10.

Becker, Howard S. 1963. *Outsiders*. New York: Free Press.

—— 1966. "Introduction." In Clifford R. Shaw, *The Jack-Roller*. Chicago: University of Chicago Press.

Beckford, George L. 1972. *Persistent Poverty*. New York: Oxford University Press.

Bell, Colin. 1968. *Middle Class Families*. London: Routledge and Kegan Paul.

Bell, Colin and Howard Newby. 1971. *Community Studies*. London: Allen & Unwin.

Bendix, Reinhard. 1954. "Social Theory and Social Action in the Sociology of Louis Wirth." *American Journal of Sociology*, 59:523–29.

—— 1960. *Max Weber*. Garden City, N.Y.: Doubleday.

Benet, Francisco. 1963a. "The Ideology of Islamic Urbanization." *International Journal of Comparative Sociology*, 4:211–26.

—— 1963b. "Sociology Uncertain: The Ideology of the Rural-Urban Continuum." *Comparative Studies in Society and History*, 6:1–23.

Bensman, Joseph and Robert Lilienfeld. 1973. *Craft and Consciousness*. New York: Wiley.

Berger, Bennett M. 1966. "Suburbs, Subcultures, and the Urban Future." In Sam Bass Warner, Jr., ed., *Planning for a Nation of Cities*. Cambridge, Mass.: M.I.T. Press.

—— 1973. "A Fan Letter on Erving Goffman." *Dissent*, 20:353–61.

Berger, Peter L. 1965. "Toward a Sociological Understanding of Psychoanalysis." *Social Research*, 32:26–41.

—— 1970. "On the Obsolescence of the Concept of Honor." *Archives Européennes de Sociologie*, 11:339–47.

—— 1973. "Sincerity and Authenticity in Modern Society." *The Public Interest*, 31:81–90.

Berger, Peter L., Brigitte Berger, and Hansfried Kellner. 1973. *The Homeless Mind*. New York: Random House.

Berger, Peter L. and Hansfried Kellner. 1964. "Marriage and the Construction of Reality." *Diogenes*, 46:1–24.

Berger, Peter L. and Thomas Luckmann. 1966. *The Social Construction of Reality*. Garden City, N.Y.: Doubleday.

Berghe, Pierre L. van den. 1970. "Pluralism and Conflict Situations in Africa: A Reply to B. Magubane." *African Social Research*, 9:681–89.

Berlin, Isaiah. 1978. *Russian Thinkers*. New York: Viking.

Berman, Marshall. 1972. "Weird but Brilliant Light on the Way We Live Now: Relations in Public." *New York Times Book Review*, February 27, pp. 10, 18.

Bernstein, Basil. 1971. "A Sociolinguistic Approach to Socialization: With some Reference to Educability." In Dell Hymes and John J. Gumperz, eds., *Directions in Sociolinguistics*. New York: Holt, Rinehart and Winston.

Berreman, Gerald D. 1960. "Cultural Variability and Drift in the Himalayan Hills." *American Anthropologist*, 62:774–94.

—— 1972. "Social Categories and Social Interaction in Urban India." *American Anthropologist*, 74:567–86.

—— 1978. "Scale and Social Relations." *Current Anthropology*, 19:225–45.

Berry, Brian J. L. 1967. *Geography of Market Centers and Retail Distribution*. Englewood Cliffs, N.J.: Prentice-Hall.

Berry, Brian J. L. and Chauncy D. Harris. 1968. "Central Place." *International Encyclopedia of the Social Sciences*. New York: Macmillan and the Free Press.

Birenbaum, Arnold and Edward Sagarin. 1973. "Introduction: Understanding the Familiar." In Arnold Birenbaum and Edward Sagarin, eds., *People in Places*. New York: Praeger.

Bittner, Egon. 1963. "Radicalism and the Organization of Radical Movements." *American Sociological Review*, 20:928–40.

—— 1967. "The Police on Skid-Row: A Study of Peace Keeping." *American Sociological Review*, 32:699–715.

Blanton, Richard E. 1976. "Anthropological Studies of Cities." *Annual Review of Anthropology*, no. 5. Palo Alto, Calif.: Annual Reviews.

Blumer, Herbert. 1939. *Critiques of Research in the Social Sciences: I. An Appraisal of Thomas and Znaniecki's The Polish Peasant in Europe and America*. New York: Social Science Research Council.

—— 1972. "Action vs. Interaction." *Society*, 9(6):50–53.

Bogart, Robert W. 1977. "Critique of Existential Sociology." *Social Research*, 44:502–28.

Boissevain, Jeremy. 1974. *Friends of Friends*. Oxford: Blackwell.

Boissevain, Jeremy and J. Clyde Mitchell, eds. 1973. *Network Analysis*. The Hague: Mouton.

Boltanski, Luc. 1973. "Erving Goffman et le temps du soupçon." *Social Science Information*, 12(3):127–47.

Bott, Elizabeth. 1957. *Family and Social Network*. London: Tavistock.

—— 1971. "Reconsiderations." In *Family and Social Network*, 2d ed. London: Tavistock.

Boulding, Kenneth E. 1963. "The Death of the City: A Frightened Look at Post-civilization." In Oscar Handlin and John Burchard, eds., *The Historian and the City*. Cambridge, Mass.: M.I.T. Press.

Braudel, Fernand. 1974. *Capitalism and Material Life 1400–1800*. London: Fontana/Collins.

—— 1977. *Afterthoughts on Material Civilization and Capitalism.* Baltimore: Johns Hopkins University Press.

Brown, Richard. 1973. "Anthropology and Colonial Rule: Godfrey Wilson and the Rhodes-Livingstone Institute, Northern Rhodesia." In Talal Asad, ed., *Anthropology & the Colonial Encounter.* London: Ithaca Press.

Bryce-Laporte, Roy Simon. 1971. "Slaves as Inmates, Slaves as Men: A Sociological Discussion of Elkins' Thesis." In Ann J. Lane, ed., *The Debate over Slavery.* Urbana: University of Illinois Press.

Bulmer, Martin, ed. 1975. *Working-Class Images of Society.* London: Routledge and Kegan Paul.

Burgess, Ernest W. and Donald J. Bogue. 1967. "Research in Urban Society: A Long View." In Ernest W. Burgess and Donald J. Bogue, eds., *Urban Sociology.* Chicago: University of Chicago Press.

Burke, Peter. 1975. "Some Reflections on the Pre-Industrial City." In H. J. Dyos, ed., *Urban History Yearbook 1975.* Leicester: Leicester University Press.

Burnet, Jean. 1964. "Robert E. Park and the Chicago School of Sociology: A Centennial Tribute." *Canadian Review of Sociology and Anthropology,* 1:156–64.

Butterworth, Douglas. 1974. "Grass-Roots Political Organization in Cuba: A Case of the Committees for the Defense of the Revolution." In Wayne A. Cornelius and Felicity M. Trueblood, eds., *Anthropological Perspectives on Latin American Urbanization,* Latin American Urban Research, vol. 4. Beverly Hills, Calif.: Sage.

Carey, James T. 1975. *Sociology and Public Affairs: The Chicago School.* Beverly Hills: Sage.

Carneiro, Robert L. 1970. "A Theory of the Origin of the State." *Science,* 169:733–38.

Caro Baroja, Julio. 1963. "The City and the Country: Reflexions on Some Ancient Commonplaces." In Julian Pitt-Rivers, ed., *Mediterranean Countrymen.* The Hague: Mouton.

Carter, Harold. 1972. *The Study of Urban Geography.* London: Edward Arnold.

Castells, Manuel. 1976. "Theory and Ideology in Urban Sociology." In C. G. Pickvance, ed., *Urban Sociology.* London: Tavistock.

—— 1977. *The Urban Question.* London: Edward Arnold.

Cavan, Sherri. 1972. *Hippies of the Haight.* St. Louis, Mo.: New Critics Press.

Christaller, Walter. 1966. *Central Places in Southern Germany.* Englewood Cliffs, N.J.: Prentice-Hall.

Chudacoff, Howard P. 1972. *Mobile Americans.* New York: Oxford University Press.

Clarke, John, Stuart Hall, Tony Jefferson, and Brian Roberts. 1975. "Subcultures, Cultures and Class: A Theoretical Overview." *Working Papers in Cultural Studies,* 7/8:9–74.

Cobb, Richard. 1975. *A Sense of Place.* London: Duckworth.

Cohen, Abner. 1969. *Custom and Politics in Urban Africa.* London: Routledge and Kegan Paul.

Cohen, Albert K. 1955. *Delinquent Boys*. Glencoe, Ill.: Free Press.

Collins, Randall. 1973. "Review of Relations in Public." *Sociological Quarterly*, 14:137–42.

—— 1975. *Conflict Sociology*. New York: Academic Press.

Colson, Elizabeth. 1977a. "The Institute under Max Gluckman, 1942–47." *African Social Research*, 24:285–95.

—— 1977b. "From Livingstone to Lusaka, 1948–51." *African Social Research*, 24:297–307.

Cornelius, Wayne A. and Felicity M. Trueblood, eds. 1975. *Urbanization and Inequality*. Latin American Urban Research, vol. 5. Beverly Hills, Calif.: Sage.

Coser, Lewis A. 1970. *Men of Ideas*. New York: Free Press.

—— 1974. *Greedy Institutions*. New York: Free Press.

Cox, Oliver C. 1969. "The Preindustrial City Reconsidered." In Paul Meadows and Ephraim H. Mizruchi, eds., *Urbanism, Urbanization, and Change*. Reading, Mass.: Addison-Wesley.

Craven, Paul and Barry Wellman. 1974. "The Network City." In Marcia Pelly Effrat, ed., *The Community*. New York: Free Press.

Cressey, Paul G. 1969. *The Taxi-Dance Hall*. Montclair, N.J.: Patterson Smith. (First published by the University of Chicago Press 1932.)

Cubitt, Tessa. 1973. "Network Density among Urban Families." In Jeremy Boissevain and J. Clyde Mitchell, eds., *Network Analysis*. The Hague: Mouton.

Dalton, George. 1960. "A Note of Clarification on Economic Surplus." *American Anthropologist*, 62:483–90.

Davis, Murray S. 1975. "Review of Frame Analysis." *Contemporary Sociology*, 4:599–603.

Dawe, Alan. 1973. "The Underworld-view of Erving Goffman." *British Journal of Sociology*, 24:246–53.

Dennis, N. 1958. "The Popularity of the Neighborhood Community Idea." *Sociological Review*, 6:191–206.

Denzin, Norman K. 1970a. "Symbolic Interactionism and Ethnomethodology." In Jack D. Douglas, ed., *Understanding Everyday Life*. Chicago: Aldine.

—— 1970b. *The Research Act*. Chicago: Aldine.

Devons, Ely and Max Gluckman. 1964. "Conclusion: Modes and Consequences of Limiting a Field of Study." In Max Gluckman, ed., *Closed Systems and Open Minds*. Edinburgh and London: Oliver & Boyd.

Dewey, Richard. 1960. "The Rural-Urban Continuum: Real but Relatively Unimportant." *American Journal of Sociology*, 66:60–66.

Dike, K. Onwuka. 1956. *Trade and Politics in the Niger Delta 1830–1885*. London: Oxford University Press.

Domhoff, G. William. 1970. *The Higher Circles*. New York: Random House.

—— 1974. *The Bohemian Grove and Other Retreats*. New York: Harper & Row.

Dore. R. P. 1958. *City Life in Japan*. Berkeley and Los Angeles: University of California Press.

Douglas, Mary. 1970. *Natural Symbols*. New York: Pantheon.

—— 1978. *Cultural Bias*. London: Royal Anthropological Institute.

Duff, Charles. 1935. *Anthropological Report on a London Suburb*. London: Grayson & Grayson.

Duncan, Otis D. 1957. "Community Size and the Rural-Urban Continuum." In Paul K. Hatt and Albert J. Reiss, Jr., eds., *Cities and Society*. New York: Free Press.

Durkheim, Emile. 1961. *The Elementary Forms of the Religious Life*. New York: Collier Books.

Eames, Edwin and Judith G. Goode. 1977. *Anthropology of the City*. Englewood Cliffs, N.J.: Prentice-Hall.

Eddy, Elisabeth M., ed. 1968. *Urban Anthropology*. Athens, Ga.: Southern Anthropological Society.

Elias, Norbert. 1978. *The Civilizing Process*. New York: Urizen Books.

Elkins, Stanley M. 1959. *Slavery*. Chicago: University of Chicago Press.

Engels, Friedrich. 1969. *The Condition of the Working Class in England*. London: Panther Books.

Epstein, A. L. 1953. *The Administration of Justice and the Urban African*. London: HMSO.

—— 1958. *Politics in an Urban African Community*. Manchester: Manchester University Press.

—— 1959. "Linguistic Innovation and Culture on the Copperbelt, Northern Rhodesia." *Southwestern Journal of Anthropology*, 15:235–53.

—— 1961. "The Network and Urban Social Organization." *Human Problems in British Central Africa*, 29:29–62.

—— 1964. "Urban Communities in Africa." In Max Gluckman, ed., *Closed Systems and Open Minds*. Edinburgh and London: Oliver & Boyd.

—— 1967. "Urbanization and Social Change in Africa." *Current Anthropology*, 8:275–84.

—— 1969. "Gossip, Norms and Social Network." In J. Clyde Mitchell ed., *Social Networks in Urban Situations*. Manchester: Manchester University Press.

—— 1978. *Ethos and Identity*. London: Tavistock.

Etzioni, Amitai. 1959. "The Ghetto—A Re-evaluation." *Social Forces*, 37:255–62.

Faris, Robert E. L. 1970. *Chicago Sociology 1920–1932*. Chicago: University of Chicago Press.

Fava, Sylvia F. 1966. "Recent Books in the Urban Field—An Essay Review." *Social Problems*, 14:93–104.

Festinger, Leon, Stanley Schachter, and Kurt Back. 1950. *Social Pressure in Informal Groups*. New York: Harper.

Feuer, Lewis. 1973. "Ideology & No End: Some Personal History." *Encounter*, 40(4):84–87.

Finley, M. I. 1977. "The Ancient City: From Fustel de Coulanges to Max Weber and Beyond." *Comparative Studies in Society and History*, 19:305–27.

Firth, Raymond. 1951. *Elements of Social Organization*. London: Watts.

—— 1954. "Social Organization and Social Change." *Journal of the Royal Anthropological Institute*, 84:1–20.

—— 1955. "Some Principles of Social Organization." *Journal of the Royal Anthropological Institute*, 85:1–18.

Firth, Raymond, Jane Hubert, and Anthony Forge. 1969. *Families and Their Relatives*. London: Routledge and Kegan Paul.

Fischer, Claude S. 1972. "Urbanism as a Way of Life: A Review and an Agenda." *Sociological Methods and Research*, 1:187–242.

—— 1975. "Toward a Subcultural Theory of Urbanism." *American Journal of Sociology*, 80:1319–41.

Fischer, John L. 1975. "The Individual as a Crucial Locus of Culture." In Thomas R. Williams, ed., *Socialization and Communication in Primary Groups*. The Hague: Mouton.

Fisher, Sethard. 1962. "Community-Power Studies: A Critique." *Social Research*, 29:449–66.

Fortes, Meyer. 1953. "The Structure of Unilineal Descent Groups." *American Anthropologist*, 55:17–41.

Fosbrooke, Henry. 1977. "From Lusaka to Salisbury, 1956–60." *African Social Research*, 24:319–25.

Foster, George M. 1953. "What is Folk Culture?" *American Anthropologist*, 55:159–73.

Foster, George M. and Robert V. Kemper, eds. 1974. *Anthropologists in Cities*. Boston: Little, Brown.

Fox, Richard G. 1972. "Rationale and Romance in Urban Anthropology." *Urban Anthropology*, 1:205–33.

—— 1977. *Urban Anthropology*. Englewood Cliffs, N.J.: Prentice-Hall.

Fox, Robin. 1973. *Encounter with Anthropology*. New York: Harcourt Brace Jovanovich.

Frankenberg, Ronald. 1966. *Communities in Britain*. Harmondsworth: Penguin.

—— 1968. "The Beginning of Anthropology: The Challenge of the New Africa to the Sociological Study of Small-Scale Social Process." *Proceedings of the VIIIth Congress of Anthropological and Ethnological Sciences*, 2:73–77.

Friedmann, John. 1961. "Cities in Social Transformation." *Comparative Studies in Society and History*, 4:86–103.

Gamson, William A. 1975. "Review of Frame Analysis." *Contemporary Sociology*, 4:603–07.

Gans, Herbert J. 1962a. *The Urban Villagers*. New York: Free Press.

—— 1962b. "Urbanism and Suburbanism as Ways of Life: A Re-evaluation of Definitions." In Arnold M. Rose, ed., *Human Behavior and Social Processes*. Boston: Houghton Mifflin.

—— 1967. *The Levittowners*. New York: Pantheon.

Garbett, G. Kingsley. 1970. "The Analysis of Social Situations." *Man*, 5:214–27.

Garfinkel, Harold. 1967. *Studies in Ethnomethodology*. Englewood Cliffs, N.J.: Prentice-Hall.

Gearing, Frederick O. 1970. *The Face of the Fox*. Chicago: Aldine.

Geertz, Clifford. 1965. *The Social History of an Indonesian Town*. Cambridge, Mass.: M.I.T. Press.

—— 1967. "Politics Past, Politics Present: Some Notes on the Contribution of Anthropology to the Study of New States." *Archives Européennes de Sociologie*, 8:1–14.

—— 1972. "Deep Play: Notes on the Balinese Cockfight." *Daedalus*, 101:1–37.

Gellner, Ernest. 1974. *Legitimation of Belief.* London: Cambridge University Press.

Gerholm, Tomas. 1977. *Market, Mosque, and Mafraj.* Stockholm Studies in Social Anthropology, no. 5. Stockholm: Department of Social Anthropology, University of Stockholm.

Gerlach, Luther P. 1970. "Corporate Groups and Movement Networks in Urban America." *Anthropological Quarterly,* 43:123–45.

Gerlach, Luther P. and Virginia H. Hine. 1970a. *People, Power, Change.* Indianapolis: Bobbs-Merrill.

—— 1970b. "The Social Organization of a Movement of Revolutionary Change: Case Study, Black Power." In Norman E. Whitten, Jr., and John F. Szwed, eds., *Afro-American Anthropology.* New York: Free Press.

Glaser, Barney G. and Anselm L. Strauss. 1964. "Awareness Contexts and Social Interaction." *American Sociological Review,* 29:669–79.

—— 1967. *The Discovery of Grounded Theory.* Chicago: Aldine.

Gluckman, Max. 1940. "Analysis of a Social Situation in Modern Zululand." *Bantu Studies,* 14:1–30, 147–74.

—— 1945. "The Seven Year Research Plan of the Rhodes-Livingstone Institute." *Rhodes-Livingstone Journal,* 4:1–32.

—— 1955. *The Judicial Process among the Barotse of Northern Rhodesia.* Manchester: Manchester University Press.

—— 1961a. "Ethnographic Data in British Social Anthropology." *Sociological Review,* N.S., 9:5–17.

—— 1961b. "Anthropological Problems arising from the African Industrial Revolution." In Aidan Southall, ed., *Social Change in Modern Africa.* London: Oxford University Press.

—— 1962. "Les Rites de Passage." In Max Gluckman, ed., *Essays on the Ritual of Social Relations.* Manchester, Manchester University Press.

—— 1963a. *Order and Rebellion in Tribal Africa.* London: Cohen & West.

—— 1963b. "Gossip and Scandal." *Current Anthropology,* 4:307–16.

—— 1965. *The Ideas in Barotse Jurisprudence.* New Haven: Yale University Press.

—— 1968a. "The Utility of the Equilibrium Model in the Study of Social Change." *American Anthropologist,* 70:219–37.

—— 1968b. "Psychological, Sociological and Anthropological Explanations of Witchcraft and Gossip: A Clarification." *Man,* 3:20–34.

—— 1971. "Tribalism, Ruralism and Urbanism in South and Central Africa." In Victor Turner, ed., *Profiles of Change.* Cambridge: Cambridge University Press.

—— 1974. "Report from the Field." (Letter.) *New York Review of Books,* November 28:43–44.

Goffman, Erving. 1952. "On Cooling the Mark Out: Some Aspects of Adaptation to Failure." *Psychiatry,* 15:451–63.

—— 1955. "On Face-Work: An Analysis of Ritual Elements in Social Interactions." *Psychiatry,* 18:213–31.

—— 1956a. "The Nature of Deference and Demeanor." *American Anthropologist,* 58:473–502.

—— 1956b. "Embarrassment and Social Organization." *American Journal of Sociology*, 62:264–74.

—— 1959. *The Presentation of Self in Everyday Life*. Garden City, N.Y.: Doubleday/Anchor Books.

—— 1961a. *Asylums*. Garden City, N.Y.: Doubleday/Anchor Books.

—— 1961b. *Encounters*. Indianapolis: Bobbs-Merrill.

—— 1963a. *Stigma*. Englewood Cliffs, N.J.: Prentice-Hall.

—— 1963b. *Behavior in Public Places*. New York: Free Press.

—— 1964. "The Neglected Situation." *American Anthropologist*, 66(6, part 2):133–36.

—— 1967. *Interaction Ritual*. Chicago: Aldine.

—— 1969. *Strategic Interaction*. Philadelphia: University of Pennsylvania Press.

—— 1971. *Relations in Public*. New York: Basic Books.

Goldkind, Victor. 1970. "Anthropologists, Informants and the Achievement of Power in Chan Kom." *Sociologus*, 20:17-41.

Gonos, George. 1977. "Situation versus Frame: The Interactionist and the Structuralist Analysis of Everyday Life." *American Sociological Review*, 42:854–67.

Goodenough, Ward H. 1971. *Culture, Language, and Society*. Reading, Mass.: Addison-Wesley.

Goody, Jack. 1977. *The Domestication of the Savage Mind*. London: Cambridge University Press.

Goody, Jack and Ivor P. Watt. 1963. "The Consequences of Literacy." *Comparative Studies in Society and History*, 5:304–45.

Gould, Harold A. 1965. "Lucknow Rickshawallas: The Social Organization of an Occupational Category." *International Journal of Comparative Sociology*, 6:24–47.

Gouldner, Alvin W. 1970. *The Coming Crisis of Western Sociology*. New York: Basic Books.

Gramsci, Antonio. 1971. *Selections from the Prison Notebooks*. London: Lawrence and Wishart.

Granovetter, Mark S. 1973. "The Strength of Weak Ties." *American Journal of Sociology*, 78:1360–80.

Gregersen, Bo., ed. 1975. *Om Goffman*. Copenhagen: Hans Reitzel.

Grillo, Ralph. 1973. *African Railwaymen*. London: Cambridge University Press.

Grunebaum, G. E. von. 1955. "The Structure of the Muslim Town." *American Anthropologist*, 57(2, part 2):141–58.

Gugler, Josef and William G. Flanagan. 1977. "On the Political Economy of Urbanization in the Third World: The Case of West Africa." *International Journal of Urban and Regional Research*, 1:272–92.

Gulick, John. 1963. "Urban Anthropology: Its Present and Future." *Transactions of the New York Academy of Sciences*, ser. II, 25:445–58.

—— 1969. "Village and City: Cultural Continuities in Twentieth Century Middle Eastern Cultures." In Ira M. Lapidus, ed., *Middle Eastern Cities*. Berkeley and Los Angeles: University of California Press.

Gutkind, Peter C. W. 1968. "Urban Anthropology: Creative Pioneer of Comparative Modern Social Anthropology—The African Case." *Proceedings of the VIIIth Congress of Anthropological and Ethnological Sciences,* 2:77–81.

—— 1969. "The Social Researcher in the Context of African National Development: Reflections on an Encounter." In Frances Henry and Satish Saberwal, eds., *Stress and Response in Fieldwork.* New York: Holt, Rinehart and Winston.

—— 1974. *Urban Anthropology.* Assen: van Gorcum.

Gutnova, Eugenia V. 1968. "Levitsky's Artisanal Theory in England." In John F. Benton, ed., *Town Origins.* Lexington, Mass.: Heath.

Hall, J. A. 1977. "Sincerity and Politics: 'Existentialists' vs. Goffman and Proust." *Sociological Review,* 25:535–50.

Handelman, Don and Bruce Kapferer. 1972. "Forms of Joking Activity: A Comparative Approach." *American Anthropologist,* 74:484–517.

Hannerz, Ulf. 1967. "Gossip, Networks and Culture in a Black American Ghetto." *Ethnos,* 32:35–60.

—— 1968. "The Rhetoric of Soul: Identification in Negro Society." *Race,* 9:453–65.

—— 1969. *Soulside.* New York: Columbia University Press.

—— 1971. "The Study of Afro-American Cultural Dynamics." *Southwestern Journal of Anthropology,* 27:181–200.

—— 1973. "The Great Chernichewski." *Current Anthropology,* 14:172.

—— 1974a. *Caymanian Politics.* Stockholm Studies in Social Anthropology, 1. Stockholm: Department of Social Anthropology, University of Stockholm.

—— 1974b. "Ethnicity and Opportunity in Urban America." In Abner Cohen, ed., *Urban Ethnicity* (ASA 12). London: Tavistock.

—— 1976. "Methods in an African Urban Study." *Ethnos,* 41:68–98.

—— 1978. "Problems in the Analysis of Urban Cultural Organization." In Joyce Aschenbrenner and Lloyd Collins, eds., *Processes of Urbanism.* The Hague: Mouton.

Hansen, Edward C. 1974. "From Political Association to Public Tavern: Two Phases of Urbanization in Rural Catalonia (Spain)." *Annals of the New York Academy of Sciences,* 220:509–21.

Harries-Jones, Peter. 1975. *Freedom and Labour.* Oxford: Blackwell.

—— 1977. " 'A House Should Have a Ceiling': Unintended Consequences of Development Planning in Zambia." In Sandra Wallman, ed., *Perceptions of Development.* Cambridge: Cambridge University Press.

Harris, Chauncy D. 1943. "A Functional Classification of Cities in the United States." *Geographical Review,* 33:86–99.

Harris, Marvin. 1956. *Town and Country in Brazil.* New York: Columbia University Press.

—— 1959. "The Economy Has No Surplus?" *American Anthropologist,* 61:185–99.

Harvey, David. 1973. *Social Justice and the City.* London: Edward Arnold.

Hauser, Philip M. 1965. "Observations on the Urban-Folk and Urban-Rural Dichotomies as Forms of Western Ethnocentrism." In Philip M. Hauser and Leo F. Schnore, eds., *The Study of Urbanization.* New York: Wiley.

Henderson, Ian. 1975. "Early African Leadership: The Copperbelt Disturbances of 1935 and 1940." *Journal of Southern African Studies,* 2:83–97.

Hepworth, Mike. 1975. *Blackmail.* London: Routledge & Kegan Paul.

Herskovits, Melville J. 1951. *Man and His Works.* New York: Knopf.

Holleman, J. F. and S. Biesheuvel. 1973. *White Mine Workers in Northern Rhodesia 1959–60.* Leiden: Afrika-Studiecentrum.

Hooker, James R. 1963. "The Anthropologists' Frontier: The Last Phase of African Exploitation." *Journal of Modern African Studies,* 1:455–59.

Horton, Robin. 1967. "African Traditional Thought and Western Science." *Africa,* 37:50–71, 155–87.

Horwath, Ronald J. 1969. "In Search of a Theory of Urbanization: Notes on the Colonial City." *East Lakes Geographer,* 5:69–82.

Hoselitz, Bert. F. 1955. "Generative and Parasitic Cities." *Economic Development and Cultural Change,* 3:278–94.

Hughes, Everett C. 1958. *Men and Their Work.* Glencoe, Ill: Free Press.

—— 1961. *Students' Culture and Perspectives.* Lawrence: University of Kansas Law School.

—— 1969. "Robert E. Park." In Timothy Raison, ed., *The Founding Fathers of Social Science.* Harmondsworth: Penguin.

—— 1971. *The Sociological Eye.* Chicago: Aldine.

Humphreys, Laud. 1970. *Tearoom Trade.* Chicago: Aldine.

Hunter, Floyd, 1953. *Community Power Structure.* Chapel Hill: University of North Carolina Press.

Ibn Khaldun. 1969. *The Muqaddimah.* Princeton, N.J.: Princeton University Press.

Jackson, Brian. 1968. *Working Class Community.* London: Routledge and Kegan Paul.

Jacobs, Jane. 1961. *The Death and Life of Great American Cities.* New York: Vintage Books.

—— 1969. *The Economy of Cities.* New York: Random House.

Jacobson, David. 1971. "Mobility, Continuity, and Urban Social Organization." *Man,* 6:630–44.

Jameson, Fredric. 1976. "On Goffman's Frame Analysis." *Theory and Society,* 3:119–33.

Janowitz, Morris. 1952. *The Community Press in an Urban Setting.* Chicago: University of Chicago Press.

Jayawardena, Chandra. 1968. "Ideology and Conflict in Lower Class Communities." *Comparative Studies in Society and History,* 10:413–46.

Jefferson, Mark. 1939. "The Law of the Primate City." *Geographical Review,* 29:226–32.

Johnsen, Tim. 1970. "The Extended Case Method—teknikk eller teori?" *Tidsskrift for samfunnsforskning,* 11:314–32.

Johnson, E. A. J. 1970. *The Organization of Space in Developing Countries.* Cambridge, Mass.: Harvard University Press.

Johnson, Sheila K. 1971. *Idle Haven.* Berkeley and Los Angeles: University of California Press.

Jones, G. I. 1963. *The Trading States of the Oil Rivers*. London: Oxford University Press.

Kapferer, Bruce. 1966. *The Population of a Zambian Municipal Township*. Lusaka: Institute for Social Research, Communication no. 1.

—— 1969. "Norms and the Manipulation of Relationships in a Work Context." In J. Clyde Mitchell, ed., *Social Networks in Urban Situations*. Manchester: Manchester University Press.

—— 1972. *Strategy and Transaction in an African Factory*. Manchester: Manchester University Press.

—— 1973. "Social Network and Conjugal Role in Urban Zambia: Towards a Reformulation of the Bott Hypothesis." In Jeremy Boissevain and J. Clyde Mitchell, eds., *Network Analysis*. The Hague: Mouton.

—— 1976. "Conflict and Process in a Zambian Mine Community." In Myron I. Aronoff, ed., *Freedom and Constraint*. Assen: van Gorcum.

Keil, Charles. 1966. *Urban Blues*. Chicago: University of Chicago Press.

Keiser, R. Lincoln. 1969. *The Vice Lords*. New York: Holt, Rinehart and Winston.

Keniston, Kenneth. 1971. *Youth and Dissent*. New York: Harcourt Brace Jovanovich.

King, Anthony D. 1974. "The Language of Colonial Urbanization." *Sociology*, 8:81–110.

—— 1976. *Colonial Urban Development*. London: Routledge and Kegan Paul.

Klockars, Carl B. 1974. *The Professional Fence*. New York: Free Press.

Kornblum, William. 1974. *Blue Collar Community*. Chicago: University of Chicago Press.

Kornhauser, William. 1962. "Social Bases of Political Commitment: A Study of Liberals and Radicals." In Arnold M. Rose, ed., *Human Behavior and Social Processes*. Boston: Houghton Mifflin.

Krapf-Askari, Eva. 1969. *Yoruba Towns and Cities*. London: Oxford University Press.

Kroeber, A. L. 1948. *Anthropology*. New York: Harcourt, Brace.

Kuhn, Thomas S. 1962. *The Structure of Scientific Revolutions*. Chicago: University of Chicago Press.

Kuper, Adam. 1973. *Anthropologists and Anthropology*. London: Allen Lane.

Kuper, Leo. 1969. "Plural Societies: Perspectives and Problems." In Leo Kuper and M. G. Smith, eds., *Pluralism in Africa*. Berkeley and Los Angeles: University of California Press.

La Fontaine, J. S. 1970. *City Politics*. London: Cambridge University Press.

Lamont, Barbara. 1975. *City People*. New York: Macmillan.

Leach, E. R. 1967. "An Anthropologist's Reflections on a Social Survey." In D. G. Jongmans and P. C. W. Gutkind, eds., *Anthropologists in the Field*. New York: Humanities Press.

Leacock, Eleanor B., ed. 1971. *The Culture of Poverty: A Critique*. New York: Simon and Schuster.

Lee, Nancy Howell. 1969. *The Search for an Abortionist*. Chicago: University of Chicago Press.

Leeds, Anthony. 1964. "Brazilian Careers and Social Structure: A Case History and a Model." *American Anthropologist,* 66:1321–47.

—— 1968. "The Anthropology of Cities: Some Methodological Issues." In Elizabeth M. Eddy, ed., *Urban Anthropology.* Southern Anthropological Society Proceedings, no. 2. Athens: University of Georgia Press.

—— 1972. "Urban Anthropology and Urban Studies." *Urban Anthropology Newsletter,* 1(1):4–5.

Lelyveld, Joseph. 1970. "Kishan Babu." In William Mangin, ed., *Peasants in Cities.* Boston: Houghton Mifflin.

Lemann, Nicholas. 1978. "Survival Networks: Staying in Washington." *Washington Monthly,* 10(4):22–32.

Lerner, Daniel. 1958. *The Passing of Traditional Society.* New York: Free Press.

Lewis, Oscar. 1951. *Life in a Mexican Village.* Urbana: University of Illinois Press.

—— 1965. "Further Observations on the Folk-Urban Continuum and Urbanization with Special Reference to Mexico City." In Philip M. Hauser and Leo F. Schnore, eds., *The Study of Urbanization.* New York: Wiley.

—— 1966. *La Vida.* New York: Random House.

Linsky, Arnold S. 1965. "Some Generalizations Concerning Primate Cities." *Annals of the Association of American Geographers,* 55:506–13.

Linton, Ralph. 1936. *The Study of Man.* New York: Appleton-Century-Crofts.

Little, Kenneth. 1965.*West African Urbanization.* Cambridge: Cambridge University Press.

Lloyd, Peter C. 1973. "The Yoruba: An Urban People?" In Aidan Southall, ed., *Urban Anthropology.* New York: Oxford University Press.

Lockwood, David. 1966. "Sources of Variation in Working-class Images of Society." *Sociological Review,* 14:249–67.

Lofland, John F. 1970a. "Morals Are the Message: The Work of Erving Goffman." *Psychiatry & Social Science Review,* 4(9):17–19.

—— 1970b. "Interactionist Imagery and Analytic Interruptus." In Tamotsu Shibutani, ed., *Human Nature and Collective Behavior.* Englewood Cliffs, N.J.: Prentice-Hall.

Lofland, Lyn H. 1973. *A World of Strangers.* New York: Basic Books.

London, Bruce and William G. Flanagan. 1976. "Comparative Urban Ecology: A Summary of the Field." In the John Walton and Louis H. Masotti, eds., *The City in Comparative Perspective.* New York: Halsted/Wiley.

Long, Norton E. 1958. "The Local Community as an Ecology of Games." *American Journal of Sociology,* 64:251–61.

Lopez, Robert S. 1963. "The Crossroads within the Wall." In Oscar Handlin and John Burchard, eds., *The Historian and the City.* Cambridge, Mass.: M.I.T. Press and Harvard University Press.

—— 1976. *The Commercial Revolution of the Middle Ages, 950–1350.* Cambridge: Cambridge University Press.

Luckmann, Thomas and Peter Berger. 1964. "Social Mobility and Personal Identity." *Archives Européennes de Sociologie,* 5:331–43.

Lupri, Eugen. 1967. "The Rural-Urban Variable Reconsidered: The Cross-Cultural Perspective." *Sociologia Ruralis,* 7:1–20.

Lyman, Stanford M. 1973. "Civilization: Contents, Discontents, Malcontents." *Contemporary Sociology,* 2:360–66.

Lynch, Kevin. 1960. *The Image of the City.* Cambridge, Mass.: M.I.T. Press.

Mabogunje, Akin L. 1962. *Yoruba Towns.* Ibadan: Ibadan University Press.

MacDonald, John S. and Leatrice D. MacDonald. 1962. "Urbanisation, Ethnic Groups, and Social Segmentation." *Social Research,* 29:433–48.

—— 1964. "Chain Migration, Ethnic Neighborhood Formation, and Social Networks." *Millbank Memorial Fund Quarterly,* 42:82–97.

Madge, John. 1962. *The Origins of Scientific Sociology.* New York: Free Press.

Magubane, Bernard. 1968. "Crisis in African Sociology." *East Africa Journal,* 5(12):21–40.

—— 1969. "Pluralism and Conflict Situations in Africa, A New Look." *African Social Research,* 7:529–54.

—— 1971. "A Critical Look at Indices Used in the Study of Social Change in Colonial Africa." *Current Anthropology,* 12:419–31.

—— 1973. "The Xhosa in Town, Revisited Urban Social Anthropology: A Failure of Method and Theory." *American Anthropologist,* 75:1701–15.

Mannheim, Karl. 1936. *Ideology and Utopia.* New York: Harcourt, Brace.

Manning, Peter K. 1973. "Review of Relations in Public." *Sociological Quarterly,* 14:135–37.

—— 1976. "The Decline of Civility: A Comment on Erving Goffman's Sociology." *Canadian Review of Sociology and Anthropology,* 13:13–25.

Marx, Karl. 1973. *Grundrisse.* New York: Vintage/Random House.

Marx, Karl and Frederick Engels. 1970. *The German Ideology.* London: Lawrence and Wishart.

Matthews, Fred H. 1977. *Quest for an American Sociology: Robert E. Park and the Chicago School.* Montreal: McGill-Queen's University Press.

Matza, David. 1969. *Becoming Deviant.* Englewood Cliffs, N.J.: Prentice-Hall.

Mauss, Marcel. 1967. *The Gift.* New York: Norton.

Mayer, Adrian C. 1966. "The Significance of Quasi-Groups in the Study of Complex Societies." In Michael Banton, ed., *The Social Anthropology of Complex Societies* (ASA 4). London: Tavistock.

Mayer, Philip. 1961. *Townsmen or Tribesmen.* Cape Town: Oxford University Press.

—— 1962. "Migrancy and the Study of Africans in Towns." *American Anthropologist,* 64:576–92.

—— 1964. "Labour Migrancy and the Social Network." In J. F. Holleman, J. Knox, J. W. Mann, and K. A. Heard, eds., *Problems of Transition.* Pietermaritzburg: University of Natal Press.

McGee, T. G. 1964. "The Rural-Urban Continuum Debate: The Preindustrial City and Rural-Urban Migration." *Pacific Viewpoint,* 5:159–81.

—— 1971. *The Urbanization Process in the Third World.* London: Bell.

McIntosh, Mary. 1975. *The Organization of Crime.* London: Macmillan.

McKenzie, Roderick D. 1968. *On Human Ecology*. Edited and with an introduction by Amos Hawley. Chicago: University of Chicago Press.

McLuhan, Marshall. 1965. *Understanding Media*. New York: McGraw-Hill.

Mead, George H. 1967. *Mind, Self, and Society*. Chicago: University of Chicago Press.

Meillassoux, Claude. 1968. *Urbanization of an African Community*. Seattle: University of Washington Press.

Merton, Robert K. 1957. *Social Theory and Social Structure*. Glencoe, Ill.: Free Press.

Messinger, Sheldon L., Harold Sampson, and Robert D. Towne, 1962. "Life as Theater: Some Notes on the Dramaturgic Approach to Social Reality." *Sociometry*, 25:98–110.

Middleton, John. 1966. *The Effect of Economic Development on Traditional Political Systems in Africa South of the Sahara*. The Hague: Mouton.

Miles, S. W. 1958. "An Urban Type: Extended Boundary Towns." *Southwestern Journal of Anthropology*, 14:339–51.

Milgram, Stanley. 1969. "Interdisciplinary Thinking and the Small World Problem." In Muzafer Sherif and Carolyn W. Sherif, eds., *Interdisciplinary Relationships in the Social Sciences*. Chicago: Aldine.

—— 1970. "The Experience of Living in Cities: A Psychological Analysis." *Science*, 167:1461–68.

Mills, C. Wright. 1961. *The Sociological Imagination*. New York: Grove Press.

Miner, Horace. 1952. "The Folk-Urban Continuum." *American Sociological Review*, 17:529–37.

—— 1953. *The Primitive City of Timbuctoo*. Princeton, N.J.: Princeton University Press.

Mintz, Sidney W. 1953. "The Folk-Urban Continuum and the Rural Proletarian Community." *American Journal of Sociology*, 59:136–43.

—— 1954. "On Redfield and Foster." *American Anthropologist*, 56:87–92.

Mitchell, J. Clyde, 1956a. *The Kalela Dance*. Rhodes-Livingstone Papers, no. 27. Manchester: Manchester University Press.

—— 1956b. *The Yao Village*. Manchester: Manchester University Press.

—— 1956c. "Urbanization, Detribalization and Stabilization in Southern Africa: A Problem of Definition and Measurement." In *Social Implications of Industrialization and Urbanization in Africa South of the Sahara*. Paris: Unesco.

—— 1957. "Aspects of African Marriage on the Copperbelt of Northern Rhodesia." *Rhodes-Livingstone Journal*, 22:1–30.

—— 1961. "Social Change and the Stability of African Marriage in Northern Rhodesia." In Aidan Southall, ed., *Social Change in Modern Africa*. London: Oxford University Press.

—— 1964. "Foreword." In Jaap van Velsen, *The Politics of Kinship*. Manchester: Manchester University Press.

—— 1966a. "Aspects of Occupational Prestige in a Plural Society." In P. C. Lloyd, ed., *The New Elites of Tropical Africa*. London: Oxford University Press.

—— 1966b. "Theoretical Orientations in African Urban Studies." In Michael

Banton, ed., *The Social Anthropology of Complex Societies* (ASA 4). London: Tavistock.

—— 1969a. "Urbanization, Detribalization, Stabilization and Urban Commitment in Southern Africa: 1968." In Paul Meadows and Ephraim H. Mizruchi, eds., *Urbanism, Urbanization, and Change*. Reading, Mass.: Addison-Wesley.

—— 1969b. "The Concept and Use of Social Networks." In J. Clyde Mitchell, ed., *Social Networks in Urban Situations*. Manchester: Manchester University Press.

—— 1973a. "Distance, Transportation, and Urban Involvement in Zambia." In Aidan Southall, ed., *Urban Anthropology*. New York: Oxford University Press.

—— 1973b. "Networks, Norms and Institutions." In Jeremy Boissevain and J. Clyde Mitchell, eds., *Network Analysis*. The Hague: Mouton.

—— 1974a. "Perceptions of Ethnicity and Ethnic Behaviour: An Empirical Exploration." In Abner Cohen, ed., *Urban Ethnicity* (ASA 12). London: Tavistock.

—— 1974b. "Social Networks." In *Annual Review of Anthropology*, no. 3. Palo Alto, Calif.: Annual Reviews.

—— 1977. "The Shadow of Federation, 1952–55." *African Social Research*, 24:309–18.

Mitchell, J. Clyde and A. L. Epstein. 1959. "Occupational Prestige and Social Status Among Urban Africans in Northern Rhodesia." *Africa*, 29:22–40.

Mommsen, Wolfgang J. 1977. *The Age of Bureaucracy*. New York: Harper & Row.

Morris, Colin. 1973. *The Discovery of the Individual: 1050–1200*. New York: Harper & Row.

Morris, R. N. 1968. *Urban Sociology*. London: Allen & Unwin.

Mumford, Lewis. 1961. *The City in History*. New York: Harcourt, Brace.

Mungham, Geoff, and Geoff Pearson, eds. 1976. *Working Class Youth Culture*. London: Routledge and Kegan Paul.

Murphey, Rhoads. 1954. "The City as a Center of Change: Western Europe and China." *Annals of the Association of American Geographers*, 44:349–62.

Murvar, Vatro. 1969. "Some Tentative Modifications of Weber's Typology: Occidental versus Oriental City." In Paul Meadows and Ephraim H. Mizruchi, eds., *Urbanism, Urbanization, and Change*. Reading, Mass.: Addison-Wesley.

Nair, Kannan K. 1972. *Politics and Society in South Eastern Nigeria 1841–1906*. London: Cass.

Nakamura, H. 1968. "Urban Ward Associations in Japan." In R. E. Pahl, ed., *Readings in Urban Sociology*. Oxford: Pergamon.

Nakane, Chie. 1970. *Japanese Society*. Berkeley and Los Angeles: University of California Press.

Newton, Esther. 1972. *Mother Camp*. Englewood Cliffs, N.J.: Prentice-Hall.

Oliver-Smith, Anthony. 1977. "Traditional Agriculture, Central Places, and Post-disaster Urban Relocation in Peru." *American Ethnologist*, 4:102–16.

Orans, Martin. 1966. "Surplus." *Human Organization*, 25:24–32.

Ottenberg, Simon. 1971. Review of J. Clyde Mitchell, ed., *Social Networks in Urban Situations*. *American Anthropologist*, 73:946–48.

Pahl, R. E. 1966. "The Rural-Urban Continuum." *Sociologia Ruralis*, 6:299–327.

—— 1967. "The Rural Urban Continuum. A Reply to Eugen Lupri." *Sociologia Ruralis*. 7:21–28.

Paine, Robert. 1963. "Entrepreneurial Activity without its Profits." In Fredrik Barth, ed., *The Role of the Entrepreneur in Social Change in Northern Norway*. Bergen and Oslo: Norwegian Universities Press.

—— 1966. "A Critique of the Methodology of Robert Redfield: 'Folk Culture' and Other Concepts." *Ethnos*, 31:161–72.

—— 1967. "What is Gossip About? An Alternative Hypothesis." *Man*, 2:278–85.

—— 1968. "Gossip and Transaction." *Man*, 3:305–08.

—— 1969. "In Search of Friendship: An Exploratory Analysis in 'Middle-class' Culture." *Man*, 4:505–24.

—— 1970. "Informal Communication and Information-Management." *Canadian Review of Sociology and Anthropology*, 7:172–88.

Park, Robert E. 1950. *Race and Culture*. Glencoe, Ill.: Free Press.

—— 1952. *Human Communities*. Glencoe, Ill.: Free Press.

—— 1955. *Society*. Glencoe, Ill.: Free Press.

—— 1967. *On Social Control and Collective Behavior*. Edited and with an introduction by Ralph H. Turner. Chicago: University of Chicago Press.

—— 1972. *The Crowd and the Public and Other Essays*. Edited and with an introduction by Henry Elsner, Jr. Chicago: University of Chicago Press.

Park, Robert E., Ernest W. Burgess, and Roderick D. McKenzie. 1967. *The City*. Chicago: University of Chicago Press. (First published 1925.)

Parkin, Frank. 1972. *Class Inequality and Political Order*. London: Paladin.

Patrick, James. 1973. *A Glasgow Gang Observed*. London: Eyre Methuen.

Pauw, B. A. 1963. *The Second Generation*. Cape Town: Oxford University Press.

Pearson, Harry W. 1957. "The Economy Has No Surplus." In Karl Polanyi, Conrad M. Arensberg, and Harry W. Pearson, eds., *Trade and Market in the Early Empires*. Glencoe, Ill.: Free Press.

Perinbanayagam, R. S. 1974. "The Definition of the Situation: An Analysis of the Ethnomethodological and Dramaturgical View." *Sociological Quarterly*, 15:521–41.

Perrings, Charles. 1977. "Consciousness, Conflict and Proletarization: An Assessment of the 1935 Mineworkers' Strike on the Northern Rhodesian Copperbelt." *Journal of Southern African Studies*, 4:31–51.

Pilcher, William W. 1972. *The Portland Longshoremen*. New York: Holt, Rinehart, and Winston.

Pirenne, Henri. 1952. *Medieval Cities*. Princeton, N.J.: Princeton University Press.

Plath, David W. 1964. *The After Hours*. Berkeley and Los Angeles: University of California Press.

Pleck, Elisabeth H. 1976. "Two Worlds in One: Work and Family." *Journal of Social History*, 10:178–95.

Plotnicov, Leonard. 1964. "Nativism in Contemporary Nigeria." *Anthropological Quarterly*, 37:121–37.

—— 1967. *Strangers to the City.* Pittsburgh: University of Pittsburgh Press.

—— 1973. "Anthropological Field Work in Modern and Local Urban Contexts." *Urban Anthropology,* 2:248–64.

Pocock, David F. 1960. "Sociologies: Urban and Rural." *Contributions to Indian Sociology,* 4:63–81.

Polanyi, Karl. 1957a. *The Great Transformation.* Boston. Beacon Press.

—— 1957b. "The Economy as Instituted Process." In Karl Polanyi, Conrad M. Arensberg, and Harry W. Pearson, eds., *Trade and Market in the Early Empires.* Glencoe, Ill.: Free Press.

Portes, Alejandro and Harley L. Browning, eds. 1976. *Current Perspectives in Latin American Urban Research.* Austin: Institute of Latin American Studies, University of Texas.

Powdermaker, Hortense. 1962. *Copper Town.* New York: Harper and Row.

—— 1966. *Stranger and Friend.* New York: Norton.

Price, John A. 1973. "Holism through Team Ethnography." *Human Relations,* 26:155–70.

Raban, Jonathan. 1974. *Soft City.* London: Hamish Hamilton.

Rainwater, Lee. 1966. "Work and Identity in the Lower Class." In Sam Bass Warner, Jr., ed., *Planning for a Nation of Cities.* Cambridge, Mass.: M.I.T. Press.

Rakove, Milton. 1975. *Don't Make No Waves, Don't Back No Losers.* Bloomington: Indiana University Press.

Ranger, T. O. 1975. *Dance and Society in Eastern Africa.* London: Heinemann.

Rayfield, J. R. 1974. "Theories of Urbanization and the Colonial City in West Africa." *Africa,* 44:163–85.

Redfield, Robert. 1930. *Tepoztlan, a Mexican Village.* Chicago: University of Chicago Press.

—— 1941. *The Folk Culture of Yucatan.* Chicago: University of Chicago Press.

—— 1947. "The Folk Society." *American Journal of Sociology,* 41:293–308.

—— 1953. *The Primitive World and its Transformations.* Ithaca, N.Y.: Cornell University Press.

—— 1955. *The Little Community.* Chicago: University of Chicago Press.

—— 1962. *Human Nature and the Study of Society.* Margaret Park Redfield, ed. Chicago: University of Chicago Press.

Redfield, Robert and Milton Singer. 1954. "The Cultural Role of Cities." *Economic Development and Cultural Change,* 3:53–73.

Reina, Ruben E. 1973. *Paraná.* Austin: University of Texas Press.

Reiss, Albert J., Jr. 1955. "An Analysis of Urban Phenomena." In Robert M. Fisher, ed., *The Metropolis in Modern Life.* Garden City, N.Y.: Doubleday.

Reitman, Ben L. 1975. *Sister of the Road.* New York: Harper & Row. (First published 1937.)

Richards, Audrey I. 1939. *Land, Labour and Diet in Northern Rhodesia.* London: Oxford University Press.

—— 1977. "The Rhodes-Livingstone Institute: An Experiment in Research, 1933–38." *African Social Research,* 24:275–78.

Riesman, Paul. 1977. *Freedom in Fulani Social Life*. Chicago: University of Chicago Press.

Rivière, P. G. 1967. "The Honour of Sánchez." *Man*, 2:569–83.

Roberts, Bryan R. 1973. *Organizing Strangers*. Austin: University of Texas Press.

—— 1976. "The Provincial Urban System and the Process of Dependency." In Alejandro Portes and Harley L. Browning, eds., *Current Perspectives in Latin American Urban Research*. Austin: Institute of Latin American Studies, University of Texas.

Rollwagen, Jack R. 1972. "A Comparative Framework for the Investigation of the City-as-Context: A Discussion of the Mexican Case." *Urban Anthropology*, 1:68–86.

Rollwagen, Jack R., ed. 1976. "The City as Context: A Symposium." *Urban Anthropology*, 4:1–72.

Rörig, Fritz. 1971. *The Medieval Town*. Berkeley and Los Angeles: University of California Press.

Rossi, Peter H. 1960. "Power and Community Structure." *Midwest Journal of Political Science*, 4:390–401.

Rubinstein, Jonathan. 1973. *City Police*. New York: Farrar, Straus and Giroux.

Saberwal, Satish. 1972. "Status, Mobility, and Networks in a Punjabi Industrial Town." In Satish Saberwal, ed., *Beyond the Village*. Simla: Indian Institute of Advanced Study.

Salaman, Graeme. 1971. "Two Occupational Communities: Examples of a Remarkable Convergence of Work and Non-Work." *Sociological Review*, 19:389–407.

—— 1974. *Community and Occupation*. London: Cambridge University Press.

Sanders, Ed. 1972. *The Family*. New York: Avon.

Sapir, Edward. 1924. "Culture, Genuine and Spurious." *American Journal of Sociology*, 29:401–29.

Scheff, Thomas J. 1967. "Toward a Sociological Model of Consensus." *American Sociological Review*, 32:32–46.

Schneider, Peter, Jane Schneider, and Edward Hansen. 1972. "Modernization and Development: The Role of Regional Elites and Noncorporate Groups in the European Mediterranean." *Comparative Studies in Society and History*, 14:328–50.

Schnore, Leo F. 1965. "On the Spatial Structure of Cities in the Two Americas." In Philip M. Hauser and Leo F. Schnore, eds., *The Study of Urbanization*. New York: Wiley.

Schwab, William B. 1965. "Oshogbo—An Urban Community." In Hilda Kuper, ed., *Urbanization and Migration in West Africa*. Berkeley and Los Angeles: University of California Press.

Scott, Marvin B., and Stanford M. Lyman. 1968. "Accounts." *American Sociological Review*, 33:46–62.

Seabrook, Jeremy. 1967. *The Unprivileged*. London: Longmans.

Sennett, Richard, ed. 1969. *Classic Essays on the Culture of Cities*. Englewood Cliffs, N.J.: Prentice-Hall.

Sennett, Richard. 1977. *The Fall of Public Man*. New York: Knopf.

Service, Elman R. 1975. *Origins of the State and Civilization*. New York: Norton.

Shack, William A. 1972. "Urban Anthropology and the Study of Complex Societies." *Urban Anthropology Newsletter*, 1(1):5–6.

Shaw, Clifford R. 1930. *The Jack-Roller*. Chicago: University of Chicago Press.

Shils, Edward. 1975. *Center and Periphery*. Chicago: University of Chicago Press.

Short, James F., Jr., ed. 1971. *The Social Fabric of the Metropolis*. Chicago: University of Chicago Press.

Short, James F., Jr. and Fred L. Strodtbeck. 1965. *Group Process and Gang Delinquency*. Chicago: University of Chicago Press.

Silverman, Sydel F. 1966. "An Ethnographic Approach to Social Stratification: Prestige in a Central Italian Community." *American Anthropologist*, 68:899–921.

—— 1975. *Three Bells of Civilization*. New York: Columbia University Press.

Simmel, Georg. 1950. "The Metropolis and Mental Life." In Kurt H. Wolff, ed., *The Sociology of Georg Simmel*. Glencoe, Ill.: Free Press.

—— 1955. *Conflict & The Web of Group-Affiliations*. Glencoe, Ill.: Free Press.

Sjoberg, Gideon. 1952. "Folk and Feudal Societies." *American Journal of Sociology*, 58:231–39.

—— 1959. "Comparative Urban Sociology." In Robert K. Merton, Leonard Broom, and Leonard S. Cottrell, eds., *Sociology Today*. New York: Basic Books.

—— 1960. *The Preindustrial City*. New York: Free Press.

—— 1964. "The Rural-Urban Dimension in Preindustrial, Transitional, and Industrial Societies." In Robert E. L. Faris, ed., *Handbook of Modern Sociology*. Chicago: Rand McNally.

—— 1965. "Theory and Research in Urban Sociology." In Philip M. Hauser and Leo F. Schnore, eds., *The Study of Urbanization*. New York: Wiley.

Skinner, William G. 1964–65. "Marketing and Social Structure in Rural China." *Journal of Asian Studies*, 24:3–43, 195–228, 363–99.

Smigel, Erwin O., ed. 1963. *Work and Leisure*. New Haven, Conn.: College and University Press.

Smith, Carol A. 1974. "Economics of Marketing Systems: Models from Economic Geography." *Annual Review of Anthropology*, no. 3. Palo Alto, Calif.: Annual Reviews.

—— 1975. "Examining Stratification Systems through Peasant Marketing Arrangements: An Application of Some Models from Economic Geography." *Man*, 10:95–112.

Smith, Carol A., ed. 1976. *Regional Analysis*. Vol. I: "Economic Systems"; Vol. II: "Social Systems." New York: Academic Press.

Smith, Raymond T. 1967. "Social Stratification, Cultural Pluralism, and Integration in West Indian Societies." In Sybil Lewis and Thomas G. Mathews, eds., *Caribbean Integration*. Rio Pedras, Puerto Rico: Institute of Caribbean Studies.

Smith, Robert H. T. 1965. "Method and Purpose in Functional Town Classification." *Annals of the Association of American Geographers*, 55:539–48.

Smith, Robert J. 1973. "Town and City in Pre-Modern Japan: Small Families, Small Households, and Residential Instability." In Aidan Southall, ed., *Urban Anthropology*. New York: Oxford University Press.

Southall, Aidan. 1959. "An Operational Theory of Role." *Human Relations,* 12:17–34.

—— 1961. "Introductory Summary." In Aidan Southall, ed., *Social Change in Modern Africa.* London: Oxford University Press.

Southall, Aidan, ed. 1973a. *Urban Anthropology.* New York: Oxford University Press.

—— 1973b. "The Density of Role-Relationships as a Universal Index of Urbanization." In *Urban Anthropology.*

Spearpoint, F. 1937. "The African Native and the Rhodesian Copper Mines." *Journal of the Royal African Society,* 36(154), Supplement, 1–58.

Spradley, James P. 1970. *You Owe Yourself a Drunk.* Boston: Little, Brown.

—— 1972. "Adaptive Strategies of Urban Nomads: The Ethnoscience of Tramp Culture." In Thomas Weaver and Douglas White, eds., *The Anthropology of Urban Environments.* The Society for Applied Anthropology Monograph Series, No. 11.

Spradley, James P. and Brenda J. Mann. 1975. *The Cocktail Waitress.* New York: Wiley.

Stein, Maurice R. 1960. *The Eclipse of Community.* Princeton: Princeton University Press.

Steward, Julian H. 1950. *Area Research.* New York: Social Science Research Council.

Stewart, Charles T., Jr. 1958. "The Urban-Rural Dichotomy: Concepts and Uses." *American Journal of Sociology,* 64:152–58.

Stone, Gregory P. 1954. "City Shoppers and Urban Identification: Observations on the Social Psychology of City Life." *American Journal of Sociology,* 60:36–45.

Strauss, Anselm L. 1961. *Images of the American City.* New York: Free Press.

Suttles, Gerald D. 1968. *The Social Order of the Slum.* Chicago: University of Chicago Press.

—— 1970. "Friendship as a Social Institution." In George J. McCall, ed., *Social Relationships.* Chicago: Aldine.

—— 1976. "Urban Ethnography: Situational and Normative Accounts." In *Annual Review of Sociology,* no. 2. Palo Alto, Calif.: Annual Reviews.

Symmons-Symonolewicz, Konstantin. 1968. *"The Polish Peasant in Europe and America:* Its First Half-a-Century of Intellectual History (1918–1968)." *Polish Review,* 13(2):14–27.

Tax, Sol. 1939. "Culture and Civilization in Guatemalan Societies." *Scientific Monthly,* 48:463–67.

—— 1941. "World View and Social Relations in Guatemala." *American Anthropologist,* 43:27–42.

Taylor, Laurie. 1968. "Erving Goffman." *New Society,* 12:835–37.

Teeffelen, T. van. 1978. "The Manchester School in Africa and Israel: A Critique." *Dialectical Anthropology,* 3:67–83.

Tenbruck, F. H. 1965. "Formal Sociology." In Lewis A. Coser, ed., *Georg Simmel.* Englewood Cliffs, N.J.: Prentice-Hall.

Thernstrom, Stephan. 1965. "Yankee City Revisited: The Perils of Historical Naïveté." *American Sociological Review,* 30:234–42.

—— 1973. *The Other Bostonians*. Cambridge, Mass: Harvard University Press.

Thomas, William I. 1909. *Source Book for Social Origins*. Chicago: University of Chicago Press.

—— 1937. *Primitive Behavior*. New York: McGraw-Hill.

—— 1966. *On Social Organization and Social Personality*. Edited and with an introduction by Morris Janowitz. Chicago: University of Chicago Press.

Thomas, William I. and Florian Znaniecki. 1918–20. *The Polish Peasant in Europe and America*.

Thrasher, Frederic M. 1963. *The Gang*. Chicago: University of Chicago Press. (First published 1927.)

Thrupp, Sylvia L. 1961. "The Creativity of Cities." *Comparative Studies in Society and History*, 4:53–64.

Toffler, Alvin. 1970. *Future Shock*. New York: Random House.

Travers, Jeffrey and Stanley Milgram. 1969. "An Experimental Study of the Small World Problem." *Sociometry*, 32:425–43.

Trigger, Bruce. 1972. "Determinants of Urban Growth in Preindustrial societies." In Peter J. Ucko, Ruth Tringham, and G. W. Dimbleby, eds., *Man, Settlement and Urbanism*. London: Duckworth.

Trilling, Lionel. 1972. *Sincerity and Authenticity*, Cambridge, Mass.: Harvard University Press.

Tsuru, Shigeto. 1963. "The Economic Significance of Cities." In Oscar Handlin and John Burchard, eds., *The Historian and The City*. Cambridge, Mass.: M.I.T. Press.

Turner, Bryan S. 1974. *Weber and Islam*. London: Routledge and Kegan Paul.

Turner, Victor W. 1957. *Schism and Continuity in an African Society*. Manchester: Manchester University Press.

—— 1969. *The Ritual Process*. Chicago: Aldine.

Uzzell, J. Douglas and Ronald Provencher. 1976. *Urban Anthropology*. Dubuque, Iowa: Wm. C. Brown.

Valentine, Charles A. 1968. *Culture and Poverty*. Chicago: University of Chicago Press.

Vatuk, Sylvia. 1972. *Kinship and Urbanization*. Berkeley and Los Angeles. University of California Press.

Velsen, J. van. 1961. "Labour Migration as a Positive Factor in the Continuity of Tonga Tribal Society." In Aidan Southall, ed., *Social Change in Modern Africa*. London: Oxford University Press.

—— 1964. *The Politics of Kinship*. Manchester: Manchester University Press.

—— 1967. "The Extended-Case Method and Situational Analysis." In A. L. Epstein, ed., *The Craft of Social Anthropology*. London: Tavistock.

—— 1975. "Urban Squatters: Problem or Solution." In David Parkin, ed., *Town and Country in Central and Eastern Africa*. London: Oxford University Press.

Vincent, Joan. 1974. "The Changing Role of Small Towns in the Agrarian Structure of East Africa." *Journal of Commonwealth and Comparative Politics*, 12:261–75.

Volkart, Edmund H., ed. 1951. *Social Behavior and Personality*. New York: Social Science Research Council.

Wallace, Anthony F. C. 1961. *Culture and Personality*. New York: Random House.

Walton, John. 1976a. "Political Economy of World Urban Systems: Direstions for Comparative Research." In John Walton and Louis H. Masotti, eds., *The City in Comparative Perspective*. New York: John Wiley.

—— 1976b. "Community Power and the Retreat from Politics: Full Circle after Twenty Years?" *Social Problems*, 23:292–303.

Watson, Jeanne and Robert J. Potter. 1962. "An Analytic Unit for the Study of Interaction." *Human Relations*, 15:245–63.

Watson, William. 1958. *Tribal Cohesion in a Money Economy*. Manchester: Manchester University Press.

—— 1960. "The Managerial Spiralist." *Twentieth Century*, 7:413–18.

—— 1964. "Social Mobility and Social Class in Industrial Communities." In Max Gluckman, ed., *Closed Systems and Open Minds*. Edinburgh and London: Oliver & Boyd.

Weaver, Thomas and Douglas White, eds. 1972. *The Anthropology of Urban Environments*. Washington, D.C.: Society for Applied Anthropology.

Webber, Melvin M. 1964. "The Urban Place and the Nonplace Urban Realm." In Melvin M. Webber, ed., *Explorations into Urban Structure*. Philadelphia: University of Pennsylvania Press.

Weber, Max. 1958. *The City*. New York: Free Press.

Wheatley, Paul. 1963. "What the Greatness of a City Is Said To Be." *Pacific Viewpoint*, 4:163–88.

—— 1970. "The Significance of Traditional Yoruba Urbanism. *Comparative Studies in Society and History*, 12:393–423.

—— 1971. *The Pivot of the Four Quarters*. Edinburgh: Edinburgh University Press.

—— 1972. "The Concept of Urbanism." In Peter J. Ucko, Ruth Tringham, and G. W. Dimbleby, eds., *Man, Settlement and Urbanism*. London: Duckworth.

White, C. M. N. 1977. "Interregna 1955–56 and 1960–62." *African Social Research*, 24:327–29.

White, Morton and Lucia. 1962. *The Intellectual versus the City*. Cambridge, Mass.: Harvard University Press.

Whitten, Norman E., Jr. 1970. "Network Analysis and Processes of Adaptation among Ecuadorian and Nova Scotian Negroes." In Morris Freilich, ed., *Marginal Natives*. New York: Harper & Row.

Whitten, Norman E., Jr. and Alvin W. Wolfe. 1973. "Network Analysis." In John J. Honigmann, ed., *Handbook of Social and Cultural Anthropology*. Chicago: Rand McNally.

Whyte, William F. 1943. *Street Corner Society*. Chicago: University of Chicago Press.

Whyte, William M., Jr. 1957. *The Organization Man*. Garden City, N.Y.: Anchor Books.

Williamson, Henry. 1965. *Hustler!* Edited by R. Lincoln Keiser. Garden City, N.Y.: Doubleday.

Wilson, Godfrey. 1941. *An Essay on the Economics of Detribalization in Northern Rhodesia*, Part I. Rhodes-Livingstone Papers, No. 5. Livingstone: Rhodes-Livingstone Institute.

—— 1942. *An Essay on the Economics of Detribalization in Northern Rhodesia*, Part II. Rhodes-Livingstone Papers, No. 6. Livingstone: Rhodes-Livingstone Institute.

Wilson, Godfrey and Monica. 1945. *The Analysis of Social Change*. Cambridge: Cambridge University Press.

Wilson, Monica. 1977. "The First Three Years, 1938–41." *African Social Research*, 24:279–83.

Wirth, Louis. 1938. "Urbanism as a Way of Life." *American Journal of Sociology*, 44:1–24.

—— 1956. *The Ghetto*. Chicago: University of Chicago Press. (First published 1928.)

—— 1964a. *On Cities and Social Life*. Edited and with an introduction by Albert J. Reiss, Jr. Chicago: University of Chicago Press.

—— 1964b. "Rural-Urban Differences." In Albert J. Reiss, Jr., ed., *Louis Wirth on Cities and Social Life*. Chicago: University of Chicago Press.

Wolf, Eric R. 1966. "Kinship, Friendship, and Patron-Client Relations in Complex Societies." In Michael Banton, ed., *The Social Anthropology of Complex Societies* (ASA 4). London: Tavistock.

Wolfe, Alvin W. 1963. "The African Mineral Industry: Evolution of a supranational Level of Integration." *Social Problems*, 11:153–64.

—— 1978. "The Rise of Network Thinking in Anthropology." *Social Networks*, 1:53–64.

Wolfe, Tom. 1970. *Radical Chic & Mau-Mauing the Flak Catchers*. New York: Farrar, Straus and Giroux.

—— 1976. *Mauve Gloves & Madmen, Clutter & Vine*. New York: Farrar, Straus & Giroux.

Wright, Rolland H. 1971. "The Stranger Mentality and the Culture of Poverty." In Eleanor Burke Leacock, ed., *The Culture of Poverty: A Critique*. New York: Simon and Schuster.

Young, Kimball. 1962–63. "Contributions of William Isaac Thomas to Sociology." *Sociology and Social Research*, 47:3–24, 123–37.

Young, T. R. 1971. "The Politics of Sociology: Gouldner, Goffman, and Garfinkel." *American Sociologist*, 6:276–81.

Zorbaugh, Harvey W. 1929. *The Gold Coast and the Slum*. Chicago: University of Chicago Press.

Index

THE FINANCIAL CENTURY

CENTURY

From Turmoils to Triumphs

Reuven Brenner

Copyright © 2001 by Reuven Brenner

All rights reserved. No part of this publication may be reproduced or
transmitted in any form or by any means, electronic or mechanical,
including photocopying, recording, or any information storage and
retrieval system, without permission in writing from the publisher.

Published in 2001 by Stoddart Publishing Co. Limited
895 Don Mills Road, 400-2 Park Centre, Toronto, Canada M3C 1W3
180 Varick Street, 9th Floor, New York, New York 10014

Distributed by:
General Distribution Services Ltd.
325 Humber College Blvd., Toronto, Ontario M9W 7C3
Tel. (416) 213-1919   Fax (416) 213-1917
Email cservice@genpub.com

05   04   03   02   01   1   2   3   4   5

Canadian Cataloguing in Publication Data

Brenner, Reuven
The financial century : from turmoils to triumphs

Includes bibliographical references and index.
ISBN 0-7737-3281-0

1. Finance. I. Title.

HG173.B73 2001   332   C00-932944-7

Jacket design: Angel Guerra
Text design: Joseph Gisini / PageWave Graphics Inc.
Page composition: Kevin Cockburn / PageWave Graphics Inc.

THE CANADA COUNCIL | LE CONSEIL DES ARTS
FOR THE ARTS | DU CANADA
SINCE 1957 | DEPUIS 1957

*We acknowledge for their financial support of our publishing program the Canada
Council, the Ontario Arts Council, and the Government of Canada
through the Book Publishing Industry Development Program (BPIDP).*

Printed and bound in Canada